AMERICAN GOVERNMENT AND POLITICS TODAY
A Concise Introduction

AMERICAN GOVERNMENT AND POLITICS TODAY
A Concise Introduction

Charles P. Sohner
El Camino College

Scott, Foresman and Company
Glenview, Illinois   Brighton, England

To Michelle

Preface

It is easy for an author to believe that his work has its own reason for being. He likes to assume that it should be read, as the mountain should be climbed, simply because it is there. But the prospective reader deserves more of an accounting.

This book was written primarily to examine American politics from the perspective of the people. It emphasizes those aspects of the political system which affect them most directly and over which they can exert the most influence. Its rationale can be summarized in a simple truism: American government involves Americans. It is they who pay the taxes to finance their government; it is they who are called into battle to protect its interests; it is they whose faith and loyalty give it the legitimacy necessary to exercise authority effectively. Even with all its power, the government must solicit the support of the people to cope with crime, resist racism, prevent pollution, and demonstrate generally that democracy works

This book, therefore, was designed to meet the most basic political needs of the average citizen. The author sees these as falling largely in two categories: Americans need to understand the nature, extent, and importance of their constitutionally guaranteed rights and they need to know the channels through which they can exert maximum influence on government policy. For these reasons, three of the eleven chapters in this book are devoted to civil rights (Part Two) and three others to pressure groups, political parties, and the campaign techniques designed to affect voting decisions (Part Three).

Such an emphasis is further justified because this text was not written for future members of exalted political elites. It assumes that more of its readers will be litigants than lawyers, pressure group members than corporate or union officials, and voters than legislators. This probability prevails for both university and community college students.

Nevertheless, the following pages ignore neither political ideas nor governmental organization. On the contrary, Part One begins with a description of fundamental concepts in empirical and normative theory and then proceeds to apply them to the American political system. Part Four consists of an integrated and concise account of the legislative, executive, and judicial branches of government at both the national and state levels. Here there are enough essential facts regarding both structure and process to free the instructor for the more discretionary elaboration and commentary that transform teaching from ritualistic recitation to creative art. To make it easier for readers to find information on particular states, this data is separately indexed.

Together, the four parts of this volume provide a basic text for an introductory course in American politics. Needless technical terms are avoided and the length permits supplementary reading dealing with various areas of government policy, for example, or a detailed treatment of the political system in a particular state or locality. In short, the book is designed to enhance people's sense of political efficacy by imparting the knowledge needed to understand and hence to influence the governments created to serve them. Consequently, much of this work may recommend itself also to broad programs of social science education and to private groups attempting to mobilize political participation.

The concept of power has been employed to unify the book both because the author believes it provides the surest key to a comprehension of the whole political process and because it lends coherence to the treatment of diverse subjects. It is defined in Chapter 1, along with other analytical options, and continuously reappears to interpret phenomena throughout the text. Since power blocs clash, conflicting interests inevitably surface in these pages, related to major political issues of the 1970s.

The reader should be alerted to the fact that the author does not write from a position of olympian detachment. As a teacher at the community college and state college and university levels, he has been a government employee for nearly twenty years. As a party official and former candidate for a state legislature, he has felt the exhilaration of partisan battle. By his selection of material and interpretations, he has betrayed his own values and priorities. The accompanying manual of test items indicates general areas both stressed and omitted in each chapter. Among the former, for example, are geographic factors, ethnic politics, women's liberation, functions of freedom, campaign organization, and criminal procedure and punishment. While the reader is invited to identify his biases (which shouldn't be difficult), the author has tried to be fair and tolerant, to keep his facts straight, and to remain within the academic tradition. These too are among the values he cherishes.

The merits of this book are due in large measure to those who have helped so generously. In both personal and professional ways, they include Will Scoggins, Gus Shackelford, Helmut Bader, and Nadine Hata. I am indebted to Professors Fred I. Greenstein and Charles Press for their encouragement and criticisms, as I am to Lance Widman, Edgar Love, Don Haley, Bob Putzel, and Dick Schwarzman among my El Camino colleagues. Two others, Jeannette Campiglia and Tom Wilson, devoted many hours and great skill to helping me translate political science into comprehensible English. How my wife, to whom this book is dedicated, could type the entire manuscript and provide sage editorial criticism while at the same time shielding me from the realities of daily life is more to be admired than understood.

I was also the beneficiary of invaluable institutional assistance. From the Dean's office at El Camino College came the tolerance and assistance of George Merrill and Helen Puckett. Scott, Foresman has far exceeded its publication commitment, thanks to the enthusiasm and expertise of Peter Quass and the wisdom and kindness of the late George Vlach. Finally, if future editors can be mass produced, let them be made in the mold of Nancy Kannappan. Authors will be chastened, but the kind of editorial diligence, practicality, intelligence, and uncompromising standards which she personifies will produce far better books.

Inescapably, however, the flaws of this text lie neither in my stars nor in those who have assisted me, but in myself.

Charles P. Sohner

Contents

AMERICAN GOVERNMENT AND POLITICS TODAY
A Concise Introduction

PART ONE

AMERICAN POLITICS IN PERSPECTIVE

Iron rusts in the atmosphere; trees bend in the wind; and nothing exists in a vacuum. That is why this book begins with a look at the broad environment within which American politics operates. Chapter 1 discusses the basic nature of politics and government, primarily in terms of power, and it contrasts the United States government with other systems. Chapter 2 explores some of the factors that make our government unique—the land, the people, the culture, the Constitution, and our own particular historical experience. In short, we begin with these chapters because politics in America requires some understanding of both the nature of politics and the nature of America.

Chapter **1**

The Nature of Politics
What's It All About?

*Families, and communities, and indeed free nations, rest not
on law and not on force but on a certain indispensable faith
and confidence, mixed with some affection and much charity,
each person for his fellow man.*

Walter Lippmann

Aristotle, often called the father of political science, wrote
that man is a political animal. There is considerable dispute about
whether this was a compliment or an insult. A public opinion poll has
revealed that most American parents do not want their children to enter
politics; yet at the same time they seem to reserve their greatest
admiration for Washington, Lincoln, and other political leaders. Is
politics a "dirty game" or a "noble calling?" Let us begin the study of
American government by noting that there are several different views of
politics and several ways of studying it. At the end, readers may
formulate their own answers to the above question.

THE STUDY OF POLITICS

*Politics refers to government action and anything designed to
affect it.*[1] It involves a bewildering array of official decisions, ranging
from building sidewalks to bombing cities. Since complexity is always

---

1 "Politics" has a diversity of meanings. See, for example, Austin Ranney's discussion of
the term in *The Governing of Men,* 3rd ed. (N.Y.: Holt, Rinehart & Winston, Inc., 1971),
pp. 4–6.

confusing, perhaps that is why politics is viewed with such mixed emotions. The study of these activities, now called political science, once seemed helplessly entangled with philosophy, economics, history, law, even religion—all subjects with which it is still concerned. But political science today tends to concentrate mostly on the state.

The State

The state, here, refers not to New York or California; *the state is the largest area under common control*—currently an entire nation. The nation-state, as it is sometimes called, is often defined as: (1) a fixed territory, (2) with a more or less permanent population, (3) ruled by a reasonably stable government, (4) which possesses the final power to make decisions, a power known as sovereignty. Yet because the state seems to encompass so much, many political scientists limit their scholarly appetites primarily to a study of government.

Government

Government is not so broad a concept as the state and excludes much that is significant about politics. For example, private organizations such as pressure groups exert great influence on important government decisions. On the other hand, the concept of government is too broad if it encompasses the administration of such organizations as churches or yacht clubs in which political scientists are seldom interested. They are concerned, instead, with *governments which make and administer the decisions of the state.* It is these which possess sovereignty.

Sovereignty

At first, the idea of sovereignty seems somewhat vague and intangible. Its essence, however, is relatively simple: It is the *ultimate power to make final decisions affecting all the inhabitants of the state.* This concept of power has had the most important influence upon the study of politics in the last forty years and is explored more fully in the following pages.

POLITICS AS POWER

Power means the capacity to alter socially significant behavior. It makes people do things which they might not do, or stops them from doing things which they might do. In other words, power involves a relationship between people which is based on dominance and submission. All the topics considered in this book can be interpreted in terms of power—how it is distributed, how it is obtained, and how it is used.

Power as Force

The most obvious source of government power is its preponderance of physical force. Governmental dominance in this area is almost a monopoly, for although private citizens may possess guns, they are subject to whatever restrictions are legally imposed. By contrast, other social institutions seem weak. A church can make rules but can only expel or excommunicate those who defy them. An employer, too, can issue orders but can at most fire the rebellious employee. Only government can use physical coercion to compel compliance to its commands.

Power as Influence

Fortunately for human dignity, government can usually gain obedience without resort to force. Schattschneider points out that only "about 5 percent of all state and local government employees are police officers" and concludes that "the internal relations of American government are not characteristically forceable."[2] Instead, government often can obtain the ends it seeks by the use of influence—a more subtle approach that involves both rewarding people with what they want (tax exemptions, medals, or defense contracts, for example) and threatening to deprive them of what they have (such as drivers' licenses, teaching credentials, or prison paroles).

Of course the capacity to bestow rewards and impose deprivations is not limited to government. Other institutions exert influence, both in their own private sphere, as when a business promotes one employee rather than another, and also in the broad political sphere, as when a union denounces a senator in its weekly newspaper. Since the process of giving (bestowing rewards) and taking (imposing deprivations) may involve honor, affection, or money, nearly everyone has at least some influence over at least a few people.

Power as Authority

No government could long survive if it had to rely exclusively upon force and influence. Policemen and prisons are too few and money and honor too scarce. Instead, most governments endure because they possess authority—that most remarkable kind of power with which people voluntarily comply because they believe it necessary, just, and therefore legitimate. If there is anything which merits description as a "law" of politics, it is that when a government loses the faith and confidence of its people, it must increase the force necessary to maintain its rule. When too much confidence is lost, there eventually comes a time

---

2 E. E. Schattschneider, *Two Hundred Million Americans in Search of a Government* (N.Y.: Holt, Rinehart & Winston, Inc., 1969), pp. 19–21.

when too little force is available to sustain continued power. Laws are obeyed, finally, because people believe they should be. It is this which converts power into authority, producing voluntary obedience.

Yet governments must share authority, as well as influence, with other institutions. The moral doctrines of a church, the examples of parents, or the impressions left by the TV screen or printed page persuade many of their correctness, more to be obeyed than questioned. For some, authority is the law, the command of the state; but for others, it is religious beliefs, family traditions, or the Columbia Broadcasting System.

Political Resources: Tools of Power

In order to exercise any kind of power—force, influence, or authority—an individual or institution must possess certain tools or capabilities. If these are used to affect government policy, they are often called political resources.

Type of Power	Political Resources
Force	Military weapons
	Police equipment
	Home-made bombs
	Riots (and revolution)
	Assassination
Influence	Votes
	Money (taxes, loans and subsidies, campaign contributions)
	Jobs (patronage)
	Honor (medals)
	Restrictions (or privileges)
	Respect (or contempt)
	Services (road repairs, fire protection)
Authority	Constitution (and laws and court decisions)
	Appeals to conscience (fasts, demonstrations)
	Holy Scriptures (and church command)
	Tradition (custom and habit)
	Family example (and early indoctrination)
	Propaganda (radio, TV, advertising, books)
	Education (schools, knowledge, expertise)
	Intelligence (reason, logic)
	High status (upper class)
	Respected role (parent, President)

Usually, both the kind of power brought into play and the particular resources used will be determined by the nature of a particular situation. In coping with a criminal, for example, government will employ force and use police equipment. But many times a tactical choice must be made. In protesting compulsory busing to achieve racial integration ordered by a school board, a group might blow up the buses (force), elect a new school board (influence), or challenge the school board decree in court (authority). When such a choice is available, the easiest course—but not necessarily the most effective—is often to invoke authority, because it entails less risk than force and is usually less costly than influence.

OTHER VIEWS OF POLITICS

Not all political scientists are pleased with this type of emphasis upon power. They acknowledge power to be an important component of politics, but insist that one must understand its other ingredients to appreciate the many functions performed by modern political systems.

Politics as Compromise

In our pluralistic society, one notable for its numerous and diverse groups, politics is often viewed largely as an instrument of compromise among them. Between white and black, the religious and the agnostic, labor and management, some sort of agreement must be reached. If we are to avoid civil war, there must be both an accommodation of interests and an agreement to disagree peacefully.

This conception of politics has been given a bad time by some in recent years. Compromise has been equated with a betrayal of principles, unethical deals, and a cynical sellout for the purpose of gaining power. Yet compromise reflects a tradition both long and strong in American politics. Jefferson, among the most idealistic of men, wrote that "We must be contented to secure what we can get. . . . It takes time to persuade men to do even what is for their own good."[3] Henry Clay of Kentucky won his place in history books as "the Great Compromiser," forestalling North-South conflict by authoring the Missouri Compromise of 1820 and the Compromise of 1850. John C. Calhoun justified in theory the kind of compromise which his Kentucky colleague had practiced. Calhoun developed the concept of the *concurrent majority,* by which the government would adopt only policies which had the support of a majority within each of the major sections or interest groupings of the nation.

More recently, the political importance of compromise has been reflected in the attempt of both the Republican and Democratic

3 Saul K. Padover, *Thomas Jefferson On Democracy* (N.Y.: Penguin Books, Inc., 1939), p. 154.

parties to gain power through the formation of coalitions of several and often differing groups. From the English playwright, George Bernard Shaw, comes one of the best defenses of compromise. He criticized a Labour Party parliamentary candidate who insisted on expressing his unpopular pacifist opinions and lost the election.

When I think of my own unfortunate character, smirched with compromise, rotted with opportunism, mildewed by expedience, . . . I do think Joe might have put up with just a speck or two on those white robes of his for the sake of the millions of poor devils who cannot afford any character at all because they have no friend in Parliament. Oh, . . . these superior persons. Who is Joe anyhow that he should not risk his soul occasionally like the rest of us?[4]

Just as Shaw asked that a candidate compromise a little in order to be elected to a position enabling him to serve the people best, so the voter is often asked to compromise. He is asked to choose the "lesser of two evils." He is reminded by honest and dedicated campaign workers that "God isn't running this year."

But compromise can also be defended as a positive good. It provides the cement, the social cohesion, which holds together diverse groups in peace, if not in total harmony. It is a sort of ransom with which we buy off bloodshed, the visible manifestation of an unseen humility, an admission that one might be wrong. However, unfortunately, crisis situations do not always permit the considerable time necessary to negotiate a compromise. Also, compromise presupposes that all groups involved have some underlying common interest, some political resources, and some reason to trust one another. If these conditions do not exist, compromise politics, the *quid pro quo* (this for that) won't work.

Politics As Continuity And Change

Another conception of politics emphasizes mediation between the forces of stability and the forces of change. Some stability is essential and is related to our psychological needs for security and predictability. If you are a barber, for example, you need confidence that commercial hair cuts will not be declared illegal tomorrow. If you are Jewish, you want the assurance that police will not suddenly impose a curfew forcing Jews off the streets after dark.

Yet if stability is necessary, it is equally true that change is inevitable. The invention of new machines, like the train or airplane, has led governments to subsidize their development, to regulate the fares charged, and to establish requirements for the licensing of pilots. Changes in the relative influence of various groups have produced such legislation as that prohibiting racial discrimination in theaters and hotels. A shift in values and moral codes has forced legal alterations in regulations governing nudity, drinking, and abortion.[5]

4 Quoted in Stephen Bailey, Howard D. Samuel, and Sidney Baldwin, *Government in America* (N.Y.: Henry Holt and Company, 1957), p. 543.
5 Alvin Toffler, *Future Shock* (N.Y.: Random House, Inc., 1970).

Many look to government to limit the scope of these changes, channel their direction, minimize their violence, aid their victims, and maintain, through it all, some comforting strains of continuity, a few strands of the yesterdays which molded our habits and shaped our minds. Sometimes, of course, changes have been bathed in the blood of violence. It was thus that we displaced the native Indians, won our independence, settled the western frontier, ended slavery, and secured the rights of working people to organize unions.

Politics as Group Dominance: Varieties of Elitism

A variety of political observers with little else in common agree that politics is the process through which governments are dominated by some sort of privileged minority, or elite class. Marxists or communists believe that politics is the process by which this "ruling class" maintains its advantages relative to the rest of the population. They assert, moreover, that the ruling class is always an economic one consisting of those persons who own the farms and factories, the means of production, in any nation. They point to the use of police and even armies to protect the ownership of private property and to preserve the unequal distribution of wealth.

This theory was shared by non-Marxists such as Charles Beard, the American historian who interpreted the Constitution of the United States as a document designed to protect the economic interests of those who wrote it, a view challenged by subsequent scholarship.[6] Considerably later sociologist C. Wright Mills criticized contemporary American politics because of its alleged control by a small "power elite" consisting primarily of corporation officials and military leaders.[7]

Other writers, sometimes called "democratic elitists," also assert that modern government is dominated by an "establishment" power structure consisting of relatively few leaders from business, unions, the professions, and the universities. Members of this establishment are believed to have so overwhelming a predominance of long-established prestige, money, specialized abilities, and other political resources, as well as such close agreement on fundamental political issues, that they are virtually impossible to dislodge from their seats of power. Yet far from deploring this state of affairs, elitists believe it is not

6 Charles A. Beard, *An Economic Interpretation of the Constitution* (N.Y.: The Macmillan Company, 1913). For divergent views, see Robert E. Brown, *Charles Beard and the Constitution* (Princeton, N.J.: Princeton University Press, 1955), Edmund S. Morgan, *The Birth of the Republic, 1763–89* (Chicago: University of Chicago Press, 1956), Forrest McDonald, *We the People: The Economic Origins of the Constitution* (Boston: Houghton Mifflin Company, 1965), and Jackson Turner Maine, *The Anti-Federalists: Critics of the Constitution, 1781–1788* (Chapel Hill: University of North Carolina Press, 1961).
7 *The Power Elite* (N.Y.: Oxford University Press, 1956). For diverse views on this issue, note the opinions of Dahl, Domhoff, Janowitz and others in Normal L. Crockett, ed., *The Power Elite in America* (Lexington, Mass.: D. C. Heath & Company, 1970).

only inevitable but in some respects beneficial. They support their position by such arguments as these:

1) Political resources such as money, knowledge, and access to the mass media are—and always will be—unequally distributed;

2) The complexity of modern problems requires that policy decisions come from those who possess specialized training rather than from an ill-informed majority;

3) Most citizens are indifferent to most public issues and unaware of their implications; such apathetic ignorance helps stabilize the political system by minimizing passionate dissent and maximizing the chances for the peaceful compromise of existing differences;

4) The mass of the people are more intolerant than the highly educated elites and often tend to support selfish demagogues who seek to violate the rights of unpopular minorities;

5) Even if the government is democratically organized, it is influenced decisively by pressure groups that are not democratically controlled;

6) Democracy requires only that the governing elite be held accountable for its performance at the next election.

In contrast to the elitists, other scholars known as pluralists maintain that political power is actually shared by many different groups interested in different policy areas; each group helps control decisions on matters of its special concern, and all interact both in occasional competition and intermittent alliance with one another. In a very general way, however, both the elitists and pluralists would agree that there is a governing class even in the most democratic of nations.[8]

Politics as Enforced Morality

Still another interpretation of the political process holds it to be a method by which rules of moral behavior may be formalized, enforced, and passed on to future generations. Often these rules have religious roots—in the Judeo-Christian tradition in the case of the United States. Although all politics is affected by the values and customs of society, it is often hard to distinguish their secular from their ecclesiastical origins. Both, certainly, have influenced government policy. When established codes of behavior based on the influence of church, family, or society break down, law becomes the ultimate source of moral authority. For if individuals are to be prevented from hurting their fellow men, some form of social control seems essential.

Governmental policies may reflect the teachings of a dominant church group. National prohibition of the manufacture, sale, or transportation of alcoholic beverages in the United States between 1919 and 1933 is a major example, as are state laws restricting business

8 Peter Bachrach, *The Theory of Democratic Elitism* (Boston: Little, Brown and Company, 1967).

operations on Sundays and gambling, abortion, and prostitution all week long. The classic illustration of the impact of religious views on politics is the government of Geneva, Switzerland, by a *theocracy,* or religious elite, dominated by John Calvin, a leader of the Protestant Reformation. In seventeenth-century New England, the government of the Massachusetts Bay Colony also bore the strong imprint of Calvinist theology. Even in the midst of the 1972 presidential campaign, two authors noted that Gallup polls have shown the Reverend Billy Graham to be the second most-admired man in America and suggested that the winning candidate would be the one whose values seem closest to his.[9]

Politics as Systems Analysis

The fifth and final conception of politics to be noted is the attempt to understand the political system without the preconceptions (or biases) implicit in the other views. According to *systems analysis* government is an institution through which certain pressures (public demands and expectations) are transformed into official programs and policies. Borrowing the language of economics and mechanics, the pressures are sometimes called "inputs" and the resulting effects are termed "outputs;" the government is thus a processing machine.[10]

The activities of parties and interest groups help channel the inputs entering the political system, while laws, executive actions, and court decisions are the outputs. Usually, any kind of governmental output alters the later needs, opinions, and other inputs into the political system through a "feedback" process. If policy outputs fail to cope with the inputs adequately (in other words, if the people aren't satisfied with government action), the maintenance of the whole system may be in jeopardy. As a general objective, advocates of systems analysis seek to establish a better understanding of the relationship between the environmental influences on government and the policies which government pursues. This approach is diagrammed in Figure 1.

GROWING POWER OF THE STATE

Whatever people believe to be the fundamental nature of politics, there is wide agreement that the state, compared with other social institutions such as the family, church, or business, has assumed increasing importance. The modern national government provides the ultimate police power necessary for the protection of life and property. It has received much of the devotion once given to religion, assumed the direction and support of education once in the hands of church or family, and provided welfare services once dispensed by private groups. There seems now to be as much government regulation of business as business control over government, and the use of over one fourth of the gross national product is determined by government allocation. In short, the

9 *Los Angeles Times,* July 22, 1972, p. 23.
10 David Easton, *The Political System* (N.Y.: Alfred A. Knopf, Inc., 1953).

Figure 1 Politics Viewed by Systems Analysis

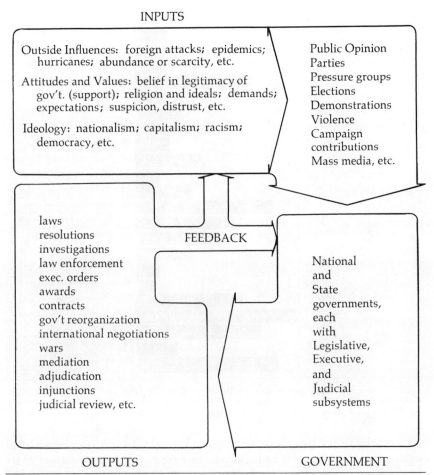

INPUTS

Outside Influences: foreign attacks; epidemics; hurricanes; abundance or scarcity, etc.

Attitudes and Values: belief in legitimacy of gov't. (support); religion and ideals; demands; expectations; suspicion, distrust, etc.

Ideology: nationalism; capitalism; racism; democracy, etc.

Public Opinion
Parties
Pressure groups
Elections
Demonstrations
Violence
Campaign contributions
Mass media, etc.

laws
resolutions
investigations
law enforcement
exec. orders
awards
contracts
gov't reorganization
international negotiations
wars
mediation
adjudication
injunctions
judicial review, etc.

FEEDBACK

National
and
State
governments,
each
with
Legislative,
Executive,
and
Judicial
subsystems

OUTPUTS

GOVERNMENT

Note that systems analysis is based on a "cause and effect" assumption. Each influence (or input) encourages the government to take some action (or output) which alters (by feedback) the subsequent influences.

so-called negative state, which "governed best" when it "governed least," has been replaced by the positive state, engaged in innumerable activities.

This is not to say that government has become the most powerful of all social institutions, but only that it is heading most rapidly in that direction. The family still has the capacity to shape the personalities of infant children in a way unlikely to be seriously rivaled, but its stability has been jeopardized by rising divorce rates, new life styles, and the generation gap. Devotion to one's employer seems little more than a nostalgic myth, and the rejection of one's ancestral religion seldom causes more than a mild reproach. In fact, all institutional loyalties have lost much of their former sanctity. Yet despite the renewed popularity of

Figure 2   The Role of Government in American Life

PRIVATE		GOVERNMENT
Gross National Product	20%	Purchased by government (1966)
Total U.S. Land Area	34%	Owned by federal government (1962)
The National Non-Farm Economy	20%	Regulated by federal agencies (1950)
All Loans To Farmers	72%	Extended by federal government (1963)
National Income	23%	Net tax revenue of government (1962)
All Debt In U.S.	30%	Net debt owed by government (1966)
Gross Corporate Profit	47%	Federal corporate taxes (1962)
Personal Income	22%	Personal taxes (1966)
All Unemployed Workers	43%	Received government unemployment (1962)
All Employed Workers	16%	Employed by government (1965)
Total Building	34%	Public construction (1966)
Bank Deposits	86%	Insured by federal government (1963)
All Medical Research	60%	Financed by federal government (1967)
Commercial Investment Holdings	54%	U.S. Government obligations (1966)
Outstanding House Mortgage Debt	34%	FHA and VA guaranteed mortgages (1965)
Revenues of State and Local Governments	15%	Federal aid (1965)
Electric Power	11%	Produced in federal-owned plants (1962)
Scientific Research	66%	Financed by federal government (1962-63)
Atomic Energy Research	99%	Financed by federal government (1954)
All Schools and Colleges	77%	Financed by government (1967)
All Medical Care Expenditures	25%	Paid by government (1965)
All Welfare Payments	88%	Paid by government (1965)

Source: Reprinted with permission of Benziger Bruce & Glencoe, Inc. (Beverly Hills, California), a Division of The Macmillan Company from *Pattern Of American Government* by Harvey M. Karlan. Copyright © The Glencoe Press 1968.

civil disobedience and political protest (in part itself a consequence of increasing state power), disloyalty to one's country or repudiation of its form of government is now the supreme and inexcusable heresy.

ORGANIZATION OF THE STATE: VARIETIES OF GOVERNMENT

The distinctive and characteristic features of American politics can sometimes be seen most clearly in contrast with other types of political systems. Such comparative analysis usually focuses on power.

Possessors of Power

Aristotle classified governments usefully, but somewhat crudely, into three broad categories based on who possessed ultimate power within them: government by one person, a few, or many. Today these types are most frequently labeled dictatorship, aristocracy (or elitism) and democracy.

Dictatorship   Governmental power controlled by one person was once found most commonly in the hands of hereditary kings, as in Saudi Arabia today. But such absolute monarchies are a dying political species, and the few remaining thrones are usually occupied by persons, like Queen Elizabeth of Great Britain, who "reign but do not rule." They are constitutional monarchs who perform ceremonial functions as head of state but do not run the government. One-man rule in modern times has usually been exercised by a dictator such as Castro in Cuba, Franco in Spain, or Hitler in Germany, often swept into power on a wave of violence.

Aristocracy Rule by a small, privileged minority of the population is sometimes called an elite, an aristocracy (when benevolent), or an oligarchy (when self-serving). It has many forms and holds most of the world's people in its sway. Indeed, it is probable that pure dictatorships may not exist at all, since even a dictator is dependent upon his servants, advisers, and especially his secret police and armed forces for continued power.

Some oligarchies have been based upon race, as in the Union of South Africa, Rhodesia, and certain areas of the American South, or upon membership in a dominating elite political party, as in the Soviet Union today. Others, like the military juntas ruling in Greece and numerous countries in Asia, Africa, and South America, are aristocracies of career army officers. Theocracy, as noted earlier, is rule by a religious elite; it dominated Geneva, Switzerland, for a time as well as the early years of the Massachusetts colony. Another common form has been plutocracy, government by the wealthy few, and there are also countless aristocracies of age and sex that have rewarded old men with political dominance. Among all the varieties of minority rule, government by the wise and just is conspicuously rare.

Democracy Governments chosen by and responsive to a majority of the adult population are called democracies. Most have emerged rather recently and they are still limited to relatively few nations. The term democracy was originally used to describe rule directly by the people—*direct democracy,* in which all participate, as in the ancient Greek city-state or New England town meeting. This was contrasted with a republic—*representative democracy,* in which actual rule was exerted by representatives elected by the people. Such a distinction is less significant than an underlying issue suggested earlier: Is any kind of real majority rule possible if various elites possess most political resources?

The Extent of Power

Broadly speaking, government power is either limited or unlimited. Since both types have been found among democracies, aristocracies and dictatorships, one must separate the question of how many people control the government from that of the scope or extent of government power.

Constitutionalism   Government power is limited where the governors as well as the governed must follow the "rules of the game" and where certain rights are guaranteed to minorities, even against the majority. Because written constitutions, like ours in America, usually contain "bills of rights" designed to protect individual freedom, governments which acknowledge such limitations upon their own power are often referred to as "constitutional" ones even where, as in England, there is no single document called a constitution. Pluralists, who emphasize the importance of distributing power among many different groups, sometimes contend that a government is constitutional only to the degree that it recognizes the autonomy (self-government) of private organizations within its jurisdiction.

Totalitarianism   Governments which reject any limitations upon their authority, either by law or practice, are called authoritarian, despotic, tyrannical, or totalitarian ones, the latter term implying a monopoly of decision-making power to the exclusion of all voluntary groups. Today such regimes severely limit individual freedom and depend upon rigid censorship and control of mass media, a secret police, and the prohibition of all political parties except the one controlling the government. The regimes of Greece, Haiti, the Soviet Union, and the People's Republic of China seem to fit this definition fairly closely.

Territorial Distribution of Power

Especially in large nations the distribution of power between the government of the whole country and the governments of the smaller parts into which it is divided is of considerable importance. There are three possible relationships between central and regional governments.

Unitary governments   Most common, especially in relatively small countries or those having a very homogeneous population with similar characteristics, is the *unitary* system. In this form the regional or local governments have only those powers which the central or national government chooses to give them. England, France, Italy, and China are leading examples of unitary systems. Moreover, if each of the fifty states in the United States is viewed as a separate political system, they too are unitary, since cities, counties, townships, and other units of local government have only the power which the various state governments delegate to them.

Confederations   The opposite of a unitary system is a *confederation*. Here, the central or national government possesses only those powers which the regional governments choose to give it. The first national constitution in America was called the Articles of Confederation, for the central government was dependent upon the thirteen states for all the authority it exerted. Confederations have become rather rare. With the possible exception of Yugoslavia and some Arab states, the

Figure 3   Methods of Distributing Power Territorially

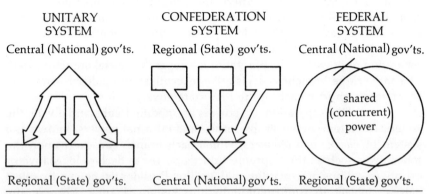

UNITARY SYSTEM	CONFEDERATION SYSTEM	FEDERAL SYSTEM
Central (National) gov'ts.	Regional (State) gov'ts.	Central (National) gov'ts.
Regional (State) gov'ts.	Central (National) gov'ts.	Regional (State) gov'ts.

Note: The nature of the federal system in the U.S. is described more fully in Chapter 2. The exact division between national and state powers has occasioned bitter political controversy.

leading—but weak—example is the United Nations, functioning at the international level.

Federalism   The third plan for distributing power territori-ally within a nation is *federalism,* an American invention first imple-mented in our present Constitution. In this system the central (national or federal) government and the regional (state) governments each have certain powers independent of one another and allocated by the Consti-tution itself. There is often cooperation between the two, but in the event of a conflict, the national government normally prevails. In addition to this country, the system is found primarily in other large nations such as Brazil, Canada, Mexico, Australia, West Germany, India, the Soviet Union, and because it is so heterogeneous even if small, Switzerland.

Functional Distribution of Power

Every government performs two kinds of functions: It makes rules and it enforces them. The former, entailing the passage of laws, is a legislative function; the second, involving the administration of laws, is an executive function. The relationship between those who pass the laws and those who enforce them may take two broad forms.

Parliamentary governments   If the same group is largely involved in the performance of both functions, one may say that there is a *fusion of power,* usually called a *parliamentary* system. Such is the case in Great Britain, Canada, West Germany, and Italy, among many other nations. In this form of government, the prime minister or premier, as the chief executive is called, must be a member of the legislative body as must all members of his cabinet. Usually, he is the head of the largest political party, or coalition of parties, in the legislature and holds office only as long as he has the support of a majority of the lawmakers.

Presidential governments   In contrast, if one group is re-sponsible for passing laws and another group for their enforcement, a *separation of powers* exists, often called a *presidential* system. This is the case in the United States, where the president and members of his cabinet are prohibited from serving simultaneously in Congress, and where he serves for a fixed term of four years, whether he has the support of a majority in Congress or not. In accordance with the separation of powers principle, there is a separate judicial branch as well. The same three branches—legislative, executive, and judicial—similarly separated, comprise each of the fifty state governments.

The separation of powers is modified substantially in the American system, however, by formal and informal powers, known as a system of *checks and balances,* which each branch can exert upon the other two—such as the Supreme Court's power to declare legislative or executive actions unconstitutional or the President's power to select judges, subject to confirmation by the Senate. France, Mexico, the Philippines, and various South American countries have presidential systems modified to one degree or another and roughly comparable to the American one. *The United States has a representative, democratic, constitutional, federal, presidential form of government.* But many other combinations of the preceding characteristics are possible.

The Purpose of Power

The language of politics remains fairly cool when discussing the forms of government described above. Nonetheless, it heats to the boiling point when the subject changes to the basic purposes of government and the philosophies on which they rest—how to interpret the pursuit of justice or the national welfare. Conservatives who view untested policies with cautious skepticism are sometimes denounced as "fascist pigs" and liberals who criticize the existing society may be branded as "commie traitors." And so, a word of caution: Labels are less important than the actual policies or personalities to which they are applied, and every group works for government policies which will advance its own interests. Yet because we use words and labels to communicate with one another, there should be some agreement on their definition.

Labels of the left   Political views are frequently described in the oversimplified terms of liberal *vs.* conservative, radical *vs.* reactionary, or left wing *vs.* right wing.

A liberal is usually believed to be one who wants change, reform, or innovation, inspired through tolerance for a wide diversity of viewpoints, including new and heretical ones. In modern times, however, self-styled liberals usually favor not only freedom of expression for differing opinions, but also a strong, active government that often limits the economic freedom of businessmen in the interests of consumers and employees, and supports government policies to improve the lot of the poor and the victims of discrimination. Especially since the 1930s, the Democratic party in America usually has been associated with such views, to the dismay of some very conservative Democrats. As a result it has developed voter support primarily among industrial workers, low-income groups and such oppressed minorities as blacks and Mexican-Americans.

The term radical is often associated with extreme liberalism and describes one who wishes great changes, frequently accomplished through violent protest or revolution. Sometimes those who want a drastic reversal of liberal policies are also called radicals, although this use of the term is rather confusing. Leftists, or left-wingers, represent a broad category often encompassing everyone from mild liberals to revolutionary Communists. The so-called New Left which gained prominence in the late 1960s, is characterized by its youth, its distrust of orthodox liberal politicians, and by a proclivity for confrontation politics, often involving illegal demonstrations. The Progressive Labor Party, the Black Panthers, and the Students for a Democratic Society (SDS) are all parts of the New Left. They tend to be anticapitalist, but often view the communist bureaucracy of the Soviet Union with equal suspicion.

The Old Left, defined very broadly, includes politicians committed to the mid-century New Deal philosophy, along with democratic socialists who favor government ownership of basic industries such as those producing electricity, mineral resources, and steel. Members of the Communist Party are committed to the doctrines of Karl Marx as interpreted by the Soviet Union. They tend to encourage participation in the traditional compromise which characterizes American electoral politics, however, while retaining the old goal of government ownership of the entire economy attained—where necessary—by violence.

Labels of the right   At the other end of the political spectrum are conservatives, reactionaries, or right-wingers. A conservative is one who wishes to conserve and perpetuate existing values and institutions. He is usually a bit skeptical of abstract logic or pure rationality, preferring instead to depend upon experience and tradition, the "tried and true," as a guide for future action. Conservatives also tend to rely primarily upon individual initiative, private enterprise capitalism, and state and local responsibility to solve social problems. They harbor a sustained distrust of comprehensive government welfare programs as a policy that destroys the freedom and self-reliance necessary for both personal integrity and national strength. Many believe that President Nixon betrayed his initial dedication to these principles. The Republican Party has typically been associated with such ideas. Its main sources of support have been businessmen and independent farmers, both with a considerable stake in existing success and therefore committed to a continuation of things pretty much as they are.

Just as radicals are considered extreme liberals, so reactionaries may be described as ultra-conservatives. They are not content with resisting new innovations but fight for a return to what they believe to be the good old days. Rightists, or right-wingers, are terms referring to a broad group that includes moderate conservatives, as well as reactionaries, and extends from organizations like the Young Americans for Freedom (YAF) to the John Birch Society and the American Nazi Party. This rightist extreme usually endorses censorship, toughness toward criminals, superpatriotism, and sometimes racial or religious bigotry.

Oddly enough, a look at the far edges of left and right reveals certain similarities in the two extremes: Both are hostile to human freedom, the left in the interests of greater equality, the right for purposes of suppressing immorality and alien ideas. Nonetheless, liberals and conservatives view the world from somewhat different perspectives. The liberal sees men as basically rational and cooperative once education has freed them from ancient superstitions and a decent standard of living has liberated them from the brutalizing effects of poverty. Both are government responsibilities. The conservative sees men as potentially impulsive and combative unless conditioned to cherish established values and restrained by firm control. These also are tasks of government.

It is important to note, however, that most Americans are not ideologically oriented. If pressed, they tend to describe themselves as middle-of-the-road, but they seldom think in terms of liberal and conservative and, with characteristic practicality, are most interested in policies that work, no matter what labels they bear. It is not surprising, then, that the government's economic and social policy is really a mixed one, a compromise between the right and the left. It is clearly moving away from individualism, however, toward a greater reliance upon collectivism, which includes economic controls, welfare programs, and socialism. Even the large private corporation is also a kind of collectivist entity whose impact on the individual may rival that of the government.

THE STUDY OF POLITICS

How can one best study a subject as complex as this? At first political science emphasized the careful analysis of political institutions and their legal foundations. Considerable stress was placed on constitutional law as enunciated in America by the Supreme Court, while the organization of Congress, political parties, and executive agencies also received much attention.

In the 1950s another approach known as behavioralism appeared more frequently in the research of political scientists. It stressed the politically significant behavior of individuals and groups more than formal structures, abstract theory, and legal authorization. Behavioralism was characterized by (1) a reliance on ideas and empirical findings derived from such other social sciences as psychology, anthropology and sociology; (2) the statistical measurement of the frequency of political actions; (3) an emphasis on the root causes and conditioning factors which may explain political phenomena; and (4) an attempt to develop a "value-free," objective, morally neutral method of political analysis.

The trend today seems away from behavioralism too, toward a sort of eclecticism combining both old and new approaches. Most particularly, there is an insistence that research be relevant to current issues and that it be related to values, to ethical standards of right and wrong. In other words, a systematic description of what *is* (empirical theory) should be associated with a conception of what *ought to be* (normative theory). With that in mind, this book will include a little of history, philosophy, law, institutions, political behavior, and other ingredients as well.

Chapter 2

The Americans
Land, Legacy, and Political Culture

God has not been preparing the English-speaking and
Teutonic peoples for a thousand years for nothing. . . . No!
He has made us . . . adept in government that we may
administer government among savage and senile
peoples. . . . And of all our race He has marked the American
people as His chosen nation to finally lead in the
regeneration of the world.

Senator Albert J. Beveridge

Americans now live in the oldest republic in the world. We have a rich political heritage—if less divinely inspired than Senator Beveridge so arrogantly asserted—and a long-established Constitution. Indeed, ours is the largest and most heterogeneous country ever to attempt to operate as a democracy. The land and history, the basic constitutional principles, the people, with their values and beliefs—all of these have shaped the contemporary American political culture. They help determine, in other words, the way we think and act in politics.

GEOGRAPHICAL INFLUENCES

Robert Frost, one of America's great literary figures, was the first person ever asked to read a poem at a presidential inauguration. Squinting out into the reflected glare of the winter sun, he spoke not of John F. Kennedy, about to take the oath of office, but of the United

States itself. "The land was ours," the old poet rasped, "before we were the land's."[1] The words sink in slowly. We understand owning the land. Only later, gradually, do we realize that the land we own begins to mold us, determine our actions, change our thinking. The very word, "land," is synonymous with country or nation in several languages. Where we live, how far apart, the way we make our money—even how we govern ourselves depends, at least in part, on the land.

Size and Location

The most obvious geographical fact about America is that it is large. When a country is large, it is almost essential that its governmental authority be decentralized. It would be absurd to regulate the speed limits in Hawaii from a Washington office. Where government services and controls are widely dispersed, then efficiency and adaptability also require dispersal of the power to make policy. This is a major justification for the federal system.

The immense size of America has contributed to its relative security, as well as to its decentralized authority. Even were an enemy army to establish an invasion beachhead on our shores, the logistical problems of supply lines thousands of miles long make successful occupation wildly improbable.

Location seems to be a geographic factor at least as important as size, although the advent of ICBM's (intercontinental ballistic missiles), making every point on the earth's surface vulnerable to attack from every other point, may have reduced its significance. America's location between oceans 3000 miles wide on the east and 6000 miles wide on the west promoted a foreign policy usually described as *isolationism*. Until this century we made few international commitments and joined no military alliances. Geographic remoteness from international power centers inhibited foreign invasion from Europe or Asia and permitted national attention to be devoted to the occupation and development of a rich, vast, and largely virgin continent. As the French, Germans, or Russians would surely testify, the advantages of a country beyond the reach of alien infantrymen are enormous.

The world is smaller now, diminished by the technology of modern communication, transportation, and weaponry. Isolationism fell victim to this new reality, with its death marked by the graves of American soldiers killed in two World Wars and in Korea and Vietnam. The emergence of the missile age has required a reevaluation of America's international position. Although sea power, so forcefully advocated by Admiral Alfred T. Mahan at the close of the last century, remains an important consideration, the air routes over the Arctic polar region have

1 From "The Gift Outright" from *The Poetry of Robert Frost,* edited by Edward Connery Lathem. Copyright 1942 by Robert Frost. Copyright © 1969 by Holt, Rinehart and Winston, Inc. Copyright © 1970 by Lesley Frost Ballantine. Reprinted by permission of Holt, Rinehart and Winston, Inc.

surpassed it in significance. The United States, isolated for so long by its location in the Western Hemisphere, now finds itself an air neighbor to the other great powers of the Northern Hemisphere. In terms of American defense, the change is not a happy one. While our security can be jeopardized from nearly anywhere, we have insufficient power to protect our interests everywhere. In the Middle East, Asia, and Europe, hard choices must be made.

Since ancient times, most significant world changes seem to have sprung from moderate climates. The United States is favored in this respect, too. Except for northern Alaska and southern Hawaii, it is located in the temperate zone. With less energy required for the physical necessities of getting warm or cooling off, more seems available for other endeavors.

Resources: People of Plenty

The political significance of America's geographic size and location has been dwarfed by the importance of its enormous riches. In quantity, variety, and accessibility of natural resources we have been favored—perhaps too much so, because the very abundance of these resources may have encouraged the rapid and wasteful depletion of far too high a proportion of them. The extensive river systems, the level of rainfall, the availability of reasonably flat farm land, and the length of the growing season also have contributed to economic wealth.

The United States grows a surplus of wheat, corn, rice, meat, and dairy products, and is a leading producer of copper, lead, sulfur, coal, iron, natural gas, petroleum, and magnesium, although known reserves of some of these minerals can support current use for only a limited future. In a world where wealth is often measured by industrialization, the U.S. manufacturing output far outstrips that of the Soviet Union, Japan, and Germany—its chief competitors.

To compare America's wealth with that of other nations, one must rely on reported production statistics for various commodities, and especially on the gross national product (GNP) per capita. This shows the value of all goods and services produced in a country if its total were divided equally among its inhabitants. Figure 4 summarizes some of this data for purposes of international comparison. Such figures demonstrate the enormous disparities between the "have" and the "have not" nations, between the American island of plenty and its surrounding sea of poverty. It is hardly surprising that the United States occasionally becomes the object of envious hatred among the destitute majorities of Asia or Latin America.

Apart from this, affluence has another important political implication. Statistical analysis demonstrates that democracy flourishes most consistently in relatively wealthy nations while poor nations, it seems, tend to trade majority rule and personal freedoms for promises of

Figure 4   Comparative National Wealth

Rank	GNP per capita Nation	Amount	Electricity Nation	Volume[2]	Steel Nation	Volume[3]	Wheat Nation	Volume[4]
1	U.S.	$4,664	U.S.	1,552	U.S.	141	U.S.S.R.	85
2	Sweden	$3,315	U.S.S.R.	689	U.S.S.R.	122	U.S.	44
3	Canada	$2,997	Japan	316	Japan	91	China	30
4	Switz.	$2,965	U.K.	238	W.Ger.	50	India	21
5	Denmark	$2,860	W.Ger.	221	U.K.	30	Canada	21
6	France	$2,783	Canada	190	France	25	France	16
7	Norway	$2,528	France	132	Italy	18	Austral.	12
8	W.Ger.	$2,512	Italy	97	China	17	Turkey	12
9	Austral.	$2,476	E.Ger.	65	Poland	12	Italy	11
10[1]	Belgium	$2,372	Sweden	58	Czech.	12	Argen.	8

[1]Other GNP figures: U.K. $1,976; Japan $1,626; U.S.S.R. $890; Mexico $566; Kenya $136; India $84. [2]In trillions of kilowatt-hours. [3]In millions of short tons. [4]In millions of short tons. Source: U.S. Bureau of the Census, *Statistical Abstract of the United States: 1971.* For U.S.S.R. GNP, *Los Angeles Times,* Nov. 21, 1968, Part II, p. 5.

economic security and material enrichment.[2] David M. Potter, in *People of Plenty,* pins down the relationship between prosperity and politics in the peculiar American experience. He argues that our economic surplus made it possible to improve the lot of the poor without substantially hurting the rich. The prevailing belief that equality could be attained by "leveling up" as well as by "leveling down" has made revolution less attractive to America's poor and reliance upon the democratic processes more appealing.[3] Nevertheless, the trend of the 1970s is toward increasing concern with redistribution of existing wealth and a disenchantment with economic growth.

HISTORICAL INFLUENCES

Our roots are sunk deep in the past. American government had already passed through three clear stages before the adoption of our present Constitution: the colonial, Revolutionary, and Confederation periods. Each of these contributed important characteristics to our present system.

Colonial Development

In spite of Spanish, Dutch, French, and American Indian influences, American history is essentially a child of English imperial expansion. From the establishment in 1607 of Jamestown, Virginia, to

2 Seymour M. Lipset, *Political Man* (Garden City, N.Y.: Anchor Books, Doubleday & Company, Inc., 1963), pp. 31–45.
3 David M. Potter, *People of Plenty* (Chicago: University of Chicago Press, 1954), pp. 111–27.

the founding in 1733 of Savannah, Georgia, England had created the thirteen colonies which became the nucleus of the United States of America. Thus, the American Revolution was a revolt against an English rule which had lasted for about a century and a half. During that time certain characteristics became so entrenched that they persist, in one form or another, to the present time.

Common law One of these enduring characteristics is the English common law tradition, which now prevails in all American states except Louisiana, still reflecting its French origins. The common law was developed before the birth of legislative bodies by judges who traveled from place to place settling disputes in a common, or uniform, manner. The judges employed a combination of old Roman legal ideas, Catholic doctrines, prevailing customs which defined what was "just," and their own ethical sensitivity. Strong reliance was placed upon precedents, or previous decisions in similar cases, to give the law consistency and continuity.

The common law established rules of court *procedure* that we still regard as essential to a fair trial. It insisted that the burden of proof in criminal cases be placed upon the prosecution and that defendants have such rights as trial by jury and access to legal counsel. It also determined certain *substantive* grounds of injury, such as contract violations or property damage, which enabled one person to sue another to gain compensation for losses.

Governmental institutions The colonial period laid the foundations for many later institutions. The separation of legislative and executive officials into distinct branches of government, the establishment of bicameral (two-house) legislatures, and the creation of towns, counties, and other units of local rule were among the most important of these.

Representative government At the time of the Revolution, eight of the thirteen colonies were royal ones. Their governors, and often members of the upper houses of bicameral legislatures were chosen—directly or indirectly—by the English king. But the Crown permitted members of the lower houses to be chosen by the voters so that government was representative at least of the people allowed to vote. The other colonies had even more elected representation. The effects of this system had immense significance.

First, in these elected houses native Americans such as Thomas Jefferson and James Madison gained the political experience and leadership training necessary to govern the nation effectively once independence had been won. This kind of training ground was sadly deficient in former Dutch, French, and Spanish colonies and may help to explain the difficulty with which stable governments have been established in those areas. Second, the election of legislators gradually created a desire for the election of still other government officials.

State loyalty Because the first thirteen states existed before there was an American national government, people focused their loyalty on the states in which they lived and only later, grudgingly, did they transfer it to the nation as a whole. When English colonial policy became harsh and restrictive in the 1760s and 1770s, Americans developed an increasing hatred for national authority and a conviction that decentralized government was the best government. Such attitudes help account for the extreme weakness of the central government provided under the Articles of Confederation, and the subsequent ambiguous compromise between national and state power represented in the federalism of our Constitution.

The continuing vigor of antinational states' rights sentiment is manifested in the support for Barry Goldwater in 1964 and George Wallace in 1968 and 1972. Devotion to decentralized, regional rule is far from dead. This preference is reflected when we speak (misleadingly but lovingly) of "states' rights," but refer (far more ominously) to "national power."

To be sure, national patriotism now supersedes state loyalty in the hearts of most Americans. Some hope that the next step, long and still more hazardous, will be the further expansion of our allegiance to embrace the entire human race. Yet, our global involvement since World War II has produced a reaction which looks inward, to unsolved problems at the state, and especially at the community, level. When presidential candidate George McGovern summoned America to "come home," some interpreted it as a new isolationism while others heard it as a plea for the kind of participatory democracy that would enable people to control their own destinies at the local level. But his real intention seemed to be to strengthen the national government, though to employ its resources more for domestic than for international purposes. Most Americans, like citizens of other lands, accept governmental action at the level best calculated to meet their needs.

Revolution and Confederation

Although the Revolution spanned only six years, its legacy would affect American government for many decades.

Independence It has been nearly two centuries since Thomas Jefferson wrote that "these United Colonies are, and of Right ought to be Free and Independent States." The freedom from imperialistic control thus proclaimed in the Declaration of Independence remains pertinent today because the American experience has similarities to the struggles against foreign colonialism that recently have swept across Africa and Asia. These revolts have often entailed subversive conspiracies (such as led by Samuel Adams), inflammatory prose (written here by Tom Paine, one of the most skilled propagandists in history), and guerrilla warfare (utilized in America by General Nathaniel Green and others). As in the American Revolution, predominantly agricultural regions have struggled against a more industrialized foe.

In any event, the American example became a source of

encouragement for oppressed peoples everywhere. In the 1820s, when Latin Americans sought to free themselves from Spanish imperialism, the United States gave support through the Monroe Doctrine, warning against repressive foreign intervention. Nearly a century later, President Woodrow Wilson enunciated the right of national self-determination as one of our aims in World War I.

In recent years, however, American dedication to the cause of independence has been compromised by our far-ranging economic interests, alliances with colonial powers, and fears that "wars of national liberation" are merely instruments of communist imperialism. The embarrassment of our dilemma was underscored in 1946 when Ho Chi Minh quoted from Thomas Jefferson in proclaiming the independence of Vietnam from French rule.

A revolutionary heritage?   There is an ageless struggle between the forces of authority and stability on one side and those of freedom and progress on the other. The American Revolution represented a victory for the latter. This triumphant treason created a radical political tradition that has been deeply troublesome to the conservative defenders of established institutions.

Some writers argue, with considerable merit, that the events of the 1770s were not a true revolution because their purpose and effect were not significantly to alter the existing relationships among social classes in America—already a basically middle-class country.[4] Assessed in terms of other characteristics of revolutions—violence, the creation of new political institutions, speed of change—there certainly was a revolution, but against an external, not internal, enemy.

New American governments   As independence became the major and most dramatic objective of the Revolution, its success required the establishment of new state constitutions and an American national government. During the Revolutionary War, the colonies drafted new constitutions as independent states. These first state constitutions, in reacting strongly against what was thought to have been the excessive power of the old royal governors, weakened the authority of the new state governors, especially with respect to money matters and appointment powers. As a result, many believe that state governors still have too little authority to meet their responsibilities effectively.

At the national level, the Second Continental Congress, consisting of delegates chosen by the various colonies, functioned to direct the war effort, but it did not have a legally secure status. Hence a committee was appointed to draft a formal constitution. This, the Articles of Confederation, was approved by all thirteen state legislatures and went into effect in 1781. In the distribution of authority throughout its far-flung territory, the British Empire was a unitary system of government, in which colonies had only that authority which the central

4 Louis Hartz, "Democracy without a Democratic Revolution," *American Political Science Review* 46 (June 1952): 321–42.

government chose to give to them. Since the American colonists came to equate a strong centralized government with arbitrary and even tyrannical power, not surprisingly they overreacted and created through the Articles of Confederation a system in which the territorial distribution of authority was arranged in exactly the opposite way. As is characteristic of a confederation, the central government was limited to that authority given it by the thirteen states.

Under the Articles, the national government, although generally quite weak, was delegated some important responsibilities. It could establish a postal system, make treaties, maintain a navy, and govern all territories outside the jurisdiction of the various states. In the long run (if its eight-year existence can be so named), the powers the national government lacked were more significant than those which it possessed. Since it could neither tax nor enlist troops into the army, it was dependent upon the states for both money and manpower—two prime ingredients of any political system. It could not prevent the states from coining money or prohibit the erection of tariffs or other trade barriers between states.

The structure of the national government under the Articles consisted only of a one-house, or unicameral, legislature in which each state had one vote regardless of population. Not only did the Confederation possess no independent executive branch and no court system, but any amendment that might strengthen it required the unanimous approval of all thirteen state legislatures. Predictably, the Articles were never amended.

Failure of the Confederation   The Confederation government had the misfortune of a wartime birth and a postwar infancy in an era later described as "the critical period" in American history. Both the state governments and the Congress had incurred heavy debts during the Revolution, and the poor farmers, forced to foot the tax bill, were already hard pressed to make their mortgage payments. They staged bitter and sometimes violent demonstrations. In 1786 the militia was called out to counter angry demands for the printing of more paper currency in New Hampshire and to suppress Shays' Rebellion in Massachusetts, an uprising designed to prevent the courts from ordering farm foreclosures.

There were other problems also. The Confederation Congress could not guarantee American territory against British and Spanish encroachments, and it was unable to get the states to make the contributions necessary to meet its own financial responsibilities, in particular to' the troops and other war claims. It was difficult to find foreign markets to supplant those temporarily lost in England, and state-imposed trade barriers simultaneously reduced the volume of goods sold within the country. Finally, there was a pervasive fear among bankers, land speculators, and other creditors that many states would follow the example of Rhode Island and adopt an inflationary currency policy to enable the poor to repay their debts in money worth less than that which they initially borrowed. Confronted with the inability of the Confederation to cope with these crises, it is little wonder that some prominent politicians began to explore the possibility of creating a stronger national government.

THE CONSTITUTION
The Constitutional Convention

While meeting for the supposed purpose of improving the Articles of Confederation, most of the fifty-five delegates to the convention assembled in Philadelphia quickly agreed to start from scratch in drafting a new document. They were partially motivated by a recognition that it would be impossible to get the unanimous state approval required to amend the Articles, and were emboldened to broaden their mandate by a decision to bar the press and public from their deliberations.

The delegates   The men who wrote our Constitution left the imprint of their minds, personalities, and vested interests upon it. As a group, they possessed certain characteristics which seem, in retrospect, most significant: (1) Their average age was only forty-two, and their youth may have contributed to their innovative vigor and sympathy for expanded national power. (2) They were an exceptionally well-educated group, with practical backgrounds covering a broad spectrum of public life. Many had served in diplomatic and military posts, seven as state governors, and thirty-nine in Congress. In short, they were seasoned politicians, adept in the skills of compromise and tactical maneuver.[5] (3) The delegates represented a relatively wealthy professional and commercial elite. Although small, independent farmers constituted a huge majority of the population, they found themselves almost unrepresented in the most vital gathering of the day. (4) Conservatism is often defined to include a distrust of the mass of the people, and by this standard, delegates were largely conservative. Elbridge Gerry, more liberal than most, asserted that the "evils were experience flow from the excess of democracy," and Edmund Randolph of Virginia argued that "our chief danger arises from the democratic parts of our (state) constitutions."[6]

The agreements   With relative ease the delegates agreed to write a new constitution in which the power of the national government would be enlarged to include the authority to tax, raise an army, regulate interstate and foreign commerce, regulate the value of currency, and control navigable rivers. The result, of course, was to diminish the relative power of the states.

This reallocation of authority required a more elaborate structure for the national government. There, to guard against despo-

5 Stanley Elkins and Eric McKitrick, "The Founding Fathers: Young Men of the Revolution," *Political Science Quarterly* 76 (June 1961): 202–16, and John P. Roche, "The Founding Fathers: A Reform Caucus in Action," *American Political Science Review* 55 (December 1961): 799–816.
6 Cited in J. Mark Jacobson, *The Development of American Political Thought: A Documentary History* (N.Y.: D. Appleton-Century Co., 1932), pp. 41 and 43.

tism, a separation of powers with built-in checks and balances was established. It was decided that the legislative branch should be bicameral, an independent chief executive should be established, and a national court system should be created. But there were important controversies still to be resolved.

The disputes   Early in the proceedings, the Virginia delegation introduced a draft constitution which provided that representation in both houses of a bicameral legislature be based on population. The small states feared that if they were outvoted in the legislative branch they would be helpless victims of large-state tyranny. From New Jersey came an alternative proposal for a unicameral Congress with one vote for each state. The deadlock between proponents of the Virginia Plan and the New Jersey Plan was finally broken by the acceptance of Benjamin Franklin's compromise as proposed by the Connecticut delegation. Now generally known as the Great Compromise, it provided a bicameral Congress, giving each state two votes in the upper house, the Senate, while apportioning seats in the lower chamber, the House of Representatives, on a population basis.

Growing directly out of the Great Compromise was another major dispute concerning direct taxes, which were to be apportioned among the states, like seats in the House of Representatives, according to population. The South did not want slaves fully counted in determining its tax burdens; the North did not want slaves fully counted in determining the number of representatives southern states could have. Eventually a compromise emerged by which each slave was counted as three fifths of a person for both purposes.

Still another controversy, concerning the term of office and manner of electing the chief executive, resulted finally in the electoral college, one of the strangest political inventions ever devised.[7]

Ratification

The ratification process was not an easy one. Those opposing the Constitution drew their strength largely from the small farmers who were generally untroubled by state trade barriers and delighted with inflated state currency that expedited the payment of their debts. Yet these were the very conditions to which the commercial and financial interests favoring the new Constitution objected most strongly. In any event, the opponents of ratification leveled three main attacks upon the Constitution: (1) It was a tool of wealthy interests to be used against the small farmers. (2) It created a danger of tyranny by transferring too much power from the states to the national government. (3) It contained no Bill of Rights to protect the individual citizens.

The supporters responded in a series of eighty-five essays appearing first in New York newspapers and later in book form. Written

7 See Chapter 10.

by Alexander Hamilton, James Madison, and John Jay, *The Federalist* (or *The Federalist Papers*) evaluated the weaknesses of the Articles and made a penetrating and highly favorable analysis of the proposed Constitution. Not only did this work win supporters for ratification but it is today regarded as one of America's most notable contributions to the literature of political theory.

Another and possibly crucial factor in getting the Constitution approved was the admission by its supporters that a Bill of Rights was desirable and their pledge to add one by amending the Constitution once it had been ratified.

The "Wonderful Work": Seven Pillars of Wisdom

The seven articles of the Constitution established a basic organization of government which was without precedent in any nation then in existence and which has survived for nearly two centuries. Before evaluating it, a distinction must be made between constitutional and statutory law. The former is the highest and most binding law and is normally confined to four topics: the creation of major governmental agencies, a description of the authority these agencies possess, amendment procedures permitting necessary changes, and a series of limitations upon governmental power (usually called a Bill of Rights). Statutory law, in contrast, is that passed by appropriate legislative bodies in exercising the authority granted them by the Constitution.

One of the frequent and unfortunate characteristics of state constitutions is that they include numerous provisions for specific government policies which are most appropriately statutory in nature. These tend to tie the hands of the state legislatures and make constitutional amendments necessary whenever certain policy changes seem desirable. The framers in Philadelphia avoided this pitfall. They wrote a Constitution consisting only of a preamble and seven articles—brief, essential, flexible.

The Constitution has endured longer than any other in any nation in recorded history. More significantly, it has proved responsive to the needs of whatever group has gained control of the government which it established. In the 1790s, for example, wealthy commercial interests used the new government to take taxes from the farmers to finance a newly created National Bank which loaned money to manufacturers. Yet in the nineteenth century that same government, yielding to farm pressures, built canals and gave away land to encourage agricultural expansion. In this century, industrial labor was able to extract from it minimum wage laws and social security benefits. Like the delicate machinery in a fine car, the political system created by the Constitution has responded to the desires of the driver, occasionally changed direction, and proceeded at varying speeds.

Constitutional amendments   If a constitution can be altered

Figure 5   An Outline of the Constitution

Preamble:	*Attributes Constitution to "We the People"* States purposes of Constitution Contains no enforceable provisions
Article I:	*Legislative Branch* Bicameral Congress: Senate and House of Representatives Membership and methods of selection Legislative procedures Powers and limitations on powers Limitations on state governments
Article II:	*Executive Branch* President and Vice President Selection by electoral college Conditions of service Powers
Article III:	*Judicial Branch* Supreme Court and provision for lower courts Selection and service of judges Powers Trial by jury guaranteed Treason defined
Article IV:	*Intergovernmental Relations* Obligations of states to one another Admission of new states Obligations of national government to states
Article V:	*Amendment Procedures*
Article VI:	*Supremacy of Constitution* Assumption of prior debts Prohibition of religious qualifications for public office
Article VII:	*Procedure for Ratifying Constitution*

too easily, its authority as the basic law is diminished and it cannot provide needed stability and continuity; if, on the other hand, it is too difficult to amend, its own rigidity may doom it to an early death. The authors of our Constitution provided four alternative amendment methods in Article V. Of these, proposal by two-thirds vote of Senate and House of Representatives, with ratification by three quarters of the state legislatures, has been used for all amendments but the Twenty-first. Altogether the document written in 1787 has been changed only sixteen times since the first ten amendments providing the Bill of Rights were added in 1791. Nothing speaks more eloquently of the work of the framers. The subject matter of the amendments and the dates they became effective are shown in Figure 6.

Figure 6   An Outline of Amendments to the Constitution

Amendment	Subject	Year of Ratification
1	Guarantees freedom of expression Prohibits establishment of religion	1791
2	Protects states' power to maintain armed militias (national guard)	1791
3	Prohibits housing soldiers in private homes	1791
4	Protects right to privacy from unreasonable searches and seizures	1791
5	Limits criminal prosecution (grand jury) Prohibits two trials for same crime (double jeopardy) Prohibits forced confessions (self-incrimination) Guarantees due process of law Limits power to take private property (eminent domain)	1791
6	Criminal trial procedures guaranteeing rights: To a speedy and public trial To an impartial jury To cross-examine witnesses To subpoena witnesses To legal counsel	1791
7	Guarantees jury trial in civil cases	1791
8	Prohibits excessive bail and fines Prohibits cruel and unusual punishments	1791
9	Guarantees rights not otherwise described	1791
10	Protects powers reserved to the states	1791
11	Reduces judicial power of national courts, modifying Article III (adopted to counteract Supreme Court decision)	1798
12	Changes method of electing Vice President, modifying Article II	1804

More than sixty years elapsed before the Civil War amendments were adopted, largely to protect black people against oppressive legislation passed by white-controlled state legislatures.

| 13 | Prohibits slavery | 1865 |

| 14 | Establishes citizenship by birth in U.S.
Guarantees due process of law against
  state interference, incorporating most of
  Bill of Rights as limitations upon state
  as well as national power
Prohibits denial by states of equal
  protection of the laws
(adopted partially to counteract Supreme
  Court decision) | 1868 |
| 15 | Prohibits denial of right to vote
  because of race | 1870 |

After another forty years, Amendments Sixteen through Nineteen were adopted within seven years. Although dissimilar in content, they were all products of the Progressive movement which, early in this century, urged experimentation and reform in all levels of government.

16	Permits national income tax levied without
	  regard to state population, modifying
	  Article I (adopted to counteract
	  Supreme Court decision)
		1913

17	Requires U.S. Senators be elected directly by voters, modifying Article I	1913
18	Prohibits manufacture, sale, or transportation of alcoholic beverages	1919
19	Prohibits denial of right to vote because of sex	1920
20	Reduces period of time between election and start of term for national officials	1933
21	Repeals Amendment Eighteen	1933
22	Limits President to two terms	1951
23	Gives Washington, D.C., electoral votes in presidential elections	1961
24	Prohibits denial of right to vote because of failure to pay taxes	1964

25	Establishes procedure to select Vice
	  President to fill vacancy in that office
	Establishes procedures for Vice
	  President to become Acting President
	  in the event of presidential disability
		1967

26	Prohibits denial of right to vote because of age to those eighteen or more	1971

The "unwritten constitution" If one interprets a constitution to mean whatever determines the fundamental scope or structure of government authority (as the British do, for example), then there is more to the United States Constitution than its short text. Under such a definition, our Constitution has other sources, some of which (again as in the English case) are unwritten.

First, there are institutions and procedures that have become deeply entrenched through custom and tradition. These include the two-party system, pressure groups, the President's cabinet, and the congressional committee system for handling legislation. They are as important as many provisions of the Constitution itself, and may be altered in practice through the years.

Second, certain actions by the state governments have had so profound an effect upon national politics as also to be of constitutional importance. The selection of presidential electors by the voters rather than by state legislatures, the abolition of property ownership as a voting requirement, and the nomination of congressional candidates by primary elections rather than party conventions are all results of state action.

Third, various parts of the Constitution have been supplemented through statutory elaboration by acts of Congress. Article III gives Congress the authority to create lower courts and Article II, at least implicitly, allows it to create executive departments. The result has been a government bureaucracy of intricate complexity and immense power. To the bones of constitutional structure, statutory elaboration has attached awesome muscles. Some would argue that it has added considerable fat as well.

Fourth, presidential action has occasionally altered the emphasis of certain parts of the Constitution, and perhaps even distorted their intent. Thus, various Presidents have used their constitutional authority as commander in chief of the armed forces to render the congressional power to declare war almost irrelevant.

Finally, the American Supreme Court, gradually entrenching itself as the final interpreter of the Constitution, has made decisions of constitutional significance. "The Constitution," as a former Chief Justice of the United States Supreme Court once wrote, "is what the judges say it is."[8] And the judges may—and do—reverse their own interpretations.

BASIC CONSTITUTIONAL PRINCIPLES
Federalism: The Middle Way

The framers of the Constitution were confronted with a dilemma: The existing Confederation, in which the states had ultimate power, was not working well; yet the people feared a strong, unitary

---

8 Saul K. Padover, *The Living U.S. Constitution* (N.Y.: Mentor Books, The New American Library Inc., 1953), p. 58.

system, such as that of the British empire, in which the national government was the source of all authority. They devised a practical compromise which provided a middle way between these extremes. This is the system of federalism, perhaps America's greatest political invention. Federalism gives authority to both the national and state governments. It forbids either from usurping the power of the other, yet provides a wide arena for cooperation and steadily expanding joint action.

The division of powers   The authority of the national government stems largely from Article I, Section 8 of the Constitution. Although this deals with the powers of Congress, it involves the executive and judicial branches as well, since they administer legislation once enacted and apply it in individual cases. In the first seventeen paragraphs of Article I, Section 8 are the *enumerated powers* expressly delegated to Congress (and also called *delegated* or *expressed* powers) while the eighteenth grants broad and vague authority to make laws "which shall be necessary and proper" to carry out the powers specifically listed. Action based on this "necessary and proper" clause is often called an exercise of *implied powers.*

The United States Supreme Court formalized the doctrine of implied powers in a decision written by our third and most influential Chief Justice, John Marshall, in the case of *McCulloch* v. *Maryland* in 1819. This concept has become the major constitutional justification for the immense expansion of national authority that has since taken place.

Such enumerated powers as those to tax and to regulate interstate commerce have had a much greater impact on our lives than others because so many implied powers have been found to be "necessary and proper" to carry them out. The power to tax, for example, implies the power to spend, and hence justifies such programs as Medicare to pay the hospital costs of the elderly, monetary grants-in-aid to state and local governments, farm price supports, and cash subsidies to corporation-owned airlines and ships. Similarly, the power to regulate interstate commerce implies the authority to pass congressional legislation concerning racial discrimination in restaurants, kidnapping, minimum hourly wages, and consumer protection. Some observers feel that the "necessary and proper" clause has by now been so stretched in its interpretation that they call it the "elastic" clause.

While the national government possesses the powers just mentioned, the Tenth Amendment states that all other powers, unless specifically prohibited elsewhere in the Constitution, "are reserved to the States respectively, or to the people." Traffic regulations, marriage and divorce requirements, the operation of the public schools, building codes, gambling laws, the licensing of lawyers and doctors, the control of crime—all these are exercises of the *reserved powers* of the states. They are not so dramatic as tragedies in Vietnam or triumphs in space exploration, but they provide the day-to-day necessities of civilized life. It should be noted that the authority of the states (as unitary systems) extends also to local governments, which have only the powers given to them by the states.

Cooperative federalism   As the national government has expanded its activities, it has intruded into matters of state jurisdiction. The result has been the growth of the area of *concurrent powers,* exercised jointly by national and state authorities. Thus, federalism has become a sharing, as well as a division, of power.

In recent years, grants-in-aid have become an increasingly important area of cooperative federalism. This form of financial assistance appropriates national tax revenue to state and local governments and permits Congress to help finance activities which it generally would have no constitutional authority to initiate. Few expenditures in our history have risen so rapidly as these. In 1964, they amounted to a little over ten billion dollars and within six years, by 1970, had increased about 150 percent, to an estimated nearly twenty-four billion dollars. The major activities assisted by grants-in-aid are shown in Figure 7.

There are two major strings usually attached to these grants. One is that the state or local governments receiving them put up some minimum of funds to help finance the same projects, and the other is that they meet nationally determined standards in administering the program receiving assistance.

While such grants accounted for only 8.2 percent of state and local revenues in 1942, this had more than doubled in the next twenty-five years, reaching 16.7 percent in 1969: In nine states, over 25 percent of government revenue came from this source, and quite significantly, five of these were among the poorest fifth of all states in per capita

Figure 7   Federal Aid to State and Local Governments in 1970

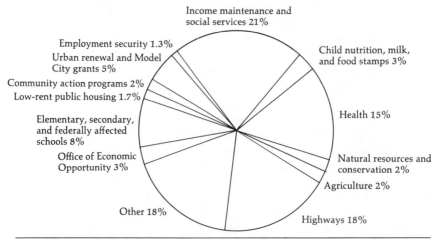

Grants-in-aid and shared revenue for selected programs in percentages of the total aid of $23,955,000.00

Income maintenance and social services 21%

Employment security 1.3%
Urban renewal and Model City grants 5%
Community action programs 2%
Low-rent public housing 1.7%

Child nutrition, milk, and food stamps 3%

Elementary, secondary, and federally affected schools 8%

Health 15%

Office of Economic Opportunity 3%

Natural resources and conservation 2%

Agriculture 2%

Other 18%

Highways 18%

Source: U.S. Bureau of the Census, *Statistical Abstract of the United States: 1971*, p. 401.

personal income. At the opposite extreme, seven of the ten richest states were among the ten for which national funds accounted for the smallest percentage of revenue. The grants-in-aid program, it seems, tends to aid poor states more than rich ones.[9]

President Nixon has instituted a far-reaching program of revenue sharing that would augment most of these grants with national tax money given to state and local governments to be used largely at their own discretion. Revenue sharing has three broad purposes. First, it is an attempt to save local governments hovering on the brink of bankruptcy; second, it seeks to decentralize control over the expenditure of public funds by transferring budgetary decisions from the national government to the states, counties, and cities; and finally, it shifts some of the financial burden of state and local government services from local property tax sources to more equitably extracted income taxes.

Intergovernmental relations: the jealous partners Numerous relationships among many governments obviously require certain ground rules, some of which are provided in Article IV of the Constitution. This sets forth three obligations of the states to one another. As people move from state to state more easily and in larger numbers, the importance of these interstate obligations has increased greatly. (1) The "full faith and credit" clause requires each state to honor the contracts, deeds, marriages, wills, and court orders (including financial settlements) authorized by the legal processes of all other states. (2) The "privileges and immunities" clause prohibits states from unjustly discriminating against citizens of other states. They may, however, charge students from other states higher college and university tuition fees on the grounds that they have not helped to pay the state taxes which largely finance these institutions. They may also require newly resident professionals (such as doctors or lawyers) to satisfy their particular standards. (3) Each state should return escaped criminal suspects to the states from which they fled. This is the process of rendition, often called extradition, but it is one which national courts have declared they are powerless to enforce, since no constitutionally guaranteed individual rights are at stake.

Article IV also requires that the national government assume three obligations to the states. The first of these obligations guarantees "a republican form of government," but the Supreme Court has held that whether a state has this kind of government is a "political question" which must be determined by Congress or the President. With incredible good fortune, the second obligation, protection of the states against invasion, has never been tested.

In actual practice, by far the most important of the national responsibilities to the states has been the protection against domestic violence whenever states have asked for such assistance. Racial conflict

9 The statistics cited in this paragraph are taken from U.S. Bureau of the Census, *Statistical Abstract of the United States: 1971,* pp. 314, 402, and 405.

on the streets of Detroit and Newark, for example, led President Lyndon Johnson to send in army units at state request. Considerably more controversial has been the presidential dispatch of troops in violation of the wishes of state officials. President Cleveland sent troops into Chicago in 1894 to end a railroad strike and resume mail transportation. Similarly, President Eisenhower dispatched armed forces to Little Rock, Arkansas, in 1957, and President Kennedy to the University of Mississippi in 1963, to avert violence which threatened to block racial integration in the schools. On all three of these occasions, however, national action was justified not by Article IV dealing with intergovernmental relations but by Article II authorizing the President to see to it that laws (including federal court orders) "be faithfully executed."

Cooperation between state governments has become increasingly meaningful. As Article I, Section 10 is interpreted, states may make interstate agreements known as compacts with the approval of Congress. Dozens of these are now in effect, and those involving oil conservation and convicts on probation or parole include most of the states. Most compacts deal with such matters as interstate boundaries, the allocation of river water, interstate bridges, forest fire prevention, and cooperative use of state-supported medical and dental schools. The Port of New York Authority, involving the states of New Jersey and New York, is the biggest business enterprise created by an interstate compact and one of the largest in the world.

Assessment   The federal division of power, like any compromise, possesses both assets and liabilities which deserve brief enumeration. Some advantages of the system are: (1) It permits unity on matters affecting the whole nation, such as foreign policy, while permitting diversity with respect to more personal matters such as gambling and abortion laws. (2) By dividing power between national and state officials it provides a possible barrier to dictatorship. (3) States may act as "social laboratories" in which new policies can be tested without damaging other states. (4) Policies may be tailored more readily to local conditions and interests. (5) State officials can gain experience which will prepare them to perform comparable functions in the national government with greater effectiveness. (6) Federalism permits the election of a large number of people, engaged personally in a kind of participatory democracy.

Offsetting these are several liabilities: (1) Federalism perpetuates unequal opportunities, since rich states can provide better schools, hospitals, and other services than poor states. (2) A division of power means mutual suspicion and jealousy and sometimes a bitter dispute over where national power ends and state power begins. (3) It encourages delay in the solution of problems by fostering "buck-passing" between national and state officials. (4) Differences among state laws in such fields as traffic regulations provide a source of embarrassment and confusion to citizens who travel across the country. (5) Fragmentation of authority makes it easier for powerful pressure groups concentrated in particular geographic areas to gain unwarranted influence. (6) State boundaries, the offspring of historical circumstance, have rendered many states too small, and others too large, for maximum administrative efficiency.

Separation of Powers: Ambition *vs.* Ambition

Although the Founding Fathers intended to create a stronger national government, they had mixed feelings, for they took a dim view of human nature and feared that more centralized power heightened the danger of its abuse. Their solution was to increase the authority of the national government but at the same time to separate it among three groups of officials—legislative, executive, and judicial—each of which was empowered to check the other two. "Ambition," in Madison's words, was "made to counteract ambition."[10] All fifty state governments are structured in much the same way.

The three branches The separation of powers provided in Articles I, II, and III of the Constitution is a separation both of personnel and of function. In terms of personnel, no one (with the exception of the Vice President) can serve in more than one branch at a time; in terms of function, each branch was assigned dominance in its particular realm: Congress was to pass laws; the President was to enforce and administer them; the courts were to interpret them in individual circumstances and punish those who violated them. The idea was borrowed from Montesquieu, a French theorist who had urged a separation of powers to give each group of officials enough independent authority to limit the power of the other two.

Checks and balances American constitutional theory assumes the three branches to be equal in authority. To assure this in practice, the framers gave each one certain checks with which to balance the power of the other two. This modifies the separation of powers principle substantially, since each branch shares some of the functions of the other two; considerable cooperation among all three is required, therefore, if the government is to function effectively. The Senate, for example, must approve presidential appointments and treaties, the President may veto acts of Congress, and the courts may declare actions of the other two branches unconstitutional.

Judicial review Perhaps the most controversial and unique of the interbranch checks is this last one, known as the power of judicial review. The Constitution does not give the courts this authority, and there is some disagreement over whether most of the framers intended that they should have it. Hamilton, however, in No. 78 of *The Federalist,* supported judicial review and others agreed. The issue was of no practical

10 *The Federalist* No. 51. Exact authorship is undetermined, and it is possible that it was written by Hamilton rather than Madison.

importance until 1803 when, in *Marbury* v. *Madison,* the Supreme Court declared a congressional law unconstitutional for the first time. The Court's opinion, written by Chief Justice Marshall, relied largely on the "supremacy" clause of Article VI of the Constitution to justify its decision. That provision states that "This constitution, and the laws . . . which shall be made in pursuance thereof . . . shall be the supreme law of the land . . ." Marshall asserted, quite simply, that the law in question came in conflict with the Constitution and was hence invalid. There were those who contended passionately that it was unconstitutional to declare a law unconstitutional, but they cried out in vain. As the Court's prestige increased, the precedent established in *Marbury* v. *Madison* became more deeply entrenched. Judicial review has now been used to invalidate nearly one hundred national and over seven hundred state laws, as well as dozens of executive acts committed by officials ranging from rookie policemen to the President of the United States. It has made American courts the most powerful in the world, is a central component in the system of checks and balances, and ranks with federalism as one of this nation's most ingenious governmental innovations.

Assessment   The separation of powers possesses several merits. First, like federalism, it helps to prevent the concentration of too much power in the hands of too few people. Second, it creates stability and continuity by guaranteeing fixed and often overlapping terms of office for congressmen and the President. Finally, it helps to balance the sometimes conflicting claims of majority rule and minority rights by permitting both the periodic election of the two "political" branches as well as lifetime tenure, immune from majority pressure, for judges in the third branch.

There are, however, liabilities as well. First, if the various branches are controlled by opposing political parties, governmental delay and even deadlock may result. Second, responsibility is so dispersed that the people may become confused, wondering who is to blame for what.

Both federalism and separation of powers relate to government structure, and both fragment government authority, the first territorially and the second functionally. The other two constitutional principles to be examined, freedom and democracy, involve not the structure of government but its relationship to the people whom it governs.

Freedom: The People's Rights

Freedom of speech, press, and assembly as well as freedom from unjust convictions and arbitrary imprisonment had been established by the common law and the English Parliament long before American independence. The Revolution, indeed, was fought in part to protect these freedoms more effectively. One of the chief reasons for dividing governmental machinery between national and state authorities and among three distinct branches was to limit the capacity of government officials to impinge upon the freedom of individual citizens. Several provisions of the original Constitution along with Amendments One through Nine, Thirteen, and Fourteen entrench freedom as a major principle in American society.

Natural rights   The idea that citizens have the rights to possess the property for which they labor and to express their individuality in action and opinion goes back to ancient Greece and Rome. This concept was refined by a famous English philosopher, John Locke, who wrote that mankind lived initially in a "state of nature" governed only by "natural law." This natural law, Locke argued, was the product of universal and unchanging reason, and it endowed the individual with "natural rights" to life, liberty, and property. In order to protect these rights more efficiently, people formed a "social compact," or contract, which created government. Granting Locke's basic assumptions, it follows logically that if the government does not protect these natural rights, the people may revolt against it and form one which will. With only minor modifications, this was the justification for revolution which Jefferson wrote into the Declaration of Independence.

Assessment   There are, of course, other arguments in behalf of freedom. It stems logically from a belief in the ultimate value of the individual and the development of his or her potential; it is necessary to control the arrogance of government officials; and it is indispensable to the search for truth upon which the creative advance of civilization depends.

Governments actually play complex roles in relation to individual freedom. They may, as Locke hoped, protect freedom from the murderer or bully or crook, or they may themselves be the biggest bullies of all. Restrictions on government power and the protection of liberty are, in this case, two sides of the same coin. All in all, the friends of freedom should remember that it can be jeopardized by both private and public power. In very effective ways, the pressures of social conformity and the demands of employers or families can erode the freedom of individual men and women most seriously. But the power of the state can imprison or kill. All this is not to endorse unrestricted freedom; each one of us must lower his voice occasionally so that another may be heard. In an increasingly congested, interdependent society, some degree of discipline, restraint, and order is necessary. It is the price society demands for efficiency, fairness, and perhaps even for survival.

Democracy: the People's Power

In its modern context, the simplest definition of democracy is majority rule. As such, this is the most recently established of the major principles of American politics. It requires two obvious conditions: that a majority of the people be permitted to vote and that they or their elected representatives be permitted to determine government policy. In the early decades of American government, however, suffrage (the right to vote) was restricted by property-ownership requirements in some states, and racial and sexual impediments persisted long after that. Further, even those who could vote were permitted to elect few of the real decision-makers. The Constitution set up a national government in which U.S. Senators were selected by state legislatures until the ratification of Amendment Seventeen in 1913; the President was elected by an electoral college which, in most states, was also chosen by state legislatures until the 1820s; judges were, and still are, appointed. Only the House of Representatives—one half of one of the three branches—was initially subject to direct popular control.

Since most of these procedural barriers have now been swept away, can we conclude that democracy will permanently flourish? Not necessarily. Democracy is not a hardy, garden-variety perennial that one can plant and then forget. Instead, it is a rare species, so delicate that it withers quickly outside a supporting environment.

Social supports   A democratic society is one in which families, churches, factories, and schools embody democratic principles. From these major social institutions individual citizens derive their attitudes and values. If social institutions are controlled dictatorially or discourage respect for minorities and human dignity, then prospects are dim for political democracy. The inability of Germany to maintain a democratic government prior to World War II, for example, has been attributed in part to the attitudes developed in the traditionally authoritarian German family. Conversely, the growth of democracy in America has been associated to some degree with the fact that many early New England churches were democratically controlled by local congregations. Some form of participatory democracy in the home, classroom, and office bolsters the chance for successful democracy in city hall and in Washington, D.C.

Economic supports   It was observed earlier that democracies seem to flourish best in fairly wealthy countries, where there is not a constant struggle for mere existence. Normally, people can't get the information they need to make intelligent political decisions unless they can read, and they can't read unless they live in a country rich enough to provide free public schools. In modern times, of course, a wealthy nation is a highly industrialized one, and although literacy, education, and industrialization may exist without democracy, democracy seldom exists without them. A large middle class appears to provide the stability requisite for democracy. If a nation is divided chiefly between the very rich and very poor, there will be no moderating force, with a stake in the system, to effect the compromises necessary to avoid violence.

Psychological supports   Analysts of individual behavior have focused their attention on psychological factors which may help to explain the relationship between democratic attitudes and certain personality characteristics. Among the traits thought to be associated with democracy are self-esteem (a good feeling about oneself which enables one to believe that others are "good folks" also), an open ego (warm, trusting, and friendly), and a multi-valued orientation rather than an obsessive preoccupation with a single interest for which one might sacrifice democratic procedures.

Cultural supports   Crucial to the survival of democracy is a culture in which its basic values are widely shared. If a society is sharply divided about such fundamental principles as religious freedom, racial tolerance, or the protection of personal property, the issue may be settled by bullets rather than by ballots. In other words, democracy can tolerate disagreements on minor issues because there is fundamental agreement on major ones.

The cultural value most central to democracy is the belief in the dignity and worth of the individual. Majority rule itself pays tribute numerically to the equal importance of each individual in the group. But the equal worth of each human being is not merely a convenient mathematical assumption for counting votes: Because it involves the assumption that all citizens are equal before the laws, it also commits us to equal justice under the laws. We want people to vote because that is the best way yet devised to guarantee that their interests will be the ultimate concern of the government. Democracy, then, is more than a procedural device to decide who will rule. It is a substantive dedication to the enhancement of human dignity. The individual is not merely a means, but an end as well.

Democracy and freedom   Democracy cannot survive without a commitment to freedom. Therefore, majority rule should not (though it sometimes does) override minority rights. For unless the majority permits the minority freedom of expression, people may be doubly deprived—deprived of knowledge that may be necessary to a wise decision on public policy, and also deprived of that choice between alternatives which permits the rejection of one proposal or one official in favor of another. Without a choice, without alternative policies and personnel, the people have no way to keep the government accountable to their wishes. Moreover, as long as today's minority is free to become tomorrow's majority, it is likely to accept the verdict of the voters without resorting to violence.

Assessment   Even under the best of circumstances, democracy is not a simple system. Sometimes the freedom of the individual conflicts with the will of a majority; sometimes the substance of justice must await the due process of democratic procedures; and sometimes liberty conflicts with the legal equality of all citizens. Each generation must meet these contradictions in some form. To do so, procedurally, at a minimum there must be universal suffrage and popularly elected policy-makers as the means to attain majority rule. Substantively, there must be a commitment to individual dignity and well-being as the ultimate ends of government policy. These must be both supplemented with and limited by a devotion to minority rights, for individual freedom is essential to a real choice by an enlightened majority.

In America, democracy must accommodate itself to federalism and to the separation of powers, both of which fragment power. Although this protects freedom by limiting power, it also requires a majority of the people to elect more representatives, perhaps, than they can intelligently evaluate. As a result, a vigilant press, competitive parties, and effective pressure groups must act on behalf of the public as watchdogs to help hold officials accountable for their performance and responsible to the voters.

The social, economic, psychological, and cultural conditions of democracy indicate that it is not merely a political system: It is a pattern of relationships in the home, a luxury product of an affluent economy, a set of collective personality patterns prone to mutual trust, and a state of mind both widely shared and deeply dedicated to common values of human worth.

The critics of democracy sometimes contend that it is so lofty an ideal, confounded by such imposing difficulties, that it can never be attained. To some, it is little more than a delusion nurtured by small elites to conceal their own political dominance. Others admit that democracy is feasible but undesirable: It works too slowly and debases cultural standards to the lowest common denominator.

The proponents of democracy counter these allegations on both theoretical and practical levels. Theoretically, they assert that if democracy is visionary, it at least is a vision that summons the best and noblest of human aspirations. Practically, they concede that democracy is an ideal that is realized only by degrees. But they point out that the societies that are most democratic are those that came out on top in both World Wars, are most productive, and fulfill most completely the individual's need for recognition and significance.

DEMOGRAPHIC INFLUENCES

Four demographic features have persisted for so long and intensified to such a degree that they are the most significant characteristics of the American population: numbers, the westward movement, urbanization, and diversity.

Numbers: Plenty of People

The American population has increased more spectacularly than that of any nation in history. From the nearly four million recorded in the first official census count in 1790, it rose to more than 204 million in 1970. The current trend, however, is toward a much lower rate of increase.

Our vast geographic area is capable of sustaining a large population with relatively little crowding. While uninhabitable mountain and desert regions make population density figures misleading, it nonetheless is significant that the United States has an average of about 57 inhabitants per square mile, compared with 200 in China, 239 in France, 426 in India, 245 in West Germany, and 720 in Japan. At the other

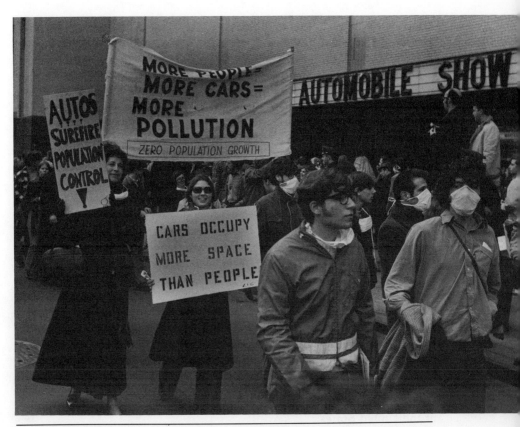

Charles Gatewood.

Young people, aware of the relationship between population and pollution, urge fewer babies, fewer cars.

extreme are 29 in the Soviet Union, 23 in Argentina, and 5 in Canada. The world average is 68.

By a coincidence convenient to human memory, America ranks fourth in both population and area among the world's nations. Although numbers alone cannot make a nation a formidable power, they are an important element in its total strength. Large numbers of combat troops are still military assets of considerable consequence, as we recently were reminded in Korea and Vietnam. Moreover, for economic diversification and a reasonable degree of national self-sufficiency there must be some minimum population to exploit the available resources most advantageously.

But exceptional growth is not an unmixed blessing, and partially counteracts the nation's geographic assets. Automobiles pollute the air, industrial wastes contaminate rivers and oceans, and an increasing population demands that government permit the leveling of hillsides for housing tracts and the construction of resort areas on previously unspoiled mountain slopes or lake shores. Although population density is relatively light, commercial, residential, and recreational needs already imperil the environment to a substantial degree. Despite these problems, world population growth will bring increasing pressures upon America to liberalize its immigration policy, since the distribution of the three-and-a-half billion people on earth is far from equitable.

Distribution: A Violent Frontier

As the American people have moved from East to West, the center of population has shifted gradually from Maryland in 1790 to a point in southwestern Illinois, not far from St. Louis, in 1970. This massive migration has been carried on in the face of many formidable obstacles, both physical and human. Its political implications have been almost as numerous. The lure of the West exerted pressures upon the government to facilitate movement by subsidizing roads, canals, and railroads, reducing the price of land on the frontier, and driving Indians from their ancestral homes.

Population has pulled political power with it. Between 1900 and 1973, for example, 55 of the 435 seats in the House of Representatives were transferred from other parts of the country to western states. California alone gained thirty-five, Washington and Arizona four, Hawaii, Colorado, New Mexico, and Oregon two, and Alaska, Idaho, Montana, and Utah each added one.[11] The shift of power was best dramatized on January 20, 1969, when one native Californian, former Chief Justice Earl Warren, swore in another, Richard Nixon, as President of the United States.

When Americans had spanned the entire continent, there followed changes in foreign policy. It seemed to many that our long Pacific coastal boundary required that we become a major power in that most vast of oceans. We acquired the Philippines and Hawaii, constructed the Panama Canal to increase both commercial and naval access to the Pacific, and developed a growing interest in Asia. In a sense, then, the westward movement has taken the United States to the Far East, and veterans of Vietnam know some of the consequences.

The frontier thesis As Americans shoved west, lured by cheap land or furs, timber or gold, they moved into that uncharted, perilous, promising domain that historians call the frontier. This, of course, was not a fixed and static place. It was the rugged, ragged cutting edge at the western limits of a civilization that was essentially European in origin and style. As the first settlers pushed the frontier steadily back, mowing down like a giant reaper the trees and Indians and wild game which obstructed their advance, they brought their European civilization with them. Their language, the faith of their fathers, their customs and laws—all were transplanted wherever they built their homes.

11 The source of statistical data here and elsewhere in "Demographic Influences" is U.S. Bureau of the Census, *Statistical Abstract of the United States: 1971.* These figures were computed from the table on p. 357.

Yet in the process of carrying an old culture to a new environment, that culture underwent a number of gradual but important changes. According to Frederick Jackson Turner, the western wilderness promoted individualism, equality, and democracy. Faced with unknown hazards, the settlers had to develop self-reliance in order to survive. They were equally good targets, regardless of social rank, race, or family wealth, for Indian arrows or a dozen other misfortunes. These common problems, Turner argued, generated the sense of brotherhood and mutual respect out of which American democracy developed.

The frontier also contributed to a kind of political stability. Whereas European malcontents and radicals posed a constant threat of revolt, the free land of the American frontier acted as a safety valve, enticing the most discontented and rebellious citizens to start new societies in the West rather than overthrow the old ones in the East.

The effects of the frontier were not always so laudable. They included a kind of crude materialism, a proclivity for violence, and a distrust of authority. In any case, both the good and the bad of the frontier seem to have persisted in modern society. Many Americans, imbued with the values of individual self-reliance, oppose most government welfare programs; "law and order" are threatened by rising crime and widespread violence; the nation is regularly accused of a preoccupation with material goods rather than broader cultural values. Yet for all its psychological impact, it is generally agreed that the actual frontier had about vanished by 1890. Later historians have contended that Turner overstated his case, but few would doubt that as Americans moved westward they became—at least in part—products of that free and lawless land which for so long was their environment.

Urbanization

A popular song of World War I asked, "How ya gonna keep 'em down on the farm, after they've seen Paree?" The answer was—whether they had seen Paris or not—that you couldn't. In fact, the steady process of urbanization began long before World War I; by 1970, 74 percent of the population was urban. The massive shift away from rural areas is as momentous as the westward movement and has the same essential cause: the continuing, consuming desire for economic improvement. The movement from rural to urban areas was, in most instances, a shift from farms to factories. Its effects had political and legal implications that no student of government can ignore.

First, it reduced the percentage of the labor force which was self-employed and increased the portion working for someone else. This led to the eventual passage of minimum-wage, workmen's-compensation, child-labor, and union-recognition laws.

Second, it created new industries which demanded and received governmental subsidies, tax advantages, and tariffs on imported goods to afford protection from foreign competition.

Figure 8   Population Growth

	Population Growth 1960–70
Central cities	6.4%
Outside central cities (suburbs)	26.7%
Nonmetropolitan areas	6.8%
Entire nation	13.3%

Source: U.S. Bureau of the Census, *Statistical Abstract of the United States: 1971,* p. 16.

Third, it increased the population density in cities, thrusting upon local governments grave new problems in such areas as zoning, public health, transportation, recreation facilities, and air pollution.

While the majority of the American people had moved to urban areas by 1920, there remain enormous differences among the states. As recently as 1970, for example, eight states were still predominantly rural. Vermont led (or trailed) the list, with only 32.2 percent of its population living in urban areas, while at the other extreme were New Jersey with 88.9 percent and California with 88.6 percent.

Until recent years, urbanization conjured up thoughts of the big city—bright and bursting with opportunity. Yet the latest population figures reveal that significant population growth is occurring not in the central cities of large metropolitan areas but in the suburban fringe cities which surround them. In fact, the major metropolises, beset by crime, pollution, and the sheer ravages of age, may be losing their vitality altogether.

Diversity: A Mixed Blessing

Franklin D. Roosevelt once mischievously teased the ancestral pride of the conservative ladies who comprise the Daughters of the American Revolution by addressing them as "My fellow immigrants." His remark contained an element of truth, for if not immigrants, our citizens are the descendants of immigrants. Even the ancestors of the Indians were probably Asians who made their way across the Bering Straits.

America: a group portrait   Americans were reasonably homogeneous only until the arrival of European invaders in the sixteenth century. Even before that, the Indian tribes displayed remarkable diversity in language and life style. The Spanish, English, Dutch, and French settlers contributed still more variety during the early colonial period, and a multiracial society was guaranteed with the importation of African laborers beginning in 1619. Thereafter, each year brought new immigrants, all carrying, duty free, their ancestral prejudices and varied ethnic backgrounds: These differences exerted a profound impact on the political behavior of Americans. The demands of blacks have led to a

Figure 9   Major American Ethnic Groups

Group	Number	Percentage
English, Scotch, Welsh	31,006,000	15.3
German	25,661,000	12.7
Negro	22,810,000	11.2
Irish	16,325,000	8.0
Italian	8,733,000	4.3
French	5,189,000	2.6
Mexican	5,073,000	2.5
Polish	4,941,000	2.4
Spanish, Puerto Rican, Cuban, other Latin American	3,883,000	1.9
American Indians, Japanese, Chinese, other nonwhite	2,412,000	1.2
Russian	2,132,000	1.1
Austrian, Canadian, Swedish, other white	59,467,000	29.3
Not reported	15,216,000	7.5
Total	202,848,000	100.0

Source: Adapted from *Congressional Quarterly Weekly Report,* March 11, 1972, p. 532. Reprinted by permission of Congressional Quarterly,Inc. Figures are based on a Census Bureau sampling taken in March 1971.

white backlash; political organizations formed by Indians, Mexican-Americans, Chinese-Americans and other groups have mushroomed rapidly; and "bloc voting" by various ethnic groups has persisted to elect (and defeat) many a candidate. To understand American politics, therefore, one should know what sorts of people inhabit the country in the 1970s. What color are they? Where did they come from?

Immigration policy The composition of the American population did not come about by sheer accident. Although no significant prohibitions were placed on immigration into the country during its first century of independence, black Americans had previously been brought here in chains and shackles, countless Indians were killed, and numbers of Chinese were brought to the United States under exploitative contracts to lay railroad tracks. In 1882, with the transcontinental railroad completed, a combination of racial prejudice and fear on the part of native white factory workers that they might lose their jobs to Asian laborers led to a prohibition of further immigration imposed by the Chinese Exclusion Act. No nation had ever before been subjected to any restriction whatever.

The Immigration Restriction Act of 1921 was the first to place general limitations on the number of new immigrants. Inspired by the antiforeign fervor generated during World War I, it established the

national origin quota system. This was designed—as amended in 1924—
to keep the proportion of new immigrants from various nations the same
as the proportion who had come from those countries before 1890. It was
justified as a measure to assist the assimilation of new arrivals into
American society, but discriminated against non-Protestants, since large
numbers of Catholics and Jews had emigrated after 1890 from countries
such as Russia, Poland, and Italy.

This religious prejudice was augumented by racial bigotry as
well. Orientals were prohibited from becoming citizens as a result of
additional legislation passed in 1924, and immigration was prohibited for
persons ineligible for citizenship. Most astonishing of all, the system
which fixed immigration quotas for each country on the basis of the
national origins of American residents prohibited the classification of
Negroes as being of African origin.

Not until 1965 was the national origin quota system abandoned and the American welcome mat largely cleansed of the stains of
ethnic bias. The new law establishes a maximum of 170,000 immigrants
each year who may enter the United States from outside the Western
Hemisphere. No more than 20,000 of this number may be admitted from
any one country, and preference is given to those who have either
relatives in the United States or special occupational skills needed by the
American economy. The 1965 Act includes another controversial change
in previous policy. Before its passage, immigrants from nations in the
Western Hemisphere were admitted "quota free" in unlimited numbers.
But present policy limits to 120,000 per year the number entering from
these areas, in addition to the 170,000 from the rest of the world.

The melting pot   Early in our history, a French immigrant
lauded "that strange mixture of blood . . . melted into a new race of
men, whose labors and posterity will one day cause great changes in the
world."[12] He thus became one of the first to propound the now famous
melting pot thesis. The diversity of the American population has no
doubt exceeded his most enthusiastic expectation, and the nation is far
richer for it. Zubin Mehta, the Asiatic Indian, has given us great music;
Albert Einstein, the German Jew, brought us genius in physics; George
Washington Carver, the Afro-American, contributed brilliance in agricultural chemistry; Amadeo P. Giannini, of Italian origin, founded the
Bank of America, largest in the world. The list is nearly endless.

Yet this is only part of the story. Although we have welded
the talents, skills, and values of many peoples into a rich and unique
amalgam, we have yet to create an alloy of happy fellowship. While
conceding that some ethnic groupings (notably German-Americans)
have diminished in solidarity, two leading scholars have concluded that
the melting pot has melted very little, and that racial and religious

12 Michel Guillaume St. Jean de Crevecoeur, *Letters from an American Farmer,* excerpted
in Oscar Handlin, *Immigration as a Factor in American History* (Englewood Cliffs, N.J.:
Prentice-Hall, Inc., 1959), p. 149.

groups—especially in New York City—retain immense political importance.[13] Thus we are confronted with a culture enriched by the creativity of diversity, yet impoverished by its accompanying rivalries.

Summary   *Population growth,* although producing a density substantially less than in many other nations, is creating an increasingly serious problem of pollution. At the same time, however, it has enabled the economic diversification and military potential necessary to a major rank among world powers.

The *westward movement* has enhanced the political power of the Pacific states and helped Asia rival Europe as a focus of the attention of foreign policy planners. The frontier period has diluted revolutionary tendencies, and contributed to the materialism, equality, democracy, individualism, and lawlessness of American society. *Urbanization* has been economically inspired, for the most part, by the lure of new jobs created by the Industrial Revolution, and has placed dramatic new demands upon governments.

Within the *ethnic diversity* of American society, northern Europeans predominate, with British descendants constituting a plurality, and those of German ancestry next in numbers. Despite overtly discriminatory immigration policies from 1882 to 1965, ours is a richly heterogeneous society. But under the melting pot there are flames of resentment as well as the warmth of fellowship.

IDEOLOGICAL INFLUENCES

The American political system operates within a context of related ideas and values which help to determine political behavior. Such ideological influences are part of the political culture. A leader identified with this ideology will most likely enjoy the widespread respect that is an essential ingredient of authority.

Americanism

Loyalty to the nation has become the overriding allegiance in much of the globe. Most Americans will forsake conflicting obligations to family, occupation, church, or political creed in order to defend their country. This loyalty is not merely the result of a threat of imprisonment; nationalism involves the identification of individual interests with the welfare of the entire country. Such an identification is strengthened by common language, traditions, and ethnic backgrounds—and yet Americans, spread over a large geographic area, possess a wide variety of racial, religious, political, and linguistic backgrounds. Why, then, are we so patriotic?

First, most Americans came to view their new homeland as

13 Nathan Glazer and Daniel P. Moynihan, *Beyond the Melting Pot* (Cambridge, Mass.: The M.I.T. Press, 1963).

an immense improvement over the rigid class structures and economic destitution of the lands from which they came. Second, the very barriers to a common loyalty have inspired extraordinary and generally successful attempts to overcome them. Thus, free public education deliberately sought to Americanize the immigrants' children by teaching them English, American history and customs, and a reverence for such symbols as the flag, the national anthem, and the patriotic mythology surrounding Washington, Jefferson, and other heroes. A 1958 survey reported that 56.7 percent of the people believed that "freedom does not give anyone the right to teach foreign ideas in our schools."[14]

In addition, the geographical divisions separating the eastern and western parts of the nation were bridged by Senator Henry Clay's "American System," providing roads, canals, and high tariffs to satisfy both sections. Even the tragedy of Civil War, nearly severing the South from the North, was diminished by the intentional postwar glorification of both Robert E. Lee, a saintly Southerner, and Abraham Lincoln, the noble Northerner. To seal the reunification bargain, the North, in 1877, quietly acquiesced in the resumption of power by the old white southern aristocracy, the violation of black voting rights, and the imposition, in the 1890s, of a rigid system of racial segregation. Lincoln himself had enunciated his priorities quite clearly: "If I could save the Union without freeing any slave," he wrote to Horace Greeley in 1862, "I would do it; and if I could save the Union by freeing all the slaves, I would do it." The great Emancipator thereby showed himself also the great nationalist. No price was too great, it seemed, to reclaim that most valued of ideals, a reunited union and an invigorated sense of national solidarity.

In America, as in all countries, the glorification of nationalism affects the conduct of American politics. First, it allows public officials to divert attention from the validity of their own ideas by associating them with patriotic pride. Thus President Nixon pleaded for support of his Vietnam policy in April 1970 by reminding a nation-wide television audience that in the "proud history" of America we had never lost a war and he did not intend that we should lose this one. His appeal was a strategically shrewd one. A 1964 poll showed 56 percent of the American people committed to the idea, "The United States should maintain its dominant position as the world's most powerful nation at all costs . . ."[15]

Second, nationalism helps to create a general public confidence in the government, investing it with a legitimacy and authority which reduces the force necessary to gain compliance with its policies. Third, patriotic devotion to the nation contributes to internal cohesion and compromise. It appeals to altruistic rather than selfish impulses and

14 Lloyd A. Free and Hadley Cantril, *The Political Beliefs of Americans* (N.Y.: Clarion Books, Simon & Schuster, Inc., 1968), p. 93.
15 Herbert McClosky, "Consensus and Ideology in American Politics," *American Political Science Review* 58 (June 1964): 361–82.

encourages labor and business, black and white, the devout and the atheist, to submerge their differences on behalf of the common good.

Fourth, and unfortunately, it increases the possibility of international conflict. Love of country can too easily become xenophobia, a fearful hatred of foreign peoples, as was skillfully accomplished in Nazi Germany. The cause of the fatherland or the mother country can flood the recruiting offices with volunteers, but the cause of the brotherhood of man has no armies. It too needs volunteers.

Capitalism

While nationalism is perhaps the dominant ideology in almost every country, capitalism has had a uniquely powerful influence on the American political system. Briefly described, capitalism is an economic system based on the ownership of business by private individuals or corporations, rather than by government. In 1776, Adam Smith argued in *The Wealth of Nations* that prosperity resulted from a government policy of *laissez-faire,* one that placed few legal restrictions upon the free competition of private business firms. A dozen generations of American capitalists have enthusiastically agreed that this would produce a division of labor resulting in a higher standard of living for the entire society. The law of supply and demand, a kind of "unseen hand" governing the economy, was believed to result in the manufacture of the variety of goods consumers wished to buy because only that would maximize sales and therefore profits as well. Moreover, each company would be forced to produce the best possible product at the lowest possible price, at the risk of losing customers to its competitors. Governmental activity could then be confined largely to the protection of life and property, and each individual left to confront life with little more than his own cleverness and initiative.

Capitalist theory was also nurtured by the Protestant ethic. Although the Catholic Church has prospered from its immense property holdings, it was the Protestants who glorified and even sanctified private profits. Specifically, the disciples of John Calvin had argued that the accumulation of earthly wealth was a probable indication of that grace of God which predestined one for eternal salvation. This religious conception, providing a sharp impetus to hard work, simple living, frugality, and business shrewdness, was implanted in colonial New England, from which it exerted a formidable influence upon all of early America.

Private capitalism was further bolstered in the last half of the last century by the ideas of social Darwinism. This theory held that the capitalistic competition for markets and jobs resulted in the "survival of the fittest." Society would be improved because its inferior members— the weak, lazy, stupid, and decadent—would be gradually eliminated through a process of natural selection; that is, they would reproduce less rapidly than the fittest. For political programs, the implication was clear: Government should neither restrain the successful nor assist the weak. It is little wonder that the United States lagged far behind Germany, France, and England in instituting such social security programs as unemployment compensation, retirement pensions, or Medicare.

Although modern times have forced numerous and substantial modifications in American capitalism, it remains the dominant theme in an economy now "mixed" with limited government ownership. A few years ago, 79 percent of the American people were found to agree with the statement, "We should rely more on individual initiative and not so much on government welfare programs."[16]

Racism

The Commission on Civil Disorders, appointed by President Lyndon B. Johnson in 1967, received considerable criticism for its conclusion that riots in Los Angeles, Detroit, Newark, and other cities were essentially the result of white racism.[17] But racism has been a pervasive and persistent ingredient of American attitudes throughout our history.

American Indians The first victims of racism in America were the first people encountered by the Europeans. The Indian population in what is now the United States is estimated to have been over a million at the time Columbus arrived in the New World. It has been substantially reduced by broken treaties, contamination with disease germs, bloody massacres by the United States cavalry, intentional inducements to chronic alcoholism, and a continual displacement to poorer lands farther West.

These first discoverers of America had initially received the white intruders with general hospitality. But after several centuries of deceit and betrayal, they fought back with vengeance and tenacity. By that time, of course, the odds against them were overwhelming and armed Indian resistance ended in 1890 at Wounded Knee, South Dakota, where several hundred Sioux, including many women and children, were killed.

Afro-Americans The first blacks were brought from Africa in 1619 as indentured servants, but their status soon degenerated into one of the most brutal systems of slavery the world has ever known. In many states it was against the law to teach slaves to read or write; some profitable plantations derived most of their income from commercial slave-breeding; theologians debated whether blacks possessed souls; and 3437 blacks were lynched between 1882 and 1951.[18]

Asian-Americans Discrimination against Asians in immigration and naturalization laws already has been noted. In addition, several massacres of Chinese occurred, and it was not until 1952 that

16 Free and Cantril, op. cit., p. 30.
17 *Report of the National Advisory Commission on Civil Disorders,* (N.Y.: Bantam Books, Inc., 1968), p. 203.
18 *Negro Year Book* (N.Y.: Wm. H. Wise & Co., Inc., 1952), p. 277.

immigrants from the world's most populous nation could be employed by
state, county, or municipal governments in California. Japanese were
also targets of those who feared the "yellow peril." They were segregated in San Francisco public schools in 1906 and, worst of all, 110,000
Americans of Japanese ancestry were herded into "relocation centers"
during World War II, although not one had been found to be disloyal.

White ethnics   The list goes on and on, embracing Mexi-
cans, Irish, Jews, Italians, Slavs, and others. Most of these ethnic
groups, one might reasonably object, *are* white; how could they be fair
game for racism? The answer is partly that racism has an insatiable
appetite for new groups to devour and partly that the concept of the white
race was compressed to a category so small as to exclude practically
anyone the categorizers didn't like. In 1924, just nine years before Hitler,
the most notorious modern racist, rose to power in Germany, a widely
used American sociology text asserted that immigrants of those days
"belong to a different race from ours. They belong to the Slavic and
Mediterranean subraces which have not shown the capacity for
self-government . . . which the peoples of northern and western Europe
have shown." It is not surprising that the author also opposed black
voting and viewed the "negro problem" as "essentially the same as the
Indian problem or the problem of any backward people or race . . .
inferior in culture and possibly also inferior in nature."[19]

Equality

In spite of the inequalities of racism, Americans have cher-
ished the ideal of equality in very meaningful ways. In 1776 when
Thomas Jefferson, a slave owner, asserted it to be "self-evident" that "all
men are created equal," even a commitment to white, largely Anglo-
Saxon equality was a truly revolutionary concept. Alexis de Tocqueville,
an observant and witty Frenchman who visited America in the 1830s,
was as impressed by the social equality which he observed here as he was
astonished by our capitalistic obsession with material possessions or
amused by our pugnaciously patriotic nationalism.

We demonstrated the commitment to equality by prohibiting
titles of nobility in Article I of our Constitution and by guaranteeing
"equal protection" of state laws in Amendment Fourteen. Equality thus
has major implications for the legal processes of government. Jurors,
judges, legislators, and voters each have an equal vote in making the
decisions entrusted to them. Yet several opinion surveys reveal considerable confusion, uncertainty, and even opposition regarding the concept
of equality.

A major study reported 58 percent agreement with the
statement that "we have to teach children that all men are created equal

19 Charles A. Ellwood, *Sociology and Modern Social Problems,* rev. ed. (N.Y.: American
Book Company, 1924), pp. 233 and 265–66.

but almost everyone knows that some are better than others."[20] Clearly we are not equal if equality means identity. People differ widely in strength, virtue, skill, ambition, and intelligence. On the other hand, all share membership in the human species: They are all similar in their biological desires for food, drink, and sex; all require shelter and warmth; all have emotional needs for approbation and respect; all must endure whatever genetic attributes, infant environment, and racial identity have been their gratuitous endowment; all, finally, must confront their inevitable mortality. Increasingly, each is dependent upon the other—butcher, mortician, plumber, and lawyer—in industrialized societies demanding ever more specialized division of labor. Equality assumes the similarities outweigh the differences.

The belief in equality springs from a variety of roots. We were, in fact, more equal in material conditions than people in other nations; the open frontier with its available land and the absence of an old feudal aristocracy were immensely important in this respect. A rapidly developing literary heritage also stressed the equality theme, with Melville, Whitman, and Twain its major contributors; the individualist philosophy of Emerson and Thoreau enhanced it too. In addition, while some religious ideas have been used to justify extreme inequalities, there are others which have opposite effects. The concept of the brotherhood of man is often rooted in a belief in the universal fatherhood of God, and the family analogy is comfortable and persuasive. Finally, equality is also part of the humanist tradition. Eugene V. Debs, an American socialist, said in 1919: "(Y)ears ago I recognized my kinship with all living things, and I made up my mind that I was not one bit better than the meanest of the earth . . . While there is a lower class, I am in it; while there is a criminal element, I am of it; while there is a soul in prison, I am not free."[21] He was sent to a federal penitentiary for opposing American involvement in World War I.

Pragmatism

While Americans are not well known for their philosophical speculation, they are internationally renowned for their practical accomplishments. They take frank pride in being "doers," not "thinkers." It is therefore appropriate that this country's most notable contribution to philosophy is pragmatism, which glorifies its most characteristic traits. Pragmatism stresses the belief that the truth of an idea is best tested by its results. Abstract conceptions have validity, pragmatists contend, only in terms of their practical consequences.

This philosophy, developed and refined in the early years of the twentieth century by Charles Peirce, William James, and John Dewey, is not so much a conscious belief embraced by the people as it is

20 McClosky, loc. cit.
21 Quoted in Ray Ginger, *The Bending Cross* (New Brunswick, N.J.: Rutgers University Press, 1949), p. 374.

an operational definition of their attitudes and behavior patterns. Its basic sources go back to an earlier period when American frontiersmen were forced to devise practical expedients to cope with their immediate, and often unexpected, needs. Gradually, a faith in the process of trial and error largely replaced more dogmatic doctrines. Pointing out that there is a discrepancy between what Americans say they believe and the actual programs they favor, two prominent pollsters concluded that "what seems to make the system continue to function as effectively as it does is its distinctly American pragmatism."[22]

Although short on political philosophers, America has been long on skillful practical politicians. The pragmatic orientation stands out clearly in almost every part of the political system. Our major political parties are not ideologically oriented, for the most part, but consist of expedient and sometimes shifting group coalitions formed to win elections. The legislative process is marked by a sort of consensus politics born of the lawmaker's concessions to his conscience, his colleagues, and his constituents. Even the courts, led by the great justices Holmes and Brandeis, have applied a sort of legal pragmatism which "follows the election returns" under the guise of sociological jurisprudence—the theory stressing the law's role as a problem solver. Finally, the "mixed economy" of America, part government owned or regulated and part privately controlled, reflects the same practical preoccupation with final results rather than formal doctrine. Our preference for democracy itself manifests a practical, empirical concern with existing realities. As Winston Churchill said, democracy is the worst form of government—except for all the others that have ever been tried. Democratic politics is above all the art of the possible. Theoretically, it is not very neat; morally, it is sometimes corrupt. But, meeting the pragmatic and typically American test, it usually works.

Political Culture, Past and Future

The symbolic importance of the Constitution demonstrates the influence of intangible elements in the maintenance of America's evolving nationhood, for human beings cannot live by bread alone. They need emblems and ideals, common hopes and shared habits, in order to endure. It is the combination of all of these that constitutes what is called political culture, and this involves the many influences and principles we have already discussed. It includes, therefore, our special brand of patriotism, our preference for capitalism, our entanglements with racism, our respect for equality, and our tendency to practicality. It is grounded on a devotion to freedom and democracy, reinforced by a tradition of self-reliant individualism, materialism and a lawless sort of antiauthoritarianism. Some of it embraces the remnants of Puritan moralism and an emphasis on hard work.

22 Free and Cantril, op. cit., p. 178.

"Courtesy Chicago Historical Society."

Campaign antics have long enlivened American democracy. Here a supporter of
the losing presidential candidate plays donkey for the triumphant backer of the
winner, Grover Cleveland, in 1892.

Popularly accepted myths, legends, heroes, and traditions all
contribute to political culture by emotionally tying the individual to the
vast multitude that shares a common citizenship in the whole nation.
Thus, the elaborate etiquette surrounding the display of "Old Glory," a
national Father who "never told a lie," and a martyr who regretted that
he had "but one life to give" for his country all became pillars of support
for the nationalism inherent in the developing political culture of the new
America. The skeptic may be right in charging that some of these
phenomena are irrational, irrelevant, even fraudulent. But they contributed immeasurably to the growth and solidarity of a nation.[23]

23 An illuminating account of some "fictions" that have infused our political culture is in
the preface to Forrest McDonald, *E Pluribus Unum: The Formation of the American
Republic, 1766–1780* (Boston: Houghton Mifflin Company, 1965).

The evolution of a common American political culture is dynamic and continuing. The War of 1812 produced the national anthem, the Uncle Sam symbol, and the successful defiance—for the second time—of English military might. Some twenty years later it was strengthened by the administration of Andrew Jackson, who linked the welfare of the lower middle class to national prosperity much as Washington and Hamilton had performed the same feat with respect to the commercial elite. Union victory in the Civil War was important in reaffirming the primacy of national rather than sectional loyalties. In the last century, America fell in love with its own prosperity and power. As we aspired to the world leadership we finally attained, we incorporated a devotion to an unexcelled standard of living and unmatched military might into our national self-image. How long can reality sustain the illusion?

Our political culture today is in a state of flux, in part because those with a substantial stake in society assimilate its values more readily than the poor, the ethnic minorities, and the alienated youth who proclaim allegiance to a real but poorly defined counterculture. Changes also result from the technological challenges and realignments of international power which no country can now escape. History provides little solace for nations seeking immortality. Whether the United States, as we know it, will survive, depends on whether its political culture can be diffused more evenly among our people and whether it can adjust to the pervasive changes which characterize our time on earth.

Conclusion to Part One

The American political system is a variation on universal political themes. To illustrate this, the first chapter has defined the world-wide nature of politics, and the second has described the geographical, historical, social, and cultural forces that have made American politics unique.

If we interpret these in terms of power, we see some of the paradoxes presented by our historical development. The Revolution signified rebellion, change, and freedom—a challenge to authority—but the Constitution adopted thirteen years later symbolized stability, order, and authority itself. The protection of individual rights, federalism, and the separation of powers have limited power more than in almost any other country, yet our national government has continuously increased its centralized authority. Furthermore, while government authority has become more concentrated, political influence has also been more widely diffused through the gradual extension of voting rights and direct elections.

There are other complexities as well: White dominance has declined but racism persists; the westward movement dispersed power geographically but urbanization has concentrated it; and political resources such as money remain unequally distributed even as votes and education are more equally allocated than ever before. The American people exert an enormous impact on the use of government power, but they have yet to control it.

Bibliography

Chapter 1

The Nature of Politics: What's It All About?

Dahl, Robert A., *Modern Political Analysis,* 2nd. ed. (Englewood Cliffs, N.J.: Prentice-Hall, Inc., 1970).

Easton, David, *The Political System: An Inquiry into the State of Political Science* (N.Y.: Alfred A. Knopf, Inc., 1953).

Ebenstein, William, *Today's Isms,* 6th ed. (Englewood Cliffs, N.J.: Prentice-Hall, Inc., 1970).

Eulau, Heinz, *The Behavioral Persuasion in Politics* (N.Y.: Random House, Inc., 1963).

Lasswell, Harold D. and Abraham Kaplan, *Power and Society* (New Haven, Conn.: Yale University Press, 1950).

Murphy, Robert E., *The Style and Study of Political Science* (Glenview, Ill.: Scott, Foresman and Company, 1970).

Ranney, Austin, *The Governing of Men,* 3rd ed. (New York: Holt, Rinehart & Winston, Inc., 1971).

Chapter 2

The Americans: Land, Legacy, and Political Culture

Beard, Charles A., *An Economic Interpretation of the Constitution of the United States* (N.Y.: The Macmillan Company, 1913).

Brown, Robert E., *Charles Beard and the Constitution* (Princeton, N.J.: Princeton University Press, 1956).

Corwin, Edward S., and Jack W. Peltason, *Understanding the Constitution,* rev. ed. (N.Y.: The Dryden Press, Inc., 1958).

DeTocqueville, Alexis, *Democracy in America,* trans. by Phillip Bradley (N.Y.: Alfred A. Knopf, Inc., 1945).

Farrand, Max, *The Framing of the Constitution of the United States* (New Haven, Conn.: Yale University Press, 1913).

Free, Lloyd A. and Hadley Cantril, *The Political Beliefs of Americans* (N.Y.: Clarion Books, Simon & Schuster, Inc., 1968).

Grodzins, Morton, *The Federal System* (Englewood Cliffs, N.J.: Prentice-Hall, Inc., 1960).

Hamilton, Alexander, *et al., The Federalist* (N.Y.: Everyman's Library, E. P. Dutton & Co., Inc., 1929).

Hofstadter, Richard, *The American Political Tradition* (N.Y.: Alfred A. Knopf, Inc., 1959).

Kammen, Michael G., ed., *Politics and Society in Colonial America* (N.Y.: Holt, Rinehart & Winston, Inc., 1967).

Lipset, Seymour M., *Political Man,* (Garden City, N.Y.: Anchor Books, Doubleday & Company, Inc., 1963).

Myers, Henry A., *Are Men Equal?* (Ithaca, N.Y.: Cornell University Press, 1945).

Potter, David M., *People of Plenty* (Chicago: University of Chicago Press, 1954).

Roche, John P., ed., *Origins of American Political Thought* (N.Y.: Torchbooks, Harper & Row, Publishers, 1967).

Smith, Adam, *The Wealth of Nations* (N.Y.: Everyman's Library E. P. Dutton & Co., Inc., 1957).

Steinfield, Melvin, ed., *Cracks in the Melting Pot* (Beverly Hills, Calif.: Glencoe Press, 1970).

U.S. Bureau of the Census, *Statistical Abstract of the United States,* published annually (Washington, D.C., 1971).

PART TWO

THE PEOPLE'S RIGHTS

Even in a democracy, relatively few people hold positions of government power, but everyone is affected by government actions. In Part Two, we examine ways in which we have tried to prevent those in possession of government power, the rulers, from destroying the rights and freedoms of the ruled.

It makes no difference how just the laws are, or how scrupulously they preserve the rights and freedoms of individual citizens, if they are applied in an arbitrary or excessive manner. There is a distinction, in other words, between the law itself and the way it is enforced, between the substance or content of a government decree, and the procedure by which it is carried out. The Constitution places limits on both by guaranteeing substantive and procedural rights alike. A law prohibiting all brothers from talking to one another, for example, would be a bad law substantively, no matter how fairly it might be enforced. Similarly, a good law prohibiting drunken driving would be procedurally intolerable if the home of every licensed driver were searched each night for alcoholic beverages. The First Amendment freedoms discussed in Chapter 3 are substantive rights to which the Supreme Court once seemed to give a preferred position. Amendments Four through Eight in Chapter 4 deal primarily with procedural requirements imposed upon police practices and the conduct of trials. Judicial interpretation now makes little distinction as to the relative importance of these two types of constitutional protections. To be either substantively or procedurally just, law in a democracy must apply equally to all citizens. None can be arbitrarily favored or disfavored. Chapter 5 discusses equal justive under law.

Chapter **3**

Freedom of Expression
First Things First

[W]hen men have realized that time has upset many fighting faiths, they may come to believe, even more than they believe the very foundations of their own conduct, that the ultimate good desired is better reached by free trade in ideas—that the best test of truth is the power of the thought to get itself accepted in the competition of the market. . . . That at any rate is the theory of our Constitution. It is an experiment, as all life is an experiment.

Oliver Wendell Holmes

It is no coincidence that the First Amendment to the Constitution protects the freedoms central to democracy: religion, speech, press, assembly, and petition. These were believed to be the very lifeblood of an enlightened society, and the authors of the Bill of Rights were simply putting first things first.

Most of these specific freedoms are dependent upon one another. Freedom of religion, for example, entails the freedom to assemble in church congregations; freedom of speech without freedom of assembly is nothing but the right to talk to oneself; and freedom of the press is often necessary to petition the government effectively (meaning to protest or request official action). This interrelatedness enables us to refer to all five of these rights as freedom of expression. Clearly a democracy requires such freedom in order that citizens may form their own opinions, propose and evaluate policies and personnel, and then organize for political action supporting or opposing the government of the day.

THE DOUBLE STANDARD FADES

Before considering specific provisions of the Bill of Rights, it would be well to distinguish those rights guaranteed against only the national government from those protected against both the national and state governments.

Although it doesn't say so, the Bill of Rights (Amendments One through Ten) was adopted to protect individuals only from the arbitrary power of the national government. The Civil War changed all that. Contemplating the potential menace presented by white-dominated southern states to the rights of newly freed blacks, a northern-controlled Congress proposed the Fourteenth Amendment to limit the powers of all state governments—north or south—to abuse any individual citizens—white or black. The words of that amendment were broad and sweeping: "No State shall . . . deprive any person of life, liberty, or property, without due process of law . . ." What, precisely, did these words mean?

Not much, for quite a while. The *Slaughter House Cases* of 1873 declined to interpret the Fourteenth Amendment as aiding the individual against the state governments.[1] Not until 1925 did the Supreme Court, in *Gitlow* v. *New York,* hold that the "due process" clause protected at least part of the First Amendment (freedom of speech) against interference by the state governments as well as by the national government.[2] Since that decision, many other cases have produced Court opinions placing more and more of the rights in the first nine amendments under protection against state as well as national threat. The Supreme Court, in effect, has used the due process provision of the Fourteenth Amendment to incorporate most of the Bill of Rights into a broad barricade against state, as well as national, power.

But the justices on the Court have disagreed on how to determine which rights are protected by the Fourteenth Amendment against the states and which are not. Clearly, any guideline establishes a double standard of superior and inferior rights. Some justices, notably the late Hugo Black, would abolish that double standard altogether and apply the whole Bill of Rights to the states. Most have adhered to the rule of Justice Cardozo, who said in *Palko* v. *Connecticut*[3] that any provision in the Bill of Rights that was essential to "a scheme of ordered liberty" limited all governments, state as well as national.

The *Palko* rule is obviously a subjective one, and some justices who endorse it have held several provisions of the Bill of Rights to be necessary to ordered liberty which Cardozo, who devised the doctrine, thought not to be. In any event, the Court has now made the rights in Amendments One, Four, most of Five and Six, Eight, and possibly Nine applicable to the states as well as the national government.

1 16 Wall. 36 (1873).
2 268 U.S. 652 (1925).
3 302 U.S. 319 (1937).

THE SEPARATION OF
RELIGION AND POLITICS

Religion has permeated nearly every aspect of American life. It has influenced our literature, music, art, and recreational activities. Among twelve leading nations the U.S. ranks highest in belief in God and a life after death.[4] For more than a decade, over 40 percent of our people have attended a religious service each week.[5] Even without an established church such as is found in many other countries, the United States may be one of the most religious nations in the world. The young "Jesus people" are the offspring of a strong tradition.

Freedom from Religion:
The "Establishment" Clause

In view of its pervasive influence, it is not surprising that religion has exerted a strong impact upon our government. Thirty-seven states have "blue laws" which require the closing of business establishments on Sundays, the armed forces employ chaplains, and legislative bodies throughout the nation begin each day's session with prayer. Even our official currency affirms that "In God We Trust," although the behavior of many citizens indicates a stronger belief in the money than in the motto.

It is more difficult to assess the likely future of religion as a factor in American politics. The election of John F. Kennedy as our first Catholic president in 1960 may signal either an increase in tolerance or a diminished importance attached by voters to religious matters. Such a decline may be inferred from the fact that church attendance has dropped by 7 percent since 1958 and by 15 percent among adults between twenty-one and twenty-nine years of age. On the other hand, political issues continue to surface, such as abortion or aid to Israel, which have unmistakable religious overtones. Richard Nixon, a perceptive interpreter of public opinion, has been the first President to hold religious services in the White House.

The secular state   Yet American government is commanded by the Constitution to remain neutral on religious issues. Although some examples above indicate official endorsement of theological principles, they have either been upheld by the courts on nonreligious grounds, as in the Sunday-closing laws,[6] or have not yet produced cases forcing the Supreme Court to rule on their constitutionality. It can be argued,

---

4 George Gallup, *Los Angeles Times,* Dec. 28, 1968, p. 19. Note that 98 percent of the people said they believe in God, up 4 percent since 1948, and 73 percent in life after death, up 5 percent.
5 *Los Angeles Times,* March 20, 1972, p. 9.
6 See, especially, *Gallagher* v. *Crown Kosher Super Market of Massachusetts,* 366 U.S. 617. Supreme Court decisions are usually documented this way. "U.S." refers to *United States Reports,* the official volumes containing the full text of Court opinions. The first number indicates the volume and the last the page on which the case begins.

Figure 10   American Religious Preferences[1]

Denomination	Percentage of Population	Denomination	Percentage of Population
Protestant	66.2	Roman Catholic	25.7
Baptist	19.7	Jewish	3.2[2]
Methodist	14.0	Other religions	1.3
Lutheran	7.1	No religion	2.7
Presbyterian	5.6	Not reported	0.9
Others	19.8		

[1]Based upon 1957 responses to the only government census of religious preference.
[2]About 40 percent of all American Jews live in New York City where they constitute about one fourth of the population.
Source: "American Religious Preferences" from *This U.S.A.* by Ben J. Wattenberg with Richard M. Scammon. Copyright © 1965 by Ben J. Wattenberg. Reprinted by permission of Doubleday & Company, Inc. and A.D. Peters & Co.

however, that the framers of the Constitution wished to create a political system which was essentially secular, or nonreligious in nature.

In the first place, the Constitution makes no mention of a Supreme Being. Secondly, Article VI clearly stipulates that "no religious Test shall ever be required as Qualification to any Office or public Trust under the United States." Finally, the First Amendment opens with the words "Congress shall make no law respecting an establishment of religion . . ."

The phrasing of this "establishment" clause is significant. It does not simply prohibit an established church—an officially favored one receiving tax support—but goes further to ban legal aid for all churches and for religion in general. There are two major reasons for this categorical rejection of government assistance. Most important is that European history was marred by innumerable and tragic wars fought over what help government was to give, and to whom, in support of religious principles. This our American forebears wished to avoid. A second reason for the insistence upon government neutrality in religious matters was the antipathy which some of our early leaders felt toward the organized churches of the day.

In addition to the constitutional restrictions, religious influence in America is partially neutralized by the immense diversity of beliefs. The expression of almost any religious sentiment is bound to antagonize some people holding contrary views, and candidates for office are well advised to remember that more than sixty separate church denominations have memberships in excess of 50,000 people in the United States.

Confusion on the Court   The Supreme Court of the United States, as final arbiter of what government can and cannot do, has been faced with many hard decisions regarding how much encouragement laws can give to organized religion without violating the First Amendment's prohibition of religious "establishment." Upon occasion it has ruled that this merely prevents some legal preference for one religion over another. But the difficulty the judges confront is indicated by their frequent inability to agree with one another. In 1947, in the case of *Everson* v. *Board of Education of Ewing Township, N.J.*,[7] the Court upheld by a 5–4 vote the constitutionality of a school district providing bus transportation for pupils attending parochial schools as well as for those attending public schools. In 1968, a six-member majority approved a New York law supplying textbooks for parochial school children. In this case, *Board of Education* v. *Allen,* the Court distinguished state aid primarily for the benefit of students from that which constitutes direct assistance to religion.[8] Three years later federal aid to construct church-owned classrooms not used for religious instruction was approved 5–4 but state subsidies for teachers' salaries in church schools was invalidated 8–1. Seven justices sustained the constitutionality of property tax exemptions for church property in 1968.[9]

In *Zorach* v. *Clauson,* a 6–3 decision in 1952, the Court held that public school students could be released part of the regular school day for the purpose of receiving religious instruction in the church or synagogue of their choice.[10] Only four years earlier the Court ruled that released-time programs for religious purposes were a violation of the "establishment" clause if the religious instruction took place on public school property.[11] It is extremely doubtful that the Supreme Court has heard its last case regarding the "establishment" clause. President Nixon has pledged himself to seek greater tax support for parochial schools than ever before proposed.

Prayer in the schools   The most controversial recent cases involving government aid to religion have dealt with religious observances conducted as a part of the daily routine in public schools. The leading case is *Engel* v. *Vitale* in which the Supreme Court decided that a nondenominational prayer written by the New York State Board of Regents and recited in every public school classroom was unconstitutional—even though no student was required to join in saying the prayer. Justice Hugo Black, who wrote the majority opinion, believed that the prayer constituted a kind of state-endorsed religious activity prohibited by the "establishment" clause of the First Amendment. It is not "the business of government," he wrote, "to compose official prayers."[12] Standing alone, Justice Potter Stewart wrote a dissenting opinion stating that he saw nothing unconstitutional in "letting those who want to say a prayer to say it."[13]

7 330 U.S. 1.
8 392 U.S. 236.
9 *Tilton* v. *Richardson,* 403 U.S. 672 (1971), *Lemon* v. *Kurtzman,* 403 U.S. 602 (1971), and *Walz* v. *Tax Commission of City of New York,* 397 U.S. 664 (1970).
10 343 U.S. 306.
11 *Illinois ex rel McCollum* v. *Board of Education,* 333 U.S. 203.
12 370 U.S. 425. The case illustrates our religious diversity, as it was brought by five parents—two Jews, a Unitarian, a member of the Ethical Culture Society, and a nonbeliever.
13 370 U.S. 445. The prayer itself was quite short: "Almighty God, we acknowledge our dependence upon Thee, and we beg Thy blessings upon us, our parents, our teachers, and our country."

Only a handful of decisions in our entire history have been met with attacks as bitter as those which assaulted the majority opinion in the *Engel* case. Even though Justice Black took great pains to point out that he saw nothing objectionable in *studying* religion, or in nondevotional or nonworship activities such as singing Christmas carols, over a hundred congressmen introduced constitutional amendments specifically to permit prayer in the public schools.

The following year, 1963, the Supreme Court handed down two more decisions consistent with its ruling in *Engel*. In one, *Abington School District* v. *Schempp,* a Pennsylvania law requiring portions of the King James Version of the Bible to be read in all public schools each morning was declared unconstitutional, and in the other, *Murray* v. *Curlett,*[14] a Maryland law authorizing classroom use of the Lord's Prayer met the same fate. Such laws established not merely religion, but the Christian religion. While outraged criticism followed the *Engel* decision, the *Schempp* and *Murray* decisions were defied. An estimated 30 percent of all public schools had required religious observances prior to 1962 and as late as 1966 nearly 13 percent were continuing them in deliberate, determined disobedience of the supreme law of the land.[15]

Freedom of Religion: The "Free Exercise" Clause

In addition to prohibiting the establishment of religion, the First Amendment also contains another clause guaranteeing "the free exercise thereof." The "establishment" and "free exercise" clauses together appear to guarantee government neutrality, neither assisting or encouraging religion, on the one hand, nor punishing or preventing it, on the other.

Yet, just as the "establishment" clause is not absolute, so also the "free exercise" clause has exceptions. Here we approach a vital but lamentable principle of our human existence: Society is so complex and our values so often contradictory that there is no freedom guaranteed in the Constitution which can be absolute—all have permissible limitations.

The limits of "free exercise"   In 1878 the Supreme Court placed some limits on freedom of religion by upholding a law prohibiting polygamy in what was then the territory of Utah, even though the Mormon religion at that time endorsed plural marriages.[16] Similarly, there seems little doubt that states can prohibit practices such as human torture or sacrifice or the use of drugs such as LSD, even though they may be sanctioned by religious groups. In a 1905 case, a Massachusetts law compelling vaccinations against smallpox was upheld, regardless of

14 The two cases were decided together. 374 U.S. 203.
15 Prof. Richard B. Dierenfield's figures, in Charles H. Sheldon, ed., *The Supreme Court: Politicians in Robes* (Beverly Hills, Calif.: Glencoe Press, 1970), p. 84.
16 *Reynolds* v. *U.S., 98 U.S. 145.*

contrary religious convictions.[17] Most of these instances involved the use of the so-called *police power* of the states (a substantial portion of the powers reserved by the Tenth Amendment) to protect the health, safety, morals, and welfare of the people. Unfortunately, sometimes such legitimate authority runs counter to religious freedom for a portion of the population and a conflict arises between two parts of the Constitution. Under such circumstances judges, forced to decide which of the conflicting provisions shall prevail, really earn their money.

The extent of "free exercise"   While freedom of religion is not absolute, the Supreme Court has guaranteed it wide latitude. A relatively small church, the Jehovah's Witnesses, has brought about thirty cases to the Supreme Court and as a result has produced official recognition of the rights to distribute religious literature without a permit, to expound religious views even to people offended by them, to sell religious tracts without payment of the license fees often required by municipalities, and to refuse to salute the flag on grounds of religious doctrine.[18] A 1972 decision upheld the right of members of the Amish church to prohibit their children from attending high school.[19] These cases produced sharp disagreement among Supreme Court justices and in a few instances represent reversals of previous decisions. Like all human beings, judges change their minds. When they do, the authoritative meaning of constitutional provisions changes also.

Religion, Conscience, and the Draft

No issue has troubled young Americans of this generation more than the undeclared war in southeast Asia, especially if they were about to be drafted into the army fighting it. Of the 22.7 million men registered under selective service regulations in 1970, some ten thousand conscientious objectors, more than three times the number in 1965, were working on civilian projects required by the selective service system, and another 28,000 had been classified as available for such work.[20] Adding to the significance of these numbers is the fact that as many as 30,000 draft-age men had fled to Canada and other countries to escape induction and that 450 went to federal penitentiaries in violation of selective service laws in 1970 compared to only 173 in 1965.[21] More men applied for conscientious objector classification in 1970 than in either World War I or World War II.

Conscientious objection   American draft laws, the first of which was enacted during the Civil War, have always been opposed by

---

17 *Jacobson* v. *Massachusetts,* 197 U.S. 25.
18 *Lovell* v. *Griffin,* 303 U.S. 444 (1938); *Cantwell* v. *Connecticut* 310 U.S., 296 (1940); *Murdock* v. *Pennsylvania,* 319 U.S. 105 (1943); *West Virginia State Board of Education* v. *Barnette,* 319 U.S. 624 (1943).
19 *Wisconsin* v. *Yoder,* 92 S.Ct. 1526 (1972).
20 U.S. Bureau of the Census, *Statistical Abstract of the United States: 1971,* p. 257.
21 Ibid., p. 151. See the estimate of columnist Stewart Alsop, *Newsweek,* July 20, 1970, p. 88.

some citizens on the ground that they represent the sort of tyranny which many immigrants came to this country to escape. Yet these laws have recognized that no person shall be compelled to serve in the armed forces if "by reason of religious training and belief [he is] conscientiously opposed to participation in war in any form." Such training and belief has been most characteristic of the so-called peace churches, *i.e.*, the Church of the Brethren, Friends (Quakers), Jehovah's Witnesses, and a great many Methodist congregations, although it has been claimed by members of many other denominations as well. If the selective service system believes "c.o." claims to be valid, it compels alternative nonmilitary service in the armed forces, or civilian work of a humanitarian nature. In every war, some people have been imprisoned because they have denied the legitimacy of any sort of government-compelled service at all.

The courts and the "c.o." The courts have been forced to consider four vital constitutional issues regarding the conscientious objector: (1) Is exemption from military combat service on grounds of religious belief an unconstitutional violation of the "establishment" clause prohibiting aid to religion? (2) Is denial of draft exemption because a man's objection is moral, but not religious, a violation of the "free exercise" clause? (3) What is religion? (4) Is one, on either religious or moral grounds, entitled to draft exemption if he opposes specific wars (*e.g.*, Vietnam), but not all war?

Three decisions have dispelled considerable uncertainty. In the 1965 *Draft Act Cases,* often cited as *United States* v. *Seeger,*[22] the nation's highest court unanimously ruled that religious belief might include not only a belief in a Supreme Being or God, but also a belief which is equal to it in genuine importance in the lives of those who hold it. Perhaps an even more important decision, extending this ruling, was handed down in 1970. Here the court decided that a sincere opposition to war based entirely on philosophic, moral, and sociological grounds warranted "c.o." classification, because of the "establishment" clause, just as much as opposition rooted in more traditional religious doctrine.[23] Finally, selective opposition to particular wars was declared legally invalid in 1971.[24]

FREEDOM OF SPEECH, PRESS, ASSEMBLY, AND PETITION

The constitutionally guaranteed freedoms of speech, press, assembly, and petition are closely related, yet each has distinguishing characteristics. Freedom of speech has sometimes been suppressed on the grounds that it might produce violence, but some nonverbal acts have been protected as "symbolic" speech. Freedom of the press is guaranteed

22 380 U.S. 163.
23 *Welsh* v. *U.S.,* 398 U.S. 333.
24 *Gillette* v. *U.S.,* 401 U.S. 437 (1971).

to a great degree by preventing censorship, although motion pictures, theoretically, have not been freed from that control. Freedom of assembly, in certain circumstances, cannot occur without prior permission; yet such permission cannot be denied arbitrarily nor in a discriminatory fashion. Freedom of petition, entailing the right to request or protest government action, is increasingly exercised by pressure group lobbyists.

Freedom of Speech

Private citizens can restrict speech in whatever way they wish in their own homes, offices, and factories. The First Amendment is a protection against government interference. Even here, however, speech has consequences affecting other people, and its freedom is not unlimited.

Restrictions on free speech   Justice Oliver Wendell Holmes, a phrasemaker who had few peers, once asserted that no man has the right to shout "fire" falsely in a crowded theater. In other words, one man's freedom of speech should not endanger another man's safety. In the same vein, he once remarked that "your right to swing your arms ends where my nose begins."

Yet it is easier to devise clever epigrams than it is to apply the First Amendment to situations in which impassioned speakers hurl inflammatory charges at angry crowds. Should violence erupt, who is at fault? The person employing his freedom of speech to provoke and denounce, sometimes without justification? Or the listeners, whose anger may flow only from their own hotheaded intolerance? The answers have not been easy, for we are again confronted with a constitutional contradiction: an individual right (Amendment One) *vs.* the authority of the state to prevent riots (implicit in Amendment Ten). Sometimes, constitutional *law* and public *order* may thus conflict.

Verbal attacks upon the government pose a more serious problem than those upon private individuals. Should those who would destroy our freedoms be entitled to use them for that purpose? Should freedom of speech be protected for those who use it to urge the overthrow of the government? Again there is a clash of principles—this time between freedom of expression and the legitimate power of national self-preservation. In 1798 Congress passed the Alien and Sedition Acts, the latter of which made it a crime, in effect, to criticize public officials. During World War I, it enacted Espionage and Sedition Acts which prohibited virtually any statement which was designed to interfere with military success. In 1940, moreover, the Smith Act made teaching or advocating the violent overthrow of the government illegal, declared the Communist Party to be committed to that very purpose, and made joining it with knowledge of that aim to be illegal also. Ten years later, the McCarran, or Internal Security Act of 1950, was passed over President Truman's veto. It created a Subversive Activities Control Board to designate organizations as subversive if it found them to be loyal to a foreign government or advocating the violent overthrow of our own. Membership in such groups was required to be registered with the Board each year. Some believe these laws betray a surprising fear that the advantages of our form of government are so few that appeals for its forceful destruction might enlist many eager recruits. Others consider these laws vital to national security in times of great peril. Whatever the truth, the application of such statutes has revealed the difficulty of balancing freedom of expression and government power.

Rights reclaimed In resolving the dilemmas presented by freedom of speech, the Supreme Court has drawn some very fine lines—some would say nearly invisible ones—in distinguishing speech that is constitutionally protected from that which is not. In 1942 it held that calling a policeman a "damned Fascist," and "God-damned racketeer" was so likely to invite violence as to lose its First Amendment protection.[25] Yet seven years later, by the narrowest of margins, it reversed a breach of the peace conviction of a speaker who denounced Jews and other minorities in highly offensive terms. Should violence break out, as it did in the latter situation, the Court apparently believed that the violent ones, and not the speaker, should be punished.[26] Another significant case involved a speaker who denounced the President and the mayor of Syracuse, New York, as "bums," and in addition urged that Negroes should "rise up in arms and fight" for equal rights. By a 5–3 vote, the Court upheld the "disorderly conduct" conviction of the Syracuse orator.[27] But it reversed the "breach of the peace" conviction against 187 blacks who marched to the South Carolina state capital carrying banners proclaiming "Down with Segregation," and chanting "We Shall Not Be Moved." Only Justice Clark dissented.[28]

Most cases involving free speech *vs.* public order have resulted from state and local prosecutions. But a new element was added in 1968 when Congress first entered the riot-control business. It passed legislation which made it a national crime to cross state boundaries for the purpose of inciting a riot, and under which demonstration leaders at the 1968 Democratic national convention were convicted.

The Supreme Court first passed on the constitutionality of subversion laws in 1919, in *Schenck* v. *U.S.*,[29] in which the "clear and present danger" doctrine was developed. The issue involved a man convicted of urging draft evasion during World War I. In an opinion written by Justice Holmes, the court based its decision on three assump-

25 *Chaplinski* v. *New Hampshire,* 315 U.S. 568. "Resort to epithets or personal abuse," the Court said, "is not in any proper sense communication of information or opinion safeguarded by the Constitution."
26 *Terminiello* v. *Chicago,* 337 U.S. 1. Justice Douglas, for the Court majority, observed that ". . . A function of free speech . . . is to invite dispute. It may indeed best serve its high purpose when it induces a condition of unrest, creates dissatisfaction with conditions as they are (and) strike(s) at prejudices and preconceptions."
27 *Feiner* v. *New York,* 340 U.S. 315 (1951).
28 *Edwards* v. *South Carolina,* 372 U.S. 229 (1963). The dissenting opinion observed that "to say that the police may not intervene until the riot has occurred is like keeping out the doctor until the patient dies."
29 249 U.S. 47. Schenck's conviction was upheld.

tions: (1) The Constitution guarantees freedom of expression but not freedom of action; (2) expression is often designed to provoke action; (3) when expression creates "a clear and present danger" that illegal action will occur, it loses its constitutional protection. This "clear and present danger" doctrine, while not consistently followed by the Court, has influenced almost all its decisions in the last half century in cases involving verbal attacks upon the government or its policies. Under this Court standard, freedom of expression is protected by the First Amendment up to that point when it results in an obvious (clear) and immediate (present) threat of "substantive evil" (illegal action) that the state has the power to prohibit.

Although criticized by those who believe that freedom of speech and press are absolute rights never to be infringed, this "clear and present danger" test, in actual application, has protected a wider area of expression than almost any of the alternative standards that have been suggested from time to time in other cases. In *Gitlow* v. *New York*,[30] for example, the Court utilized what has come to be known as the "bad tendency" (or "dangerous tendency") doctrine. Over the dissents of Justices Holmes and Brandeis, this held that free expression lost its constitutional protection if it created a tendency toward illegal acts.

The necessity of drawing the delicate line between personal freedom and state power was presented again in 1950 by the prosecution of the eleven top leaders of the Communist Party under the Smith Act provision prohibiting advocacy of violent revolution. The Supreme Court majority, in *Dennis* v. *U.S.*,[31] upheld the conviction of these defendants under a diluted version of the "clear and present danger" test, sometimes called the "grave and probable" doctrine. This made it sufficient cause to limit free expression if it created a probable danger of some grave evil. In the following years, more than seventy other Communists were convicted under the Smith Act, but in 1957 such prosecutions ceased when the Supreme Court held in *Yates* v. *U.S.*[32] that the First Amendment protected all political expression except that which urges "one to *do* something . . . rather than merely to *believe* in something." This emphasis upon incitement to action rather than abstract advocacy moves the Court closer to the "clear and present danger" test as originally propounded by Holmes.

Just as the *Yates* case defused the Smith Act as a weapon for jailing Communists or other alleged subversives, so the Internal Security Act of 1950 was rendered largely useless when the Court held that its ultimate registration requirement compels people to testify against themselves in violation of the Fifth Amendment.[33] Since the old 1798 Sedition Act was enforced for only two years, and the World War I legislation is

30 268 U.S. 652 (1925).
31 341 U.S. 494.
32 354 U.S. 298.
33 *Albertson* v. *Subversive Activities Control Board,* 382 U.S. 70 (1965). This constitutional provision is examined in greater detail in the next chapter. The Internal Security (or McCarran) Act is also known as the Subversive Activities Control Act.

operative only in time of declared war, no significant congressional legislation designed to suppress subversive propaganda is now being enforced.

This does not mean that the government is helpless; it can still prosecute those who cross state lines to incite riots, or those who bomb banks, derail troop trains, dodge the draft, sabotage weapon production, spy, and engage in other overt acts of rebellion. It does mean that the Supreme Court in many instances has defended the First Amendment from abuse by the other two branches and, at least partially, has reclaimed for all Americans some of the rights which are too quickly threatened by paranoid patriots who would sacrifice freedom under the guise of protecting it.

Symbolic speech   Whereas antiriot or antisubversion laws tend to restrict freedom of speech, the courts have recently accepted a doctrine which tends to expand it. This is the concept that silent, nonverbal communication can be used as a vehicle for the transmission of ideas in a sort of symbolic speech protected by the First Amendment.

The idea of symbolic speech has been used in a number of relatively minor cases, such as those in which California courts have held that nude dancers in public bars are engaged in a kind of freedom of expression which exempts them from prosecutions for lewd conduct. In a case involving not only civil rights, but more specifically student rights as well, the Supreme Court held in *Tinker* v. *Des Moines* that the wearing of black arm bands to class as a gesture of antiwar sentiment is protected by the First Amendment even in the face of prohibitive action by school authorities. This 1969 decision[34] tended, in some slight degree, to offset a decision one year earlier that the public burning of a draft card was not a constitutionally permissible exercise of freedom of expression.[35] The extent of constitutionally protected symbolism is still largely undetermined.

Freedom of the Press

From a practical point of view, it is difficult to censor what is said, verbally, in advance of its utterance. Yet this is a distinct possibility with respect to the written word. The constitutional meaning of freedom of the press, therefore, has been clarified to a substantial degree by the case of *Near* v. *Minnesota*,[36] which ruled that censorship before publication, or what is called "prior restraint," is normally unconstitutional, and can be undertaken only to prevent revelations endangering national security such as the description of future troop movements. Possible abuse of this press freedom can be prevented, the court argued, because publishers can be sued or perhaps prosecuted *after* publication, for instance for libel or obscenity.

34 *Tinker* v. *Des Moines Independent Community School District,* 393 U.S. 503.
35 *United States* v. *O'Brien,* 391 U.S. 367.
36 283 U.S. 697 (1931).

The prohibition of "prior restraint" of the press was further strengthened by the 1971 Pentagon Papers case involving a secret history of the Vietnam War. Here, the Court ruled 6–3 that the government could not suppress the publication of documents provided to newspapers by Daniel Ellsberg. But some observers believe that freedom of the press was weakened in 1972 by a 5–4 decision requiring journalists to divulge confidential news sources when questioned by grand juries. All news reporters—for the press, radio, and television—are further frustrated by the excessive application of "secret" classifications to official documents, the closed sessions of many legislative committees, and other government actions carried on privately. Freedom of the press is of little value without free access to significant information.

The movies go to court In 1952 the Supreme Court expanded the constitutional guarantee of freedom of the press to encompass motion pictures, previously considered entertainment rather than serious communication. It has not, however, extended to them the protection of no "prior restraint." Movies can, therefore, be censored in advance,[37] although only a few states have done so. In addition, the court has refused to permit the banning of films either on the ground that they were "sacrilegious" (treating religion with "contempt, mockery, scorn and ridicule") or because they depict "sexual immorality (adultery, in this case) as desirable."[38] To date, the court has approved of film censors but paradoxically has reversed every act of censorship which has been brought to its attention.

Freedom of the press *vs.* trial by jury Just as the "free exercise" clause may conflict with the prohibition of the establishment of religion, or freedom of speech may interfere with the power to control domestic violence, so too, freedom of the press may interfere with the right to trial by an impartial jury, guaranteed in Amendment Six. If newspapers, radio, and television inflame readers' emotions and reveal selective information or allegations about a pending trial, it may be impossible to find jurors who can deliberate with calm and open minds and render a verdict based only on evidence disclosed in court.

The English tend to solve this problem by contempt of court actions against the press. Thus far, American courts have tended to nullify the conviction of those found guilty by juries potentially brainwashed by earlier publicity.[39] On the constitutional level, conflicting rights must somehow be compromised; on a practical level we need a press capable of exercising responsible restraint.

Freedom of the press *vs.* slander and libel: what price a good

---

37 *Times Film Corp.* v. *Chicago,* 365 U.S. 43 (1961). The vote was 5–4.
38 *Burstyn* v. *Wilson* 343 U.S. 495 (1952) and *Kingsley Pictures* v. *Regents of the University of New York,* 360 U.S. 684 (1959). The vindicated film in this case was a screen adaptation of *Lady Chatterley's Lover.*
39 Two major cases in point involve a former aide to the U.S. Senate, *Estes* v. *Texas,* 381 U.S. 532 (1965) and a well-known doctor accused of murdering his pregnant wife, *Sheppard* v. *Maxwell,* 384 U.S. 333 (1966). On this topic, see the discussion by Henry J. Abraham, *Freedom and the Court* (N.Y.: Oxford University Press, Inc., 1967), pp. 127–32.

name?   A person's reputation is his most valuable possession. At stake may be his job, his friends, even his family. Slander and libel laws are designed to protect individuals from irresponsible accusations. Slander is an oral, and libel a written, statement which maliciously injures the reputation of another person. Although there are criminal laws prohibiting such statements, they result in few prosecutions; most court cases are brought under state civil codes which permit the person allegedly injured to sue the person who purportedly made the damaging statement for a specified amount of money. This amount may compensate a person for suffering and loss, and may also include punitive damages designed to teach the offender a lesson.

As a general rule, the truth of the alleged statement is an adequate defense for the beleaguered defendant, especially in criminal cases, although there are occasions in which even this will not help him. If, for example, one person charges another with some scandalous action (e.g., "Smith is always half-drunk"), the person so insulted and maligned may collect money, even if he *is* half-drunk, in the absence of any proof that the accusation served any useful purpose or was motivated by anything other than purely personal malice. Correspondingly, a false statement does not necessarily make one vulnerable to a successful libel suit if the statement was made without spite or deliberate deception.

Now, if one is threatened with a slander or libel suit, that fact will surely act as a restraint upon one's freedom of expression. Yet the courts have held that laws in this area do not violate the First Amendment because they were a part of the common law long before that amendment was proposed and would doubtlessly have been prohibited expressly if that had been the intention of those who wrote the Bill of Rights.

There is less danger of being successfully sued for libel if you criticize a public figure than if you make allegations against a generally unknown citizen. Former President Harry Truman is said to have remarked to one complaining about attacks on government officials, "If you can't stand the heat, stay out of the kitchen." The Supreme Court, in effect, has adopted the same logic with respect to libel suits involving public figures in general. This is the essence of the Court's decision in *New York Times* v. *Sullivan*,[40] in which a libel judgement in favor of a Montgomery, Alabama, city official was set aside on the grounds that "erroneous statement is inevitable in free debate" and that discussion of public issues "should be uninhibited, robust, and wide open." In *Associated Press* v. *Walker*[41] the Court expanded this same doctrine to protect those who write of prominent citizens who engage in debate on vital public controversies. A 1971 decision extended the protection against

---

40 376 U.S. 254 (1964).
41 388 U.S. 130 (1967). In another case decided with this one, *Curtis Publishing Co.* v. *Butts*, the Supreme Court upheld a $460,000 libel suit won in a lower court by Butts, athletic director of the University of Georgia, against the *Saturday Evening Post*, a magazine which had accused him of giving pregame information to the University of Alabama football team.

slander suits to a radio station that made unintentionally false charges against a little-known person whose business was the object of a police raid.

All of this does not mean that the Court has declared open season on anyone involved with some matter of public concern. As former Chief Justice Warren observed in the *Walker* case, "Freedom of the press . . . does not include absolute license to destroy lives or careers."

Obscenity: The Uncertain Crime   The reserved powers of the states, guaranteed by the Tenth Amendment, always have been assumed to include the "police power" necessary to protect, among other things, public morality. Thus, the states tended to punish the sale or distribution of sexually explicit books and pictures since early in the last century. In 1873 the national government joined the crusade against obscene materials by banning them from the mails. Although the exact definition of obscenity was rather vague, American courts usually followed the Hicklin obscenity test which hinged upon "whether the tendency of the matter . . . is to deprave and corrupt those whose minds are open to such immoral influences and into whose hands a publication of this sort may fall."

Not until 1957 did the Supreme Court confront the incompatibility of obscenity laws and freedom of expression. Although the case, *Roth* v. *United States*,[42] upheld a conviction for sending obscene materials through the mail, and even though Justice Brennan's majority opinion asserted that "obscenity is not within the area of constitutionally protected speech or press," it had the effect of permitting open distribution of materials previously confined to men's locker rooms or the back alleys of Paris.

It had this effect because first, the *Roth* decision explicitly repudiated the Hicklin doctrine which barred everyone from access to publications which might have an undesirable influence on anyone. Second, it established a new test of obscenity: "whether to the average person, applying contemporary community standards, the dominant theme of the material taken as a whole appeals to prurient interest." Thus obscenity was made a dynamic concept, shaped always by the changing standards recognized by "average" people. "Prurient interests" is defined in such a way as to involve only "lustful thoughts," or "a shameful or morbid interest in nudity, sex or excretion."[43] It in no way includes violence, greed or other indications of immorality.

The permissive society   The *Roth* case was the crack in a censorship wall which has since been widened to an open door. In 1959, for example, the Court held that a book seller could not be convicted unless he knew he was selling an obscene publication,[44] and seven years

---

42 354 U.S. 476 (1957).
43 The definitions are cited and discussed in Eberhard and Phyllis Kronhausen, *Pornography and the Law* (N.Y.: Ballantine Books, Inc., 1959), pp. 147–48.
44 *Smith* v. *California*, 361 U.S. 147.

later, in *Memoirs* v. *Massachusetts*,[45] it was decided that no publication could constitutionally be deemed obscene unless it was "utterly without redeeming social value." The most permissive decision of all came in 1969 in the case of *Stanley* v. *Georgia*, in which the Supreme Court upheld the right of a man to possess admittedly pornographic films in his own home. In 1971, however, a divided Court upheld prohibitions against the mailing or importation[46] of obscene materials.

Only one case has significantly tightened the state's control over obscenity since the Roth decision in 1957. In *Ginzburg* v. *U.S.*,[47] with four judges each filing individual dissents, the Court upheld an obscenity conviction on the grounds that works were *advertised* in a way which appealed to prurient interests, even though the publications themselves were not obscene.

Freedom of Assembly

Freedom of speech and press have generally enjoyed fewer restrictions than freedom of assembly. This is because assembly often entails large crowds and/or such physical demonstrations as marches and picketing. Local governments, therefore, may require permits or licenses for rallies and parades so long as they are granted on an impartial basis under local regulations which prohibit arbitrary administrative discretion. A permit application for a peace march, in other words, must be treated the same as one for an armed forces parade. Either may be denied if a busy highway would have to be closed during a workday rush hour, or either may be granted. But they cannot be treated differently, nor could they be refused on capricious, unreasonable grounds.

The Court also has held that if freedom of assembly is unconstitutionally denied by a licensing agency such as a park department or police commission, the legal remedy is to seek a court order requiring the license rather than assemble without it.[48]

A more difficult problem in this area, and one which divided the Court badly, was posed when thirty-two students from Florida A. & M. University entered the jail grounds in Tallahassee to protest both racial segregation in the prison and the earlier arrest of some fellow students. Police arrested the protesters under a "malicious trespass" law. At issue was whether trespass laws may be applied to restrict assembly on public as well as private property. In a 5–4 vote, the Court held that they could.[49]

Picketing, a particularly important form of assembly in labor disputes, generally has been held to be constitutionally protected if the

45 383 U.S. 413 (1966). The "Memoirs" are those of a "Woman of Pleasure," a book more commonly known as *Fanny Hill*.
46 89 S. Ct. 1243.
47 383 U.S. 463 (1966).
48 *Poulos* v. *New Hampshire*, 345 U.S. 395 (1953).
49 *Adderley* v. *Florida*, 385 U.S. 39 (1966).

picketers do not block the entrances of the institution picketed. The Court has ruled, however, that a shopping center may bar distributors of antiwar leaflets from its premises, but not labor pickets.

Freedom of Petition

The First Amendment right to "petition the Government for a redress of grievances" was designed to guarantee the people some access to government officials, some medium of communication with those in charge. Increasingly, large groups of citizens hire professional lobbyists to contact officials in their behalf, and most recent court cases involving the right to petition have arisen from congressional attempts to regulate lobbying activity.[50] The right to petition guaranteed in the First Amendment is not related to the initiative petitions by which some states permit propositions to be placed on the ballot for approval by the voters.

THE FUNCTIONS OF FREEDOM

It is disturbing that the strong emphasis on freedom of expression found in both the Constitution and many court decisions seems to have relatively little support among the American people. Surveys during the past two decades indicate that about three fourths would not allow groups to organize peaceful antigovernment demonstrations, 60 percent would prohibit speeches against churches or religion, 45 percent would forbid socialists from publishing newspapers, 40 percent would ban peaceful anti-Vietnam war demonstrations, and 36.7 percent believed that "a man oughtn't to be allowed to speak if he doesn't know what he's talking about."[51]

Few Americans know much about the Bill of Rights (21 percent according to a 1945 poll)[52] and even fewer are familiar with the Declaration of Independence (only one person out of fifty signed it in the form of a typed petition in 1970).[53] There seems to have been a failure of political socialization, an inability of families, schools, and other institutions to teach new generations the political values and traditions of the old ones. The importance of freedom of expression clearly requires renewed emphasis.

50 For a good discussion of this subject, see the editor's essay in Robert F. Cushman, ed., *Cases in Civil Liberties* (N.Y.: Appleton-Century-Crofts, 1968), pp. 490–92. This casebook is one of the best, containing condensations of many Supreme Court decisions, along with interesting editorial commentary.
51 Herbert McCloskey, "Consensus and Ideology in American Politics," *American Political Science Review* 58 (June 1964): 367.
52 Robert E. Lane and David O. Sears, *Public Opinion* (Englewood Cliffs, N.J.: Prentice-Hall, Inc., 1964), p. 61.
53 *Los Angeles Times*, July 5, 1970, p. 2. Two called it "Commie junk," one "the work of a raver," another "rubbish," and yet another "meaningless."

Human Dignity: Are Natural Rights Self-Evident?

The Declaration of Independence contends that it is a self-evident truth that governments were created to protect, among other things, the natural right to liberty. The chief trouble arising from this natural rights philosophy is that it cannot be empirically proved; no one can feel or see the rights that are claimed. Yet whether or not there is a natural right to liberty the *theory* of natural rights elevates the individual human being to a position of supreme importance. It assumes that he *has* rights, that the state is supposed to protect them, and that society exists for the purpose of enhancing his dignity, rather than he for the purpose of serving its needs. Indeed, if there were no natural rights of man (and there may not be), we would surely have to invent them if we are to save the individual human being from all the governments, churches, families, corporations, and movements ever ready to sacrifice him to some "greater good."

The characteristic of democracy which most sets it apart from communist or fascist regimes is the belief that there is no greater good than the dignity and nobility of the individual. Love and compassion may lead him to sacrifice himself for other individuals, but his essential integrity and worth must never be bartered away by others in behalf of some abstract class, creed, or flag. Freedom is important, then, because without it the individual is stripped of his basic dignity and subject to the control of those more interested in class consciousness, national honor, the one true faith or racial pride.

The belief in natural rights philosophy may be essential to freedom, just as freedom is necessary to human dignity. But it is a belief that cannot be proved. Like confidence in God's mercy, a belief in man's dignity requires an act of faith.

Social Progress: The Search for Truth

In the last century, the case for individual freedom has relied largely on the value of its social contributions, rather than on its protection of individual rights. This line of reasoning was expressed most influentially by the great English philosopher John Stuart Mill in his long essay, *On Liberty*. Mill defended freedom of expression as necessary to the search for truth on which human progress depends. Through the clash and combination of differing viewpoints, he believed, new insights are possible. Even the expression of bad ideas is socially valuable, he argued, because they stimulate the further improvement of good ones, make the truth easier to ascertain by comparison with them, and by their challenge convert dead dogmas too easily taken for granted into living faiths rationally understood and more vigilantly defended. Moreover, it is often difficult to distinguish truth from falsity, good ideas from bad ones. Socrates and Jesus, perhaps the two most honored figures in the

Western World, were put to death because the authorities—and remarkably enlightened ones at that—believed their ideas to be blasphemous and subversive. Galileo was forced to retract a scientific truth of surpassing importance (the belief that the earth revolves around the sun) in order to escape the same fate. Even the wisest of men occasionally suppress the wrong ideas and would-be censors would do well to heed Mill's reminder that "all silencing of discussion is an assumption of infallibility."

In the century and more since its publication, *On Liberty* has been vindicated many times. Yesterday's "dangerous heresies," such as biological evolution or birth control, have become accepted parts of today's "truth." Freedom is clearly a prerequisite for maximum progress.

Personal Improvement and Intellectual Growth

In a free society, there are many opinions among which men and women are asked to choose. Such choices are often difficult, and require the maximum use of our intellectual capacities. But the very freedom which makes choice necessary, also affords us the practice which makes wise choice possible. Just as a child learns to walk by standing, stepping, and falling, over and over, learning from his mistakes, so we learn to make wise choices by choosing over and over, learning finally from our bad ones.

John Dewey, the famous pragmatist, was primarily an educational philosopher. As such, he was also a leading defender of freedom as essential to personal growth and mental development. "Learning by doing," as his theory was often described, is impossible in a totalitarian society where choice is impossible and one may do only what he is ordered to do. Freedom, on the other hand, exercises the mental muscles.

Varieties of Freedom

This discussion thus far has focused upon but one kind of freedom—the absence of governmental or social restraint. Vital as this is, freedom is too slippery and complex a concept to be confined in so narrow a definition. The truth is that there are several different conditions which various people call "freedom." One, certainly, is the lack of external control just mentioned. Another, not so pertinent to politics, is the absence of compulsive drives, as when one is "free" of nicotine or alcohol. These are essentially negative freedoms; they are freedom *from* something. Equally important is freedom of opportunity—a more positive aspect that involves the freedom to make a choice among two or more realistically available alternatives.

One more point is relevant: One person's freedom limits another's. The freedom to have a party extending until 3:00 A.M. in a crowded apartment building destroys the freedom of other tenants to sleep; the freedom to manufacture or drive a car may restrict the freedom to breathe clean air; the freedom to sell your house to whom you wish (say a white family) limits the freedom of others (say a black family) to buy a house they can afford. Dewey put the matter plainly:

"There is no such thing as the liberty or effective power of an individual, group, or class, except in relation to the liberties, the effective powers, of *other* individuals, groups and classes. . . . (L)iberty is always a *social* question, not an individual one."[54]

The fact that freedoms come in conflict poses society's most difficult dilemma: Whose freedom is to prevail? There is no easy answer or pat formula, but two suggestions may be in order. One is the traditional democratic solution of counting noses: Restrict the freedom of the minority in the interests of the majority. The other, more difficult to apply, is to determine which of the conflicting freedoms is most important. It is a subjective test. Try applying it to the examples cited earlier. In any event, chances are that government will finally decide.

54 John Dewey, *Philosophy of Education* (Totowa, N.J.: Littlefield, Adams Company, 1956), pp. 112–13.

Chapter 4

The Defendant's Rights
Criminal Justice in America

*Solon, asked how justice could be secured in Athens, replied,
"If those who are not injured feel as indignant as those who
are."*

       What happens to the citizen who is arrested? This chapter is
mainly devoted to the procedural rights guaranteed him in Amendments
Four through Eight. But as a preliminary, there is a more general
provision in the Fifth Amendment which is of fundamental significance:
"No person shall . . . be deprived of life, liberty, or property, without
due process of law . . ."

       As we have seen, the "due process" clause in the Fourteenth
Amendment has been interpreted to mean that most of the provisions of
the Bill of Rights limit state governments as well as the national government. Yet the fact that the Bill of Rights itself, in Amendment Five, has a
clause almost identical in wording suggests that "due process" has
further meaning. Our whole legal history, however, reveals that few
phrases in the Constitution are so difficult to define.

       Its origins lie obscured in the ancient common law of En-
gland; as recently as 1952, due process was described by the Supreme
Court in such general terms as "civilized conduct," "a sense of justice,"
and "the community's sense of fair play and decency."[1] The concept of
due process has both substantive and procedural aspects—it limits the
content of laws as well as the procedures by which they are enforced.

---

1 *Rochin v. California,* 342 U.S. 165 (1952).

Substantively, laws may not be so vague that no one is sure of their purpose nor so arbitrary and capricious that they cannot be defended on reasonable grounds. Procedurally, the rulers cannot attain their objectives by using just any means they may find convenient against the ruled. In *Rochin* v. *California,* the 1952 case just referred to, the Court dealt with a denial of procedural due process. It decided that morphine, a narcotic, could not be used to convict a drug suspect because it was obtained by pumping his stomach despite his vigorous resistance.

The "due process" clause comes very close, then, to providing constitutional affirmation that we are a government of laws and not of men. Although it is true that laws are made, enforced, and administered by men and women, the authority of these officials is limited by legal and constitutional restrictions. They do not have unlimited power merely because they won an election, wear a badge, or wield a gavel. To put it in theoretical terms, the agents of the law must not be permitted to violate the law; in practical terms, officials must neither use more force than is necessary to perform their duties, nor presume to enlarge those duties. This is what makes us a constitutional democracy.

SUBSTANTIVE SAFEGUARDS IN THE ORIGINAL CONSTITUTION

Although most of the rights that protect the person accused of crime are procedural, to be found in the Bill of Rights, there are also three provisions of the original Constitution that insure substantive rights because they limit what the legislature can do in dealing with crime.

The old adage that "ignorance of the law is no excuse" is obviously not applicable to laws not yet passed. The citizen cannot be expected to behave today in anticipation of what may be declared illegal tomorrow. This elementary logic underlies the prohibition against *ex post facto* laws. Such laws make some action a crime that was not a crime when the action was performed, or make it easier to convict someone of a crime committed previously, or retroactively increase criminal punishment.[2] They are fortunately unconstitutional. Motorists, for example, could not be arrested for driving without seat belts on January 1, if the law requiring them was not passed until January 2. Article I, Section 9 forbids Congress from passing such laws and Article I, Section 10 extends this prohibition to the states.

"Equal justice under law" is one of humanity's highest aspirations and is the motto inscribed on the Supreme Court building in Washington, D.C. A society that has one law for the rich and another for the poor, one for me and another for you, is clearly unjust. The ban on *bills of attainder,* laws which inflict punishment on specific persons or groups without a conviction in court, was meant to prohibit such unequal

2 The leading case in this matter is an old one, *Calder* v. *Bull,* 3 Dallas 386 (1798).

justice. They are specifically forbidden in Article I, Sections 9 and 10. Laws withholding salary from three allegedly subversive government employees and prohibiting Communists from serving as officers of labor unions have been declared unconstitutional bills of attainder even though they were not criminal statutes in the usual sense of that term.[3] The claim that the relocation of Japanese-Americans in World War II concentration camps constituted a bill of attainder (while no action was taken against German-Americans) was not upheld by the courts.

A writ is a court order and a writ of *habeas corpus* is intended to prevent arbitrary imprisonment. The writ, in effect, requires public officials holding a person in custody to either "put up or shut up"—to release him, charge him with some criminal act, or demonstrate in some way why he should be held. If a writ of habeas corpus is issued, the suspect will be released on bail (an amount of money deposited with the court) pending a trial, or held in custody under some specific legal provision.

The Constitution contains no provision relating this writ to the states, but Article I, Section 9 provides that the national government shall not suspend it "unless when in Cases of Rebellion or Invasion the public Safety may require it." Since the Civil War, the writ has been suspended only in Hawaii when martial law (military rule) was invoked during World War II. The Supreme Court, however, has declared this permissible only if the regular civilian courts are unable to function.[4]

PROTECTING THE SUSPECT

The common law required the government to assume persons to be innocent of criminal charges until it had proved them guilty. But this noble ideal needed to be translated into specific day-to-day practices. Some of these protect persons who are simply "suspicious characters"; others protect them should they become actual defendants in a criminal case.

Policing the Police: The Right to Privacy

"A man's house is his castle," says an old English proverb. But if the police are to be given maximum authority to capture criminals it is certain that they will occasionally batter down the castle walls. The two horns of the dilemma, adequate power for the police and reasonable privacy for the people, deserve brief examination.

The thin, blue line   Confronted with a soaring crime rate, society looks more and more to the police as a barricade against the apparent barbarism that seems to threaten it. Certainly, the police are the first line of defense against the criminal hordes, and a thin blue line

---

3 *U.S.* v. *Lovett,* 328 U.S. 303 (1946) and *U.S.* v. *Brown,* 381 U.S. 437 (1965).
4 *Ex parte Milligan,* 4 Wall 2 (1866) and *Duncan* v. *Kahanamoku,* 327 U.S. 304 (1946) are perhaps the most important judicial interpretations.

they are, expected to enforce the laws yet insulted by cries of "pig" and continuously accused of needless brutality.

The lot of the "cop" appears to be getting worse. Underpaid and often undereducated, his profession is among the most dangerous in the world. In 1968 patrolmen's pay in big cities averaged about $7500 a year, only two-thirds that of union plumbers and far less than they received thirty years earlier relative to those in other occupations. But police salaries rose about 9 percent between 1969 and 1970. Whereas over half of the police recruits in New York City were college graduates in 1940, this proportion had fallen to about 5 percent in less than thirty years and reflected trends in other cities as well.[5]

As police pay and preparation have become comparatively poorer, their jobs have become more difficult. Between 1960 and 1966 the number of law enforcement officers rose about 20 percent, but the crime rate during the same period increased 62 percent.[6] While there has been some dispute about the reliability of official crime statistics, records show a 144 percent increase in the rate of serious crime between 1960 and 1970. Policemen themselves were often the victims: 48 were killed in 1960, 88 in 1964, and 125 in 1969. A 1971 Harris poll showed that more people feared crime in the streets (55 percent) than at any time in six years, even though the annual increase in the rate of crime had dropped from 17 to 7 percent since 1968.

As crime continued to increase, so did its political importance. In 1968 Congress passed a Safe Streets Act establishing a Law Enforcement Assistance Administration (LEAA) to supervise financial grants from the national government to aid in the "war on crime." President Nixon persuaded Congress to pass an Omnibus Crime Control Act in 1970, and by 1972 LEAA grants were more than eleven times larger than in 1969.[7] Increasingly fearful voters turned to law-and-order candidates. In 1971 the mayors of Philadelphia, Detroit, and Minneapolis were former police officials. Many citizens demanded that society stop "coddling crooks," "handcuffing the cops," and even that we "curb the courts" in their leniency toward criminal defendants. As a result of President Nixon's judicial appointments it was clear by 1972 that the courts were getting the message. But there is another side to the story, called privacy.

The Fourth Amendment: protecting the castle   The Constitution does not explicitly mention privacy, but it is a value long enshrined

5 Jerome H. Skolnick, *The Politics of Protest:* A report to the National Commission on the Causes and Prevention of Violence (N.Y.: Clarion Books, Simon & Schuster, Inc., 1969), pp. 151–54 and 384. Low educational backgrounds are noted also for new policemen in Berkeley, California, and Washington, D.C.

6 *Report of the National Advisory Commission on Civil Disorders* (N.Y.: Bantam Books, Inc., 1968), p. 269. Sometimes known as the Kerner Commission, the group responsible for this report was appointed by President Johnson to study the causes of big city riots.

7 Fred P. Graham, "A Contemporary History of American Crime," Hugh Davis Graham and Ted Robert Gurr, *Violence in America* (N.Y.: A Signet Book, The New American Library, Inc., 1969), pp. 460–78. See also U.S. Bureau of the Census, *Statistical Abstract of the United States: 1971,* pp. 140 and 143, and *Crime and the Law* (Washington, D.C.: Congressional Quarterly, Inc., 1971), pp, 2, 30, and 54.

Figure 11   The Increase in Crime, 1960-1970

VIOLENT CRIMES

	20 40 60 80 100 120 140 160 180 200 220 240 260
Murder[1]	76%
Forcible Rape	121%
Robbery	224%
Aggravated Assault	117%

CRIMES AGAINST PROPERTY

Burglary	142%
Auto Theft	183%
Larceny[2]	245%

Source: U.S. Bureau of the Census, *Statistical Abstract of the United States: 1971*, p. 140.
[1]Includes non-negligent manslaughter. [2]$50 and over.

in American tradition. Justice Brennan spoke for the Supreme Court majority when he wrote that "The overriding function of the Fourth Amendment is to protect personal privacy and dignity against unwarranted intrusion by the State."[8]

But what intrusions are unwarranted? It is a hard question, and even the Fourth Amendment provides little more than loose guidelines in formulating an answer. "The right of the people," it stipulates, "to be secure . . . against unreasonable searches and seizures, shall not be violated, and no Warrants shall issue, but upon probable cause, . . . and particularly describing the place to be searched, and the persons or things to be seized."

Clearly, the provision involving warrants, which are court permits authorizing police action, is designed to limit the procedures used by law enforcement officers. It is also generally agreed that a search or seizure (including an arrest) accomplished without a warrant is unreasonable *except* in one of the following circumstances:

1) The crime is committed in the presence of the policeman (or person making a "citizen's arrest");

2) There is "probable cause" to believe that a felony (or major crime) has been committed, and there is no time to get a warrant;

3) There is probable cause to make an arrest and a search of the person is necessary to seize weapons which might endanger the arresting officer or to prevent the destruction of evidence.

On many occasions, these rules are easy enough to apply. If a patrolman hears a gun shot from inside an apartment followed by a bloodcurdling scream, most reasonable men would admit he has probable cause to believe a crime has been committed and that it would be

8 *Schmerber* v. *California*, 384 U.S. 757 (1966).

folly to prohibit his immediate entry into the building—warrant or not. Yet there are borderline cases in which decisions about what is reasonable, about what constitutes probable cause to suspect crime, would confound the wisest of judges, let alone the policemen who must make instantaneous choices in an atmosphere of perilous excitement. If the officer decides there is no probable cause, a criminal may escape; if he decides there is, a court may disagree and release the suspect.

Three Supreme Court cases decided in 1968 indicate some of the complexities involved. In the major one, *Terry* v. *Ohio*,[9] police "stop and frisk" procedures were upheld with respect to a suspect whose behavior indicated he might be about to hold up a store. The detective "patted down" the outside of the suspect's clothes, felt a revolver, removed it, and arrested him for carrying a concealed weapon. Similarly, the Court approved another frisking without a warrant when a policeman discovered burglar tools on a suspect who was tiptoeing down an apartment hall and began to run when a door was slammed. These cases indicate Court approval of at least modified searches when there was enough cause to suspect criminal activity, although no reasonable or probable grounds for arrest. Yet the Court reversed a conviction on the grounds that the mere fact that the defendant had talked to known drug addicts did not justify his being searched (successfully) for narcotics.[10]

Most arrests take place without a warrant,[11] although this part of the Bill of Rights now limits state and local officers as well as the national government.[12] Moreover, an "exclusionary rule" has been propounded which prohibits materials unconstitutionally seized from being used as evidence in criminal court prosecutions.[13] No warrant is needed for a search of an automobile or other moving vehicle if there is probable cause for an arrest,[14] but even when there are sufficient grounds for an arrest without a warrant inside a house, the police must confine their search to the suspect and the area within his reach. Warrants must usually specify items to be seized, although officers entering a home with a warrant to search for one object (for example, forged checks) may seize something else (draft cards belonging to others), but only if possession of the latter is itself a crime.[15] The implication for drug or marijuana users is clear and ominous.

Finally, it is well to remember that police entry into a private dwelling, even without a warrant, is permissible if it can be justified in terms of "practical considerations of everyday life."[16] Loud noises or

9 392 U.S. 1 (1968).
10 The cases were *Peters* v. *New York,* involving burglary, and *Sibron* v. *New York,* narcotics. 20 L. Ed. 2d 917 (1968).
11 Paul W. Tappan, *Crime, Justice and Correction* (N.Y.: McGraw-Hill Book Company, 1960), p. 329.
12 *Wolf* v. *Colorado,* 338 U.S. 25 (1949), and *Mapp* v. *Ohio,* 367 U.S. 643 (1961).
13 *Weeks* v. *U.S.,* 232 U.S. 383 (1914) and *Mapp,* loc. cit.
14 *Carroll* v. *U.S.,* 267 U.S. 132 (1925).
15 *Harris* v. *U.S.,* 331 U.S. 145 (1947).
16 In this connection, see *Johnson* v. *U.S.,* 333 U.S. 10 (1948) and, more importantly, *Brinegar* v. *U.S.,* 338 U.S. 160 (1949).

suspicious smells emanating from a late night party, for example, are probably sufficient to justify such action. With respect to general criminal investigation in Washington, D.C., and suspected drug offenses throughout the nation, Congress has authorized the issuance of "no knock" warrants which permit police to enter a building without prior warning if they believe evidence would otherwise be destroyed or personal safety endangered.

Taking the Fifth: self-incrimination   Closely related to the Fourth Amendment, is a provision in Amendment Five which specifies that "No person . . . shall be compelled in any criminal case to be a witness against himself . . ." This protection against compulsory self-incrimination has become one of the best known of our constitutional rights, and one may "take the Fifth" in refusing to answer any questions about oneself whether they are posed by policemen, prosecuting attorneys, legislative committees, or any other government officials. An exception in which persons *may* be compelled to testify about their own activities occurs when they are offered immunity from prosecution involving related criminal behavior.

Police brutality: the "third degree"   Although a refusal to reveal facts about one self is obviously a protection of privacy, it may also jeopardize one's safety while being questioned by police. A clear purpose of the Fifth Amendment is to prevent law enforcement officers from extracting confessions by force, the so-called "third degree," yet such techniques seem to persist in the privacy of a few police station back rooms in spite of the constitutional prohibition. Forced confessions once involved physical torture, replaced in many instances with psychological pressures including the loss of sleep, deprivation of tobacco, use of bright lights, and promises of leniency if the suspect confesses. Police training manuals have also advised the use of such deception as false claims that an alleged accomplice had confessed or that nonexistent evidence has been obtained.[17]

Pretrial procedure   The usual procedure in an arrest varies somewhat from state to state but it always entails *detention* by an officer, often only for the purpose of asking questions.[18] Next, assuming the answers are unsatisfactory to the policeman, the suspect is *arrested* and transported to the police station. There one is *booked*, with name recorded, and thus saddled with a "police record." Within a certain period after arrest and booking, averaging from forty-eight to seventy-two hours, the suspect is brought before a magistrate, or judge, for a *preliminary examination*. During the period between the booking and examination most police questioning takes place, and "as many as 40 percent of those arrested are released without being charged before a

---

17 Fred E. Inbau and John E. Reid, *Criminal Interrogation and Confessions* (Baltimore: The Williams & Wilkins Co., 1962), p. 28.
18 Questionable police practices sometimes occur at this point. See Diane Schroerluke, *Police Personnel Complaints and Redress Remedies* (Berkeley, Calif.: American Civil Liberties Union, Berkeley-Albany Chapter, 1970). Mimeographed.

magistrate.[19] Finally, one may be *arraigned* and ordered to stand trial either through a complaint from a private citizen, the police, or the prosecuting attorney, or else through action of a grand jury.

In the long process described above, the police have viewed the opportunity to obtain pretrial confessions as essential to effective crime control. In defense of suspect questioning, they have asserted that about 80 percent of all felony convictions result largely from confessions.[20] Then what legal guarantees does the suspect have in protecting himself against attempts to extract confessions? The answer lies in a series of recent court decisions regarding the right of the suspect to remain silent.

The Supreme Court held in 1964 that the Fifth Amendment's prohibition of forced self-incrimination applies to both state and national government.[21] Most significantly, in *Miranda* v. *Arizona*,[22] it was decreed that any confession obtained was inadmissible evidence unless the suspect was first informed of his constitutional rights to remain silent and to obtain legal counsel. The *Miranda* decision has been much criticized. The case against the right to refuse to testify against oneself is that it tends to protect the guilty and restricts the police too severely. The argument in its defense is not only that it protects the individual from invasion of privacy and painful police coercion, but also that it encourages difficult and detailed police investigation. An Indian policeman put it well when he said "It is far pleasanter to sit comfortably in the shade rubbing red pepper in some poor devil's eyes than to go about in the sun hunting up evidence."[23] But perhaps the strongest argument for the right to remain silent is that it helps to prevent the conviction of innocent people. In 1964, in New York City alone, three men confessed to murders, under police questioning, of which they were later proved innocent.[24]

The defense of the Fifth Amendment is not meant to suggest that policemen are clever fiends intent upon sending innocent people to jail. On the contrary, they are members of understaffed institutions expected to solve more crimes than they can adequately investigate. Both their prestige and potential for promotion are dependent on producing, as nearly as possible, a probable culprit for every crime. Under these circumstances, they try to get the quickest confession from the most probable suspect. The people need protection from the police not because they are evil but because they are—like all officials to whom we grant vast powers—human.

Technological tyrants The framers of the Constitution no

19 Ed Cray, *The Big Blue Line* (N.Y.: Coward-McCann, Inc., 1957), p. 73, and A. C. Germann, Frank D. Day, and Robert R. J. Gallati, *Introduction to Law Enforcement* (Springfield, Ill.: Charles C Thomas, Publisher, 1962), pp. 164–65.
20 Cray, op. cit., p. 70 and note 8, p. 231.
21 *Malloy* v. *Hogan*, 378 U.S. 1.
22 384 U.S. 436 (1966).
23 Cited in Robert F. Cushman, ed., *Cases in Civil Liberties* (N.Y.: Appleton-Century-Crofts, 1968), p. 242.
24 Cray, op. cit., pp. 77–82.

doubt believed that the prohibitions on unreasonable searches (Amendment Four) and forced confessions (Amendment Five) were sufficient to protect the privacy and dignity of innocent suspects. But they reckoned without knowledge of the twentieth-century technology which has produced such skilled snoopers as electronic eavesdropping devices and chemical blood tests.

The Supreme Court met the problem of telephone wiretaps in 1928 in the case of *Olmstead* v. *U.S.* and held, 5 to 4, that they were constitutionally acceptable because they involved no seizure of material things nor any physical trespass.[25] Since then, electronic listening has had a stormy history and is no less controversial today than it was forty years ago. In 1934 Congress declared the practice illegal, but in 1941 the law was interpreted by the U.S. Justice Department (which includes the Federal Bureau of Investigation) to permit the use of wiretaps if the information gained were not used in court. Law enforcement officials contended it provided valuable "leads" to other information which was admissible in court.

In 1961 and 1967[26] the Court began a retreat from the *Olmstead* ruling and held that the Fourth Amendment's prohibition against seizing things extended to intangible things such as conversations. The constitutionality of wiretapped evidence was rejected entirely in *Katz* v. *U.S.*[27] which involved an F.B.I. listening device attached outside a public telephone booth. Here the Court ruled that conversations were not only things but that their seizure without a warrant was normally unconstitutional even though (as in this case) the search involved no physical entrance, penetration or trespass. Although the *Katz* decision seemed to overrule the old *Olmstead* doctrine, only a short time later, in the summer of 1968, Congress passed the Omnibus Crime Control and Safe Streets Act which appeared to repeal the old 1934 law outlawing electronic eavesdropping. The new legislation authorized judges to issue warrants permitting the use of wiretapping and listening devices, or "bugs" as they are called in the trade, and in addition permitted the use of certain confessions in ways which some thought to violate the *Miranda* ruling cited earlier. Clearly, in its eagerness to fight crime, Congress was responding to political pressures and was all too eager to pass the buck back to the Courts for delicate decisions involving constitutionality.

At last report, the bugging business was flourishing, although presumably with the blessings of court warrants. New York officials authorized 191 wire taps in 1969 and U.S. Attorney General John Mitchell revealed that midway through 1970 the national government had obtained permission for "more than double . . . the previous year's total of 33."[28] The Nixon administration suffered a setback in 1972,

---

25 277 U.S. 438 (1928). In dissent, Justice Holmes called wire tapping a "dirty business."
26 *Silverman* v. *U.S.*, 365 U.S. 505, and *Berger* v. *New York*, 388 U.S. 41.
27 389 U.S. 347 (1967).
28 "The Assault on Privacy," *Newsweek*, July 27, 1970, p. 17.

however, when a unanimous Court declared the use of wiretaps in domestic security cases to be unconstitutional unless court authorization had been first obtained. The government had argued that when the safety of the nation was menaced internally, no warrants were necessary to obtain evidence in this way.[29]

There are other weapons in the total technological arsenal poised against individual privacy. Blood tests to determine whether motorists are drunk do not involve unreasonable search and seizure because they entail emergency situations in which it is reasonable to suspect that the alcoholic content of the blood would diminish during the time required to obtain a warrant. Nor do they constitute compulsory self-incrimination, the Court has held, since they consist of "physical evidence" rather than "testimony" or some "communicative act or writing." On the same grounds, traffic officers may require suspects to "assume a stance, to walk, or to make a particular gesture."[30]

The threat of government intrusion upon private affairs is heightened by the use of computers that are capable of recording, combining, and exchanging information about individual citizens almost instantly. The Army has the criminal and "loyalty" records of seven million servicemen, contractors, and civilian employees on file, as well as data on anti-Vietnam war protesters such as folk singer Joan Baez and pediatrician Benjamin Spock. Even the Internal Revenue Service in the Treasury Department has been active in the peering-and-peeking business with regard not only to tax records but also to "militant and subversive" books individual citizens have borrowed from public libraries.

We are confronted, it seems, with a sort of pollution of our privacy often associated more with totalitarian dictatorship, and unparalleled in our history. It is not only government agencies which have pried into our conversations, criminal records, political attitudes, and reading habits. They have been joined in their intrusions upon our personal lives by private peekers such as the Pacific Telephone and Telegraph Company which monitored 27 million phone calls in 1965, the Retail Credit Company of Atlanta which has files on seventy million installment buyers, and psychological testing experts who inform employers about the bed-wetting histories and sexual attitudes of job applicants.[31]

These threats to privacy cannot be thwarted by the Constitution alone, for they are products of an increasingly urbanized, congested, economically interdependent society. But whatever their origins, they threaten the integrity of individual citizens who may wish, in Thoreau's words, to "march to the beat of a different drum." They threaten also the progress and ingenuity of a nation whose greatness has required the resourceful inventiveness of people who were a little bit strange. Ein-

29 *Los Angeles Times,* June 20, 1972, p. 1.
30 *Schmerber* v. *California,* 384 U.S. 757 (1966).
31 "The Assault on Privacy," op. cit., p. 16.

stein, for example, seldom wore socks. The computers might go crazy with that one.

   A constitutional "catch-all": Amendment Nine   One of the least-invoked guarantees of the Constitution is Amendment Nine which assures us in mysteriously general terms that the people have other rights in addition to those specifically mentioned. At least by implication, it seems to rival the broad guarantees of due process discussed above. Nonetheless, most Americans would probably agree that it is a valuable safeguard, and that citizens should indeed enjoy rights other than those specified in the Constitution. One expects to be able to choose his occupation, for example, or the color of his shoes, without government interference. Yet a constitution which attempted to enumerate all such rights would be both interminably long and patently absurd. Hence, the Ninth Amendment. The most important case involving matters such as this is *Griswold* v. *Connecticut*,[32] which declared unconstitutional a state law prohibiting the use of birth control devices. The decision elicited six different opinions, including one endorsed by three justices who asserted that such a law impinged upon a right of marital privacy such as the Ninth Amendment was designed to guarantee.

The Difficult Choice

   As we have seen, to help protect the citizen from the occasional excesses of police procedure, Amendment Four forbids unreasonable searches and seizures, Amendment Five prohibits compulsory self-incrimination, and Amendment Nine guarantees additional, unspecified rights. Moreover, both the Fifth and Fourteenth Amendments require national and state officials respectively to employ "due process of law" in their contacts with private citizens.

   When confronted with these constitutional handicaps in their attempts to enforce the laws, the police naturally become frustrated. After careful study, one finally must confront the sad truth that crime detection and personal privacy are sometimes incompatible. Although the police search, arrest, and question many innocent people, often with casual indifference to their constitutional rights, many more who are subjected to the same treatment are indeed guilty. In short, if we want all criminals captured, the rights of some innocent people will be sacrificed; but if we want the rights of all innocent people preserved, some criminals will escape. It is a hard choice, to be sure, on balance well handled by the courts. No one ever claimed that it was easy to run a society which promised "liberty and justice for all."

PROTECTING THE ACCUSED

   Thus far we have been concerned with those constitutional provisions which protect the people in their homes, on the street, or in

32 381 U.S. 479 (1965).

the police station. We come now to the nation's courtrooms and the rights of those who must stand trial as criminal defendants.

Prelude to Prosecution

It is said that the wheels of the gods grind slowly, but they grind exceeding fine. The same could be said of American justice, in spite of both the constitutional requirement of a speedy trial and public accusations of inadequate fineness or fairness.

Trial without error   To be a defendant in a criminal trial is a terrible and traumatic experience. It forces the accused person to endure social embarrassment, entails time sacrificed to prepare a defense, and often costs money necessary to hire a good lawyer. Ideally, then, no one should be tried unless he or she is guilty. This ideal, like most others, can never be fully attained, but the American legal system tries at least to make sure that no one is tried without good cause.

The Fifth Amendment deals with this by providing that no person can be tried for a serious crime except through "indictment of a grand jury." A grand jury is a group of one to two dozen citizens, which can issue formal criminal accusations—known as *indictments*—to bring suspects to trial, if the evidence against them, presented by the police and prosecuting attorneys, indicates probable guilt. In practice, the grand jury seems to be most important in cases involving criminal charges against government employees and those otherwise favored by the power or prestige of their positions.

In many states, however, grand juries have been abolished, or are important only in investigating local government agencies such as the welfare department or coroner's office. The reference to them in the Fifth Amendment is one of the few provisions of the Bill of Rights which the Supreme Court has not held to limit state as well as national action. Even in the most serious of crimes, therefore, states may bring persons to trial either through grand jury indictments or through charges brought by prosecuting attorneys known as bills of information, or *true bills*.

No excessive bail   Anglo-American law insists that no person be considered guilty of a crime unless guilt has been proved in a court of law. The burden of proof is on the government prosecutors. The defendant has no obligation to prove his innocence.

This presumption of innocence raises a difficult problem. Since a suspect is presumed innocent until proven guilty, he should not have to languish in jail until his trial. Yet if he is released, he must be provided with some motivation to appear for the trial rather than to run away. Therefore, *bail* is required—an amount of money which must be deposited with the court in return for which the defendant may be released from jail until the trial begins. If he shows up for the trial the bail money is returned; but if he has "jumped bail" and evaded prosecution, a warrant for his arrest is immediately issued by the judge.

Amendment Eight prohibits excessive bail, an amount which

generally depends on the seriousness of the alleged crime and the previous record of the defendant. Suggestions that the amount of bail be influenced by the wealth of the accused have been judicially ignored. But if one can't raise bail, it is usually possible to go free by paying a fee to a bail bondsman who then posts the bail. Occasionally, judges allow an accused person to be released without bail on his *own recognizance,* or in the event the crime was quite serious, deny the accused bail and retain him in prison until the trial.

One of the controversial aspects of the crime-control law that Congress enacted for Washington, D.C. in 1970 is a "preventive detention" provision that permits judges to hold defendants without bail for sixty days if they believe the defendants might commit a crime if released. The constitutionality of such an unprecedented departure from our tradition is yet to be tested.

A Fair Trial

The Sixth Amendment contains as impressive a list of defendants' rights as can be found anywhere in the world.

How fast is speedy? The first command of the Sixth Amendment is that "the accused shall enjoy the right to a speedy . . . trial." The longer it takes to bring a man to trial the less reliable will be the memory of key witnesses and the greater likelihood that they will have died or disappeared. But how fast is speedy? In an age of increasing crime and overworked courts, the only reasonable answer is, "as soon as possible." Courts have usually held that this constitutional requirement has been met if there has been no deliberate delay in bringing a case to trial although in some areas they have set six-month limits. In 1970 there were over 140 people in Washington, D.C., jails who had been awaiting trial for over a year.[33] To facilitate the demand for speed, criminal cases are given precedence over civil ones and statutes of limitations have been passed prohibiting prosecutions, except in murder cases, if no arrest warrant has been issued within a specified period of time, usually from one to seven years, after the crime has been committed.

How exposed is public? The Sixth Amendment also demands public trials, on the assumption that secret, or "star chamber," proceedings are less apt to be fair than those illuminated by the floodlights of publicity. But judges can clear the courtroom if spectators behave in ways which jeopardize the serious and thoughtful decorum necessary to ascertain the truth. To maintain such an atmosphere, photographs of the trial and live radio and television coverage are almost always banned.

Confrontation The accused has the additional right "to be confronted with the witnesses against him," on the theory that his

---

33 Richard L. Strout, "The District's Crime Bill," *The Christian Science Monitor,* July 24, 1970, p. 14. Such conditions contributed to the Washington prison revolt in 1972.

accusers, testifying under penalty of perjury (lying under oath), and subject to cross-examination by the defense counsel, will be more likely to tell the truth.

This provision has prohibited second-hand hearsay testimony and created two additional problems. First, it limited the use of secret witnesses (sometimes called "faceless informers" or "stool pigeons") by the prosecution. If such persons were forced to appear in court, they might be murdered later by criminals who had confided in them. The testimony of these witnesses, often paid by the police, is sometimes of dubious validity anyway, although it is often of real value in the capture, if not the actual conviction, of dangerous criminals.

Another problem involving the right to confront witnesses is raised by defendants whose wild behavior makes it difficult or even impossible to continue their trials. It gained national attention in 1969 when Federal District Court Judge Julius Hoffman ordered Bobby Seale, a defendant in the case involving incitement to riot at the 1968 Democratic National Convention, to be chained and gagged because of his insulting and disruptive courtroom shouts. Although Judge Hoffman apparently believed he could not constitutionally remove Seale from his own trial, the Supreme Court later ruled, in another case, that such action is permissible under certain extreme circumstances.[34]

The right to subpoena witnesses Since the prosecution may summon witnesses in an attempt to prove guilt, Amendment Six gives the accused the right "to have compulsory process for obtaining witnesses in his favor." Subpoenas are the compulsory process available. They are court orders requiring people upon whom they are served to appear in court and answer questions (not involving their own possible guilt) regarding the alleged crime. If the person subpoenaed does not testify, the judge may rule him in contempt of court and punish him, without trial, by fine or imprisonment.

The right to legal counsel No Sixth Amendment right has been more strengthened or expanded by recent court decisions than the right to professional legal advice. In 1963 *Gideon* v. *Wainwright* applied it to state as well as federal courts.[35] Then, in 1964, the Court ruled in *Escobedo* v. *Illinois*[36] that legal counsel had to be provided when the defendant requested it at the time of his arrest, and not solely for trial. The *Miranda* decision required the police not only to inform the defendant of his right to remain silent, as mentioned regarding the Fifth Amendment, but also to tell him, before questioning, of his right to be represented by an attorney. A 1972 decision required that legal counsel be made available to anyone threatened with even a single day in jail.

But how can the accused obtain legal counsel? He may, of course, hire his own lawyer. The *Miranda* decision also insisted that he

34 *Illinois* v. *Allen,* 397 U.S. 337 (1970).
35 372 U.S. 335. An intriguing account of the case appears in Anthony Lewis, *Gideon's Trumpet* (N.Y.: Random House, Inc., 1964).
36 378 U.S. 478.

must be informed that an attorney will be provided for him if he cannot afford to hire one. This is done in two different ways. In federal courts, and in most state courts, a judge will appoint some local attorney to represent the indigent defendant. Alternatively, especially in major cities, public defenders offices have been created and staffed by full-time lawyers who are recruited and paid on the same basis as those working in the prosecuting attorney's offices. These public defenders, devoted exclusively to representing the poor, seem to provide a higher caliber of legal counsel than is otherwise available in such cases.

No double jeopardy   With only a few exceptions, criminal defendants may be tried only once for a single act. This is the result of the Fifth Amendment's assurance that no person shall be "twice put in jeopardy of life or limb." The exceptions are: (1) Persons in the armed services are subject both to military law and civilian law. There are situations, therefore, permitting both a military court martial and a prosecution in a regular state court for the same offense. (2) If, for example, one robs a bank of funds insured by the national government, he has broken both national and state laws and theoretically could be tried in both national and state courts. In practice this seldom happens. (3) One may be tried twice for the same crime if convicted the first time as a result of some unconstitutional procedure and on appeal, a higher court orders a second one. Hence convicted criminals are not always set free on some technicality, as is often supposed, when the Supreme Court or some other appellate tribunal finds that the conviction was obtained in an unconstitutional manner.

Trial by jury   Trial by jury is mentioned three times in the Constitution. Article III establishes it, Amendment Six specifies an impartial jury, and Amendment Seven extends the right from criminal cases to civil cases involving more than $20. Sir William Blackstone, an eighteenth-century English legal scholar, wrote in his famous *Commentaries* that ". . . the trial by jury ever has been, and I trust ever will be, looked upon as the glory of the English law."[37]

Yet jury trials are not mandatory; they are simply a right the accused may exercise, except in petty cases, if he wishes to do so. Either a judge or a jury may render a verdict and the defendant has the choice. If judges are corrupt or hopelessly prejudiced, as during the colonial period in America, then trial by jury is indispensable. But if judges are believed to be honest, competent, and fair—which seems to be the prevailing view today—then trial by jury is not essential to procedural fairness. In fact, the right of trial by jury has been utilized less and less. Judges now render the verdict in 40 percent of criminal cases going to trial.[38] As long as jury trials exist, however, the constitutional requirement of impartiality is of vital importance, and that guarantee is enforced in a number of ways:

37 Quoted by Justice Black, *Reid* v. *Covert,* 354 U.S. 1.
38 Justice Harlan, in dissent, *Duncan* v. *Louisiana,* 20 L. Ed. 2d 491 (1968).

1) If the defendant in a case has received so much adverse publicity that it would be impossible to find enough jurors who are not already biased against him, then the judge should issue a *change of venue,* an order transferring the trial to some area where there has been less coverage of the case by TV, radio, and the press.

2) No group may be systematically excluded from jury duty because of race, sex, nationality, or attitude toward capital punishment (the death penalty).

3) Attorneys for both defense and prosecution may disqualify prospective jurors after questioning each of them. These *voir dire* examinations permit an unlimited number of disqualifications for adequate cause, and usually from five to thirty peremptory challenges for which no explanation need be given.

In 1970 the Supreme Court upheld the constitutionality of Florida's six-member jury, repudiating a centuries-old tradition that juries must consist of twelve persons. A more important issue was whether juries could hand down a verdict in criminal cases by less than the unanimous vote prescribed by common law custom. It was resolved in 1972 when all four justices appointed by President Nixon were joined by one other in a 5–4 decision sustaining the Louisiana law that permitted convictions by a 9–3 margin. Only Oregon, Montana, and Oklahoma allowed similar verdicts but defendants throughout the country feared that other states would join them.[39]

OF CRIME AND PUNISHMENT: VENGEANCE, DETERRENCE, REHABILITATION

Once the criminal suspect has been searched, arrested, interrogated, and formally charged with a crime, he is an accused person. As such, he has certain constitutional protections spelled out primarily in the Sixth Amendment but also in the double jeopardy and grand jury provisions of Amendment Five and the prohibition of excessive bail in Amendment Eight. But, in spite of all this, what happens to him if he is convicted?

Americans, perhaps like other peoples, aren't quite sure what to do with their criminals. The oldest theory was that they should be punished in a manner commensurate with their crime; this follows the Old Testament rule of "an eye for an eye, a tooth for a tooth." It is a concept rooted in revenge.

An alternative criterion for punishment rests upon the assumption that its purpose is not for revenge but to discourage or deter others from committing crime. Those holding this opinion often believe that the harsher the penalty, the more effective the deterrent.

---

39 *New York Times,* May 28, 1972, p. 6. The ruling affected only state court procedures; federal court verdicts must still be unanimous.

The newest theory is that convicts should be punished only to the degree that is necessary to reform them, to make sure that their rehabilitation is sufficient for safe release into the society at large.

The Criminals: A Group Biography

Before discussing what to do with criminals, it would be well to find out who they are. That is not easy because less than one fourth of all crimes lead to arrests, and many of these do not result in convictions.[40] We do know, however, that cities of over 250,000 population have crime rates from two to six times higher than those with populations under 10,000.[41] Moreover, judging from the persons arrested by the police we can see some characteristics of the "typical" criminal. In 1969, five out of six persons charged with a serious crime were male, three out of four were under twenty-four years of age, and more than six out of ten were white. Although no exact statistics are available, it seems nearly certain that an overwhelming number were poor.

How did they go wrong? Beware of the single, simple explanation. Among the possible "causes" for crime are poverty, permissiveness, television violence, overcrowding, racism, a lawless social heritage, leniency of the courts, inept police work, broken homes, increased (and expensive) drug addiction, and inadequate gun control laws. Whatever the reasons, the crime crisis is urgent.

"To Keep and Bear Arms:" A Right or a Wrong?

One of the most misunderstood provisions of the Constitution is Amendment Two, which seems to guarantee "the right of the people to keep and bear arms." It is also one which many people believe to be related to the high crime rate in America. The fact is that this right was actually designed to guarantee to the states the authority to maintain their own military and police forces. This is indicated by the opening words of the Second Amendment, seldom quoted, which refer to "A well regulated Militia, being necessary to the security of a free state . . ." Only the national guard, sheriffs' deputies, and other law enforcement officers, therefore, have a right to carry guns.

While many people sincerely believe that private citizens *should* be allowed to own firearms, this issue is essentially a political one on which the Constitution maintains a silent neutrality. Only after the assassinations of President John F. Kennedy, Dr. Martin Luther King, and Senator Robert Kennedy, did gun control become a major public controversy. President Lyndon B. Johnson requested more stringent national restrictions than had ever been proposed previously, and the

40 Reo M. Christenson, *Challenge and Decision,* 3rd ed. (N.Y.: Harper & Row, Publishers, 1970), pp. 216–17.
41 U.S. Bureau of the Census, *Statistical Abstract of the United States: 1971,* p. 142.

resulting legislation placed severe restrictions upon the mail order and other interstate sale of firearms. It also prohibited the sale of guns to convicts and minors, but did not require that gun owners be licensed or that the firearms themselves be registered.

Outside of Congress, the National Rifle Association, a powerful private pressure group, and extremist groups on both the left and right, the Black Panthers and the predominantly Caucasian Minutemen, all insist that they need guns for hunting, target shooting, or self-defense. Opposing them are several prominent police officials, the U.S. Conference of Mayors, Common Cause, Americans for Democratic Action, and various union and church groups.

The issue of gun control touches emotions rooted in the soil of our unique history. Americans have been a frontier people, accustomed to rely on self-defense and fond of glorifying the cowboy, sheriff, or even the crook who shot first and asked questions later. That the issue will not soon disappear is suggested by the facts that gun controls are weaker here than in any other major nation and that private ownership of hand guns quadrupled between 1962 and 1968. The most reliable estimates indicate that there are at least thirty-five million rifles, thirty-one million shotguns, and twenty-four million hand guns in civilian possession.[42]

Types of Sentences

No cruel and unusual punishment   Although the Constitution contains many provisions aimed at helping criminal defendants, it includes only one for the person finally convicted—the Eighth Amendment's prohibition against cruel and unusual punishments. The courts have not found it easy to say precisely what such punishments are, but their decisions indicate a belief that the severity of sentences should be related to the seriousness of the crime.

In *Robinson* v. *California*,[43] the Court ruled that *any* criminal punishment for being a narcotics addict was cruel and unusual. While a state may punish possession or use of narcotics, addiction was held to be an illness, not a crime. In *Powell* v. *Texas*,[44] however, the conviction of a chronic alcoholic for being drunk in a public place was sustained.

Capital punishment   In the darkest days of World War II, Winston Churchill paid tribute to the British air force by asserting that never before in human history had so many owed so much to so few. Before June 29, 1972, never in American history had as many as six hundred people owed their lives to a single court decision. Those saved were not freedom-loving citizens resisting tyranny; they were 517 mur-

42 The National Commission on the Causes and Prevention of Violence, *To Establish Justice, to Insure Domestic Tranquility* (Toronto: Bantam Books, Inc., 1970), p. 158.
43 370 U.S. 660 (1962).
44 20 L. Ed. 2d 1254 (1968).

derers, 79 rapists, and 4 armed robbers. What had happened, of course, is that the death penalty had been declared unconstitutional in the case of *Furman* v. *Georgia*[45]—at least as applied to all persons then on death row. They were an intriguing group: 329 blacks, 257 whites, 10 Mexican-Americans, 2 Puerto Ricans, and 2 Indians.

The historic decision was announced in conflicting voices: The vote was 5–4, nine different opinions were written, and the long-term impact was far from certain. Justices William Brennan and Thurgood Marshall seemed to believe the death penalty to be a cruel and unusual punishment under almost any circumstances. Justices Potter Stewart, Byron White, and William O. Douglas objected to the arbitrary and uncertain standards by which some felons were doomed to death and others guilty of the same offenses were given lesser sentences. The four dissenters were the Nixon appointees, voting together as they had on other 5–4 decisions which permitted less than unanimous jury verdicts and denied the right of reporters to conceal their sources of information from grand juries. Although the decision spared the lives of those already sentenced to death, most justices seemed willing to withhold judgment on capital punishment in situations in which the judge or jury was permitted less discretion in imposing the death sentence. Because the future is in doubt, the opposing arguments require mention.

Those who defend the ultimate penalty claim that it serves as a deterrent to murder and assert that it has been sanctioned by centuries of religious tradition and legal precedent. Critics argue that the death penalty is immoral, an affront to human dignity, and of questionable importance as a deterrent, since in eleven of the fifteen states where it was abolished, the homicide rate was below the national average. Perhaps certainty and speed of convictions would be more of a deterrent than the stiffness of the sentence. Finally, opponents of capital punishment allege that it has been inequitably imposed, selecting a disproportionately large number of its victims from the poor, the black, and the male.

Imprisonment   Until recently, there was general agreement that the easiest way to deal with the convicted criminal was to lock him up. Yet by the end of September 1971, prison violence in state penitentiaries at San Quentin, California, and Attica, New York, had resulted in nearly fifty deaths, claiming inmates and guards alike. Suddenly penal problems became a major social and political controversy. Although black militancy and political radicalism may have contributed to these tragedies, they focused belated attention on such issues as overcrowding, abuse by prison guards, inadequate facilities for recreation and job training, and the general brutalization of inmates. Of the jails maintained by local governments in 1970, 86 percent had no facilities for exercise, 89 percent lacked education, 49 percent lacked medical care, and 26 percent were without provisions for visitors. In addition to spawning acts of

45 92 S.Ct. 2726 (1972).

dangerous desperation, imprisonment has two other disadvantages: It is expensive and it fails to rehabilitate the criminal.

In part, its expense is due to the number of people imprisoned, more than 360,000 in 1970, or about one person out of every 570 in the nation. It can be attributed, also, to relatively long sentences imposed in this country in comparison with most other Western nations.[46] For the more than 8000 federal prisoners released for the first time in 1970, the average time served was almost twenty months. The per prisoner cost of all government correctional programs amounted to more than $4000 per year, an amount capable of maintaining a family of four above the poverty level outside prison.[47]

Even this price would be cheap enough if imprisonment rehabilitated the criminal. Yet the evidence indicates that this is not the case. One expert notes that "Two thirds of the men and women now imprisoned are repeaters,"[48] and another asserts that in Oklahoma those convicts receiving short sentences actually committed proportionately fewer crimes upon their release than those who had been imprisoned longer.[49]

All too often, it seems, prolonged imprisonment simply allows criminals to develop more efficient techniques by exchanging ideas with one another, or it contributes to homosexuality by cutting them off from contact with the opposite sex. In any event, since "85 percent of the nation's crime is committed by repeaters,"[50] a reexamination is required of the usefulness of imprisonment as an effective anticrime device. The major alternatives to jail seem to be probation or parole.

Probation and parole   In most states, judges may release convicted persons on probation, rather than sending them to prison. This entails certain restrictions on their travel, associates, and behavior during a specified period, and places them under the supervision of a probation officer. Parole is a similar arrangement by which persons already in prison are given a conditional release requiring them to fulfill certain requirements and report periodically to parole agents.

Probation and parole have clear advantages over long imprisonment in that they permit the convict to earn a living, enjoy normal sex relations, support a family, and minimize correctional expenses for the taxpayer. Their success is somewhat difficult to assess, but seems related to the types of persons selected for such treatment and the adequacy of their supervision. Of prisoners paroled in New York, New

46 *Crime and the Law,* op. cit., pp. 11–14, (the prisoner figure includes 21,000 in federal prisons, 185,000 in state prisons, and 160,000 in local jails) and Hoyt Gimlin, "Street Crimes in America," *Editorial Research Reports on Challenges for the 1970's* (Washington, D.C.: Congressional Quarterly, Inc., 1970), p. 78.
47 Computed from U.S. Bureau of the Census, *Statistical Abstract of the United States: 1971,* p. 148, and previously cited data.
48 Gimlin, loc. cit.
49 Ronald L. Goldfarb, *Washington Post,* reprinted in *Los Angeles Times,* July 26, 1970, Section G, p. 1. See also Christenson, op. cit., p. 216.
50 Christenson, op. cit., p. 221.

Jersey, and California, between 40.5 and 50.9 percent had violated the conditions of their parole within three to five years.[51]

Justice for Juveniles

Beginning with Illinois in 1899, all states have authorized special methods of dealing with alleged delinquents under the age of 18. They were intended to spare children the embarassment and disgrace which accompany criminal proceedings against adults, and to save them "from a downward career." But the realities of juvenile court operations often left minors as helpless pawns who could be assured only of the "right" to whatever form of custody the court felt best, without the benefit of constitutional guarantees enjoyed by adults as a matter of course.

These conditions were suddenly changed by the Supreme Court in 1967. *Re Gault*[52] involved a fifteen-year-old Arizona boy who was on probation because he had been with another boy who stole a lady's purse and who, nearly two years earlier, had stolen a baseball glove from another boy. The appeal to the Supreme Court resulted from an allegedly obscene phone call for which young Gault was sentenced to up to six years in a so-called "industrial school." Had he been an adult (at least three years older), his maximum sentence for the crime, were he guilty, would have been imprisonment for two months. In an eight to one decision, the Court reversed the sentence and decreed that juveniles, as well as adults, were entitled to notification of charges against them, legal counsel, the right to refuse to testify against themselves, and the right to confront and cross-examine their accusers—all constitutional guarantees that had been denied to Gault and his parents. The Court took great pains, however, to affirm its belief that juveniles should be accorded special treatment, so long as such treatment does not deprive defendants of the procedures essential for "due process of law."

51 Tappan, op. cit., p. 749.
52 387 U.S. 1 (1967).

Chapter 5

Equal Justice Under Law
Of Dreams Deferred

What happens to a dream deferred?

Does it dry up
like a raisin in the sun?
Or fester like a sore—
And then run?
Does it stink like rotten meat?
Or crust and sugar over—
like a syrupy sweet?

Maybe it just sags
like a heavy load.

Or does it explode?*
            Langston Hughes

Human equality is the underlying and often unspoken assumption supporting many rights guaranteed in the Constitution. Freedom of the press, for example, is not restricted only to writers who belong to the Democratic Party, and the right of trial by jury is available to women as well as men. This chapter is devoted to the broad concept of equality itself, and the gap that still exists between that ideal and the practical realities of every day American life.

*Copyright 1951 by Langston Hughes. Reprinted from *Selected Poems of Langston Hughes* by permission of Alfred A. Knopf, Inc.

EQUAL PROTECTION OF THE LAWS: JUSTICE IN BLACK AND WHITE

Following the "due process" clause in the Fourteenth Amendment is another crucial clause, the one that stipulates that no state shall "deny to any person within its jurisdiction the equal protection of the law." In the last quarter of a century, no part of the Constitution has had a more explosive impact on American life than this one.

A Color-blind Constitution

We have already noted that in 1873 the Supreme Court declined to interpret the Fourteenth Amendment as aiding the individual against the state governments. In 1883, the Court also ruled unconstitutional much of the 1875 Civil Rights Act which had penalized discrimination in places of public accommodation.

Separate but equal Some years later, in 1896, the Court held in *Plessy* v. *Ferguson*[1] that a Louisiana law requiring separate but equal railroad coaches for white and black passengers did not deny Negroes their constitutional right to equal protection. The result of this "separate but equal" doctrine was to enable the spread of "legal" segregation of blacks and whites in almost every area of southern life—in schools, theaters, restaurants, court houses, rest rooms, and marriage chapels, as well as in railroad coaches. Only Justice John Marshall Harlan, in a lonely dissenting opinion, sounded a cry largely unheeded for over half a century. "Our Constitution," he wrote, "is color-blind."

A segregated nation Whether or not the Constitution was color-blind, most white Americans had no such eye trouble. While the South relied chiefly on legally compelled segregation to keep the races apart, the North was more subtle. White businessmen simply refused to serve blacks or to employ them in any positions of prestige or prominence.

The ranks of America's leading opera companies, for example, were closed to black singers until Camilla Williams appeared in a New York City Center production in 1946, and the next year Jackie Robinson became the first black to play on a major league baseball team.[2] Blacks and whites were segregated from the cradle to the grave, from birth in segregated neighborhoods to burial in segregated cemeteries.

The "separate but equal" rule which the Supreme Court endorsed in 1896 was remarkably effective in permitting states to ensure

1 163 U.S. 573.
2 Edgar A. Toppin, "Breaching the Old Walls of Prejudice," *The Christian Science Monitor,* June 5, 1969, p. 12. This article is one of an excellent series by a professor of history at Virginia State College.

the racial dominance of white people. In 1899, the Court approved the maintenance of a high school for whites only on the plea that the county in question could not afford another one for blacks;[3] in 1927 it sanctioned the requirement that a Chinese student attend a school for colored children rather than one for whites closer to her home;[4] and not until 1940 were school boards required to pay black teachers as much as white ones of equal training and experience.[5]

Most shameful of all was the role of American government, which declined to lead or even set an example. While a number of blacks had served in positions of some prominence in the half-century following emancipation, President Woodrow Wilson's inauguration in 1913 marked a discouraging setback for the supporters of equal opportunity. The number of black presidential appointees dropped from thirty-one to nine and the segregation of offices and toilet facilities was suddenly introduced for employees of the Post Office, the Treasury, and the Navy. The armed forces were not integrated until the administration of President Harry S. Truman (1945–53).[6] Finally, at the pinnacles of power, no cabinet position escaped Caucasian control until 1966, when President Lyndon B. Johnson designated Robert C. Weaver as Secretary of the newly created Department of Housing and Urban Development. The next year Thurgood Marshall became the first black on the Supreme Court. Mexican-Americans, Asian-Americans, and American Indians are still waiting.

The decline of compulsory segregation   The "equal protection of the laws" clause persisted, however, as a rebuke to the hypocrisy of prevailing legal standards. Back in 1886 the Supreme Court used it to declare the application of San Francisco business licensing laws to be an unconstitutional discrimination against Chinese laundry operators.[7] Much later, it was invoked to permit black people to vote in Democratic party primary elections,[8] serve on juries,[9] and attend previously all-white state law schools.[10]

But it was not until 1954 that the Fourteenth Amendment began to fulfill its initial promise of racial justice, when the case of *Brown* v. *Board of Education of Topeka*[11] repudiated the "separate but equal" doctrine. The *Brown* decision produced profound changes in American society. In the first place, its immediate purpose was to declare racial segregation in the public schools to be an unconstitutional violation of the "equal protection of the laws" clause of Amendment Fourteen. Second, it established a precedent, soon followed, for ending compulsory

3 *Cumming* v. *County Board of Education,* 175 U.S. 528.
4 *Gong Lum* v. *Rice,* 257 U.S. 78.
5 *Allston* v. *School Board,* 112 Fed. 2d 992.
6 Leslie H. Fishel, Jr., and Benjamin Quarles, eds., *The Negro American* (Glenview, Ill.: Scott, Foresman and Company, 1967), pp. 390, 484–85.
7 *Yick Wo* v. *Hopkins,* 118 U.S. 356.
8 *Nixon* v. *Condon,* 286 U.S. 73 (1932).
9 *Norris* v. *Alabama,* 294 U.S. 587 (1935).
10 *Sweatt* v. *Painter,* 339 U.S. 629 (1950).
11 347 U.S. 483.

racial segregation in all government facilities, such as public parks, beaches, prisons, and municipally owned buses.

Third, the decision constituted a moral victory for blacks, which inaugurated a period of rapidly rising expectations embodied in the civil rights movement led by Martin Luther King. During the next few years blacks made major gains, but by 1955 the gap between expectation and change transformed hope into disillusionment and converted much of the civil rights movement into a crusade for "Black Power." A fourth effect of the *Brown* decision, although perhaps a temporary one, was to increase tensions between the South, where racial prejudice had been most obvious, and the rest of the nation. In 1957 President Eisenhower sent troops into Little Rock, Arkansas, to enforce a court order requiring the integration of a local high school and five years later, President Kennedy responded the same way to insure the enrollment of James Meredith, the first black ever admitted to the University of Mississippi.

The Court's desegregation command is still the subject of bitter dispute and diverse interpretations. Its application has been extended to certain districts in the North and West where segregation in the schools reflects the racial composition of residential neighborhoods. The Supreme Court has yet to review fully these cases of *de facto* segregation, and in view of the busing controversy, it would be well to examine the reasoning of the Court in its unanimous opinion.

The case involved situations in which white and black children were attending schools that were legally segregated, but without any significant differences "with respect to buildings, curricula, . . . and other 'tangible' factors." If the black schools were admittedly as good as the white ones, how could the mere fact of segregation violate the equal protection clause? The Court conceded that there was little historical evidence indicating that the framers of the Fourteenth Amendment intended it to ban segregation in the public schools, since few existed at the time it was written. But the contemporary effect of segregation, the Court contended, creates among black children "a feeling of inferiority as to their status in the community that may affect their hearts and minds in a way unlikely ever to be undone." This feeling of inferiority, moreover, adversely "affects the motivation of a child to learn."

The conclusion of the Court has been most bitterly criticized on the basis that it rested more on a number of studies by psychologists and sociologists, cited in the decision, than it did on historical records or legal precedent. Nonetheless, there seems little doubt that when segregated schools were first established, they were created by white state legislators and white school board members who in fact did believe that blacks were inferior. Moreover, there were at least a few cases, at the graduate-school level, in which the Supreme Court had held segregation unconstitutional even before the *Brown* decision.

But the most important evidence supporting the Court ruling came twelve years after it was handed down, in *Racial Isolation in the*

Public Schools, a report issued by the United States Commission on Civil Rights.[12] This report, based largely on a 1966 study of thousands of black students in the ninth and twelfth grades,[13] concluded that racial segregation in schools tends to lower students' achievement and restrict their aspirations. The chief reason for the improved academic progress of black students in integrated schools seems to be the superior educational backgrounds of their classmates' parents and the resultingly higher occupational goals of the classmates themselves.

One of the major barriers to interracial understanding has been a fantastic array of traditions, rumors, fantasies, and fears centering around sex. The importance of this whole matter to the vast majority of Americans is indicated in a nation-wide poll showing that whereas only 21 percent of white people would object to using the same rest rooms as blacks, a whopping 88 percent would oppose their teen-aged child dating them.[14] In 1968, moreover, an international Gallup Poll found that American opposition to white-nonwhite marriage, 72 percent, was highest among the thirteen nations surveyed.[15] Judicial interpretation of the Constitution, of course, should not depend on public opinion, and in 1967, a unanimous Supreme Court declared state laws prohibiting racial intermarriage (miscegenation) to be an unconstitutional violation of both the "equal protection" and "due process" clauses of the Fourteenth Amendment.[16]

Racial Politics

The historical record indicates that if constitutional prohibitions are to be enforced, and if private individuals are to be prevented from discriminatory behavior, then court decisions must be supplemented by legislative and executive action. But the potential of such political action for solving a particular problem is determined largely by the attitudes of those who elect the politicians. The issue of civil rights, therefore, begins with the nature and extent of prejudice among the people. If prejudice influences politics—and surely it seems to—the explanations for it point to contradictory conclusions regarding its future importance. With respect to the condescending portrayals of minority groups in history books and the mass media, substantial changes have been made which should diminish antagonism and promote harmony. The psychological need for belonging to a group—"we" *vs.* "they"—and the need to bolster bruised egos by looking down on someone "worse" are deep-seated and enduring, however.

12 U.S. Commission on Civil Rights, *Racial Isolation in the Public Schools* (Washington, D.C.: U.S. Government Printing Office, 1967).
13 James Coleman, *et al., Equality of Educational Opportunity* (Washington, D.C.: U.S. Government Printing Office, 1966).
14 *Newsweek,* August 22, 1966, p. 26.
15 *Los Angeles Times,* Nov. 11, 1968, p. 6. Sweden with 67 percent, was highest in approval. "A slight majority" of American Negroes approved of mixed marriages, "but as many as three in ten disapproved."
16 *Loving* v. *Virginia,* 388 U.S. 1.

Economic considerations are also discouraging. After World War II, two researchers found that veterans who slid downward in socioeconomic status (those who had to take poorer jobs, for example) were more prejudiced than those who were more successful.[17] In view of this finding it is not surprising that nearly twenty years later a new survey found that racial prejudice was most prevalent among the troubled "middle Americans" who were hardest hit by inflation, high taxes, and rising unemployment. "The more precarious a family's hold on economic security," the study revealed, "the more menaced it feels by . . . black militancy."[18]

Most of these people felt that blacks had greater opportunities than they did, and only a quarter of them favored increased racial integration of the public schools. Although traditionally aligned with the Democratic party, they are prime targets for President Nixon's appeal to the "silent majority." They are worried about losing their jobs—who can blame them?—and blacks often seem to threaten these jobs most severely. Politically, candidates such as Louise Day Hicks in Boston and Lester Maddox in Georgia hover over them, eager to peck the political flesh of desperate men. Racial prejudice may have its price after all: economic prosperity for white America.

In any event, statistics produced by public opinion polls show an unmistakable increase in tolerance toward ethnic minorities. Between 1967 and 1969, to cite but one example, the percentage of the American people who would vote for a Jew for President jumped from 82 to 86, and those willing to vote for a Negro climbed even more, from 54 to 67.[19]

State action   While the Fourteenth Amendment's "equal protection" clause prohibited state discrimination, it did nothing to compel private institutions to afford equal treatment. Yet by 1947, without court compulsion, eighteen states had prohibited discrimination because of race in places of public accommodation such as privately owned restaurants, hotels, and theaters.[20] This, apparently, was racism's most vulnerable barrier and the first one to be cracked—but not the last. By 1962 twenty-one states had passed laws forbidding racial discrimination in employment, beginning with New York in 1945, and in 1963 discrimination in at least a portion of the housing market had been barred in nineteen states and fifty-five cities, including New York City, Pittsburgh, and Toledo.[21] However, a 1972 Supreme Court decision

17 Bruno Bettelheim and Morris Janowitz, "Prejudice," *Scientific American* (October 1950): 11–13.
18 *Newsweek,* October 6, 1969, p. 32, 45. The Archie Bunker stereotype is a bit unfair in the opinion of several recent observers.
19 These figures are from Gallup polls reported in the *Los Angeles Times,* June 4, 1967, Section G, p. 2, and April 3, 1969, p. 31.
20 Gustavus Myers, *History of Bigotry in the United States,* ed. by Henry M. Christman (N.Y.: Capricorn Books, G. P. Putnam's Sons, 1960), p. 443.
21 United States Commission on Civil Rights, *Freedom to the Free* (Washington, D.C.: U.S. Government Printing Office, 1963), pp. 132–33, 144.

upheld the power of a state to issue liquor licenses to private lodges (the Moose, in this case) which refused to serve black guests.[22]

Population changes and political power These state prohibitions against racial discrimination, sometimes badly enforced, were imposed in northern and western states. This may be explained largely by the steady exodus of black people from the South to other sections of the country, and from rural areas to urban ones. World War II accelerated the move. The percentage of all blacks in the nation who resided in the eleven southern states dropped from 77 in 1940 to 53 in 1970. By the latter year, each of the four cities with the largest black population—New York, Chicago, Detroit, and Philadelphia—were northern ones. Most of the emigrants who left southern rural areas seem to have moved to these and other cities. The 1960 census revealed that for the first time in American history a higher percentage of blacks than whites had urban homes.[23]

One effect of these population changes was to increase black political power. Not only were voting restrictions fewer in the North and West than in the South, but the black voters were more heavily concentrated in cities, and hence better able to elect black candidates and influence the passage of civil rights laws. As a result of the 1970 congressional elections there were eleven blacks in the House of Representatives, more than at any time since the Reconstruction period following the Civil War. All were Democrats from big cities, and none were from the eleven southern states. Perhaps most prominent among them was Rep. Shirley Chisholm of New York, the first black woman ever elected to Congress and a 1972 candidate for the Democratic presidential nomination. In the Senate was Edward W. Brooke, Republican from Massachusetts, who in 1967 became the first black to sit in that august body in this century. Such encouraging progress should not obscure the fact that even now blacks, with 11 percent of the population, have less than 3 percent of the members of Congress. The situation at the state level is similar. In 1970, 174 blacks were serving in thirty-four state legislatures; they held the most seats in Illinois, Missouri, Georgia, Ohio, and Michigan.[24]

Other ethnic minorities have fared little better than blacks, at least in national politics. There were four congressmen of Asian parentage, all from Hawaii (including Rep. Patsy T. Mink, a woman), and five Mexican-Americans, (two each from New Mexico and Texas, and one from California). Of this group, seven were Democrats, and two Republicans.

Congressional action After decades of inaction, Congress finally enacted a civil rights law in 1957, followed by others in the next decade. The 1957 act created the United States Commission on Civil

22 The case involved K. Leroy Irvis, a Pennsylvania legislator. *New York Times,* June 18, 1972, p. 6.
23 U.S. Bureau of the Census, *Statistical Abstract of the United States: 1971,* pp. 16, 21–24, 27.
24 *Congressional Quarterly Guide to Current American Government* (Fall 1970), p. 138.

Rights and authorized it to investigate voting discrimination prohibited by the Fifteenth Amendment as well as alleged violations of the "equal protection of the laws" clause of the Fourteenth. It also prohibited attempts to prevent persons from voting, empowered the U.S. Attorney General to intervene in voting-rights cases, and banned discrimination in jury selection.

The Civil Rights Act of 1960 outlawed the possession of explosives designed to blow up a vehicle or building and allowed the federal courts, in suits filed by the Attorney General, to declare persons qualified to vote. Although two laws thus pushed a congressional foot in the discrimination door, it was the passage of the 1964 legislation that seemed to unhinge it completely. This legislation followed the spectacular and often violent events of the early 1960s which dramatized the need for further congressional action.

The record of those events, written in bravery and blood, still commands respectful attention. In February 1960, students from the North Carolina Agricultural and Technical College began a "sit-in" at a Greensboro, North Carolina, lunch counter where blacks had been refused service. In spite of their arrest, the movement rapidly reached out across the South, sometimes in the form of widely publicized "Freedom Rides." In 1961, for example, when black and white bus passengers defied the local requirements of seating segregation in a journey across Alabama and into Mississippi, riots broke out, a bus was burned, and the riders were attacked by enraged whites. On April 23 1963, William Moore, a white civil rights marcher, was shot to death in northeast Alabama. In May, protest marches were launched in Birmingham seeking an end to discrimination in public accommodations and access to better jobs. The demonstrators were confronted with police dogs and fire hoses, and a few days later bombs were thrown in attempts to kill Rev. Martin Luther King, Jr., and his brother, Reverend A. D. King. On June 12, Medgar Evers, the head of the National Association for the Advancement of Colored People in Mississippi, was fatally wounded by a gunman outside his home in Jackson.

Against this background of tension and fear, President Kennedy, on June 19, 1963, submitted to Congress the proposal which was the basis for the Civil Rights Act of 1964. It was passed by Congress exactly one year later. The events of the intervening twelve months elicit memories both painful and important. In August, 200,000 people streamed into Washington, D.C., in the largest civil rights demonstration in history; in September, four black girls were killed by a bomb exploded in a Birmingham Sunday School. "It was," as the *Congressional Quarterly* observed, "the 21st time in eight years that Negroes had been the victims of bombings in Birmingham, and like the previous cases, the crime went unsolved."[25] In October, congressional committees debated

25 Shirley M. Seib, ed., *Revolution in Civil Rights,* 3rd ed. (Washington, D.C.: Congressional Quarterly, Inc., 1967), p. 11.

the most recent civil rights proposals, but on November 22, the man who made them was assassinated. Five days later his successor, President Lyndon B. Johnson, urged Congress to pass the pending legislation to honor his memory. Without these tear-stained traumas, the most sweeping civil rights legislation of this century might never have been enacted.

Its time had come   On eleven occasions between 1938 and 1962, civil rights legislation was defeated because the Senate, normally permitting unlimited debate on a bill, refused to invoke the *cloture* rule to shut off further discussion and bring the matter to a vote. Therefore, even after the House of Representatives had passed the 1964 bill by an overwhelming margin, there was fear that it would be talked to death by a filibuster on the floor of the Senate. Just as depressing to supporters of the bill was the possibility that it would die in the Senate Judiciary Committee, traditionally exercising jurisdiction over such matters, before the entire Senate had an opportunity even to consider it. Bills are normally referred to the appropriate committee before they are considered by either house, and in the preceding ten years the Judiciary Committee, under the chairmanship of Senator James Eastland of Mississippi, had been the graveyard for no fewer than 120 out of the 121 civil rights bills referred to it.

Senate passage was assured by sending the bill to the Commerce Committee and by imposing limitations on debate. It was the first time in history that cloture had been voted on a civil rights bill. Nine days after the vote on cloture (71 to 29), the Senate passed the bill itself, 73 to 27. As the late Senator Everett Dirksen (R–Ill.), essentially conservative and flamboyantly colorful, put it, nothing is more powerful than "an idea whose time has come."

The Civil Rights Act of 1964   The idea whose time had come was a complex law divided into eleven parts, called titles. Two are of particular importance. Title II prohibits discrimination based on race, color, religion, or national origin in restaurants, gas stations, theaters, stadiums, hotels, and similar "public accommodations." Title VII forbids discrimination in employment practices based on race, color, religion, sex, or national origin by employers with twenty-five or more workers. Other provisions make a sixth-grade education sufficient proof of literacy for purposes of state voting requirements; cut off federal financial assistance from programs, including schools, which practice discrimination; and allow the U.S. Attorney General to bring suit against schools defying court decisions on desegregation.

The battle for the ballot   The Fifteenth Amendment, adopted in 1870, prohibited voting requirements based on race. Yet many states, especially in the South, displayed remarkable ingenuity in getting around it. Laws imposed ridiculously complex "literacy tests" as a prerequisite for voting and "white primary" elections excluded blacks from the selection of party candidates. Poll taxes also kept poor people (including most blacks) from the ballot boxes, and simultaneously laws had "grandfather clauses" which suspended certain other voting requirements if one's grandfather had been able to vote. Over the years several of these devices were invalidated, but they had all done their share to make the southern polling booth off limits to most blacks prior to 1965. Earlier civil rights laws changed this situation very little, and President Johnson, therefore, asked for additional legislation in this area. Assisted by a vastly expanded liberal Democratic majority resulting from the 1964 elections, Congress responded favorably with the Voting Rights Act of 1965. Its major provision permitted the national government to appoint voting examiners who, in effect, could register persons to vote in any area where there was a state literacy requirement and less than 50 percent of the persons of voting age had actually voted in the last election. It also prohibited poll taxes as voting requirements in state elections, thereby supplementing the Twenty-fourth Amendment to the Constitution which had forbidden poll taxes in the election of national officials.

The Voting Rights Act is perhaps the most effective civil rights legislation ever passed. As a result, the percentage of blacks registered to vote in the eleven southern states zoomed from 36 to 65 between 1964 and 1968.[26] While there were only thirty-six black state legislators in the entire nation in 1960, their number had grown to 205 after the 1970 elections, and Arkansas was left as the only state in the South with an all-white legislative branch. Lounds County, Alabama, exemplifies the dramatic change: In the spring of 1965, it had not a single black registered voter; in the fall of 1970, it elected a black sheriff.[27]

Further congressional action   Ironically, civil rights laws also stimulated more violent bigotry. In 1964 three young men, Michael Schwerner and Andrew Goodman (white) and James Chaney (black) were killed in Mississippi as a result of their civil rights activities. The next year, the Rev. James Reeb and Mrs. Viola Liuzzo (both white) were murdered for similar reasons in Alabama. In 1966, James Meredith— who had gained fame as the first black person admitted to the University of Mississippi—was wounded in the course of a voter registration campaign. On April 4, 1968, Martin Luther King, Jr., was assassinated in Memphis, Tennessee, while attempting to gather support for the strike of that city's predominantly black rubbish collectors. The death of Rev. King, winner of the Nobel Peace Prize and the most influential black man in America, helped to precipitate two important developments; militant black demands shifted from racial integration to "Black Power," discussed in the following chapter, and Congress passed another civil rights law.

The Civil Rights Act of 1968 contained several provisions, including harsh penalties for those who cross state lines to incite a riot or who interfere with a person's exercise of his civil rights. What seemed most significant when the law was passed was a fair housing provision

26 U.S. Bureau of the Census, *Statistical Abstract of the United States: 1971,* p. 365.
27 *Los Angeles Times,* November 29, 1970, Sec. F, p. 8.

which prohibited racial discrimination in the sale or rental of nearly 80 percent of all housing units in the nation. Less than three months after the enactment of this legislation, however, a Supreme Court decision rendered the housing section obsolete by holding that an old law passed over a hundred years earlier barred discrimination in disposing of all property.[28] The civil rights legislation passed in 1970 extended and broadened the 1965 Voting Rights Act.

Racial Realities

Any attempt to assess intelligently the attitudes attributed to either race in the 1970s requires some facts regarding the conditions of minority life.

Employment   In spite of persistent obstacles, nonwhite Americans (mostly black) seem to be making important advances in getting better jobs. Between 1957 and 1970, for example, the percentage of whites working in professional and technical jobs increased 4.0 percent while their nonwhite counterparts increased 5.4 percent. More impressive is the fact that the percentage of whites engaged in clerical occupations rose 2.8 percent while the nonwhite figure went up 7.2 percent.[29] Perhaps the employment provisions of the 1964 Civil Rights Act are beginning to pay off, although progress in this area is far from consistent. An officially authorized study of the U.S. Department of Housing and Urban Development has revealed that as late as October 1970, that agency discriminated against blacks in the promotion of its own employees.[30] Moreover, the Nixon administration's "Philadelphia plan" to provide minority jobs in the construction industry has fallen short of initial expectations.

Police treatment   It is almost impossible to assess changes, if any, in the behavior of police toward racial minorities. This issue has been a hot one for a long time and it caught fire with the somewhat extravagant charges of police brutality hurled by several militant groups in 1970. The Black Panther Party especially declared war on the police, and "off the pigs" (kill the cops) became a call to arms for radical groups, both white and black.

Charges of racial prejudice among law enforcement officers have had no effect upon congressional legislation thus far, but have led to demands for police review boards, staffed by civilians, in major metropolitan centers. In 1966, Mayor John Lindsay established such an agency in New York City, only to have it abolished four months later by an overwhelming vote of the people in a referendum election. The police

28 *Jones* v. *Mayer Co.*, 392 U.S. 409 (1968).
29 Computed from U.S. Bureau of the Census, *Statistical Abstract of the United States: 1971*, p. 223.
30 *Los Angeles Times*, Oct. 22, 1971, p. 20.

themselves led the attack against it. In St. Louis, where such an agency exists, it has also produced police hostility.[31]

Education Ten years after compulsory racial segregation in the public schools was declared unconstitutional, over 90 percent of the black students in seventeen southern and border states were still attending all-black schools.[32] Progress had been so slow primarily because the Supreme Court ordered desegregation to be accomplished "with all deliberate speed," recognizing that practical problems—worse in some districts than in others—would take time to solve. The result was that additional law suits were required to integrate school districts that refused to do so voluntarily.

The years since 1964 have seen changes of immense magnitude. Spurred by threats to cut off federal financial assistance and additional court decisions that condemned too much deliberation and too little speed, the pace of southern desegregation accelerated so quickly that by 1970 there was more school integration in the South than in the nation as a whole. The proportion of black students attending schools that had a white majority was nearly 40 percent in the eleven states of the deep South but only about 33 percent throughout the entire nation.[33]

This situation is one of the most ironic in the tormented history of American race relations. Its explanation lies primarily in the fact that the *Brown* desegregation case applied only to *de jure* segregation (required by law and confined primarily to the South), but not to *de facto* segregation (based upon residential housing patterns and most common in the North and West).

The school segregation controversy has now shifted to two relatively new focal points: Is *de facto* segregation also unconstitutional and is compulsory busing of students a legitimate means of overcoming it? On the first issue, a California judge insisted that there was little difference between *de jure* and *de facto* segregation in Los Angeles because the school board had drawn school attendance boundaries and located new schools in a way which resulted in an all-white enrollment in 120 of the district's 428 elementary schools and an over 80 percent black enrollment in another 64 schools.[34] The issue seems still in doubt. On the matter of forced busing, President Nixon has taken a negative view, lauding the concept of the "neighborhood school," although in 1971 the Supreme Court upheld such busing, at least on a limited basis.

Under election-year pressures, Congress enacted a law in 1972 which reflected the President's recommendations, although in drastically diluted form. It postponed the authority of the courts to order involuntary busing for purposes of racial balance. Since about 40 percent of all students take a bus to school anyway, the controversy seemed laden with racist implications. There were no impassioned pleas for

31 Jerome H. Skolnick, *The Politics of Protest* (N.Y.: Ballantine Books, Inc., 1969), pp. 278–81.
32 U.S. Bureau of the Census, *Statistical Abstract of the United States: 1970*, p. 118.
33 *Los Angeles Times,* June 18, 1971, p. 4.
34 Los Angeles County Commission on Human Relations, *Report of the Housing Committee to the Commission,* June 5, 1967, p. 6. (Mimeographed).

Bruce Roberts from Rapho Guillumette Pictures.

Cross-town busing in Charlotte, North Carolina, 1971.

Figure 12   White Parent Opinion on School Integration

Percent Objecting to Children Attending Integrated Schools

	Northern	Southern
With a few Negroes		
1963	10%	61%[1]
1970	6%	16%
With half Negroes		
1963	33%	78%
1970	24%	43%
With Negro majorities		
1963	53%	86%
1970	51%	69%

[1] Gallup calls the rapid drop in southern opposition, revealed in this column "one of the most dramatic shifts in the history of public opinion polling, bringing North and South closer together on this issue (as one can see by reading across the 1970 columns) than at any other time in recent years." While this shows considerable progress, a poll taken in 1969 showed that 44 percent of the American people believed that school integration was going "too fast." Ibid., Aug. 17, 1969, Sec. F, p. 8.

Source: Gallup Poll, *Los Angeles Times,* May 3, 1970, Sec. H, p. 4. Reprinted by permission of the American Institute of Public Opinion (The Gallup Poll).

tedious trips to crime-infested neighborhoods, but those who valued racial harmony asked two questions that were hard to ignore. Why was there no white opposition to the busing that maintained school segregation for so many years? More important, how else can black and white children overcome centuries of racial antagonism, if segregated neighborhoods prevent them from knowing one another?

Mexican-Americans are the second largest racial minority in America, and their problems are most obvious in the field of public education. Of the 1.4 million Chicano school children in Colorado, Texas, New Mexico, Arizona, and California, nearly half (635,000) are attending predominantly Mexican-American schools. Moreover, while Chicano pupils comprise 17 percent of the public school enrollment in these five southwestern states, Mexican-Americans account for only 10 percent of the school board members, 4 percent of the teachers, and 3 percent of the school principals.[35] In California, "Spanish surname persons" (mostly Chicano) achieved a median educational level of 8.6 years in 1960, compared with 10.5 for nonwhites (mostly black), and 12.1 for Anglo-American (white).[36] In five southwestern states, the U.S. Civil Rights Commission reported in 1972 that 80 percent of Mexican-American students were receiving education which showed little respect for their culture or the Spanish language, and which was inadequate to their needs. American Indians are confronted with educational disadvantages that are even greater. Ten percent of those over age fourteen have never been to school at all and more than half never completed the eighth grade.

Housing   School segregation outside the South is largely a reflection of discriminatory housing patterns. These have persisted in spite of the fact that local ordinances prohibiting blacks from inhabiting certain residential areas were declared unconstitutional in 1917.[37] In addition, "restrictive covenants" barring blacks, Orientals, and Jews from certain neighborhoods, through private deed restrictions, were invalidated in 1948.[38]

These legal advances did little to forestall increasing residential segregation in cities throughout the nation. Predominantly black areas have become more overwhelmingly black, and white regions even whiter, in such cities as Buffalo, New York; Louisville, Kentucky; Evansville, Indiana; and Raleigh, North Carolina. The black population of central cities (those at the heart of metropolitan regions) increased 31.6 percent between 1960 and 1970, while the white population dropped 1.3 percent.[39]

35 U.S. Civil Rights Commission, United Press International release, *Los Angeles Times,* August 21, 1970, p. 11.
36 A Report of the California State Advisory Committee to the U.S. Commission on Civil Rights, *Education and the Mexican-American Community in Los Angeles County,* April 1968, p. 3. (Mimeographed).
37 *Buchanan* v. *Warley,* 245 U.S. 60.
38 *Shelley* v. *Kraemer,* 334 U.S. 1.
39 U.S. Bureau of the Census, *Statistical Abstract of the United States: 1971,* p. 16.

Explanations for this growing segregation, with blacks in the big cities and whites elsewhere, are tentative and complex. For one thing, the end of the plantation or tenant farm system has abolished the need for rural blacks to live near white landowners. In urban areas, electric dishwashers and similar laborsaving devices, along with industrial mechanization, have also diminished the need for large numbers of black workers living close by. Very generally, one might conclude that automation—on the farm, in the home, and in the factory—has reduced the necessity for a large black labor force and therefore has permitted increased residential segregation. Phrased differently, what economic necessity no longer demands, racial prejudice has prohibited.[40]

From a white point of view, higher living standards have permitted moves to more expensive, cleaner, less crowded, more modern suburban environments. Black concentration in the central cities is viewed, correspondingly, as an inevitable consequence of older, cheaper housing units attracting generally poorer inhabitants.

In the final analysis, it is hard to separate racial prejudice and the disappearance of economic necessity as causes of housing segregation. If one is wealthy enough, by and large, one can afford to be a practicing segregationist.

While it is generally true that modern technology has contributed to residential segregation, another factor has helped to produce the same result. This one, however, is based upon a belief that is almost totally false: It is generally assumed that if a black family moves into a white neighborhood, property values will fall. Except for a brief period in which white home owners, inspired by this myth, try quickly to sell their houses, this is simply not true. A study of 10,000 home sales over a five-year period in San Francisco, Oakland, and Philadelphia, revealed that property values are usually at least as high in racially integrated areas as in all-white ones.[41] The contrary belief is often fostered by real estate salesmen, called "block-busters," who spread the rumor in order to sell more houses.

Institutional racism   When governmental commissions or sociologists speak of "white racism," they are talking about more than the effects of individual racial prejudice. In fact, there is considerable evidence that such bigotry is declining, and it surely would be unjust to attribute it to all whites. Instead, the experts are referring to "institutional racism," a situation in which significant social differences exist between racial groups. This condition may exist without any prejudice,

40 J. William Stinde, a perceptive Los Angeles land developer has observed that the recent availability of cheap used cars has permitted both the economic exploitation of black labor and increasing residential segregation. He notes that the percentage of black-occupied housing units in the south Los Angeles ghetto without auto use dropped by 29.5 percent between 1960 and 1965. U.S. Bureau of the Census, Current Population Reports, Series P–23, No. 18, *Characteristics of the South and East Los Angeles Areas: November 1965* (Washington, D.C.: U.S. Government Printing Office, 1966), pp. 36–37, and conversations with the author.
41 Luigi Laurenti, *Property Values and Race* (Berkeley, Calif.: University of California Press, 1960).

or even any racial discrimination, and may be illustrated by three examples: (1) Predominantly white public schools in large cities are usually in better condition and more modern than others, not because of discrimination but because racial minorities in search of cheaper housing live in older neighborhoods, with older schools; (2) Proportionately more battle casualties are suffered by minority groups because their members have less education to gain them draft exemptions or noncombat army jobs; (3) Nonwhites are often the first to be fired during times of recession, not because of lack of ability or employer prejudice, but because they have been the most recently hired, and union contracts protect the seniority of older workers. Other important differences, stemming chiefly from institutional racism, are shown in Figure 13. A racist society is one that permits such differences to continue.

Figure 13   Racial Differences

	Infant Death Rate[1]		Median School Years Completed		Unemployment Rate		Median Family Income	
	1960	1968	1960	1970	1960	1970	1960	1969
White	22.9	19.2	10.9	12.2	4.9%	4.5%	$5835	$9794
Non-white	43.2	34.5	8.2	10.1	10.2	8.2	3233	5999

[1] Per 1000 live births
Source: U.S. Bureau of the Census, *Statistical Abstract of the United States: 1971,* pp. xviv, xxv, xxvi, and 53; and *Los Angeles Times,* July 16, 1970, p. 22.

EQUAL PROTECTION OF THE LAWS: ONE MAN, ONE VOTE

One of the nation's leading authorities on constitutional law has observed that "Negroes would probably constitute a minority of those who have invoked the equal protection clause against discriminatory treatment."[42] Indeed, the largest group to benefit from this provision is not racial but geographic—those who live in and around the nation's major cities.

Rural Dominance

Farm interests have dominated American government for most of our history. This was quite proper until urban dwellers began to outnumber the rural population shortly before 1920, but the situation persisted until the 1960s and still does, to some degree.

Legislative apportionment   Perhaps the chief reason for the

42 Robert F. Cushman, *Cases in Civil Liberties* (N.Y.: Appleton-Century-Crofts, 1968), p. 541.

excess political power of rural areas lies in the way in which seats in Congress and the state legislatures are distributed, or apportioned.

The United States Senate, with two members per state, gives the farmers an enormous advantage because the small states, mostly rural, have as many votes as bigger ones with huge metropolitan centers. The fifty-two senators from the twenty-six states with the fewest people represent fewer people than the four senators from California and New York.[43] This imbalance, or malapportionment, of Senate seats seems destined to get worse. Nothing can be done about it since the only provision of the Constitution which cannot be amended, according to Article V, is the one which guarantees an equal number of senators from each state.

Seats in the upper houses of the state legislatures have also been apportioned to benefit rural areas since most state constitutions allocated state senate seats among counties or other local units of government in a way similar to that in which U.S. senators' seats were allocated among the states in our federal union. Such representation schemes produced a number of state senates in which urban majorities fared even worse than in the U.S. Senate. In Nevada, for example, senators from the two largest urban counties, with 62 percent of the population, amounted to only 12 percent of the total membership of the state senate. Similarly, urban counties with over half of the state population had only 38 percent of the state senate seats in New Jersey, 24 percent in Florida and Delaware, and 10 percent in California.[44]

The state legislatures themselves have had the responsibility for drawing the boundaries of districts from which members of their own lower houses are elected. They determine as well the boundaries for congressional districts, from which members of the U.S. House of Representatives are chosen. Since these legislatures were initially under farm control, it is not surprising that they apportioned these districts—or refused to reapportion them—in such a way as to keep their own jobs and, on occasion, to help to insure the election of some of their members to Congress. Consequently, even as rural areas were losing thousands of people to the lure of the city and suburban life, they were able to retain most of their legislative seats.

The failure of the state legislatures to pass reapportionment laws to insure that equal numbers of people would elect equal numbers of lawmakers produced predictably bizarre results. In Tennessee, which had not changed the district boundaries for over sixty years, legislators from Nashville represented districts averaging over 54,000 people in 1961, while a representative from a rural area represented only 3948 people—along with 8611 cows and 4739 pigs and horses.[45] Less than 29 percent of the people could elect a majority of the members in the

43 Glendon Schubert, ed., *Reapportionment* (N.Y.: Charles Scribner's Sons, 1965), p. 169.
44 Gordon E. Baker, *Rural versus Urban Political Power* (Garden City, N.Y.: Doubleday & Company, Inc., 1955), p. 16.
45 Editorial, *New Republic*, January 29, 1962; p. 3.

Tennessee General Assembly. The situation in many other states was similar, and often worse. In Vermont, 11.6 percent of the population could elect over 50 percent of the members in the lower house of the legislature, as could 12 percent in Florida, 18.5 in Kansas and Delaware, and 22.6 in Georgia.[46] Congressional districts as drawn by state legislatures revealed the same sort of population disparities. In 1962 thirteen states had at least one congressional district over twice the population of its smallest one.

Gerrymandering   State legislators have been in the habit of drawing election district boundaries to their own advantage for at least a century and a half. During that time, the weirdly shaped results have been known as *gerrymanders,* after Governor Elbridge Gerry of Massachusetts who signed a reapportionment bill in 1812 containing a district whose shape resembled a legendary animal called the salamander. More will be said of this in Chapter 10.

Not until 1946 did the Supreme Court face the issue of the constitutionality of a gerrymander which created districts with huge population differences, each selecting a single official. The case before it involved obvious bias in favor of agricultural regions: Southern Illinois, mostly rural, elected proportionately more congressmen than the larger populations of northern Illinois concentrated in and around the Chicago metropolitan area. The high court decided it could do nothing about it. In Justice Frankfurter's words, the apportionment issue was a "political thicket," a nonjusticiable question that the Constitution intended to be decided not by the courts but by the popularly elected legislative and executive branches.[47]

". . . People, not trees or acres"   But sixteen years later in *Baker* v. *Carr,*[48] the Court ruled that legislative apportionment *was* an issue properly subject to judicial attention. If equal numbers of voters could not elect equal numbers of legislators, they could scarcely expect the constitutionally guaranteed "equal protection of the laws." The *Baker* case involved the lower house of the Tennessee legislature, and was interpreted by lower courts to require that at least one house of all state legislatures had to be chosen from equally populated districts.

Two years later, there followed *Wesberry* v. *Sanders* in which the Court voted, 6–2, that state legislatures must also apportion congressional districts in a way that permitted equal numbers of voters to elect equal numbers of members of the House of Representatives.[49] Completing the process, the Court concluded its 1964 session by ruling that the "equal protection" clause required *both* houses of a state legislature to be elected from districts with approximately the same

46 Schubert, op. cit., p. 82.
47 *Colegrove* v. *Green,* 328 U.S. 549 (1946).
48 369 U.S. 186 (1962).
49 376 U.S. 1 (1964). *Wesberry* did not impose the equal population rule on the basis of the "equal protection" clause of Amendment Fourteen, but on the basis of Article I, Section 2, which requires that members of the House Representatives be elected "by the People"— presumably in equal numbers.

population. The key case, *Reynolds* v. *Sims,* produced the "one man, one vote" formula which held that a person's vote in any district should have as much influence in electing a candidate as any other person's vote in any other district. Or as Chief Justice Warren put it: "Legislators represent people, not trees or acres."[50]

Just as the *Baker, Wesberry,* and *Reynolds* cases required substantial equality in the populations which elected certain national and state officials, so *Avery* v. *Midland County,* a case from Texas, demanded the same standards in the selection of "a city council, school board, or county governing board."[51]

In 1962, Justice Frankfurter indicated in his *Baker* dissent that this initial reapportionment decision simply would not be obeyed. He confidently predicted that the Court ruling was "merely empty rhetoric, sounding a word of promise to the ear, sure to be disappointing in the hope."[52] Yet Frankfurter, for all his cynical realism, was dramatically wrong. Eight years after his pessimistic prediction, ninety-five of America's ninety-nine state legislative bodies had been reapportioned to meet the "one man, one vote" standard.[53] Similar progress seems indicated in congressional districting. The result is a substantial increase in the political power of the cities and suburbs.

Equal Protection in other Areas

The importance of the "equal protection" clause of Amendment Fourteen extends beyond questions of race or legislative apportionment. Under this constitutional provision, various courts have also held that states may not designate males over females in the administration of wills, require jail sentences of those too poor to pay fines, or keep the names of candidates who can't afford filing fees off the ballot. Most important, perhaps, is that courts in California, Minnesota, Texas, and New Jersey have ruled that public schools can no longer be financed primarily by a local property tax because such a scheme denies equal educational opportunity to students in poor districts.

50 377 U.S. 533.
51 390 U.S. 474 (1968).
52 *Baker* v. *Carr,* 81 S.Ct. 691, at 739.
53 George B. Merry, "U.S. Census Promises Fresh Wave of Redistricting," *The Christian Science Monitor,* July 23, 1970, p. 1. Only the South Carolina and Alaska lower houses and both houses of the Oregon legislature were apportioned so fairly before 1962 as to require no change. There are only ninety-nine legislative bodies at the state level because Nebraska has a unicameral legislature.

Conclusion to Part Two

The Constitution exalts the free mind and commits the government to no creed but tolerance. As a result, it guarantees the freedom in which a new idea or an unpopular cause may grow and even flourish. It also provides the protection of fair procedure for the defendant confronting the awesome power of criminal prosecution, and it seeks to guarantee equal legal treatment. Yet fairness and equality, in life as well as in law, proceed not only from official policy but from the widely shared conviction that all humanity is precious. Unless the constitutional safeguards protect each of us, no matter how despised or even truly despicable, the rights of all of us someday may be in jeopardy.

Like all great constitutional standards, those described in the last three chapters are sometimes abused in the rough and tumble of legislative and executive processes. Their chief protection, therefore, has come primarily from the courts. More than most of us, judges have recognized that if the rights of the people are to be preserved, the power of government must be limited.

Bibliography

Chapter 3

Freedom of Expression: First Things First

Abraham, Henry J., *Freedom and the Court* (N.Y.: Oxford University Press, Inc., 1967).
Chafee, Jr., Zechariah, *Free Speech in the United States* (New York, Atheneum Publishers, 1969).
Cushman, Robert F., ed., *Cases in Civil Liberties* (N.Y.: Appleton-Century-Crofts, 1968).

Meiklejohn, Alexander, *Free Speech and Its Relation to Self-Government* (N.Y.: Harper & Row, Publishers, 1948).
Mill, John Stuart, *On Liberty* (Chicago: Gateway Edition, Henry Regnery Co., 1955).
Sheldon, Charles H., ed., *The Supreme Court: Politicians in Robes* (Beverly Hills, Calif.: Glencoe Press, 1970).

Chapter 4

The Defendant's Rights: Criminal Justice in America

Campbell, James S., *et al.*, *Law and Order Reconsidered*, A Staff Report to the National Commission on the Causes and Prevention of Violence (N.Y.: Bantam Books, Inc., 1970).
Cray, Ed, *The Big Blue Line* (N.Y.: Coward-McCann, Inc., 1967).
Crime and the Law, (Washington, D.C.: Congressional Quarterly Service, 1971).
Fellman, David, *The Defendant's Rights* (N.Y.: Holt, Rinehart & Winston, Inc., 1958).
Germann, A. C., Frank D. Day, and Robert R. J. Gallati, *Introduction to Law Enforcement* (Springfield, Ill.: Charles C Thomas, Publisher, 1962).
Inbau, Fred E., and John E. Reid, *Criminal Interrogation and Confessions* (Baltimore: The Williams and Wilkins Co., 1962).
Tappan, Paul W., *Crime, Justice and Correction* (N.Y.: McGraw-Hill Book Company, 1960).

Chapter 5

Equal Justice Under Law: Of Dreams Deferred

Baker, Gordon E., *Rural versus Urban Political Power* (Garden City, N.Y.: Doubleday & Company, Inc., 1955).
Fishel, Jr., Leslie H., and Benjamin Quarles, eds., *The Black American* (Glenview, Ill.: Scott, Foresman and Company, 1970).
Myers, Gustavus, *History of Bigotry in the United States*, ed. by Henry M. Christman (N.Y.: Capricorn Books, G. P. Putnam's Sons, 1960).

Schubert, Glendon, ed., *Reapportionment* (N.Y.: Charles Scribner's Sons, 1965).
Seib, Shirley M., ed., *Revolution in Civil Rights*, 3rd ed. (Washington, D.C.: Congressional Quarterly , Inc., 1967).
Silberman, Charles, *Crisis in Black and White* (N.Y.: Random House, Inc., 1964).
U.S. Commission on Civil Rights, *Racial Isolation in the Public Schools*, vol. 1 (Washington, D.C.: U.S. Government Printing Office, 1967).

PART THREE

POLITICAL BEHAVIOR

A democracy does what a majority of the people wants it to do. Effective methods of communication, therefore, are indispensable to democratic government, so a majority on any particular issue can inform government officials of its wishes. The next three chapters describe the most effective communication channels available in American politics. Chapter 6 stresses the importance of concerted group action, suggesting how opinions are formed and how pressure groups transmit those opinions to the government through various kinds of lobbying techniques. Chapter 7 deals with political parties, the groups which are formed specifically for the purpose of electing officials, and which help to formulate policy alternatives. Since communication is a two-way process, Chapter 8 considers the campaigns in which politicians attempt to win the people's favor, and the voting process by which majorities are won at the polls. In all three of these chapters, we thus deal with behavior that links the citizens to the government and transmits policy preferences back and forth between the people and the politicians.

Chapter **6**

The People's Influence
Public Opinion and Pressure Groups

If there is no struggle, there is no progress. Those who profess to favor freedom, and yet deprecate agitation, are men who want crops without plowing up the ground. They want the rain without thunder and lightning. . . . Power concedes nothing without a demand. It never did and never will.
                                                            Frederick Douglass

Power is a two-way street. Government can alter the behavior of the people, and in a democracy the people can alter the direction of government policy as well. But what do the people want and how can they get it? This chapter may give some clues.

THE DYNAMICS OF PUBLIC OPINION

Democracy has been described as a government chosen by and responsive to a majority of the adult population. This is simply another way of saying that it rests upon public opinion, defined as the beliefs shared by large numbers of people regarding some issues of public importance.

Political Socialization:
The Transfer of Opinion

How do people acquire their opinions? How are the attitudes and values that make up their political culture transferred from one generation to the next? Answers to these questions lie in the study of political socialization, a relatively new research area.

The family   Even while many people (mostly parents) are worrying about the "generation gap," there is considerable evidence that most persons—at least in political matters—have views substantially similar to those of their elders. One study, for example, disclosed that only 12 percent of the people whose parents were both Democrats identified themselves as Republicans, and only 16 percent of those whose parents were both Republicans were traitorous enough to become Democrats.[1] The influence of the older generation, moreover, is apparent at an early age. Greenstein found that by the age of ten over 60 percent of a group of Connecticut children were able to express a party preference, even though only "little more than a third . . . could name even one (leader) of either of the two major parties."[2]

Any political ideas tend either to stabilize the status quo by perpetuating established values, or to promote change by challenging the existing order of things. There is little doubt that ideas obtained in the family, or at least somewhere before the child reaches high school, are primarily of the former variety. Children seem to have viewed the United States government as the next best thing to Disneyland and have attributed to government officials qualities of power and goodness usually imputed only to saints. A study of pupils in grades three through eight in the Chicago area revealed that from 70 to 84 percent of them agreed that "The government usually knows what is best for the people."[3] The Connecticut research mentioned earlier disclosed that nearly all children view the President and mayor very favorably. The President, somewhat typically, was thought by a fifth-grade girl to "stop bad things before they start," and a fourth-grade boy believed that the mayor "helps everyone to have nice homes and jobs."[4]

In view of this general acceptance of "the best of all possible worlds," one scholar concluded that the "early family socialization process is . . . one of the most important factors making for the resistance to social and political change."[5] Adult dissatisfaction with the Vietnam war, however, has forced a reexamination of some of these conclusions. A study released in 1971 confirms family influence on children's political views, but shows, as a result, that 45 percent of elementary school pupils doubted that the President always tells the truth about the conflict in southeast Asia.[6]

1 Angus Campbell, Gerald Gurin, and Warren E. Miller, *The Voter Decides* (N.Y.: Harper & Row, Publishers, 1954), p. 99.
2 Fred I. Greenstein, *Children and Politics* (New Haven: Yale University Press, 1965).
3 David Easton and Jack Dennis, "The Child's Image of Government," *The Annals of the American Academy of Political and Social Science* 361 (September 1965).
4 Fred I. Greenstein, "The Benevolent Leader: Children's Images of Political Authority," *The American Political Science Review* 54 (December 1960): 934–43.
5 Gabriel A. Almond, "A Functional Approach to Comparative Politics," Gabriel A. Almond and James S. Coleman, eds., *The Politics of Developing Areas* (Princeton: Princeton University Press, 1960), p. 27.
6 *Los Angeles Times,* October 17, 1971, Sec. F, p. 2. The research was under the direction of Professor Howard Tolley.

The schools It is generally agreed that compulsory school attendance affects political socialization, and that it does so in a way which bolsters the prevailing norms, or standards, of our society. This simply indicates that the schools do what we want them to do. "Nationalistic values," as two observers have written, "permeate the entire school curriculum . . ."[7]

After examining teaching materials used in Los Angeles County, Will Scoggins, a leading labor historian, concluded that "the United States as portrayed in high-school social studies textbooks would seem very near paradise for a man who was blind to economic and social facts."[8] The texts most commonly used are more objective than was once the case, however. A study by Edgar Litt indicated that students in three Boston area high schools showed greater support of democratic ideals as a result of a semester course in civics, but the effects of the course depended in considerable part on the nature of the community in which it was taught.[9] School influence far exceeds the impact of textbooks and subject matter, of course. In extracurricular activities and patriotic rituals it infuses the minds of the students with the political attitudes and values of their elders. That's what the socialization process is all about.

Peer groups But individual Americans do not simply respond passively to the programming of organized institutions such as family and school. They seek and usually share the opinions of their friends and fellow workers—those whom sociologists call their peers. One study showed that 88 percent of those whose three best friends were Republicans voted Republican, and 85 percent of those whose best friends were Democrats voted Democratic.[10] It is difficult to tell, of course, whether our choice of friends determines our political views, or whether our political views determine our choice of friends. In either event, the desire to belong, to be accepted, may convert one's social circle into a sort of filter, straining out those ideas that are either unacceptable or unknown to the group as a whole.

The Mass Media: Information Dissemination

Newspapers, magazines, radio, television, and other methods of mass communication are also sources of political socialization. Although their impact is not so personal or intimate as that of a family member, teacher, or friend, they reach a far larger audience.

Newspapers Thomas Jefferson wrote to a friend in 1816

7 Richard E. Dawson and Kenneth Prewitt, *Political Socialization* (Boston: Little, Brown and Company, 1969), p. 147.
8 *Labor in Learning* (Los Angeles: U.C.L.A., Institute of Industrial Relations, 1966), p. vii.
9 Edgar Litt, "Civic Education, Community Norms, and Political Indoctrination," *American Sociological Review* 28 (February 1963): 69–75.
10 V. O. Key, Jr., *Politics, Parties, and Pressure Groups,* 5th ed. (N. Y.: Thomas Y. Crowell Company, 1964), p. 120.

that "Where the press is free, and every man able to read, all is safe."[11] Yet recent experience suggests that perhaps newspapers are not quite so important as Jefferson believed. The evidence, at least, seems mixed. On the one hand, the paid circulation of daily papers is over sixty-two million.[12] President Nixon has sent personal letters praising editorials he admires,[13] and, in an earlier day, when he had just been defeated for the California governorship, he blamed the press for his loss. President Kennedy was so unhappy with the *New York Times'* coverage of the Vietnam war that he suggested to the publisher that its reporter in that country be assigned elsewhere.[14] Important officeholders have more or less regular press conferences, and the legendary "fearless reporter" is believed to have struck frequent terror into the hearts of corrupt local politicians. It was the work of newspaper reporters that revealed the medical history of Senator Thomas Eagleton, which led to his withdrawal from the vice-presidential race in 1972. In addition, newspapers can influence people indirectly because they are widely read by "opinion makers" such as politicians, authors, teachers, and clergymen.

On the other hand, radio and television have replaced the newspapers as a prime source of information for many Americans; consequently, the impact of the press on election results is of doubtful importance. One indication of this is that although most newspapers usually endorse Republican party candidates editorially, the Democrats controlled Congress for all but four years between 1930 and 1972. In 1960, John F. Kennedy was elected president with the support of less than one third of the nation's daily newspapers, and even these had only 16 percent of the total daily circulation.[15] But while most editorial writers support Republican candidates, the working reporters who write the front-page stories tend to favor the Democratic party[16] and may—as President Nixon once implied—slant their stories to reflect that bias.

Three trends in the newspaper field require brief mention. First, the total number of papers declined by over seven hundred between 1950 and 1971[17] largely because of increased operating costs and the resulting mergers—prevalent in other industries as well.

Second, an increasing percentage of newspaper space is filled by syndicated material sold to hundreds of papers throughout the country and proportionately less is devoted to locally produced journalism. The result may be that the public receives more information about national and international affairs but less about state and local political issues. The same news stories written by reporters for the Associated

11 Saul K. Padover, ed., *Thomas Jefferson On Democracy* (N. Y.: Pelican Books, Penguin Books Inc., 1946), p. 89.
12 U. S. Bureau of the Census, *Statistical Abstract of the United States: 1971*, p. 490.
13 *Time,* August 31, 1970, p. 45.
14 David Halberstam, *The Making of a Quagmire* (N. Y.: Random House, Inc., 1965), p. 268. Halberstam was the reporter in question.
15 *New York Times,* November 4, 1960, p. 24.
16 Seymour Martin Lipset, *Political Man* (Garden City, N.Y.: Anchor Books, Doubleday & Company, Inc., 1963), pp. 339–40. This was true both in the mid-1930s and mid-1950s.
17 U.S. Bureau of the Census, *Statistical Abstract of the United States: 1971*, p. 491.

Press (AP) and United Press International (UPI) appear in papers all over the country. A similar situation exists with respect to the work of editorial cartoonists and political columnists.

Third, there has been a notable decrease in locally owned newspapers, not only because there are fewer newspapers but because many of those that remain are owned by the same corporation. These newspaper chains often control other mass media outlets as well. The most famous is that founded by William Randolph Hearst which "includes 12 newspapers, 14 magazines, three television stations, six radio stations, a news service, a photo service, a feature syndicate, and Avon paperbacks."[18] Another communications octopus is the Knight chain which owns papers in Miami, Detroit, Akron, and Charlotte.

All of these developments are parts of the same problem: more and more people are acquiring information and attitudes from fewer and fewer sources. To some extent, the same problem exists with respect to magazines.

Television and radio   Television and radio stations are licensed by the Federal Communications Commission and neither has been given the special freedom guaranteed to the press by the First Amendment. Both television and radio are required by the Federal Communications Commission to give equal time to different candidates for the same office and to honor the *fairness doctrine* in presenting both sides of important issues. It is generally agreed that television now reaches more people than any other medium. It is the only one of the mass media that reaches the child early enough and often enough to rival his family in shaping values and molding opinions. It first gained political notice in 1948, and by 1960 it had become the most important single vehicle for campaign propaganda. It is widely credited with a decisive role in determining the outcome of the 1960 Kennedy-Nixon presidential race since the two candidates met in four nationally televised face-to-face debates. After the first of these confrontations, public opinion polls show that Kennedy picked up 4 percent of the probable vote and thereby took a narrow lead which he never lost.[19]

A survey completed in the mid-1960s reveals that television is the chief source of information for most people and that they have considerable confidence in its reliability.[20] In view of the pervasive impact of this newest of media (98 percent of all American homes had at least one set in 1971),[21] it is not surprising that a philosopher should emerge to try to explain its significance. "A new form of 'politics' is emerging," wrote Marshall McLuhan,

18 G. William Domhoff, *Who Rules America?* (Englewood Cliffs, N.J.: Prentice-Hall, Inc., 1967), p. 81.
19 See Hugh A. Bone and Austin Ranney, *Politics and Voters* (N.Y.: McGraw-Hill Book Company, 1963), p. 38, Table 8.
20 James D. Barber, *Citizen Politics* (Chicago: Markham Publishing Co., 1969), pp. 124–25.
21 U.S. Bureau of the Census, *Statistical Abstract of the United States: 1971*, p. 677.

and in ways we haven't yet noticed. The living room has become a voting booth. Participation via television in Freedom Marches, in war, revolution, pollution, and other events is changing *everything*.[22]

There are signs, however, that television's impact is not unlimited. The general public is becoming aware that this medium is even more monopolized than newspapers. Three networks, NBC, CBS, and ABC, have a virtual stranglehold on national and international news. One may reject, therefore, the views of David Brinkley, Walter Cronkite, and Howard K. Smith (all liberal to moderate in their interpretations), and still claim that his own personal attitudes are "correct." Vice President Agnew has attacked TV news reporters as "a tiny enclosed fraternity of privileged men" who are "supersensitive, self-annointed, supercilious electronic barons of opinion." His view that the mass media in general, and television in particular, have an anticonservative bias is shared by a significant percentage of the general population.[23]

Additionally, the opinions and attitudes developed over a lifetime form a sort of selective sieve that permits us to see primarily that which we wish to see, whether on television or in direct observation. Thus, we often do not perceive those impressions which might challenge our values or beliefs to an emotionally disturbing degree.

Whereas the family, school, and peer group largely tend to reinforce prevailing opinions and thereby strengthen the *status quo,* this is not so much the case with the mass media. Although the latter have a conservative bias in behalf of maintaining the conditions under which they presently exist, they are also committed, by their essential function, to report the new and different. Nevertheless, at least one expert believes that political opinions are so firmly rooted in social and psychological influences that newspapers, radio, and television serve mostly to reinforce existing attitudes.[24]

Public Opinion and Political Activity

Public opinion has political significance when it is translated into overt behavior. This could be negative, as in not voting or in expressing cynicism about the whole political process. If widespread, such alienation might severely diminish respect for government and hence the authority it exercises.

Normally, however, public opinion results in various kinds of positive behavior, each with a different degree of impact on the political system. For example, the individual may vote, urge friends to vote, write letters to the press and public officials, "walk a precinct" for a

22 Marshall McLuhan and Quentin Fiore, *The Medium Is the Massage* (N.Y.: Bantam Books, Inc., 1967), p. 22.
23 *Newsweek,* November 9, 1970, pp. 22–25.
24 Joseph T. Klapper, *The Effects of Mass Communication* (N.Y.: The Free Press, 1960), pp. 8–15.

political candidate, join a pressure group, make a campaign contribution, or run for office. What the individual does will be determined not only by his or her political resources (time, money, role, skills) but also by the intensity of his or her opinions about public matters. Consequently, the intensity of public opinion is as important a dimension as its content. If Jones thinks Smith would be a good governor, but doesn't believe this with much intensity or conviction, he may not even bother to vote. But if Green believes this very strongly she will not only vote for Smith but campaign for him with vigor. Politicians resort to highly emotional appeals more to increase the intensity of convictions than to change them. Public opinion polls often acknowledge the importance of this factor by asking their respondents whether they "strongly favor," "mildly favor," "mildly oppose," or "strongly oppose" a particular candidate or proposal. The distinctions indicate the kind of behavior which is likely to ensue.

The influences which determine the intensity of public opinion are the same as those which determine its content (family, friends, press, and so forth), plus an additional one—a sense of political efficacy. In other words, if one believes that what one does can make a difference, one is more likely to do it than if it seems that it will not matter anyway. A sense of political efficacy appears to be related both to social status and personality characteristics.

GROUP POLITICS

The United States has a population so vast that the voice of the individual can easily get lost. In fact, were it not so, government agencies would be widely and properly denounced for yielding to the wishes of a single person. Most political participation, therefore, is a collective phenomenon, because groups of individuals—bound together by mutual need and common interests—attempt to influence government policy.

Just as the people influence the government largely through group politics, so also government policy concerns itself almost entirely with groups, with types of activity, instead of with the individual citizen. Therefore, the analysis of group politics is essential to an understanding of modern democracy.

The Types of Groups

One must first distinguish those groups that are politically meaningless from those that are politically relevant. The former are sometimes called *categoric* and are based on certain shared characteristics that have little political importance. People with red hair or people with sisters are examples in point. By contrast, politically relevant groups are based on some common *interest* as a result of which their members are affected by certain government policies in much the same way. Indians, veterans, and doctors are interest groups. Students of politics are concerned with interest groups, which in turn can be subdivided into unorganized (or informal) and organized (or formal) groups.

The importance of organization Unorganized groups tend to be relatively impotent in influencing the important conditions that affect their lives. Children, the insane, and poor people are examples, exerting little political clout. Indeed, some of the most important political changes throughout our history have come about when previously unorganized groups "got themselves together" through formal organization. Slavery was ended only after those opposed to it formed abolition societies, the work day was shortened after laborers unionized, and civil rights laws were passed after minority groups organized.

This raises a question which is of the utmost tactical importance: What ingredients must be added to simple group membership for effective group organization? Six factors seem paramount:

1) Group consciousness: The members must realize that they are a group with common interests and common wants.

2) Leadership: At least a few members must possess the knowledge, intelligence, dedication, efficiency, persuasiveness, and popularity to create the organization and articulate its goals.

3) Communication: There must be a way for the members to communicate with each other, either through meetings or through mimeographed pamphlets, newspapers, radio, or television.

4) Money: It may not take much, but there must be financial resources to defray leadership expenses and the cost of whatever communications media are used.

5) Hope: An air of hopelessness blights the prospects for effective group action. Any sign of possible improvement—any "light at the end of the tunnel"—may engender what has been called a revolution of rising expectations and inspire more consolidated group effort.

6) Ideology: Most people will sacrifice very little—even organizational dues—on behalf of a common cause unless it can be justified by some idea or doctrine. It may be as simple as "brotherhood" or "justice," but it is necessary to legitimize the organization, to assure the members that it is "right."

The important organized interests discussed later in this chapter possess in varying degree these basic characteristics.

Membership groups and reference groups For a long time foreign observers have been commenting on the strong tendency of Americans to seek group associations. These associations may be personal ones that involve membership in organizations such as unions, or clubs, or they may be vicarious ones that the individual respects and identifies with (feels he is similar to), even though he may not belong to them. The former are *membership groups* and the latter *reference groups*. The influence of a group in which one is a member is more or less direct but the importance of reference groups requires a few more words.[25] A reference group is one from which a person derives his values or standards, whether he belongs to it or not. For the most part, individuals adopt the opinions of reference groups because they admire people in those groups, fulfill certain emotional needs to "belong" in that manner, or hope to obtain personal advantage as a result. Some white people, for example, support predominantly black organizations, while many blacks adopt the values of white society; rising young business executives model their opinions on those of the top management of the companies for which they work.

Primary groups and secondary groups   In some groups, people have regular face-to-face relationships with each other. These *primary groups* include the family, the local parish congregation, and one's job associates. As a rule, such primary groups have a greater influence on our political ideas than the *secondary groups* of which we are also members, but which are bigger, more impersonal, and may involve little or no personal contact. The United States Chamber of Commerce, the Catholic Church, and the National Rifle Association are examples of secondary groups. In this sort of classification, the small (primary group) is often mightier than the large (secondary group).

Ingroups and outgroups   There seems to be a natural inclination to divide people into "we" and "they" or—as the sociologists would put it—into ingroups and outgroups. One generally views with indifference, suspicion, or hostility the "outs" to which one does not belong, but shares the opinions of the "ins" to which one does. Although this sort of division is nearly universal, it may spring less from a natural inclination than from the conscious attempts of each group to instill a feeling of loyalty among its own members. Figure 14 depicts the various kinds of groups.

Economic Pressure Groups

In politics, as in nearly everything else, the wheel that squeaks the loudest gets the grease. *Pressure groups are organized interest groups that attempt to influence government policy,* and are among the biggest wheels in the American political machine. Their squeaks rarely go ungreased by some sort of government service. Among the major pressure groups are those that represent the chief elements of the American economy—business, labor, agriculture, and the professions.

The nation's business   Of those who speak for business, the National Association of Manufacturers (NAM) and the U.S. Chamber of Commerce are the most prominent. The NAM, founded in 1895, consists of large industrial corporations—what might loosely be called big business—and the Chamber of Commerce, established in 1912,

25 Heinz Eulau, *The Behavioral Persuasion in Politics* (N.Y.: Random House, Inc., 1963), pp. 53–54.

Figure 14   Types of Groups

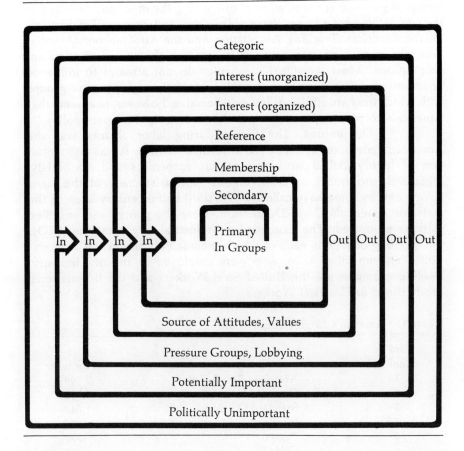

is made up chiefly of retail merchants, or small business firms.[26] While these two groups occasionally differ, they share a basic conservatism that leads them to join in opposition to most welfare programs, to the relatively high taxes necessary to pay for such benefits, and to most proposals made by labor unions.

Each kind of business also normally maintains its own specialized pressure group. Among the many examples, the American Petroleum Institute has assisted oil companies and mineral producers in obtaining depletion allowances that have resulted in lower taxes; the National Association of Real Estate Boards has lobbied hard for government-guaranteed loans for house buyers; and the Association of American Railroads has fought for authorization from the Interstate Commerce Commission to raise freight rates. There is often a clash of competing economic interests between specific groups. The natural gas industry and

26 Harmon Zeigler, *Interest Groups in American Society* (Englewood Cliffs, N.J.: Prentice-Hall, Inc., 1964).

electric power companies are inevitable foes, for example, with more stringent government regulation of one giving the other an advantage in the competition for a larger share of the stove and oven market. Similarly, the American Trucking Association and the Air Transport Association take opposing views on such issues as highway construction appropriations. Most individual companies do not attempt to influence government policy directly, but work instead through pressure groups with which they are affiliated. It would be naive, however, to assume that America's corporate giants exert no influence on government policy.

The unions   The first enduring labor alliance was the American Federation of Labor (AFL) formed in 1886. It was an association of highly skilled workers, such as carpenters and machinists, organized into trade, or craft, unions—the aristocracy of the labor movement, as some have called it. Not until half a century later, in the midst of America's Great Depression, were the poorer and unskilled workers unionized. The Congress of Industrial Organizations (CIO), was a group of unions each of which included all production workers, skilled and unskilled alike, who were employed in any one industry. Leading examples are the United Steel Workers and the International Brotherhood of Electrical Workers.

Figure 15   America's Largest Corporations

1969 Rank	Company	Net Profits[1]
1	American Tel. & Tel.	2,199
2	General Motors	1,711
3	Standard Oil (N.J.)	1,048
4	Int. Business Mach.	934
5	Texaco	770
6	Gulf Oil	611
7	Ford Motor	547
8	Standard Oil (Calif.)	454
9	Sears, Roebuck	441
10	Mobil Oil	435
11	Eastman Kodak	401
12	Du Pont, E.I.	356
13	Standard Oil (Ind.)	321
14	Shell Oil	291
15	General Electric	278
16	General Tel. & Elec.	237
17	International Tel.	234
18	Atlantic Richfield	227
19	United States Steel	217
20	Proctor & Gamble	187

[1] In millions of dollars.
Source: *The New York Times Encyclopedic Almanac* 1971, p. 637. Note: Five of the ten largest are oil companies, due in part to the tax depletion allowance mentioned in the text. Each of the three largest have net profits exceeding the total revenue of 27 states in 1969. U.S. Bureau of the Census, *The Statistical Abstract of the United States: 1971*, p. 410.

After some twenty years of rivalry, mutual animosity between the craft unions and the industrial unions declined enough that a single giant labor federation could be formed in 1955 by a merger of the AFL and CIO. Although it encompassed more than a hundred groups, neither the Teamsters Union nor the United Auto Workers, now the two largest in the entire nation, belong to the AFL-CIO. Other independent unions are various railroad brotherhoods, the United Mine Workers, and the International Longshoremen's and Warehousemen's Union.

There are now about twenty million union members in America, constituting approximately one quarter of the total labor force.[27] Automation has cut heavily into the jobs available in many of those industries which were once most effectively unionized, such as newspaper printers and typesetters, sheet metal workers, and musicians. Offsetting this downward trend, however, is union growth among farm laborers, white-collar workers, and government employees such as social workers and teachers. The old distinction between craft and industrial unions has become blurred and some unions are ignoring their traditional jurisdictional boundaries in much the same way as business conglomerates are now diversifying their activity. Thus, the Teamsters Union, which initially consisted of wagon and truck drivers almost exclusively, now embraces many warehouse and processing employees, taxi drivers, airline workers, and people in other occupations as well.

Unions have been largely liberal: They have worked persistently for larger pensions and medical care through the social security program, passage of civil rights laws, higher miminum wages and lower maximum hours, and more expenditures for public schools. Union leadership is divided and somewhat confused regarding its proper role. Some officials, like George Meany, president of the AFL-CIO, seem content to concentrate on such bread-and-butter issues as higher wages and job security for those already unionized. As part of the "establishment," they dine at the White House and usually support the administration's foreign adventures. In contrast, men like the late Walter Reuther of the UAW and Cesar Chavez of the United Farm Workers have had a broader vision of organizing the dispossessed and powerless.

The voices of the farmer   The major agricultural pressure group is the American Farm Bureau Federation, founded in 1919 and possessing a reported membership of about a million and a half. Its members are concentrated largely in the corn and cotton belts of the Midwest and South and include many of the richest farmers with the largest agricultural acreage in the nation. It has enjoyed unusually close relations with agricultural agencies in both the national and state governments.[28] The National Grange, the oldest of the major farm groups, is

---

27 Estimates based largely on data in U.S. Bureau of the Census, *Statistical Abstract of the United States: 1971*, pp. 233–34. Much of the material in this section reflects the erudition and insight of Paul Perlin, a former member of the Executive Board of the International Longshoremen's and Warehousemen's Union.
28 Theodore Lowi, "How the Farmers Get What They Want," *The Reporter*, May 21, 1964.

Figure 16   America's Largest Unions

Union	Members[1] 1964	1968
Teamsters[2]	1,507	1,755
Automobile workers[2]	1,168	1,473
Steelworkers	965	1,120
Machinists	808	903
Electrical (IBEW)	806	897
Carpenters	760	793
Laborers[2]	432	553
Retail clerks	428	552
Garment, ladies'	442	455
Hotel and restaurant	445	459
Clothing workers	377	386
Meatcutters	341	500
Building services	320	389
Engineers, operating	311	350
Communications workers	294	357
Electrical (IUE)	271	324
Plumbers	256	297
State, county	235	364
Railway and steamship clerks[2]	270	280
Musicians	275	283
Mine workers, District 50[2]	210	232
Painters	199	200
Government (AFGE)	139	295
Letter carriers	168	210
Railroad trainmen[2]	185	185

[1] In thousands
[2] All unions except these are affiliated with the AFL-CIO.
Source: U.S. Bureau of the Census, *Statistical Abstract of the United States: 1971*, p. 234.

strongest in the East and has about half the membership of the Farm Bureau.

The National Farmers Union is the smallest of these three groups with about 250,000 members, most of whom live in the wheat, dairy, and cattle country of Wisconsin, Minnesota, Montana, Colorado, and the Great Plains states. This group is substantially more liberal, and hence more receptive to government intervention in farm affairs, than the more moderate Grange or the increasingly conservative Farm Bureau. Just as these organizations frequently differ with one another on questions of government policy, so also do the more specialized agricultural groups, such as the American Livestock Association, the National Apple Institute, and the National Wool Growers Federation.[29]

The chief concerns of nearly all farm organizations are government-guaranteed prices, acreage restrictions, and tariffs on for-

29 Key, op. cit., pp. 31–40.

eign imports. Even on these issues, however, their divergent views reflect opposing economic interests. Corn farmers naturally want high grain prices and poultry farmers low ones. Similarly, citrus growers may favor free international trade, because of their large export market, while dairy farmers or beef producers may want rigid restrictions because of the competitive threat of foreign imports.

Two overriding and related issues now confront American agriculture: the displacement of the small, privately owned family farm by far larger, corporately owned, "factories in the field," and the remarkably rapid growth of the United Farm Workers Organizing Committee, AFL-CIO, in unionizing agricultural laborers. In the near future, agriculture may be dominated by business corporations as farm employers, with workers largely organized in unions.

The professions Jobs in America have usually been classified into occupational and professional categories, although this distinction may be more one of status considerations than of economic, educational, or ethical differences. At any rate, many professional organizations are enormously influential pressure groups.

Most lawyers belong to the American Bar Association (ABA) and through that organization exert considerable influence on such matters as the appointment of judges, court organization and procedure, and—to a lesser extent—changes in certain legal codes. The American Medical Association (AMA), representing an even greater percentage of the nation's medical doctors, successfully opposed tax-supported medical care (Medicare) for more than fifteen years and continues to restrict the supply of doctors and exert influence on health legislation.

Like the ABA and AMA, there are groups of barbers, morticians, insurance salesmen, cosmetologists, teachers, and many others who are permitted by state laws to establish entrance requirements for new members of their professions. Again like the ABA and AMA, most of them tend to be somewhat conservative where protecting their own interests is concerned.

Ethnic Solidarity: Lumps in the Melting Pot

Economic interests have been forced to share the stage of group politics with many organizations representing Americans of various races and national origins.

"If you're white, you're all right" Prowhite groups can be divided into those based on prejudice and those designed to promote the interests of particular ethnic groups. Both have little influence at the national level and scarcely more in state and local politics. The former include the Ku Klux Klan, formed after the Civil War and of some influence as late as the 1920s, the American Nazis, the white Citizens' Councils that led the more sophisticated southern attack on racial integration in the 1950s and 1960s, and the Christian Nationalist Crusade

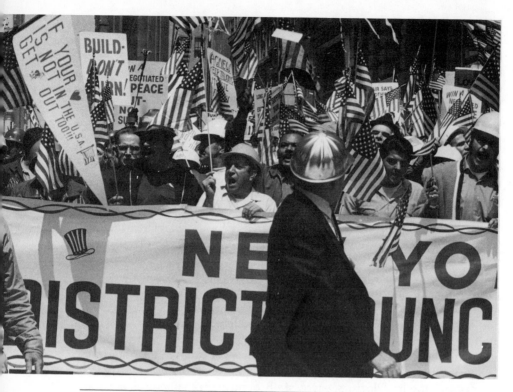

Burt Glinn © 1970 Magnum Photos.

Many Americans enthusiastically support their country's policies, both foreign and domestic, although many others urge basic changes.

led by the Rev. Gerald L. K. Smith of California.[30] These organizations are nearly always antiblack, usually anti-Jewish, often anti-Catholic, and seldom capable of acting effectively in the arena of nation-wide pressure politics.

Those groups that seek to advance their own group more than to attack others have more respectability than those based on bigotry. One of the most militant is the Jewish Defense League which has staged demonstrations against the anti-Semitism practiced in the Soviet Union. Irish-American groups have traditionally held St. Patrick's Day parades and Polish-Americans have organized Pulaski Day dinners.[31] A common denominator of many such groups in recent years has been a desire to counteract the growing influence of black organizations, in order to retain their share of job training and college scholarship

30 For a general survey of racist groups, consult Gustavus Myers, *History of Bigotry in the United States,* ed. and rev. by Henry M. Christman (N.Y.: Capricorn Books, Random House, Inc., 1960). For more detailed recent information, see George Thayer, *The Farther Shores of Politics* (N.Y.: A Clarion Book, Simon and Schuster, Inc., 1968), Part One.
31 Edgar Litt, *Ethnic Politics in America* (Glenview, Ill.: Scott, Foresman and Company, 1970), p. 64.

programs. A National Confederation of American Ethnic Groups has been established for this purpose.[32]

There is little doubt that the last ten years have seen an increase in ancestral pride, especially vocal among the descendants of those Americans from southern and eastern Europe whose ancestors arrived in the United States most recently, often to be derided as "hunkies" and "wops." White ethnics such as these are not free of prejudice—who among us is?—but they reveal a genuine fear that they somehow may be lost in the continuing shuffle of a competitive economy and status system in which they have only recently found a reasonably prosperous place. They learned that whites from the old American families are somewhat more "all right" than those who arrived more recently. Having been scorned by the upper classes, they now feel caught in a vise tightened by the increasing militancy of the lower classes—the racial minorities who covet the respectability that Americans of Irish, Italian, Polish, Slovak, Greek, and Russian ancestry have struggled so hard to attain.

"If you're brown, stick around"   The five million Mexican-Americans, most of whom have some Indian ancestry, constitute the second-largest racial minority in the United States. In a sense, theirs is a double disability: They are often identifiable by their physical characteristics, and their Spanish language environment, especially in areas near the Mexican border, makes it difficult for them to learn English. Throughout the Southwest they attend schools whose teachers and administrators are, for the most part, alien to their culture, ignorant of their language, and often indifferent to their aspirations.[33] In Los Angeles, where more persons of Mexican ancestry live than in any metropolis except Mexico City and Guadalajara, there is a substantial amount of residential segregation. The "Chicano barrios," or Mexican-American neighborhoods, are characterized by lower incomes, higher unemployment, and poorer medical care than in the county as a whole.

In recent years Chicanos have developed new organizational weapons in their struggle for equal opportunity and new leaders to provide inspiration and direction in waging it. In Denver, Rodolfo "Corky" Gonzalez, a colorful and articulate ex-boxer, formed the Crusade for Justice to help meet the needs of Colorado's substantial Chicano population. In south Texas, where Mexican-Americans are a majority in twenty-six counties, a political party, *La Raza Unida* (the United People), has elected two mayors. In Crystal City, the "spinach capital" of the nation, it won a majority on both the city council and school board.[34] In California's rich San Joaquin Valley, Cesar Chavez, the nonviolent head of the United Farm Workers Organizing Committee, AFL-CIO, has

32 *Newsweek*, October 6, 1969, p. 36.
33 See Chapter 5, p. 118.
34 Frank del Olmo, "Chicano Group Seeks Control of South Texas," *Los Angeles Times*, August 23, 1970, Sec. F, p. 3.

brought more gains for migratory laborers in five years than they had achieved in the preceding fifty.

Older organizations, such as California's Community Service Organization, established in 1947, or the American G.I. Forum, founded in Texas in 1948, function much like other pressure groups which wish to work by traditional methods and in fairly close alliance with sympathetic Anglos. Although the Mexican-American Political Association (MAPA) and the Political Association of Spanish-Speaking Organizations (PASSO) have much in common with these groups, they are newer and emphasize the election of Mexican-Americans to office in California and Texas respectively.[35] Finally, there are radicals who favor militant direct action or even revolutionary measures. The Brown Berets in California and the native Indian *Alianza Federal de los Pueblos Libres* (Federal Alliance of Free City States) in New Mexico, although quite small, are leading examples.[36]

Behind these disagreements on tactics there is another barrier to Mexican-American unity that involves a problem of identity. As a group, they differ about what to call themselves—Mexican-Americans, Chicanos, Spanish-Americans, browns, or something else. This psychological confusion reflects very real and sometimes deep divisions among the people themselves. Some have been in this country for many generations, while 17 percent are foreign born; some speak little Spanish, while 47 percent speak little English;[37] some are legal entrants into the United States, while others are *wetbacks* who crossed the border illegally; and some are relatively prosperous while many are very poor. Yet with few exceptions, they are united by a common religion, a common cultural heritage, and a common problem: aloof toleration by, or active hostility from, the dominant Anglo society. At best, they have been permitted to "stick around."

Some of the problems confronting Mexican-Americans, concentrated in the southwestern states, are similar to those of the one and three-quarter million Puerto Ricans living principally in New York, and the 565,000 Cubans residing mainly in Florida. All persons of Latin American origin average three years less schooling and a 30 percent smaller family income than other Americans. In October 1971, a "Brown Power" conference attempted to map a common political program on

35 Ralph Guzman, "Politics and Policies of the Mexican-American Community," Eugene P. Dvorin and Arthur J. Musner, eds., *California Politics and Policies* (Reading, Mass.: Addison-Wesley Publishing Co., Inc., 1966), pp. 373–81.
36 The members of the *Alianza*, along with others of Indian ancestry in New Mexico, are often called Hispanos. In many cases their forebears lived in what is now New Mexico as long ago as 1540 when the Spanish explorer Coronado became the first European to set foot in this region. For an account of the *Alianza* and Reies Lopez Tijerina, its dynamic and unorthodox leader, see Carroll Cagle, "The Great Land Grab Game," *The Black Politician* 1 (April 1970): pp. 17–21.
37 *The World Almanac and Book of Facts* 1972 Edition (N.Y.: Newspaper Enterprise Association, Inc., 1971), p. 656, and U.S. Bureau of the Census, *Statistical Abstract of the United States: 1971*, p. 29.

which Americans of both Mexican and Puerto Rican ancestry could unite.[38] One of the difficulties it confronted was a disagreement on the ultimate ends to be sought. Some cherish the traditional American dream of full integration into the mainstream of Anglo society; others, disillusioned by prejudice or fearful of losing unique characteristics of their own heritage, wish to progress as a separate and largely autonomous subculture within the nation as a whole.[39]

"If you're black, get back" Some of the difficulties confronting blacks in America have been depicted in Chapter 5.[40] The present discussion is confined to a consideration of the organizations that cope with such difficulties. The significance of the subject transcends the black community, since the strategies they have used have inspired many members of other minorities to seek solutions to their own problems in similar ways.

The first important civil rights organization to work in behalf of racial justice was the National Association for the Advancement of Colored People (NAACP), founded in 1909. In many ways, the group was an organizational reaction to the doctrines of Booker T. Washington, the black educator who opposed, on tactical grounds, work toward integration and social equality. To W. E. B. Du Bois and other leaders of the NAACP, on the contrary, these goals seemed the minimum essentials of individual dignity and social justice. The organization's most important contribution has been its legal leadership in getting segregation laws declared unconstitutional.

The National Urban League, formed in 1910, has been concerned as much with equal opportunity in housing and employment as with governmental policy. In recent years, Roy Wilkins, executive director of the NAACP, and the late Whitney M. Young, Jr., holding the same post for the Urban League, have epitomized the moderate and responsible leadership that has linked the white liberal to the black community, and the black community to the decision-makers who hold government power.[41]

In 1941 the Fellowship of Reconciliation, a predominantly white organization consisting primarily of religious pacifists, broadened its antiwar preoccupation to embrace the cause of racial harmony. For this purpose, it organized the Congress of Racial Equality (CORE) which developed nonviolent civil disobedience as an effective technique for fighting racial segregation. In the mid-1960s CORE lost much of its initial white pacifist support because it abandoned nonviolence in the face of increasingly brutal reactions by white racists. Simultaneously, it

38 *Los Angeles Times*, October 22, 1971, p. 18.
39 The separatist movement is described by del Olmo, loc. cit.
40 See pp. 115–120.
41 For background information on the NAACP and Urban League, see Arna Bontemps, *One Hundred Years of Negro Freedom* (N.Y.: Dodd, Mead & Co., 1961), Chs. 9–13, and Langston Hughes, *Fight for Freedom, the Story of the NAACP* (N.Y.: Berkley Publishing Corporation, 1962).

suffered defections by many blacks to similar groups and more militant organizations.[42]

Prior to the assassination of Rev. Martin Luther King in 1968, the Southern Christian Leadership Conference (SCLC) was, in large measure, a reflection of his magnetic leadership. He was a scholar influential among intellectuals and a preacher effective in mobilizing the indignation of the multitude. The SCLC, influenced by CORE, was born in 1957 after the Montgomery bus boycott, touched off when Mrs. Rosa Parks was denied a vacant seat in the front of a bus in December 1955. Subsequently, through massive marches, illegal sit-ins, and placid perseverance in the face of billy clubs, electric cattle prods, and police dogs, the SCLC succeeded in capturing the essence of that which seemed "best" in the civil rights movement.

The Student National (formerly Non-Violent) Coordinating Committee (SNCC, or "Snick") was founded in 1960 and moved rapidly from moderate militancy to left-wing agitation. The organization began as a sort of junior CORE, helping to register black voters. Under the leadership of Stokely Carmichael, it was the first leading civil rights group to embrace the slogan and ideology of "Black Power." This idea, also propounded with great vigor and effectiveness by Malcolm X, the former Black Muslim leader, signaled the temporary abandonment of racial integration as a major black objective. Instead, it sought the election of black officials to represent black ghettoes and black ownership of businesses that have predominantly black customers.[43]

At the left-wing extreme is the Black Panther party, formed in Oakland, California, in 1966. It is not a party in the usual sense, since it nominates no candidates for office. But it is deeply political in its commitment to a modified Marxist philosophy and has formulated a specific program that includes full employment, the exemption of black men from military service, and a United Nations-supervised plebiscite to determine "the will of black people as to their national destiny."[44] Panther tactics have ranged from a free breakfast program for ghetto children to armed confrontations with police and prison officials. The group has been badly damaged by a leadership split between Eldridge Cleaver, in exile in Algeria, and Huey Newton.

By 1969 most blacks displayed greater racial pride than ever before, but rejected the tactics and goals of extremist groups; 63 percent believed equality was possible without violence, 74 percent favored integration, and 70 percent felt that blacks had made progress in the preceding five years.[45] There was also a change among whites. Their

42 For a brief summary of post-World War II civil rights organizations, see *Report of the National Advisory Commission on Civil Disorders* (N.Y.: Bantam Books, Inc., 1968), pp. 223–36.
43 The most detailed and sophisticated analysis is in Stokely Carmichael and Charles V. Hamilton, *Black Power* (N.Y.: Vintage Books, Random House, Inc., 1967).
44 The full, ten-point program of the Panthers is found in every issue of its weekly newspaper, *The Black Panther*, and is reprinted in William M. Chace and Peter Collier, eds., *Justice Denied* (N.Y.: Harcourt Brace Jovanovich, Inc., 1970), pp. 534–37.
45 *Newsweek*, June 30, 1969, p. 19.

stereotype of the superstitious and cowardly Negro had been destroyed, a victim of the civil rights and "Black Power" movements of the 1960s. The choice of an integrated and united America, or separate and mutually suspicious racial blocs is still before us.[46] It requires both races to choose the first alternative, but either one can compel the second. Blacks will "get back" no longer.

   The red agony   Informed observers have little doubt that the native Indians now suffer greater deprivations than any other ethnic group.

The indicators of Indian suffering are appalling. Their life expectancy is 44 years, compared with 71 for white Americans. The average income for each Indian family living on a reservation—and more than half do—is only $1,500. The average years of schooling are 5.5, well behind that of both the black and the Mexican-American. Some officials rate 90 percent of reservation housing as substandard. Unemployment ranges from 20 percent on the more affluent reservations to 80 percent on the poorest.[47]

These statistics apply to a total reservation population of over 425,000— more than the populations of Oklahoma City, or Portland, Oregon. What is even more depressing is that the red man has been unable to form groups sufficiently strong to bring about any substantial changes in this situation. The reasons for this lack of organization include geographic dispersion, ignorance, feelings of futility, a pronounced shyness common among Indian cultures, and the disunity fostered by fragmentation among nearly three hundred tribes. One should derive no comfort from a notion that the Indians, although poor and disorganized, are happy. On the contrary, among young Indians the suicide rate is three times the national average.[48]

   There are some bright clouds on the horizon, although they are few and faint. For the first time in this century, President Johnson appointed an Indian to head the Bureau of Indian Affairs, and President Nixon has followed suit. Furthermore, in 1970 Mr. Nixon asked Congress to appropriate an additional $250 million for Indian economic development, to grant Indians more control over reservation affairs, and to rescind the "termination" policy of the 1950s designed to lure Indians off the reservations.[49]

   More importantly, there have been signs of organizational activity among Indians themselves. In 1961, 460 Indians from ninety tribes met to issue a "Declaration of Indian Purpose";[50] an Indian Patrol has been formed in Minneapolis in an attempt to minimize police mistreatment; La Donna Harris, the part-Comanche wife of a United

46 For several different points of view expressed by prominent blacks, see "Which Way Black America?," a special issue of *Ebony* magazine, August 1970.
47 *Time,* February 9, 1970, p. 16.
48 *Los Angeles Times,* July 5, 1970, Sec. G. p. 3.
49 *Christian Science Monitor,* July 14, 1970, p. 13.
50 Wilcomb E. Washburn, ed., *The Indian and the White Man* (Garden City, N.Y.: Anchor Books, Doubleday & Company, Inc., 1964), pp. 400–407.

Paul Conklin.

Navajo men learn stone masonry in a self-help housing program in Arizona.

States senator, has organized a group called "Oklahoma for Indian Opportunity" to attract antipoverty funds from the national government; and there is a Congress of American Indians headquartered in Washington, D.C. An increased impatience and a growing militancy is apparent among a portion of the Indian population, directed in part against the loss of water rights on Indian land. The most dramatic manifestation of the new activism was the Indian seizure of Alcatraz Island, site of a former federal prison, in 1969. One thing seems sure: The problem will not go away. A high birth rate has resulted in a 50 percent increase in the Indian population during the last ten years.

      Asian-Americans; a "yellow peril?" Americans of Asian ancestry—Japanese, Chinese, Filipinos, and Koreans, in order of their numerical strength in this country—generally have stayed out of politics. Their lack of involvement can be attributed to many factors, including a fear of white retribution and their small numbers. Even in the San Francisco-Oakland region, with its world famous Chinatown, Chinese-Americans constitute only about 2 percent of the population.[51] (In Hawaii, however, the situation is different. There, Asian-Americans

51 Hon. Alfred H. Song, California State Assemblyman, "Politics and Policies of the Oriental Community," in Dvorin and Misner, op. cit., p. 389, Table 14–3. One exception is Ken Nakoaka, a Japanese-American who served as mayor of Gardena, California, a Los Angeles suburb.

comprise over three quarters, and Japanese-Americans about two thirds, of the state legislature.)

An additional reason for the political inactivity of Asian-Americans is their fragmentation into Chinese, Japanese, Filipino, and other communities, geographically isolated from one another and each with relatively unique problems and dissimilar outlooks. They came to the United States during different time periods, entered various occupations in different proportions, and to some degree reflected in their mutual suspicions the rivalries that existed between the nations from which they came. The Chinese, who arrived first, reacted to white bigotry by attempting to maintain their cultural traditions intact, and gradually tended to specialize in wholesale and retail trade. The Japanese arrived later, tried hard to adapt to American cultural norms, and engaged in agriculture much more frequently. Filipinos, the last to come in significant numbers, are racially distinct from Chinese and Japanese, and work in disproportionately large numbers as migratory farm laborers and in domestic capacities.

The result of all these factors has been the emergence of very few pressure groups specifically for the purpose of articulating the peculiar needs and desires of Asian-Americans. By far the most important organization is the Japanese American Citizens League (JACL), founded in 1930, which maintains direct lobbying relationships with officials in Washington.[52] The situation, especially among young, college-educated Asians, is changing however, particularly in the direction of greater militancy and increasing unity among nonwhite minorities. In 1970 their activism was expressed in its most extreme form by the Red Guards, a San Francisco-based, communist-oriented organization whose members have denounced the traditional Six Companies that have long dominated Chinese economic and social activity in America.[53] The Six Companies grew out of associations of family-based clans and control a substantial number of restaurants, banks, and sweatshop factories. The sharpened sense of kinship among all Americans of Asian descent has led the Wah Ching, a group of Hong Kong-born Chinese, to work with the Asian-American Political Alliance[54] as well as with blacks and browns in the Third World Liberation Front, which is committed to the overthrow of white colonialism wherever it is found—either in foreign imperialism or domestic oppression.[55]

While nearly all Asian-Americans identify totally with the United States, they remember the World War II internment of Japanese-Americans in concentration camps, and they realize the uneven nature of their present prosperity. As recently as 1960, Filipinos in

52 Bill Hosokawa, *Nisei: The Quiet Americans* (N.Y.: William Morrow & Co., Inc., 1969), pp. 198–99, and passim.
53 Min Yee, "Chinatown in Crisis," *Newsweek,* February 23, 1970, pp. 57–58.
54 Kenneth Lamott, "The Awakening of Chinatown," Los Angeles Times *West Magazine,* January 4, 1970, pp. 7–15.
55 Amy Uyematsu, "The Emergence of Yellow Power in America," *Gidra* 1 (October 1969): pp. 10–11.

California had a median income of $2925, Chinese $3803, Japanese $4388, and Caucasians $5109—in spite of the fact that a higher percentage of both Chinese and Japanese had completed college than had whites.[56] In San Francisco's Chinatown the rate of substandard housing is over three times the city average and the rate of suicide is three times the national average. The situation there is not likely to improve for some time, because more than 33,000 Chinese, largely poor people from Hong Kong, have arrived since immigration quotas were abandoned by Congress in 1965.[57] In 1972 Chinatown was beset by a serious wave of extortion and violent crime.

Despite considerable improvement in their overall public image, Asian-Americans still encounter occasional social ostracism (especially with respect to intermarriage), some housing discrimination, and a competitive disadvantage in obtaining semiskilled and skilled industrial jobs. In the opinion of some observers, American economic competition with Japan could produce repercussions of prejudice against Japanese-Americans. Nonetheless, there has been immense improvement in the lot of most Asian-Americans—largely achieved by their own tenacity and hard work—since the days when whites viewed them as part of a vast and menacing "yellow peril." Because problems still exist, the nation cannot, in good conscience, ignore their plight.

Figure 17   Leading States in Minority Population

Rank	Indians	Japanese	Chinese	Mexicans	Negroes
1	Oklahoma	Hawaii	California	California	New York
2	Arizona	California	Hawaii	Texas	Illinois
3	California	Washington	New York	New Mexico	Texas
4	New Mexico	Illinois	Illinois	Arizona	California
5	No. Carolina	New York	Massachusetts	Colorado	Georgia

Source: Computed from U.S. Bureau of the Census, *Statistical Abstract of the United States: 1971*, pp. 27 and 31, *The New York Times Encyclopedic Almanac*, 1971, p. 288, and *The World Almanac and Book of Facts*, 1972 Edition (N.Y.: Newspaper Enterprise Association, Inc., 1971), p. 149.

"Sexual Politics": The Women's Liberation Movement

Few social movements in our history have received so much publicity as that which has accompanied the struggle of the female majority to attain equal rights. With steady persistence, the fiery feminists have gained a grudging acknowledgement that American society, like others, is dominated by men.

Along with nationalism, racism, and the other ideological influences that have shaped our politics, sexism is an important ingredient of modern society. Consider the following facts regarding the three branches of the national government:

56 Uyematsu, op. cit., p. 9.
57 Yee, loc. cit.

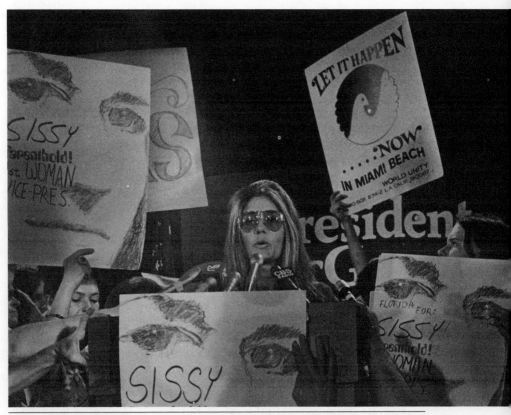

© George W. Gardner, 1972.

Gloria Steinem, in the forefront of the effort to increase women's representation in politics.

1) In early 1972 there was only one woman among the one hundred United States senators (Margaret Chase Smith, R–Maine), and there never have been over twenty women among the 435 members of the House of Representatives;

2) There has never been a woman President or Vice President, and during our entire history only two women have ever served in the President's cabinet.

3) There has never been a woman on the Supreme Court of the United States and of 8750 judges—at all levels of government—only three hundred are women.

In the teaching profession (and it is important to note that most teachers are government employees) women represent 88 percent of the total at the elementary school level, yet only 22 percent of all principals. At the high school and college levels their plight is even worse. Such statistics can be piled up almost endlessly. Women are only 7 percent of doctors, 3 percent of lawyers, and 1 percent of engineers. More depressing is evidence that the situation has been getting worse. In

Figure 18   Median Earnings of Men and Women, by Occupation of
Longest Job Held, During the Year 1969

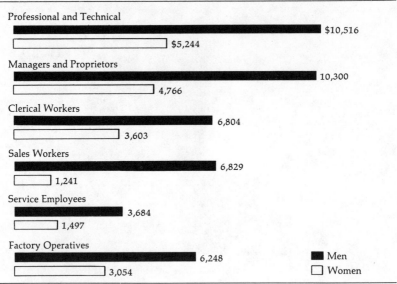

Source: U.S. Bureau of the Census, *Statistical Abstract of the United States: 1971*, p. 229.

the field of dentistry, women have slipped from 3 to 1 percent in the last
half-century and in university teaching from 30 to about 20 percent in
little more than thirty years.[58] From 1961 to 1972, the number of women
in Congress dropped from nineteen to thirteen.

Worst of all, working women make less money than men
who have similar jobs, and the discrepancy is widening. According to the
Women's Bureau of the U.S. Department of Labor, the median income of
working women was 63.9 percent of that of their male counterparts in
1955, but had slipped to 58.9 percent in 1970.[59] Yet the percentage of
women in the total labor force has increased; in 1970, 53 percent of single
women and 41 percent of married women were working outside their
homes.[60]

In 1848 the first organized attempt to improve the status of
women culminated in a women's rights convention in Seneca Falls,
N.Y., but progress was slow, and it was not until 1869 that the right to
vote was first won in Wyoming, and not until 1920 that the Nineteenth
Amendment forbade sex discrimination in voting booths throughout the
nation. After the long decades of effort and agitation—even the arrest of
women who chained themselves to the White House fence—the extension of voting rights to women inaugurated a period of general apathy
regarding the relative roles of the sexes. For forty years only the National

58 *Time*, August 31, 1970, p. 17, and Dorothy Townsend, "Women's 'Lib' Groups Plan
Nationwide Strike," *Los Angeles Times*, August 23, 1970, Sec. C., pp. 1 and 5.
59 *Congressional Quarterly Weekly Report*, March 18, 1972, p. 599.
60 U.S. Bureau of the Census, *Statistical Abstract of the United States: 1971*, p. 212.

Federation of Business and Professional Women's Clubs and a few smaller groups worked actively, although with dignified discretion, for equal opportunity. A turning point came in 1963 with the publication of Betty Friedan's *The Feminine Mystique,* and in 1966 this was followed by the formation of NOW, the National Organization for Women. Within a few years more militant groups such as Bread and Roses, Female Liberation, and SALT (Sisters All Learning Together) were established. Of these, NOW is the largest, least militant, and most broadly based—what some have called the NAACP of women's liberation.

In 1970 the movement gained impetus from the passage of a constitutional amendment by the House of Representatives (approved by the Senate the following year), and from a women's one-day strike. The proposed amendment provides that "equality of rights under the law shall not be denied or abridged . . . on account of sex" and was promptly ratified by a number of states. The strike, primarily symbolic in nature, was called to mark the fiftieth anniversary of women's suffrage, and demanded abolition of abortion laws, free child-care centers, and equal employment at equal pay. In 1971 the National Women's Political Caucus was formed in Washington, D.C., to encourage the election and appointment of more women to public office.

Groups in the Government

Pressure groups are usually thought of as private organizations seeking government action, or trying to prevent it. But governments themselves consist of people and these, like other citizens, often have conflicting interests. The result is that there are pressure groups within the government as well as outside it.

Government employees Among the more important government groups are the American Federation of State, County, and Municipal Employees, the American Federation of Government Employees, and unions for letter carriers, teachers, firefighters, and social workers. Some of these are among the most rapidly growing unions in the AFL-CIO, and tend to be among the most militant. While the right of public employees to strike against the government is the subject of heated dispute, the fact is that they are striking with increasing frequency. Postal workers, school teachers, air traffic controllers, college professors, and occasionally even policemen and nurses have all engaged in work stoppages of one kind or another—sometimes under the guise of mass sick-ins. From 1958 through 1965, there were no more than fifty work stoppages by government employees in any single year, but in 1966 the figure was 142, and in 1968 it climbed to 254.[61]

Level against level Not only do government employees lobby against their employers (with work stoppages only a fraction of that activity), but governments lobby against governments as well. The

61 *American Teacher,* May 1970, p. A–6.

National League of Cities attempts to get increased assistance from the state and national governments, and it is sometimes joined by the Council of State Governments in seeking to influence Washington policy makers. Moreover, a number of states and large cities have lobbyists working for them in Washington.[62] Even at the same level of government, various federal departments and agencies vie with one another for appropriations and other benefits bestowed by legislative bodies.

The Politics of Shared Attitudes

Since life consists of more than money-making, race, and sex, many pressure groups are concerned with the wide variety of other interests that enrich life but may also lead to conflict with others' interests.

Religious groups   The constitutional provision banning the establishment of religion does not prohibit church organizations from attempting to influence public policy. The largest of these is the National Council of Churches, which was formed in 1950 and includes most major Protestant denominations. It has supported reduced American military action abroad and civil rights and Medicare legislation at home. On the conservative side, both theologically and politically, is the American Council of Christian Churches, a much smaller organization. Other Protestant groups are the Women's Christian Temperance Union, long a proponent of the prohibition of alcoholic beverages, and the Friends Committee on National Legislation, a Quaker organization promoting pacifism, foreign economic aid, and a liberal domestic program. Roman Catholics often express their views on political questions through such groups as the Social Action Department of the National Catholic Welfare Conference and Jews, ever alert to the problems of anti-Semitism, through the Anti-Defamation League of B'nai B'rith and the American Jewish Congress. All are predominantly liberal in orientation. While these and many other religious groups are still interested in matters of public morals, most of them now have concerns far broader in scope.[63]

Veterans' groups   After World War I, returning servicemen formed the American Legion, one of the nation's most influential lobbies, with a membership now exceeding two and one-half million. The Veterans of Foreign Wars, about half the size of the Legion, is the second largest such group, with the Disabled American Veterans ranking third. The major objectives of all three involve pensions, educational assistance, and other GI benefits, although the Legion has also lobbied for larger military appropriations, a more militant foreign policy, and a continuation of the Subversive Activities Control Board.

---

62 Congressional Quarterly Service, *Legislators and the Lobbyists,* 2nd ed., (Washington, D.C., Congressional Quarterly, Inc., 1968), p. 63. The states are California, Florida, Illinois, Indiana, Maryland, Massachusetts, New York, Ohio, Pennsylvania, Texas, and West Virginia; the cities are New York, Los Angeles, San Francisco, Boston, Dallas, New Orleans, San Diego, and Seattle.
63 Key, op. cit., pp. 116–21 and Thayer, op. cit., pp. 217–61.

After World War II, two new organizations sprang up, both relatively small, to challenge their older counterparts. They are the moderate AMVETS (American Veterans of World War II and Korea), and the liberal American Veterans Committee. Both have placed more emphasis upon assistance to those in need than on blanket increases to all veterans. There are also smaller ex-servicemen's groups based on the common bonds of religion and ethnic origin: the Catholic War Veterans, Jewish War Veterans, Polish Legion of American Veterans, and Italian-American War Veterans.[64] Finally, the Retired Officers Association has been extremely active in recent years.

Foreign policy groups A wide variety of small but often influential organizations are interested in altering America's international outlook. Some, such as the Fellowship of Reconciliation and the American Friends Service Committee, are committed to pacifism to one degree or another. Others, such as the Council for a Livable World and the Committee for a Sane Nuclear Policy (known often as SANE), have worked for a relaxation of world tensions through disarmament. The United Nations Association and the United World Federalists seek a stronger world organization, and other groups have arisen from passionate opposition to the Vietnam War, including the National Mobilization Committee, The Resistance, and Another Mother for Peace. In contrast to these are the highly nationalistic Daughters of the American Revolution, and other groups with heavy commitments to the interests of some foreign country. Examples include the "China lobby" of the 1950s, dedicated to strengthening the Nationalist Chinese regime on Formosa; the National Council of American-Soviet Friendship in the 1940s; and the German-American Bund of the 1930s.

Ideological groups Organizations like the Communist party, National States' Rights party, and Socialist Workers party seldom nominate candidates for office. When they do, campaign activity is more for propaganda purposes than in genuine hope for victory in the polling booths. Most such groups that are wedded to a particular ideology, however, make no pretense of being separate political parties, but instead either engage in lobbying activity or, occasionally, employ illegal and sometimes violent techniques. At the far right are the Minutemen and the more respectable John Birch Society, nearly obsessed with a fear of internal communist subversion. Closer to the center, but still conservative, are the Americans for Constitutional Action and the Liberty League.

All of these groups have roughly analogous counterparts on the left end of the political spectrum. Most radical are the young Weathermen, with liberal groups such as the Americans for Democratic Action, the Urban Coalition, and Common Cause less distant from the center.

64 Membership figures for these and other groups, along with the addresses of their national headquarters, may be found in *The New York Times Encyclopedic Almanac, 1972,* pp. 334–38 and 576.

Single-issue groups Many other groups have interests involving one or only a few issues. Among these are the Sierra Club and other conservation groups leading the ecological crusade; the American Civil Liberties Union, which concentrates on defending First Amendment rights (but has recently taken left-wing stands on public issues), and public service law firms, such as that organized by Ralph Nader for the defense of consumer interests against careless manufacturers and ineffective government regulation. Still more specialized are the American Cancer Society, National Rifle Association, Gay (homosexual) Liberation Front, American Automobile Association, and countless others. Wherever people are united by a common goal affected by government policy, a pressure group is likely to be found. Altogether, 269 organizations attempting to influence legislation were registered with Congress in 1969.[65]

Although pressure groups are as varied as they are numerous, they usually share certain common characteristics. Many of them are national in scope, but with local affiliates; they often serve their members in other ways than influencing government policy; and they usually work against, though sometimes with, other pressure groups on specific issues. Unfortunately, some are governed rather undemocratically and therefore do not always express the wishes of their membership.

LOBBYING TECHNIQUES

We come now to what is perhaps the most important question of this chapter: How can the groups just described obtain their objectives? There are three broad choices available. Pressure can be exerted through access, confrontation, or violence.

The Politics of Access: Traditional Methods

Most pressure groups in the United States exert influence on government policy by gaining access to government officials. This involves a communication process called lobbying, and the pressure group spokesmen who engage in it are termed lobbyists, although some prefer more elegant titles such as legislative counsels or advocates. The fragmentation of governmental authority inherent in both federalism and the separation of powers gives lobbyists many different points of potential access at which they can direct their influence.

The lobbyists The public image of the lobbyist falls somewhere between that of a dope pusher and a sideshow barker at a carnival. It is almost totally erroneous. Lobbyists are probably as honest (or dishonest) as teachers or butchers, and a good deal better informed about the major issues of the day. They come from all walks of life, but their

---

65 *Congressional Quarterly Guide to Current American Government* (Fall 1970), p. 107.

backgrounds frequently fall into three broad categories: pressure group members who have worked their way up in their organizations, lawyers who have a legal specialty coinciding with the interests of a particular group, and former public officials who have been defeated in seeking reelection.[66] Whatever their background, it is imperative that they know the problems of the groups they represent. A lobbyist for the Farm Bureau, for example, probably knows more about international wheat prices, the average size of farms, and the amount of money spent on agricultural research than most of the members of Congress. Equally important, lobbyists for the larger pressure groups are assisted by Washington office staffs that include statisticians, attorneys, and whatever other specialists may be needed. It would be a foolish lawmaker indeed who did not avail himself of the information that lobbyists are eager to make available about the problems a proposed bill is designed to solve.

In human terms, the most effective kind of access to public officials is through personal trust and friendship, and this results in a considerable amount of socializing between lobbyists and legislators. There is nothing necessarily corrupt about lobbyists taking congressmen out to lunch or to a weekend yachting cruise on the Potomac River. While lobbyists often entertain legislators, their purpose is not bribery but a discussion of pending legislation at greater length and in a more informal atmosphere than is possible in offices or capitol building lobbies (the origin of the term "lobbyist"). In any event, few public officials will trade their votes for a pitcher of martinis or a few days of fun: Most are too honest; some have a higher price. One other point needs to be made. Some lobbyists work only for a single pressure group, often one with which they have had a lifetime association, while others are for hire and may represent as many as twenty-five different organizations.

Legislative contacts   A more significant legislative contact comes through committee testimony or the authorship of bills. In both state legislatures and Congress, bills are referred to appropriate legislative committees, where open public hearings usually will be held; lobbyists are among the most frequent witnesses giving testimony at such hearings. It is there, perhaps, that pressure groups perform their two most valuable services to our political system: They contribute to more enlightened legislation by transmitting their specialized knowledge, and they act as direct channels of communication between the thousands of group members for whom they speak and the most powerful government decision-makers in our national and state capitols. The benefits to the groups themselves are fairly obvious: Committee testimony permits lobbyists to argue for or against the bills in which they are most interested before those legislators most likely to determine passage or defeat.

66 Between 1946 and 1967, twenty-three former senators and ninety former representatives served as lobbyists for one or more pressure groups. *Legislators and the Lobbyists,* op. cit., pp. 45–49.

Occasionally, lobbyists will not only affect the passage of bills, but also will assist in writing them. The Association of American Railroads drafted legislation exempting freight rate agreements from antitrust laws, for example, and unions shaped part of the language written into the National Industrial Recovery Act in 1933. Most legislators, especially those who are not lawyers, do not personally write the bills they introduce. They are too busy, or lack the technical vocabulary required. As a result, even though the idea for some new legislation is their own, they may seek assistance in drafting the exact language from sympathetic lobbyists who have been urging such legislation anyway.

Campaign contributions   Much of the money required for political campaigns comes from pressure groups. They contribute not because it will guarantee that the candidate, if elected, will always vote the way they wish, but because it will at least assure access to him. Few lawmakers slam down the receiver when they get a phone call from the group that contributed $5000 to the last campaign.

There are, however, certain general principles that govern financial contributions from pressure groups. For one, help is given to individual candidates rather than political party organizations. The reason for this is that lobbies wish to retain some influence regardless of which party controls the government. In the 1970 congressional races, the Committee on Political Education (COPE), speaking for the AFL-CIO, endorsed 341 Democrats, one Independent, and nineteen Republicans.[67] In a few instances, the same pressure group may quietly contribute funds to two opposing candidates, if the views of both are acceptable, just to cover its bets.

Another rule governing campaign contributions is that pressure groups support their friends, rather than trying to buy off their enemies. There are two reasons for this. If a contribution is made in the hope of changing the vote of a legislator on some important bill, then the fine line between bribery and campaign support becomes even more blurred and criminal prosecution might result. A second consideration is that it often costs little more to elect a candidate who agrees with you than to bribe one who doesn't.

A last principle of financial donation is to give preference to the incumbent when in doubt. He has already compiled a voting record, which is a better indication of his intentions than the promises of the challenger, and he usually has a better chance of winning simply because he has the greater publicity accorded to one already in office. Moreover, his experience and seniority will probably make him a more effective ally than a green, first-term legislator.

Mobilizing the public   In addition to legislative contacts and campaign contributions, pressure groups try to influence government officials indirectly through the manipulation of public opinion. This

---

67 *The Washington Lobby* (Washington, D.C.: Congressional Quarterly, Inc., 1971), pp. 49–50.

can be done by urging group members to write or wire their state legislators or congressmen, asking them to vote a certain way on a particular bill. In 1971 various environmental protection groups, led by Friends of the Earth, launched such a campaign to defeat the appropriation of additional money to finance the costly supersonic transport plane. Senator Clinton Anderson (D–N.M.), a former supporter of the SST, changed his vote because, he said, "I read my mail."[68] Or a more ambitious attempt can be made to gain support from the broader public through advertising campaigns in the mass media, usually designed by professional public relations firms. These appeals are more often calculated to win general sympathy than to influence action on a particular bill.

Executive and judicial influence Lobbying is usually associated with attempts to influence the passage of laws, but it also may involve access to the executive agencies that enforce laws and the courts that apply them. Pressure group influence upon executive or administrative officials seems most pronounced in the case of business and professional organizations. Television representatives keep a close eye on the Federal Communications Commission, for example, especially when they are under attack. In 1971 CBS broadcast a controversial documentary critical of Defense Department public relations programs. The FCC, in this instance, defended the network when it was accused of distortion and bias by certain congressmen and administration officials. The American Medical Association is widely credited with preventing the appointment of a liberal doctor, John F. Knowles, to the post of Assistant Secretary of the Department of Health, Education and Welfare in 1969.

Lobbyists pay only a little less attention to the judicial branch. Few political battles in recent history have equaled the intensity of the successful attempts by labor unions and civil rights groups to block Senate confirmation of two of President Nixon's appointments to the Supreme Court. AFL-CIO President George Meany denounced the nomination of Court of Appeals Judge G. Harrold Carswell as a "slap in the face" to blacks, and the lobbyist for the NAACP gave highly critical testimony before the Senate Judiciary Committee considering the appointment. Most lobbying activity directed toward the courts, however, entails the submission of written arguments known as *amicus curiae* ("friend of the court") briefs by parties not directly involved in a case. These are often used to persuade judges that a particular law or executive act is unconstitutional. Two pressure groups have enjoyed noteworthy success in this respect: the NAACP in its struggle against racial segregation and, to a lesser extent, the ACLU in its opposition to restrictions upon individual freedom.[69] Between 1945 and 1960, the Supreme Court ruled as the NAACP wished in fifty cases, including one that declared

68 Ibid., p. 108.
69 Henry J. Abraham, *The Judicial Process* (N.Y.: Oxford University Press, Inc., 1962), pp. 209–12.

racially discriminatory real estate deeds to be unenforceable. In this one, no fewer than twenty-five *amicus curiae* briefs were accepted by the Court. In 1972 the ACLU was successful in persuading a Court of Appeals to strike down a provision of the Hatch Act which barred government employees from engaging in campaign politics.

Reservations and regulations The case for the traditional lobbying techniques described above seems to be fairly persuasive. They contribute to the democratic ideal of popular control over government by providing a link between millions of group members and government officials; they help to educate legislators; and in addition they can infuse fresh ideas into the stagnant waters of stand-pat politics. Yet access politics poses some real perils. While the power of most pressure groups tends to be counterbalanced by the power of others, with some opposing each measure that others favor, this is not always the case. Some interests don't get represented, and others get overrepresented. Even when opposing groups are equally well organized, one side is often much better financed than its opposition.

There are no foolproof remedies for these problems, in part because of the First Amendment's guarantee of the right to petition the government. But Congress has shown some sensitivity to the situation.

Figure 19   Pressure Groups Spending $50,000 per Year for Six or More Years (1946–1966) on Lobbying Activity

Group	Number of Years
AFL-CIO	20
American Legion	20
American Farm Bureau Federation	18
National Housing Conference	17
United Federation of Postal Clerks	17
National Assn. of Real Estate Boards	15
U.S. Savings and Loan League	15
International Assn. of Machinists, District Lodge No. 44	14
National Farmers Union	14
American Medical Assn.	13
Assn. of American Railroads	13
National Assn. of Electric Companies	13
National Assn. of Letter Carriers	12
National Education Assn.	11
American Trucking Assns.	10
National Assn. of Home Builders	10
International Brotherhood of Teamsters	8
National Federation of Independent Business	7
Brotherhood of Locomotive Firemen and Enginemen	6
Central Arizona Project Assn.	6

Source: *Legislators and the Lobbyists,* 2nd ed., (Washington, D.C., Congressional Quarterly, Inc., 1968), p. 34. Reprinted by permission of Congressional Quarterly, Inc. Omitted are groups that did not report spending over $50,000 since 1959.

It has prohibited the use of corporation profits and union dues for direct campaign contributions, and it passed a Regulation of Lobbying Act in 1946 which requires lobbyists to register and file financial reports four times a year. Although this act has many loopholes and few enforcement provisions, it brought to light far more data regarding traditional pressure group politics than had ever before been available.

The AMA alone spent over one million dollars in each of three years, and the AFL-CIO, Farm Bureau, Committee for Constitutional Government, and National Association of Electric Companies each have spent more than half a million dollars in a single year.[70] Access politics is an expensive business.

The Politics of Confrontation: Lobbies in the Streets

When traditional lobbying seems to work so well, why would certain groups resort to raucous street demonstrations which often entail confrontations with the police? One answer is that the usual pressure group tactics are sometimes unsuccessful,[71] and another lies in the ideological preferences of specific groups.

Challenge and change Confrontation techniques may seem desirable if a group is small, poor, or disenfranchised. If it is small, few lawmakers will pay much attention to what it wants. This preoccupation with numbers is one of the characteristics of a democratic society. Election statistics or group membership figures reveal quantity rather than quality. Thus, 51 percent of the voters with a mild preference for a particular candidate will defeat an opponent strongly favored by the other 49 percent.

Yet a group can sometimes compensate for its meager numbers by dramatic actions that demonstrate the intensity of its convictions. To do this successfully, it must gain a wide audience for its grievances and prick the conscience of the majority. It must appeal, in other words, to a kind of moral authority. Thus, although opposition to the Vietnam war was small in 1967, a series of rallies, teach-ins, and other activities was instrumental in attracting wide television and newspaper publicity that by 1968 had helped reverse the tide of public opinion.

If a group has sufficient funds, even if it is small, it stands a good chance of utilizing the old-fashioned type of access lobbying with some effectiveness. A poor group, on the other hand, regardless of its size, is forced to rely upon dramatic demonstrations—what has been called the politics of confrontation—to influence government policy. Vivid illustrations of such actions were the sit-ins and mass marches employed by the civil rights movement of the early 1960s, and the fasts of Cesar Chavez, leader of the farm workers, in later years.

70 *Legislators and the Lobbyists,* op. cit., pp. 28–31.
71 Lewis Anthony Dexter, *How Organizations are Represented in Washington* (Indianapolis: The Bobbs-Merrill Co., Inc., 1969), especially Ch. 7.

George Ballis, Black Star.

Cesar Chavez leads agricultural workers in a strike.

A third kind of group that usually finds access politics ineffective is one that is disenfranchised—whose members cannot vote. Recognizing this, women demanding the right to vote in the early part of this century utilized picketing and widely publicized protest demonstrations to win the sympathy of those who were already enfranchised. Students, many of whom were too young to go to the polls, have used similar techniques in trying to advance their causes.

Change has come about in our political system not only through pressures exerted in the private offices of lobbyists and legislators, but also in response to street demonstrations, sit-ins, strikes, and fasts. Such activities counterbalance quantities of people and dollars with personal commitment, risk, and exposure. It is unlikely that the Civil Rights Act of 1964 could have been enacted without them.

Civil disobedience The significance of confrontation politics lies in its possible effectiveness for groups that find the more orthodox methods of access politics to be impossible or unproductive. One form that confrontation politics may take is civil disobedience—a deliberate violation of the law that entails nonviolent acts designed to bring about social change and usually involving willingness to accept whatever punishment the law may prescribe for the disobedience.

Civil disobedience, both as a theoretical concept and as a consciously contrived tactic, owes much to Henry David Thoreau. In 1849 the American essayist published a short book, *On Civil Disobedience*, justifying his refusal to pay a tax in protest against the Mexican War. In it he argued that it was morally wrong to obey an unjust law and insisted that the citizen must measure government policy against the dictates of his own conscience. Justifiably or not, civil disobedience has played a supporting role on the American political stage. The successful sit-down strikes of auto workers in 1937 were carried on in defiance of a court injunction. More recently, this tactic was popularized by Rev. Martin Luther King, who was inspired in part by the example of Mahatma Gandhi in India. CORE, SNCC, and the SCLC defied segregation laws in the struggle for civil rights; thousands of young men have chosen federal penetentiaries rather than the U.S. Army. Nothing dramatizes the depths of one's convictions more convincingly than the willingness to risk imprisonment for them.

The Politics of Violence: From the Barrel of a Gun

The outcome of the 1968 presidential race may well have been decided on June 5 of that year—five months before the general election. It was then that Sirhan B. Sirhan assassinated Senator Robert F. Kennedy on the night of his victory in California's presidential primary. A single bullet nullified millions of ballots.

A decade of death Senator Kennedy's death marked the culmination of one of the bloodiest decades in our history, and led President Johnson to appoint a Commission on the Causes and Prevention of Violence. There was much for it to study. Since 1960 Medgar Evers, head of the Mississippi NAACP, President John F. Kennedy, Malcolm X (leading "Black Power" spokesman) George Lincoln Rockwell (American Nazi party boss) and Martin Luther King, Jr., had also been killed. Race riots had left thirty-four dead in Los Angeles, twenty-three in Newark, and forty-three in Detroit. Dozens of other cities were ravaged by similar, smaller riots, and the 1968 Democratic National Convention brought bloody encounters to the streets of Chicago. Violence, both political and nonpolitical was increasing steadily. By 1969 the murder rate had reached 7.2 per 100,000 people in the United States, compared with 3.3 in West Germany, 2.6 in Israel, 2.2 in Japan, 0.6 in Sweden, and 0.4 in England and Wales.[72] A comparative international study revealed that in the 1960s the U.S. ranked twenty-fourth among

72 *The New York Times Encyclopedic Almanac, 1972*, p. 231.

114 nations in "total magnitude of strife" and first among the seventeen Western democracies.[73]

The 1970s were off to a tragic start with the deaths of two students in Jackson, Mississippi, and four at Kent State University in Ohio, at the hands of law enforcement officers. A few months later, four persons, including a judge, were killed in a jail break attempt in northern California, and forty-two died in the Attica, New York, prison revolt. In 1972 Governor George Wallace came within inches of death from another assassin's bullet.

The quest for causes   What has gone wrong? How can this tragic toll be explained in a nation whose Constitution is designed, in part, "to insure domestic tranquility?" The answers are entangled in a complex web of history and contemporary social movements. Some of the historical roots of American violence may be our revolutionary heritage, the brutal legacy of slavery, our lawless frontier tradition, the attempt to exterminate native Indians, frictions generated by ethnic and racial diversity, unusually intense conflict in the annals of labor-management relations, and the population pressures accompanying urbanization. American violence has also been explained in terms of the polarization of opinion regarding the Vietnam war, the relative ease with which guns can be acquired, increasing permissiveness in bringing up children, the lurid depiction of violence in the mass media, a rapid rise in the aspirations of the disadvantaged, the psychological necessity of oppressed peoples to prove their manhood, archaic prison conditions, and the fears and frustrations entailed in rapid social change.

Some of these factors are peculiarly American while others are characteristic of much of the modern world. Those that seem indigenous suggest that violence is a product of cultural conditioning in the United States, while the more universal factors suggest that human beings are biologically equipped with hostile impulses that make them, along with ants and rats, one of the most violent species in the animal kingdom. Although the human capacity for cruelty is terrifying, its potential for compassion and reason is encouraging. The challenge lies in creating a culture more conducive to the latter than the former. Whatever its causes or motivation, the resort to brute force challenges the authority of government, the stability of society, and the fundamental democratic doctrine of human dignity.

From a practical political standpoint, a crucial issue is this: Does violence work? It obviously succeeded in securing independence from England by the Revolution and in preserving the nation while freeing the slaves by the Civil War. Yet in these situations the tactical advantages or military strength were on the winning side. When those who resort to violence are outgunned, outmanned, and out-maneuvered—militant students or ghetto blacks, for example—they lose.

73 Hugh Davis Graham and Ted Robert Gurr, *Violence in America* (N.Y.: A Signet Book, The New American Library, Inc., 1969), pp. 775–76. This is an official report to the presidential commission on violence.

On college campuses, it is the students who usually get killed. In big city riots, it is the blacks who suffer 90 percent of the casualties.

Yet to a great extent, the politics of violence remains a mystery not subject to simple analysis. In totalitarian states such as the Soviet Union, it is almost certain to be totally unsuccessful; in free societies such as ours, ironically, it may result in some beneficial change. In both instances, the violent ones will die, but in America, their death commands attention, however briefly, to the grievances which led to such terrible acts of desperation. Who can say whether the voting age was lowered and student freedom increased because—or in spite—of youthful acts of rebellion? Who can be sure that educational and job opportunities for blacks have been expanded because—or in spite—of the bloodshed on city sidewalks? But if violence buys progress, it does so at a price both tragic and incalculably high. In addition to death, it tends to produce a backlash of resentment and repression directed against those whom the public believes to have instigated it; freedom and justice then become trampled in the rush for law and order. Moreover, most violence is counterproductive, even when it may appear successful. Perhaps this is because it brutalizes, or at least desensitizes, those who resort to it. Thus, the French Revolution led to a Reign of Terror and the Russian Revolution produced the Stalin dictatorship. Violence has an insatiable appetite, devouring friend and foe alike. It may come to liberate, but it stays to dominate.

Chapter **7**

Government by the People
Political Parties

I have great confidence in the common sense of mankind in general.

Thomas Jefferson

People cannot expect to get what they want from government simply by supporting their favorite pressure groups. Important as these organizations are, citizens can maximize their political influence only by also engaging in political party activity and voting as intelligently as they can.

PARTY SYSTEMS

Political parties play a crucial role in governments all over the world. Nevertheless, they aren't even mentioned in the Constitution; Washington and Madison opposed the formation of parties as a matter of principle, fearing that people might develop greater loyalty to them than to the nation as a whole. Yet even before Washington left the presidency, the seeds of the first two parties had already been planted.

The Functions of Parties

Political parties would not have lasted so long or spread so widely if they did not perform useful functions that are central to the democratic process. These deserve enumeration.

Candidate recruitment When national party conventions meet to select candidates for President and Vice President, the typical nominating speaker traditionally refers to his favorite as "the man who . . ." will do wondrous things, without mentioning his name until the end of the speech. This oratory points up one of the major functions of political parties: They act as political talent scouts, nominating the candidates who will run in the general election. If the parties did not, the voters might be confronted with incredible confusion and perhaps dozens of candidates for some offices but none for the others.

Figure 20   Pressure Groups and Parties: How They Differ

1. Pressure groups are chiefly interested in influencing government policies.	1. Parties are chiefly interested in controlling government personnel.
2. Pressure groups aid any person or party who promotes their goals.	2. Parties select candidates, conduct campaigns, and staff government.
3. Citizens may support several pressure groups.	3. Citizens support one party or are independent.
4. Pressure groups are not accountable for actions to general public.	4. Parties are accountable for actions to general public at elections.
5. Pressure groups represent minority factions concerned with specific policies related to a few interests.	5. Parties seek majorities comprised of aggregations which must achieve broad compromises related to many interests.
6. Pressure groups devise and publicize new policy proposals.	6. Parties advocate or carry out policies already popular.
7. Pressure group organization is subject to few democratic legal controls.	7. Party organization is subject to many democratic legal controls.
8. Pressure group unity is usually based on shared interests and characteristics within population segments (women, factory workers, etc.).	8. Party unity is usually based on shared ambitions and broad attitudes within geographic areas (districts, states, etc.).
9. Pressure groups operate by many techniques sometimes involving extra-legal demonstrations.	9. Parties operate almost entirely by seeking election victories.

Campaign conduct   Parties not only select nominees for office but also organize their campaigns. They obtain the money for campaign advertising and help determine campaign strategies. All this makes democracy exciting, and in the process of generating so much heat, sometimes light is shed on the major issues confronting the nation, although most candidates tend to be as vague as possible to avoid antagonizing voters.

Policy alternatives and peaceful change   One major problem confronting every political system is how to change government policies (or personnel) without resorting to bloody rebellion. When free elections permit a choice between two or more political parties, that problem may be largely solved, especially if the parties represent genuine policy alternatives. When the voters chose McKinley, the Republican, over Bryan, the Democrat, in the presidential election of 1896 they were opting for high tariffs and the gold standard, and when they elected

Lyndon Johnson rather than Barry Goldwater in 1964, they chose civil rights legislation, Medicare, federal aid to education, and (they were told) nonintervention in Vietnam. Thus party competition at the polling booths permits the voters a peaceful choice among policies as well as personalities; it then enables a peaceful transfer of power.

Sometimes in the U.S., however, the major parties pursue a middle course so desperately that their policy pronouncements are virtually indistinguishable. They often do this because they believe the voters favor a moderate position; they may also do it when social conflicts are acute and the parties seek to reconcile these conflicts by a compromise satisfactory to a majority.

The existence of competing parties also helps to keep them fairly honest. In their competition for votes, each watches the other, perhaps less like a hawk than a vulture. The result is a system of political checks and balances which is just as important as the governmental one.

Policy coordination   The separation of powers among various agencies of the national government, and the division of powers between the national and state governments can cause friction and rivalry. But if several governmental branches or levels are in the hands of the same party, that party can help bridge the gaps among them and coordinate government activities on behalf of the same policies. On the other hand, if different parties dominate different parts of government, competition among them may result in a political deadlock, as happened on welfare reform and other issues involving President Nixon and the Democratic-controlled Congress. Vigorous action, therefore, usually requires the legislative and executive branches under the control of the same party.

Citizen involvement   Political parties provide an institutional link between the voters and the government. Because their committees and conventions include both public officials and private citizens, parties, like pressure groups, give people some direct and personal access to the centers of governmental power. At the same time, they provide government officials additional opportunities to gauge public opinion and strengthen their popular support. Parties also link government and people in the imperfect but important mechanism by which government is held accountable to the citizens.

Latent functions   Finally, some less apparent functions of parties are of importance. They define problems and structure the views of voters who identify with them. Likewise they provide a relevant reference for the political behavior of individual citizens who seek government services, jobs, or contracts.

The Number of Parties

Much is revealed about the stability and the democratic character of a modern political system by the number of parties which operate within it. We can distinguish three variations.

One-party politics   Some nations, such as the U.S.S.R. and Spain, have only one major party because it is illegal to form another one. Obviously, choice, accountability, and free political activity are minimal in such nations. Occasionally, however, one party will dominate the government because of peculiar historical circumstances and in spite of the existence of several other weak parties. This is the case in Mexico, India, and parts of the United States.

Two-party politics   Taken as a whole, America has a two-party system. But this does not mean that there are only two parties, nor that this situation prevails to an equal degree everywhere in the nation. It does mean that only the Republican and Democratic parties have a realistic chance of obtaining congressional majorities or electing a President.

How has such a situation come about? For one thing, an example of a two-party system had been established in Great Britain even before the Revolution. For another, congressmen and most state legislators are elected by simple pluralities rather than majorities, from *single-member* rather than from larger *multi-member* districts. As a result, candidates who finish second or third lose, which tends to discourage vigorous campaigns by small third parties. (By contrast, in some Western European nations where three or four candidates are elected from each of several large, multi-member districts, small parties have a chance to elect a lawmaker who finishes third or fourth.) Finally, the Constitution requires that the President be elected by a majority vote (over 50 percent) in the electoral college, and this also discourages small parties.

Once established, our two-party system has been sustained both by the habits of the people and by practical political realities. Most voters are Republicans or Democrats largely because their parents were. The relative strength of the two leading parties varies substantially from place to place. In only about half the states do they compete on a relatively equal basis,[1] although recent trends seem to indicate growing Democratic strength in such hitherto Republican strongholds as Maine and Vermont, while Republicans have begun to crack the traditionally Democratic "solid South." Nonetheless, a survey of the party affiliations of state legislators in 1971 revealed that political systems in many states are still close to the one-party variety. The Republicans dominated legislatures 116 to 49 in Kansas, and 118 to 62 in Vermont. And if the South is no longer solid, it remains remarkably firm. There, Democrats controlled state legislatures by a margin of 139 to 2 in Alabama, 142 to 2 in Louisiana, and 169 to 12 in Texas.[2] In presidential races, however, neither party can take the South for granted.

Most congressional districts reveal a lack of genuine competition. Two leading scholars have estimated that from 75 to 80 percent of

1 V. O. Key, Jr., *Politics, Parties, and Pressure Groups,* 5th ed. (N.Y.: Thomas Y. Crowell Company, 1964), pp. 284–87.
2 *Congressional Quarterly Guide to Current American Government* (Spring 1971), p. 18.

all seats in the House of Representatives are "safe" for one party or the other.[3] Yet the central fact remains that the two-party system has dominated national politics during nearly all of our history. As state and local issues become more similar in all sections of the country, this trend will probably spread to these levels.

Multi-party politics Since there are numerous possible opinions on political issues, many nations where there is considerable personal freedom have three or more relatively strong parties. Multi-party systems have a major disadvantage, however. By fragmenting political groups along doctrinaire lines, political compromise is more difficult, and an unstable situation often results in which no single party has a legislative majority. Hence several parties form an uneasy coalition in order to pass laws or support the executive effectively. In some parliamentary systems, such as Italy, this has caused frequent changes in executive leadership.

The Types of Parties

Aside from sheer habit, why do voters support a particular party? As a partial answer, three major types of parties, each with a distinctive appeal, may be identified.

Charismatic parties Some political parties are formed largely to support a popular and magnetic candidate—one who is said to have "charisma." That quality is an intangible one, entailing the capacity to inspire confidence and enthusiastic devotion among large numbers of people. It is hard to define, but, like sex appeal, most people know it when they see it.

Few American parties have been primarily charismatic. Those that have come closest to it, such as Theodore Roosevelt's short-lived Progressive party in 1912, have been unable to get their leaders elected. Nevertheless, there is no doubt that both Franklin D. Roosevelt in the 1930s and Dwight D. Eisenhower in the 1950s possessed some charismatic appeal. It may well be that charisma will be more important in the future than in the past because of the dramatic vividness with which television can project the personalities of leading candidates into millions of living rooms. There is a danger in this, for charismatic leadership, like romantic love, can obscure real issues and divert attention from the hard problems ahead.

Doctrinaire parties While a few parties have rested on charismatic leadership, many have been based on a political principle, doctrine, or ideology. Thus, the German Nazi party was founded on the doctrine of anti-Semitic Aryan supremacy, communist parties on anti-

---

3 William J. Keefe and Morris S. Ogul, *The American Legislative Process: Congress and the States* (Englewood Cliffs, N.J.: Prentice-Hall, Inc., 1968) pp. 109–14.

capitalist Marxism, the Prohibition party on opposition to alcoholic beverages, and socialist parties on a belief that certain industries should be nationalized (owned and operated by the government).

The major political parties in the United States are not doctrinaire. Both include citizens as well as public officials who hold widely diverse points of view. Nonetheless, the Democrats, with the notable exception of many in the South, tend to be vaguely liberal in orientation. Either they may be slightly more permissive with respect to personal behavior, or they may favor a larger role for the government in overcoming poverty or prejudice, or both. But many bread-and-butter Democrats are conservative on such issues as abortion and drugs. Republicans, in not-so-sharp contrast, are generally conservative. They are inclined to favor tighter controls on personal morality and to stress the importance of individual responsibility rather than government action in overcoming social problems. Since most Americans are nonideological moderates, it is widely held that if either party becomes too doctrinaire, as when Barry Goldwater espoused a rigidly conservative brand of Republicanism in 1964, the other party will probably win. Many attributed George McGovern's defeat in 1972 to his excessively liberal image.

Broker parties If American parties are primarily neither charismatic nor doctrinaire, what are they? The answer is phrased in different ways. They are pragmatic, interested in winning elections; they are consensus oriented, attempting to gain enough agreement on as few issues among as many groups as is required to get a majority of the votes; they are willing to "rise above principle" in order to get into office; they are flexible, bending their positions with the changing winds of public opinion.

In other words, American parties are broker parties. A broker is essentially a middleman, one who helps people get together for a mutually beneficial deal on which he too can make a profit. Thus real estate brokers bring buyers and sellers together and stockbrokers bring investors and business corporations together. In this sense, the Republican and Democratic parties are political brokers, compromising diverse and often conflicting demands. The Democratic coalition welded together in the 1930s is a classic example of broker politics. It included blacks, Southerners, the unions, urban ethnic groups, and the big city political "bosses." Each party tries to assemble a combination of voters from various geographic sections, from ethnic and religious groups, and from diverse occupations, ages, and income categories that will add up to a majority on election day. To do this, they will put together as attractive a "package" as they can, including as charismatic a candidate as possible and as many proposed government programs as necessary without binding themselves to a specific ideological principle.

A number of important results stem from the broker nature of the two major parties:

1) Since both Republicans and Democrats usually appeal to

a wide variety of groups, they tend to unify the country, rather than to divide it as Washington and Madison had feared.

2) In their search for a majority of votes, the two parties often appeal to the same groups (especially small businessmen, farmers, and skilled workers), and thus the party programs may sound very much alike. This Tweedledum and Tweedledee effect has often led third parties to argue, with some justification but little success, that they provide the only meaningful alternatives.

3) On the other hand, the similarities between the Republicans and Democrats have persuaded many pressure groups that they can work reasonably well with either party and therefore need not form one of their own.

4) Whenever a new third party has increased rapidly in popularity, especially when it has received more votes than had been expected, at least one of the two major parties has shifted its position closer to that of the brash young upstart, thereby thwarting the growth of the latter.

5) The most frequently criticized effect of the broker nature of American parties is that it makes it more difficult to hold the government responsible to the people. Because this serious charge involves a central mechanism for maintaining democracy, it deserves a careful analysis.

Democracy, Responsibility, and Parties

By definition, a democracy should provide a government responsible to a majority of the people. But the word "responsible" has a double meaning. It means that the people should be able to hold government officials *accountable* for their conduct, reelecting them if they deserve it and "turning the rascals out" if they don't. It also means that government officials should be *reliable* in the sense that they do what the people expected them to do when they elected them. But genuine responsibility, in terms of either accountability or reliability, is hard to come by in American government.

Accountability   The principal difficulty in holding elected officials accountable is that there are simply too many of them. In the 1970 general election, the present author was confronted with a ballot listing thirty-six candidates running for eleven national and state offices, plus four more seeking local judgeships. He knew nothing about sixteen of the candidates, except for their party affiliations listed on the ballots. For the judicial candidates, he lacked even that knowledge. Unfortunately, this situation is somewhat typical of conditions throughout the country. Voters are more than voters; they are also employees, family members, bowlers, Elks, and stamp collectors. They have neither the time, the information, nor the desire to hold all public officials accountable.

Reliability   The failure of public officials to be reliable may be caused by unrealistic voter demands or by conflicting pressures on the official. For instance, the voters may expect more government programs and also a tax cut, or the newly elected congressman may discover that a tax cut will truly endanger important government activities. But if the congressman votes for a tax cut, it is still possible that such a bill will be defeated in either the House or Senate or vetoed by the President. Even if the taxes imposed by the national government were reduced, this could be more than offset by increases in state taxes.

The point is that power is so widely dispersed among so many officials in American government that no one of them (with the possible exception of the President in the area of international relations) is easily able to accomplish what a majority of voters want done. The elected official is thwarted in his attempts to carry out the wishes of the people by at least four characteristics of our political system: bicameral legislatures, allowing one house to oppose the other; the separation of powers, permitting one branch to frustrate the efforts of another; federalism, enabling the national and state governments to pass the buck back and forth so as to create a political stalemate; and the constitutional principles of individual freedom and legal equality thwarting the intentions of an intolerant majority. Those who framed the Constitution, fearful of concentrating too much power in the hands of too few people, distributed authority so widely that few officials can fairly be charged with unreliability for not doing what they said they would try to do.

Party responsibility   Since the voter is expected to elect more officials than he possibly can keep track of, and since power is fragmented among them so as to pit one against another, many argue that the political parties are responsible for government action. If particular officials are not fully responsible for what finally happens, why not hold the winning party at the last election responsible? Although voters may know little of the individual candidates for whom they vote, at least the ballot usually indicates the party to which those candidates belong.

But complete party responsibility would require that all candidates of the same party favor the same government policies, and that there be some methods of party discipline to persuade all party members to vote the same way on important bills. For broker parties, by definition consisting of loose coalitions embracing widely divergent views, this situation simply does not exist. In 1967, for instance, *Congressional Quarterly* reported that a conservative coalition of Republicans and southern Democrats in the House of Representatives repeatedly defeated the Democratic President, Lyndon Johnson, on many of his key proposals. This occurred in the face of a sixty-one member Democratic majority in that chamber. Although southern Democrats were most notable in their defection to the opposition party, eight northern Democrats voted with the Republicans on at least 54 percent of the crucial roll calls.[4]

One is forced to conclude that substantial numbers of voters

4 *Congressional Quarterly Guide to Current American Government* (Spring 1968), pp. 88 and 91.

are probably frustrated by voting for Republican candidates, hoping for a conservative government, or for Democratic candidates, hoping for a liberal one. The major parties in American politics impose no effective loyalty tests, nor can they control their own members.

Yet to emphasize legislators who vote against their party's majority tends to distort the picture. The fact remains that most Democrats are liberal and most Republicans are conservative, and one major survey shows this distinction to be considerably more pronounced among party leaders than among the rank and file party members.[5] Were there no ideological differences whatever between the parties, candidates might just as well run without party labels. But democracy requires some basis for determining what—as well as whom—most people prefer. Imperfect as it is, the party system permits us to conclude, after most elections, that a majority prefers either the conservative ideas propounded by most leading Republicans or the liberal ideas advocated by most prominent Democrats. And when, in the same election, the voters choose a Republican President and a Democratic-controlled Congress— as they did in 1956 and again in 1968 and 1972—the only victor is a party system that is essentially irresponsible.

PARTIES IN AMERICA

As we have seen, two major parties have been dominant in America during most of its history. We must now examine their evolution and organization.

Party Origins: The Major Parties

The first important parties were the Federalists, led by Alexander Hamilton and John Adams, and the anti-Federalists, or Democratic-Republicans, championed by Thomas Jefferson and James Madison. The Federalists favored a strong national government, drew support from commercial interests, and were pro-English, while the Democratic-Republicans favored state power, were supported by farmers, and were pro-French.

By the early 1820s, initial party loyalties had disintegrated, largely because of a split among the Federalists regarding the War of 1812. The next decade witnessed a new political alignment in which the supporters of Andrew Jackson constituted what is now known as the Democratic party, while his opponents formed what was called the Whig party. As the Civil War moved ominously closer, the issue of whether to permit slavery in the western territories killed the Whigs, who were badly divided on the matter. The northern ex-Whigs were chiefly responsible for the present-day Republican party. And so the situation

5 Herbert McClosky, et al., "Issue Conflict and Consensus among Party Leaders and Followers," American Political Science Review 54 (June 1960): 406–27.

remains, more than a century later. So entrenched was the dominance of the two parties in 1972 that only two of the 535 members of Congress had been elected without the benefit of nomination by either party.

Between 1861 and 1933, the Republicans occupied the White House for fifty-six years and the Democrats, during the administrations of Grover Cleveland and Woodrow Wilson, for only sixteen. Since 1933, however, Democratic Presidents have held office for twenty-eight years and Republicans, led by Dwight Eisenhower and Richard Nixon, for twelve. Democrats boast of guiding the nation through two World Wars and the Great Depression, while enacting legislation providing for minimum hourly wages, union recognition, pensions and Medicare through the social security program, guaranteed price supports for farm crops, and enforcement of black voting rights. The "Grand Old Party" (GOP), as the younger Republican party is inappropriately called, claims credit for ending slavery, acquiring Alaska, Hawaii, and Puerto Rico, building the Panama Canal, passing pure food and conservation laws, ending the Korean conflict, constructing the St. Lawrence Seaway, and withdrawing ground combat forces from Vietnam.

In the 1972 campaign most Democratic candidates argued for income supplements for the poor, national health insurance, closing tax loopholes for corporations, and reduced military expenditures, while Republicans generally defended the Nixon program of revenue sharing with state and local governments, a high level of defense spending, expanded aid for law enforcement, and opposition to compulsory school busing for racial integration. On a few issues, the two parties offered clear-cut alternatives, but on many more their differences were the more customary disagreements about the relative priority of various national needs.

Neither party has remained entirely loyal to the principles for which it initially stood. Broker parties, if they are to survive, cannot afford that moral luxury. They must be flexible, often in the face of strong challenges from minor third parties.

Winning Causes and Losing Candidates: Minor Parties

Like pressure groups, third parties in America have influenced our politics in a number of important respects. Most important, they have been among the first to champion new causes. Many of these were later adopted by the Republicans and Democrats—once their popularity had been demonstrated. The People's (or Populist) party, perhaps the most significant minor party in our history, provides the best example. Formed in 1892, the Populists were among the first to advocate the popular election of U.S. senators, women's suffrage, a flexible expansion of currency, and other liberal reforms. When they won three governorships and elected half a dozen congressmen, mostly at the

Figure 21   Party Platforms, 1972
How Some of the Republican and Democratic Planks Contrast

	Democrats	Republicans
Vietnam War	Immediate complete withdrawal of all U.S. forces in Indochina, all P.O.W.'s to be returned. No more military aid to Indochina.	Withdrawal 4 months after internationally supervised cease-fire in effect in Indochina and all prisoners returned.
Amnesty	Amnesty after war to draft resisters who refused to serve.	No amnesty to those who evaded military service.
Defense	Reduce military spending where consistent with national security and reduce overseas forces and bases.	No meat-ax slashes, but prudent reductions in defense spending; will not let America become second-class power.
Foreign Policy	Reemphasis on UN and Congress. Help to Israel; pursue with U.S.S.R. mutual force reductions in Europe; reduce military aid in Latin America; opposition to policies of regimes in Rhodesia, Greece, Portugal, and South Africa.	Maintenance of strength in Europe and Mediterranean, but seek agreement with Warsaw Pact nations for mutual reduction of forces; increased contacts with China and Eastern · Europe; help to Israel; opposition to policies of regime in Cuba.
Taxes	Tax reform to distribute cost of government more fairly, close loopholes such as special favors for oil industry, capital gains, fast depreciation, and expense accounts.	Tax reform to include revenue sharing, fair distribution of tax burden, simplification, but no sharp increase in middle-income taxes.
Welfare	Income security program, guaranteeing an income substantially above poverty level. Expansion of public employment to guarantee jobs for all.	No government guaranteed income. Reform of welfare system, provision of day care.
Labor	Minimum wage of $2.50; no compulsory arbitration.	Discourage location of plants in foreign countries.
Education	Increased federal aid and equalization of spending among school districts.	Channeling aid to education so as to enable parental choice of public or nonpublic schools, as through income tax credits.
Desegregation and Busing	Desegregation to be pursued by various means including busing.	End *de jure* segregation, but no busing for racial balance.
Health Care	Establish system of universal national health insurance to cover all Americans.	No nationalized compulsory health insurance. Support comprehensive health insurance financed by employers, employees, and federal government.
Housing	Provide financing for decent homes. Promote free choice in housing through development of new communities with diversified housing and enforcement of fair housing laws.	Housing programs aimed at decent homes for all, but not for use of housing or community-development programs to impose arbitrary housing patterns on unwilling communities.

expense of the Democrats, the Democratic National Convention in 1896 nominated William Jennings Bryan, a Populist hero, for the presidency, and adopted a platform that advocated many Populist ideas.

The Socialist party also has had an effect on the policies of its far larger rivals. Organized in 1901, it was years ahead of them in its call for a graduated income tax, unemployment compensation, and old-age pensions. Such reforms would surely have come anyway, but one suspects the process was hastened by the 900,000 votes cast for Eugene V. Debs, the Socialist presidential candidate in 1912 and again in 1920. Four years later, the Socialists joined various farm groups, the AFL, and the independent railroad brotherhoods to support the newly created Progressive party. Under the leadership of Senator Robert M. ("Fighting Bob") La Follette, a liberal Republican from Wisconsin, the party urged government support for agriculture, collective bargaining for labor unions, and other proposals to which the Democratic New Deal was destined to give birth in the next decade. The Progressive ticket garnered 16.6 percent of the popular vote—a figure not since surpassed by any third party candidate.

Closely related to the policy innovation associated with minor parties is their effect in determining what ideas are considered to be politically extreme. When Alabama Governor George Wallace ran for President, for instance, he took positions on school desegregation and on law and order that made the policies of the Republicans in these areas seem quite moderate in comparison. In shifting the center of the political spectrum to the right in 1968, Governor Wallace not only forced both the Democrats and Republicans to advocate more conservative positions, but also led both major parties, in their fear of losing votes to him, to focus their campaigns on the issues (mostly law and order) which he was emphasizing.

It is probably safe to assume that any time a third party threatens to get over 5 percent of the vote, and Wallace received 13.5 percent, it will have considerable impact on the two major contenders. One does not necessarily throw away one's vote, therefore, if it is cast for minor party candidates. They cannot win, but their ideas may prevail.

One other effect of third parties must be noted: If they take most of their votes away from one major party, they may well guarantee victory for the other. In 1912, for example, dissident Republicans formed a Progressive party to support the candidacy of Theodore Roosevelt, who had failed in his attempt to get the GOP nomination. As a result, the Democratic candidate, Woodrow Wilson, was elected.

Party Organization

Parties in the United States, at least in comparison with those in England and Western Europe, are highly decentralized. National party organizations have small staffs with little control over state parties, and state parties, in turn, have little control over the organizations at the county or city level. Yet the national parties are major cogs in the machinery of American politics.

National conventions: the people's choice?   The national parties' most remarkable activity is the staging of national conventions. Every four years some four thousand delegates to the Republican and Democratic national conventions nominate the two presidential candidates between whom more than seventy million voters make a choice. More remarkable still, they congregate in a colorfully raucous atmosphere, arranged in part for maximum television impact, and often resembling a carnival more than a convention.

How these delegates are chosen is clearly a matter of fundamental importance. It is also one of incredible complexity, since no two states select convention delegates in exactly the same way. In some the procedure is determined by state law and in others it is decided upon by the state committee of each party. There are about ten states in which Republican delegates are chosen differently than Democratic delegates. With a few exceptions, however, two general methods are employed: Delegates are either elected by the voters in presidential primaries or they are chosen by party conventions at the state or district levels.

Even among the twenty-three states that have presidential primaries, there are wide variations in procedure. The election of convention delegates may be separate from a presidential preference poll in which voters can indicate their personal choice for their party's nomination. In New Jersey and West Virginia, for example, the result of the preference poll is not binding on the state's delegates, while in Indiana and Oregon it is. Another important distinction among the primary states is the extent to which the delegates elected to the national convention are pledged in advance to vote for a particular presidential candidate. New York does not even permit the presidential preference of the prospective delegate to appear on the ballot. In Florida, those seeking to become delegates may list themselves as favoring a certain presidential contender but if elected to the convention, they may vote for someone else. Delegates from New Hampshire are elected as either pledged to a particular candidate, favoring a candidate, or expressing no preference. In Wisconsin, only the names of the presidential candidates appear on the ballot and delegates supporting the winner are pledged to vote for him at the convention. Most presidential primaries select at least a few of the delegates from districts into which the states are divided, but in South Dakota, the District of Columbia, and California all the delegates are chosen in "winner-take-all," at-large elections. As a result, when George McGovern led the field in the 1972 California primary with 45 percent of the vote, he garnered all 271 delegates from that state in spite of the indignant protests of Hubert Humphrey, with 40 percent of the total.

Among states in which district or state conventions select delegates to the national convention, there is little uniformity in the methods by which convention membership is chosen. Some such as

Colorado and Texas, allow wide voter participation while Kansas and a few others are far less democratic. Illinois selects some of its delegates by state convention and some by primary, and a few other states use a similar combination of methods. If the student of national conventions thinks the whole matter of delegate selection is somewhat confusing, he has learned the most outstanding point about it. Complicating matters still more, many states change their selection methods with bewildering frequency.

The number of delegates to which each state is entitled at a national convention is not governed by law but is determined by rules adopted by each party. Although the Republicans and Democrats differ from one another in the apportionment of convention delegates, both use formulas based on state population, but reward those states where they have enjoyed recent election victories with extra bonus delegates.

At each party's national convention a candidate must receive a majority of the delegates' votes in order to win the nomination. Balloting is conducted by a roll call of the states, allowing the chairman of each state delegation to announce with a dramatic flourish how many votes the state casts for each candidate. If none of the contenders receives a majority on the first ballot, additional votes are taken until someone clears the magic hurdle of 50 percent plus one. Well-organized nation-wide preconvention campaigns have made it increasingly probable that the leading candidate will win on the first ballot, however, and not since 1952, when the Democrats nominated Adlai E. Stevenson on the third ballot, has it taken more than one roll call.

Nonetheless, there is always an air of excited uncertainty about a national convention, and in politicians' breasts hope springs eternal. In the first place, many of the delegates are not legally pledged to vote for any particular candidate and those informally committed may be persuaded by some last-minute break (say, a new public opinion poll) to change their minds. Furthermore, there·are usually half a dozen or more candidates seeking the nomination, making a clear majority difficult to obtain. Some of these candidates are "favorite sons" of their native states who may be running to polish their political images back home or to force one of the major candidates to make some concession, such as the promise of a cabinet appointment, in return for their withdrawal from the race. But they hope, too, for a situation in which the front-runners will be deadlocked and the convention, after three or four ballots, will turn to them as a compromise, or "dark horse" candidate. It doesn't happen often, but an obscure Ohio senator named Warren G. Harding was nominated on the tenth ballot by the 1920 Republican convention and went all the way to the White House.

Few political institutions in America have received more criticism than the national party conventions. Although polls reveal that they usually nominate the candidate favored by most members of their party, they have been indicted as unrepresentative elites, with most of the delegates chosen by undemocratic methods. In 1968, for example, only 41 percent of the delegates to the Democratic National Convention were chosen in presidential primaries. When Hubert Humphrey captured the nomination without campaigning in any primary, the demands for reform could not be contained even by the Chicago police force. In 1969 the chairman of the Democratic National Committee appointed George McGovern to head a twenty-eight member commission to devise guidelines that would be binding on all state party organizations in the selection of future convention delegates. The result was a requirement that the process of delegate selection take place the same year as the convention and involve a maximum number of Democratic voters. More important, the reform commission imposed a modified quota system on the selection of convention delegates to insure that young people, women, and some ethnic minorites would have convention representation in rough proportion to their total numbers.[6]

Although these guidelines were not enforced uniformly, they profoundly altered the power structure of the Democratic party and made a vital contribution to the nomination of Senator McGovern. Compared with the 1968 Democratic National Convention, in that of 1972 the percentage of delegates under thirty jumped from 4 to about 20, of women from 13 to 40, and of blacks, Chicanos, and Indians from less than 8 to 35. Not surprisingly, these were the very groups to which McGovern had appealed most strongly.

The winds of change are no respecter of party, and Republicans, too, felt a breeze. A special committee created by the GOP convention in 1968 made nonbinding recommendations for revised methods of delegate selection. As a result, the percentage of delegates under thirty at the 1972 Republican convention rose from 1 to nearly 10, of women, from 17 to about 30, and of racial minorities from less than 3 to approximately 6.[7] Preparations were made to extend these trends in selecting delegates for 1976.

Although the system remains imperfect, it must be assessed in terms of the available alternatives. It is surely more democratic than nomination by caucuses (meetings of members of the same party in Congress) which was the method used prior to the first major party convention in 1832. Similarly, a nominating convention has at least one advantage over a nation-wide presidential primary, which is the alternative most frequently recommended. A national primary would give an increased edge to the most well-financed candidates, since all-out campaigns throughout the country would then be necessary. Now such massive drives need be launched only in the presidential primary states, and usually only in some of these.

Besides nominating a presidential candidate, a national party convention performs other functions. It elects members of the national committee, although this simply confirms the persons nominated by

6 Commission on Party Structure and Delegate Selection, *Mandate for Reform* (Washington, D.C.: Democratic National Committee, 1970).

7 Ibid., pp. 26–28, and *Los Angeles Times,* July 28, 1972, pp. 14–15.

each of the state delegations. It also adopts a platform, which sometimes precipitates a convention's most exciting controversies. The platform sets forth policies the party favors, usually in a series of vaguely worded planks, but it is not binding on the candidates. Far less time is spent on another convention task, the selection of a vice-presidential candidate.

By tradition, the national convention follows the recommendation of its presidential nominee in selecting a vice-presidential running mate. But both campaign politics and the convention agenda often require that a decision on the vice-presidential nominee be made so quickly that it cannot be made very wisely, as happened in the case of Senator George McGovern's selection of Thomas Eagleton in 1972.

When McGovern was nominated on the night of June 12, he had less than twenty-four hours to pick a suitable running mate. Senator Edward Kennedy had to be asked because he would bring the most strength to the ticket. He declined. Hubert Humphrey had to be asked because his selection would strengthen both party unity and an old, but severely strained, friendship. He too declined. The other imperatives were those impersonal but contradictory ones of a balanced ticket and ideological compatibility. Since McGovern was a farm-state Protestant, he needed an urban Catholic or Jew. He must select someone who could placate union opposition, entice Chicago's Mayor Daley to back the ticket, reassure women of his support, and in addition counteract his radical image without alienating his most liberal supporters among young people and blacks. Yet a running mate would also have to share McGovern's values, his priorities, and his vision of the future.

Only five hours before the roll call was to begin for the vice-presidential nomination, George McGovern telephoned Thomas Eagleton to offer him the second spot on the ticket. Eagleton neglected to mention his electric shock treatments for depression and his three periods of hospitalization for nervous exhaustion which soon threatened to obscure the vital issues requiring campaign debate with a continued discussion of one man's mental health. Twelve days later, he withdrew from the race. In the aftermath of the 1972 controversy it seemed obvious that some change was desirable, and a Democratic party committee began studying possible future reforms.

National committees: prestige without power The national committee of each party is chosen for a four-year term and is the highest party authority during the interval between conventions. Traditionally, both the Republican and Democratic committees have been chosen by the various state delegations to the national conventions and have consisted mainly of a man and a woman from each state. The Republicans enlarged their National Committee a number of years ago to include the chairman of the Republican state committee from each state which was carried by the last Republican presidential candidate, or which has a majority of Republican congressmen, or which has a Republican governor. Starting from the same two members per state basis, the Democratic National Committee was enlarged to 303 members in 1972 to make it more representative of the entire party. The committee of each party elects a chairperson, usually on the recommendation of its presidential candidate for whom he or she acts as a major campaign coordinator and advisor. When Jean Westwood was chosen to head the Democratic National Committee in 1972, it was the first time either party had conferred this responsibility on a woman.

The national committees discharge three major responsibilities: (1) They raise money to finance the national campaign and assist in campaign research, management, and strategy planning; (2) They try to promote cooperation among party organizations in the various states; and (3) They select the city in which the next national convention will be held, appoint necessary convention officers and committees, plan the agenda, make all necessary arrangements for the housing and transportation of delegates, and arrange for TV and other media coverage. In 1972 the Democratic National Committee was required to perform a fourth function when vice-presidential candidate Thomas Eagleton withdrew from the race. When a nominee for either President or Vice President dies or resigns, the rules of both parties stipulate that a new nominee be selected by the national committee.

Although national committee membership normally carries considerable prestige and great responsibility, it entails little real power over state and local party organizations. In addition to the national conventions and national committees, each party has campaign committees for the Senate and for the House of Representatives. Their sole function is to raise funds for the candidates seeking election or reelection to Congress.

State and local organization: politics as patronage   State and local party organizations are not as powerful as they once were. In spite of this, many of them remain stronger than their counterparts at the national level. At one time, party strength was most apparent in the politics of city and county government. The boss-controlled "machines" such as those of Ed Crump of Memphis, Tom Pendergast of Kansas City, and "Boss" Tweed of New York may have been greased with corruption but they ran exceedingly well on election day. And all were examples of local organizations on which the state and national parties were largely dependent.

Most observers believe that the declining influence of political machines in the past thirty years is due to several factors. As more government jobs were awarded on the basis of civil service examinations, fewer were available as rewards for loyal service to the winning party. In addition to this decline in patronage jobs, machine influence has been weakened because more cities are electing officials on a nonpartisan basis, and are substituting primary elections for local party caucuses in the selection of candidates. The availability of welfare benefits and a general increase in the standard of living have diminished the dependence of poor people on partisan political groups and thus weakened the parties at the local level even more.[8] It is also possible that the increasing effectiveness of the mass media has made the door-to-door precinct work that is so characteristic of traditional party organization, particularly in the cities, no longer as important as it once was.

But here one must be wary of generalizations: The youthful supporters of Senator McGovern fashioned astonishingly successful campaign organizations before the primary elections which paved the way to his presidential nomination. In local politics, Albany, New Haven, and Chicago still have highly efficient party organizations, while Los Angeles, Detroit, and Seattle do not. At the county level, it would be difficult to find a more engrossing example of effective, although informal, party organization than that of Nelson County, Kentucky,[9] or one of more widespread state patronage than in Centre County, Pennsylvania.[10]

While some of the same factors that have weakened the parties at the local level are also present on a state-wide scale, many state party organizations are still held together by throngs of workers and campaign contributors motivated less by a firm belief in the party platform than by a fervent desire for government contracts or jobs. Among the variables that affect the strength of parties at the state level are the degree of party competition, the scope of the civil service system, the level of prosperity, the influence of pressure groups, the urban-rural balance, and the degree to which the traditional political culture demands a strict code of ethics.

Most states have a party organization that begins in the precinct, township, or ward—political units that usually include from a few hundred to several thousand voters. Officials at these lowest of political levels usually select city and/or county committees, which in turn choose district and/or state central committees. State party conventions are still common, and before the advent of the direct primary in the early years of this century, they nominated candidates for governor and other state offices. This was the practice in New York until 1968.

But many states have party structures that deviate widely from the general pattern. In California, for example, there are no official party organizations below the county committee level, and most members of the state committee are appointed by party nominees for Congress and various state offices.

Volunteer groups: politics as principle As many official party organizations declined in vigor, a political void developed. Increas-

8 Fred I. Greenstein, *The American Party System and the American People*, 2nd ed. (Englewood Cliffs, N.J.: Prentice-Hall, Inc., 1970), pp. 47–54.

9 John H. Fenton, *People and Parties in Politics* (Glenview, Ill.: Scott, Foresman and Company, 1966), pp. 67–70.

10 Frank J. Sorauf, "State Patronage in a Rural County," *The American Political Science Review* 50 (December 1956): 1046–56. The situation described may be fairly typical of the entire state of Pennsylvania, where the state civil service system covers only about 20 percent of its employees.

ingly candidates looked elsewhere for support. Those with enough money often turned to professional public relations firms and to greater television exposure. Some relied more heavily upon pressure group support. More idealistic aspirants were delighted to find that new political volunteer groups were springing up around the country, more interested in policy decisions than patronage dispensation, and eager to support candidates genuinely committed to the principles in which they believed.

Much as these volunteer groups differed, their members tended to be disillusioned with established party organizations, relatively young, remarkably well educated, ideologically sophisticated, and—too often—politically naive.[11] They had one appeal that is especially alluring to millions of citizens: Being both new and opposed to "machine politics," these groups were relatively unstructured and eager for the support and encouragement of new recruits.

These groups have tended to be farther to the left (or right) than the official organizations of the parties with which they are associated. This is not difficult to explain, since moderates do not work very hard in any volunteer group (unless motivated by personal gain) because they usually don't see too much wrong with society. Ideological purists, on the other hand, exert enormous energy because they are seriously convinced that if they don't society will surely collapse.

The future of American parties   The party system in America has been a crucial force which has molded and oriented the political beliefs of the people. Yet there are some compelling reasons to suspect that the strength of the Republicans and Democrats is slipping and that we may be entering an age of party decline or realignment. Ticket splitting, for example, has reached epidemic proportions. In the 1970 off-year elections there were twenty-three states in which both U.S. senators and governors were elected and in eleven of them the voters chose a senator of one party and a governor of the other. Moreover, the number of independents has increased steadily, and according to a Gallup Poll, among college students the percentage of political independents rose by 13 between 1966 and 1970, while Republicans declined by 8 percent and Democrats by 5 percent.[12]

The major reasons for the disintegration of traditional party loyalties may be summarized:

1) Television has enhanced the importance of personal charm and charismatic leadership to the detriment of party loyalty.

2) Public relations and professional campaign management firms have assumed some of the functions of party organizations.

3) The emotional impact of social issues such as crime, abortion, and school busing, along with the growing importance of foreign policy, has eroded the economic foundations (rich Republicans

11 Greenstein, op. cit., pp. 57–59.
12 Gallup Poll, *Los Angeles Times,* Feb. 14, 1971, Sec. H., p. 5.

Figure 22   Party Affiliations of the People

	Republican	Democrat	Independent
1973	27%	42%	31%
1968	27	46	27
1960	30	47	23
1950	33	45	22
1940	38	42	20

Source: Reprinted by permission of the American Institute of Public Opinion (The Gallup Poll).

vs. poor Democrats) of party preference. This was especially apparent in the refusal of the AFL-CIO, for the first time in twenty years, to endorse the Democratic presidential candidate in 1972. Many individual unions, however, remained securely in the fold.

4) The growth of civil service systems has deprived the parties of much patronage as a reward for campaign support.

5) Nonpartisan elections and the adoption of the direct primary have diminished the influence of party leaders in choosing the candidates for public office.

6) The increasing speed of social change makes it more difficult for parents to transmit old party loyalties to their children.

7) The intensification of attitudes rooted in racial and ethnic differences has accentuated the internal divisions within both major parties.

8) Since parties are weakest in those states where pressure groups are strongest, the continuing availability of campaign contributions from generous lobbyists has perpetuated a high degree of financial independence from both major parties among candidates for office.

9) Because both Republican and Democratic candidates have provided fewer new ideas or policy innovations than either pressure groups or minor parties, increasingly sophisticated and well-educated voters may view the major parties as somewhat irrelevant to the solution of contemporary problems.

It would be both brazen and misleading to conclude that funeral arrangements should be undertaken for the two-party, broker-oriented politics of the United States. Habits die hard. Yet it is difficult to escape the feeling that both the Republican and Democratic parties are confronted with a difficult challenge: Although still strong and seldom attacked, will they be increasingly ignored?

Chapter **8**

The Price of Democracy
Campaigns and Elections

Politics is the gentle art of getting votes from the poor and campaign funds from the rich, by promising to protect each from the other.

Oscar Ameringer

A political campaign is the dramatic climax of the democratic political process. It magnifies everything we have examined in the last two chapters: Public opinion becomes more intense, pressure groups grow more active, and party candidates wither or shine under the spotlight of the mass media. Part of the fascination of a campaign is that it can be a time of changed alignments and erupting emotions. The year 1972 was no exception. Many Catholics, Jews, and important union officials refused their customary support for the Democratic presidential candidate, a former security consultant for the Republican National Committee was arrested for attempting to bug the headquarters of the Democratic National Committee, a would-be assassin crippled the governor of Alabama, and a vice-presidential candidate withdrew from his ticket for the first time in history. But campaigns also display some reasonably stable characteristics, to which we will direct our attention.

POLITICAL CAMPAIGNS

The final outcome of an election depends to a considerable extent on the candidates chosen in the primaries, the money and other resources they have at their disposal, and the skill they employ in waging their campaigns.

The Primary Process

The selection process by which parties recruit their nominees has taken several forms. During our early history, small groups of party leaders, known as caucuses, picked the party candidates. In Andrew Jackson's time, in the 1830s, larger groups of party members began meeting in conventions for the same purpose. But full democracy demanded that *all* voters be permitted to select the candidates of their party.

Primaries first appeared in Crawford County, Pennsylvania, when Democrats were allowed to vote for their party nominees as early as 1842.[1] The idea didn't catch on until Wisconsin required that candidates be chosen by a direct vote of the people in 1903.[2] Since then, these preliminary elections, or primaries, have replaced the old convention system throughout the nation. The party primary is one of America's most important contributions to democracy.

At two political levels, however, the party primary has not yet played a determining role. Ironically, they are at opposite ends of the political scale—in the selection of candidates for President and Vice President and in the nonpartisan local elections in many cities. In between, at the state level, are two interesting exceptions: In Nebraska and Minnesota candidates for the state legislatures are not chosen by party primaries nor are their party designations listed on the ballots.

Closed primaries Most states have laws that permit only persons who are registered as members of a certain party to vote in that party's primary. Thus, the primary is closed to outsiders. In the North, the closed primary tends to produce relatively clear-cut policy differences between the nominees of the two parties since candidates for the Democratic nomination will have to appeal to most liberal voters and those seeking the Republican nomination must make themselves acceptable to a more conservative electorate.

Outside the South, the candidate who has a plurality usually wins the party's nomination even though he or she may not have a majority (over 50 percent). In the South the situation is somewhat different. Since the candidate who gets the Democratic nomination is almost certain to be elected there, the nominee is required to get a majority of the primary votes. If no one does, there is a second, or *runoff*, primary between the two leading candidates. So it is quite possible that an elected official in a southern state has been through three elections: the primary, the runoff primary, and the general election.

Open primaries A few states have open primaries in which the voter can help select either Republican or Democratic nominees, regardless of his or her own party preference. In Wisconsin, for example,

1 Hugh A. Bone and Austin Ranney, *Politics and Voters* (N.Y.: McGraw-Hill Book Company, 1963), p. 111.
2 Howard R. Penniman, *The American Political Process* (N.Y.: Van Nostrand Reinhold Company, 1962), p. 83.

he or she may simply ask for the primary ballot of either party upon arriving at the polls. This situation often produces many *crossovers*. For instance, if a Democrat is running for reelection to the U.S. Senate with no opposition in the Democratic primary, many Democrats may ask for the Republican primary ballot and vote for the most liberal of the candidates seeking the Republican Senate nomination, or—perhaps—the one they believe would be easiest to defeat in the general election. In the state of Washington, all primary voters are confronted with a *blanket* ballot listing all candidates seeking the nominations of all parties. The voter may vote for one candidate of any party for each office.

Open primaries may produce nominees who have appealed to voters of all parties, and who consequently display relatively few policy differences. The voters in the general election in such situations are often confronted with a barely distinguishable choice between two moderate candidates.

Nonpartisan primaries   In races for many local offices, and in the nonpartisan election of the state legislatures in Nebraska and Minnesota, candidates are chosen in primaries in which the party affiliations are not indicated on the ballots. Usually, if no candidate receives a majority of the total votes cast, there is a runoff election between the two front-runners, regardless of party.

Running for office   What must you do if you wish to run for office? Requirements vary from state to state, but normally the process is rather simple. Whether you are seeking the nomination of a political party or are running for a nonpartisan job, all you have to do is get a nominating petition signed by a certain percentage of voters and—in some states—pay a small filing fee. If you wish to run as an independent, or to organize a new party, election laws require a far higher number of signatures on the appropriate petition. Although ballots normally permit voters to write in the names of persons not printed there, write-in candidates almost never win, because voters have the habit of deciding among names already printed on the ballot, and because any technical error, such as misspelling a name, will invalidate the vote.

Campaign Resources

A huge registration advantage for one party or the other, the long-established reputation of a popular incumbent, or some overwhelming issue can make the outcome of some campaigns a foregone conclusion. Let us assume, however, that a campaign will make the difference between victory and defeat—as is often the case. What will be needed to win?

The candidate   The first ingredient in the victory recipe is a good candidate, with the following characteristics:

1) Intelligence. Americans admire common sense but are contemptuous of too much scholarship. Depending on the district, the fact that a candidate has "been an Oxford scholar may be a help or

something to be hidden."[3] The voters want someone with whom they can identify—someone who mirrors them at their best.

2) A wide acquaintance. Colonel Jacob M. Arvey, a long-time Democratic Party leader in Chicago, once remarked, "It's tough to vote against a man you know—especially if you like him."[4] At the congressional district or state level, this may be of less importance than in a race for the local school board or city council, where many political careers begin. The ideal candidate, therefore, is a joiner, since the more organizations one belongs to the more people one knows. In addition to a wide acquaintance, having many group affiliations offers subsidiary benefits: It develops skillful ease in interpersonal relations and a familiarity with parliamentary procedures and group behavior.

3) A concern for people. The successful politician is usually one who finds a certain exhilaration in handshaking, backslapping, and small talk, along with a sense of camaraderie with the person with a problem—no matter how trivial. The demands of a campaign require candidates to compromise ideals less often than emotions. Unless they genuinely like people, they will find it difficult to appear interested when bored, enthusiastic when indifferent, or hopeful when dejected.

4) Fluency. A candidate who is glib, who can talk easily and quickly, has an immense advantage, especially when answering unexpected questions from an audience, or in face-to-face exchanges with his or her opponent or news reporters.

5) Determination. What the "killer instinct" is to a boxer, determination is to a candidate. He must *want* to win with a nearly inexhaustible persistence. As a former candidate for the Indiana senate put it:

You put all your personality into a campaign. You give it your time, your effort, your money, your heart, and your soul. . . . My friends who were defeated with me knew the rules and played the game and had no regrets. Would we do it again? If we had the time and . . . the money we would.[5]

6) Good health and family support. The rigors of a campaign can be physically and emotionally exhausting. The candidate gets endless opportunities to eat and drink, but too little chance to sleep. Unfortunately, a diminished family life or even divorce are also among the occupational hazards of the chronic campaigner.

From the various attributes above, plus others intangible or unique to each candidate, come success and—in rare instances—genuinely charismatic leadership. But other factors also influence a campaign.

Money   It was Jess Unruh, former candidate for governor

3 Stimson Bullitt, *To Be A Politician* (Garden City, N.Y.: Anchor Books, Doubleday & Company, Inc., 1961), p. 82.
4 Quoted in Michael J. Kirwan, *How to Succeed in Politics* (N.Y.: Macfadden-Bartell Corp., 1964), p. 33.
5 James B. Kessler, "Running for State Political Office," Cornelius P. Cotter, ed., *Practical Politics in the United States* (Boston: Allyn & Bacon, Inc., 1969), p. 141.

in California, who said "money is the mother's milk of politics." Although he came to regret his candor, his observation is essentially correct.

The cost of political campaigns has skyrocketed even more rapidly than the cost of living. The presidential race in 1964 probably cost in the neighborhood of $38 million, or approximately fifty-four cents per vote,[6] while the amount spent at all levels of politics was over four times that figure. In 1968 national campaign expenditures climbed to over $62 million,[7] or eighty-five cents per vote, and total campaign outlays (national, state, and local) reached $300 million.[8] A serious presidential campaign cannot be launched for less than $15 million, and a race for governor or U.S. senator in a large state will cost well over a million.

Campaigns for the House of Representatives are less expensive, but still range from a low of $15,000 to a high of more than $125,000.[9] This wide discrepancy can be attributed to the fact that some districts are safe for the majority party incumbent, while in others there are close contests in which the opposing parties are tempted to believe that a few more dollars will convert defeat into victory. In races for the state legislature, the spread in possible campaign costs is, for the same reason, equally great. From $1000 to $50,000 would cover the vast majority.

Where does the money come from? At the national level from 25 to 75 percent came from fewer than 1 percent of the voters—the "fat cats" who contributed over $500—between 1948 and 1964. In the 1968 campaign, 424 persons contributed $10,000 or more to the party of their choice, and seventeen gave more than $30,000.[10] In most instances, the Republicans have benefited from the generosity of wealthy businessmen and conservative pressure groups, but labor contributions, mostly to Democratic coffers, reached nearly $8 million in 1968. This money was raised through appeals in union newspapers and meetings, as well as in person-to-person solicitation in plants and factories throughout the nation.

The inventiveness with which campaign funds are raised sometimes delights the imagination. The fund-raising dinner is an old standby, and entails appearances by prominent politicians and popular entertainers. The costs, depending on the fame of the attending dignitaries, may range from a few dollars to $500 per plate, and the menu—from box lunches to filet mignon—varies accordingly. On the eve of the 1972 Democratic convention, a telethon featuring dozens of entertainment, sports, and political celebrities netted over two million dollars. Both

6 *Politics in America, 1945–1966,* 2nd ed. (Washington, D.C.: Congressional Quarterly, Inc., 1967), p. 88.
7 U.S. Bureau of the Census, *Statistical Abstract of the United States: 1971,* p. 367.
8 Daniel S. Berman and Louis S. Loeb, *Laws and Men* (N.Y.: The Macmillan Company, 1970), p. 149.
9 Kirwan, op. cit., p. 10.
10 Herbert E. Alexander, "The Cost of Presidential Elections," Cotter, op. cit., pp. 281–82, and *Newsweek,* Dec. 13, 1971, pp. 23–32.

parties seem to assume public endorsements by such stars can be translated into votes and money. At the local level, rummage sales, wine-tasting parties, benefit theater performances, and raffle tickets have all been used to fatten the campaign coffers.

In spite of the variety of contribution sources, both major parties have worried about excessive dependence on a narrow financial base. Both have recognized that legislation in this field is woefully inadequate. As a result, Congress enacted early in 1972 the most sweeping campaign finance reform in half a century. It limits total spending, with the exception of postage for mass mailing and phoning by volunteer workers, to no more than ten cents per potential voter. No more than six cents of this total may be spent for radio or television advertising. Furthermore, any contributions exceeding $100 must be disclosed in periodic reports. Candidates for national office are limited in the amount of money they may contribute to their own campaign: $50,000 for presidential aspirants, $35,000 for those seeking Senate seats, and $25,000 for House candidates.

One result of the new legislation was to limit to $8.4 million the amount permitted for radio and television time to each presidential candidate in 1972, compared with the $12 million spent in Mr. Nixon's 1968 campaign. If democratic government is to reflect the desires of people rather than the demands of dollars, other reforms may be needed, such as tax-supported campaigns, shortened periods of campaigning, and free postal delivery and television time for campaign messages.[11]

The organization In addition to a good candidate and an adequate amount of money, an effective campaign organization is indispensable to most successful races. For partisan contests in states where there are strong parties, the organization may be ready-made, eager to support the party nominee. But in nonpartisan races, in states with weak parties, and in primary fights for the party nomination, a new one may have to be developed from scratch. In either case, it is here that the average citizen becomes most involved in the democratic process. The blueprint for a good organization should include the following basic components:

1) Precinct workers who will go door-to-door to find persons not yet registered to vote, distribute literature (thereby saving on mailing expense), sometimes solicit campaign contributions, and get persons to the polls on election day.

2) A headquarters staff that disseminates buttons, bumper strips, and campaign brochures; stuffs and addresses envelopes for campaign literature; makes phone calls soliciting support and reminding people to vote; and organizes and directs precinct workers. There is usually some building contractor, realtor, or other landlord who will

---

11 Berman and Loeb, op. cit., p. 157. In 1971, Congress passed legislation authorizing limited tax support for campaigns, but it was not to take effect until 1976.

donate a vacant store that can be used as a campaign headquarters for a few months.

3) A squad of people, often teen-agers, to put up small campaign posters along major streets. Such persons may also drive people to the polls on election day, distribute literature at shopping centers, and baby-sit for other campaign workers and voters.

4) Members of a finance committee to raise money from the "fat cats" who are potentially large contributors. Contributors worth $25 may be important at the local, grass-roots level; "fatness" is relative.

5) Occupational or special-interest committees that appeal for votes and other campaign support, usually by letter, from groups such as lawyers, teachers, veterans, farmers, ethnic organizations, and clergymen.

6) Publicity and advertising personnel to design billboards, newspaper advertisements, and campaign brochures, as well as to write stories for newspaper release.

7) Research and statistics workers who will prepare the candidate with information regarding major issues, as well as provide him or her with data regarding the opponent.[12]

A campaign manager who can pull all these together and free the candidate from personal concern with small yet often important details could be a campaign asset of incalculable value. And just what is effective campaign organization worth? One of the few relevant studies has found that in a midwestern industrial city "the increment to a party from the best, as compared with the worst, precinct workers amounted to about 5 percent in the 1956 presidential election"[13]—a figure that could make a difference in many a close contest. Yet the above question, like so many others in social science research, requires the exasperating answer: It all depends. If the candidate is well enough known and admired, money and organization may be clearly secondary. If there is enough money to promote the candidacy effectively, other factors may matter little. But all other factors being equal, organization may be decisive.

Of the three considerations—candidate, money, and organization—the candidate may be most important in the smallest electoral districts where he or she can be widely known. At the other extreme, in state-wide or national politics, there is evidence that money counts most. The U.S. News and World Report asserted in 1968 that "eight times out of ten, the man who spends the most money is the winner."[14] It is probable that organization is most important at the intermediate level, in the election of state legislators or members of

12 Some of this material is discussed in more detail in Paul P. Van Riper, Handbook of Practical Politics, 3rd ed. (N.Y.: Harper & Row, Publishers, 1967), pp. 45–63. I am indebted, also, to Dorothy Le Conte, a campaign manager with few peers, who taught me much regarding the material in this chapter.
13 Philips Cutright and Peter H. Rossi, "Grass Roots Politicians and the Vote," American Sociological Review 23 (April 1958).
14 Quoted in We the People (n.p.: California State Chamber of Commerce, 1970), p. 45. This Chamber of Commerce election pamphlet asserts that "One of every five United States Senators is a millionaire."

the U.S. House of Representatives. But effective organization means the recruitment of campaign workers, and it is one of the ironies of politics that legislators, to whom workers may be most important, have the fewest government jobs with which to reward the faithful.

Campaign Strategy: How to Win

Elections may be won or lost by the skill with which the candidate, money, and organization are combined for maximum effectiveness. These are questions of strategy.

Getting around   Even if a large amount of money is available, it must be budgeted carefully. One of the biggest expenditures in a national or state-wide race is apt to be the transportation cost of flying the candidate, press secretary, a few staff men, and dozens of reporters from one place to another. Buses and trains are still used occasionally, but they too require money.

TV or not TV?   Television has had a greater impact on campaign budgets than any other factor in recent history. In the course of the 1964 presidential campaign, $4.1 million was spent for time on the three national television networks, and by 1968 this figure had spiraled to $8.9 million.[15] In addition to television time itself, political commercials cost a lot of money to produce. Joseph Napolitan, former campaign manager of Pennsylvania's Governor Milton Shapp, has strong feelings on this subject:

When some candidates have, say $100,000 for television, they put maybe $5,000 into production so they can spend more on time. I'd rather spend $30,000 on production and only $70,000 on time. . . . (Y)ou just can't make good cheap films.[16]

Increasingly, political broadcasting comes in small doses— spot announcements as short as twenty seconds that are over before the viewer has time to switch channels. By the beginning of the 1970s, thirty seconds between the Jim Nabors show and the Thursday night movie cost about $3500 for a single Los Angeles channel, and a five-minute spot would go "well into six figures if bought for network use."[17]

Is it worth the price? Most of the experts seem to think so, and can provide at least a few examples to help prove it. In 1966 the first Republican ever elected to Congress from a district in Houston put 80 percent of his campaign budget into advertising, of which 59 percent went for television and only 3 percent to newspapers.[18] In 1970, however, Governor Dale Bumpers of Arkansas and Senators Lawton Chiles of Florida and Adlai Stevenson of Illinois all defeated candidates

15 *The New York Times Encyclopedic Almanac, 1970,* p. 155.
16 Quoted in Herbert M. Baus and William B. Ross, *Politics Battle Plan* (N.Y.: The Macmillan Company, 1968), pp. 331–32.
17 Bill Boyarsky, *Los Angeles Times,* Oct. 13, 1970, p. 1, and Baus and Ross, op. cit., p. 329.
18 Joe McGinniss, *The Selling of the President, 1968* (N.Y.: Pocket Books, 1970), pp. 37–40.

Paul Sequeria, Rapho Guillumette
Pictures.

Campaigning among minority groups: Senators Charles Percy and George McGovern pass out free groceries for Reverend Jesse Jackson's Operation Breadbasket and the Uptown People's Coalition in Chicago.

who outspent them for media time.[19] The costs of television to the American political process may be more than monetary. Its critics say that it substitutes images for ideas, personality for principle, glamour for wisdom.

The price of polls   Reliable public opinion polls, developed by George Gallup and Elmo Roper in the 1930s, serve many purposes. Initially they are used to determine whether the potential candidate has any chance of winning, what his strength is in various geographic regions, and what issues the voters are most worried about. Along with air travel and TV, the polls have pushed up the costs of modern campaigning enormously. Louis Harris, whose fame was first established as John F. Kennedy's private pollster, estimates that no more than $75,000 was spent for polls in the 1946 and 1948 campaigns combined. By 1960 the figure had probably reached a million and a half, and in a single congressional district, the minimum cost for a public opinion poll is $2000.[20] According to one estimate, three fourths of the candidates for

19 *Newsweek*, Nov. 16, 1970, p. 77.
20 Van Riper, op. cit., p. 130.

governor, two thirds of the candidates for the U.S. Senate, and one tenth of the candidates for the House of Representatives used polls in 1962.[21] "A candidate," writes a man who was one, "now pays less attention to district leaders than to opinion polls."[22]

Professionalized campaigns   Karl von Clausewitz, a famous Prussian general, once declared that war is too important to leave to generals. Adapting this idea, two professional campaign managers have asserted that "political campaigns are too important to leave to the politicians."[23] The advent of professional public relations and advertising firms specializing in campaign management has provided candidates with help in four areas.

1) They perform many functions which in the past were commonly the responsibility of party organizations. These include the issuance of press releases, recruitment of campaign workers, fund raising, and research on issues. Political parties still assist their candidates with all these, but with the decline in patronage, the weakening of party loyalties, and the gradual elimination of corruption, the party machinery is no longer capable of doing what it once did. Professional management firms have rushed to fill the void.

2) They are knowledgeable about television technicalities, such as editing or staging, on which the old-fashioned party leader has little expertise.

3) Similarly, they are aware of the specialized knowledge required for public opinion polls, involving sampling techniques, question phraseology, demographic comparisons, computer processing, and statistical interpretation. Here, again, the politician has little competence.

4) They have the advertising skill to make the sophisticated budgeting decisions to get the most votes for the money in choosing among the ever-growing media possibilities. As Leonard Hall, former chairman of the Republican National Committee, put it, "You sell your candidates and your programs the way a business sells its products."[24]

For all its effectiveness, however, some worry about the desirability of this advertising approach to politics. Adlai E. Stevenson, a twice-defeated nominee for President, said that the "idea that you can merchandise candidates for high office like breakfast cereal . . . is the ultimate indignity to the democratic process."[25]

The use of professional campaign consultants began in San Francisco in the late 1930s, with the public relations firm of Whitaker and Baxter, a husband-and-wife team. In 1952 a New York company— Batten, Barton, Durstine and Osborn—became the first involved in a

21 Kirwan, op. cit., p. 30.
22 Bullitt, op. cit., p. 65.
23 Baus and Ross, op. cit., p. 258.
24 Quoted in McGinniss, op. cit., p. 21.
25 Quoted in Vance Packard, *The Hidden Persuaders* (N.Y.: Pocket Books, 1958), p. 172.

national race, that of Dwight D. Eisenhower.[26] It is no coincidence that this was the year when "(t)elevision and the airplane came of age as campaign agencies."[27]

Today campaign management firms have become firmly entrenched as well-paid allies of both major parties, and Madison Avenue, the New York address of many advertising and public relations firms, has become synonymous with a professionalized approach to politics. A 1969 survey revealed twenty-nine businesses classifying themselves as professional campaign management firms. They do not come cheap. A "well-known Democratic consultant" estimates that his firm asks about $80,000 for "an average campaign for a U.S. House candidate." His personal services cost $500 a day.[28]

The issues: an adventure in prophesy   The road to victory does not always lead down Madison Avenue. Most candidates for a city council or state legislature do not need and cannot afford the services of professional consultants. Those seeking the bottom rungs of the political ladder usually must rely on their own popularity and their ability to assess correctly the issues that most concern the voters.

Sometimes compelling issues arise that are beyond the immediate control of candidates for even the highest offices. The Depression in 1932, and the communist offensive in Vietnam in 1967–68 are cases in point. Yet sometimes candidates can make their own issues. In 1961 Sam Yorty was elected mayor of Los Angeles in part because he promised to end the requirement that bottles and cans be separated from other garbage for trash collection purposes. In 1958 the decision of many Republicans to support "right-to-work" proposals bitterly condemned by labor unions was believed to have caused the loss of thirteen seats in the U.S. Senate, forty-nine in the House, and control of seventeen state legislative chambers.[29] More recently, issues such as changes in land zoning and school busing have affected the outcome of many local elections. At the state and national levels, Republican losses of governorships and House seats in 1970 have been attributed to too much emphasis on the law and order "social issue" and too little stress on economic problems.[30]

Although public opinion polls help to identify the problems that most concern the people, the selection of effective campaign issues is still a challenge to even the most gifted of seers and prophets. There is some evidence that the closeness of a campaign influences the choice of issues. In a lopsided race in which the outcome is a foregone conclusion, the issues may be sharply drawn; the probable winner attempts to "educate" the voters while the opponent speaks out, even in the face of

26 By the mid-1950s, Whitaker and Baxter had managed seventy-five campaigns and won seventy of them. For a brief account of some of their successes, along with the importance of BBD&O, see Packard, ibid., pp. 155–63.
27 Jasper B. Shannon, *Money and Politics* (N.Y.: Random House, Inc., 1959), p. 61.
28 *Congressional Quarterly Guide to Current American Government* (Fall 1970), pp. 131–32.
29 Kirwan, op. cit., p. 136.
30 Jules Witcover, *Los Angeles Times,* Nov. 7, 1970, p. 10.

obvious scorn for his or her opinions. In a close contest, however, candidates have a pragmatic tendency to moderate their views, and to emphasize only those issues designed to win the crucial but undecided vote.[31]

The best time and the proper place Some candidates, notably President Nixon, believe that a campaign should begin slowly, gradually pick up momentum, and finally peak on election day. Others believe in what has been called a "scrambling" technique in which an all-out effort is made for the entire duration of the campaign.[32]

There is also the question of where the candidate should concentrate most of his attention. As a general rule, the probable winner is well advised to cultivate the most fertile fields—those counties, towns, or neighborhoods in which he or his party are strongest. The reason is simple: Supporters do no good if they stay home on election day. The candidate who is trailing, on the other hand, must spread himself a bit more thinly, campaigning where he is popular in order to motivate his supporters to get out the vote, but reaching out into opposition territory as well.

Another decision confronting every campaign organization is how to spend the limited amount of money available. Television and travel expenses have already been mentioned. There may also be newspaper ads. A basic leaflet with one or two folds is considered well-nigh essential. It can be distributed in door-to-door precinct work, at factory gates, and in shopping centers, or used in direct mailings.

A recent innovation in campaign technology is the use of computerized letters which appear to be directed to each voter personally. If material is distributed by mail, it is worth the money to send it first class, so it will not be thrown out with the junk mail. That can cost $60 or $70 per 1000 voters. In comparison, a spot radio announcement—although not as selective as mail in its coverage—costs about a dollar or two per 1000 listeners.[33] Billboards are substantially more expensive, but many observers believe a few of them are necessary especially if the candidate is not well known and needs to establish name-recognition as a major contender.

There are literally dozens of products that can gobble up a campaign budget, including cards, matchbooks, straw hats, and other gimmicks, all bearing the candidate's name. In the 1968 campaign the Nixon forces, for example, ordered over half a million balloons, over twenty million buttons, and nine million bumper strips. The latter, at a little more than three cents each, cost $300,000.[34] For some of these items, their relative cheapness may be exceeded only by their uselessness. Fifty coffee hours during which candidates appear briefly in private

31 John W. Kingdon, *Candidates for Office* (N.Y.: Random House, Inc., 1966), p. 133.
32 Kirwan, op. cit., pp. 152–67.
33 Van Riper, op. cit., pp. 185–87.
34 Dale E. Wagner, "The Relationship between Party Campaign Finance and Campaign Materials," unpublished paper prepared for delivery at the 1970 Annual Meeting of the American Political Science Association in Los Angeles, September 11, 1970.

homes to talk with twenty or thirty neighbors may be worth all the campaign buttons ever pinned to a lapel.

The incumbency factor   In 1970 over 85 percent of the 435 members of the House of Representatives won reelection. In part, this illustrates the campaign advantage possessed by the incumbents already in office. As public officials, they command more publicity than the private citizens who may run against them; they know personally many lobbyists working for influential pressure groups; and often their names appear first on the ballot. Moreover, the boundaries of their districts may have been drawn to help them, and they can stress what they have done, rather than what they promise to do. They can claim that their constituents would benefit by their experience and the power advantages which seniority often brings. As officeholders, finally, they can get speaking invitations before nonpartisan groups that would never invite a mere candidate. These are formidable assets.

What can the challenger do? He must be aggressive, even offensive, in denouncing the most vulnerable portions of the incumbent's record. And he can pray for a landslide on behalf of his party.

ELECTIONS
Voting Behavior

Many influences converge upon the voters on election day. They have been subjected to the political attitudes of family, friends, and schools; they have absorbed (or ignored) the political information dispensed by the mass media; and they have been surveyed, categorized, computerized, and analyzed by census statisticians, poll takers, news commentators, public relations experts, and political candidates. Their support has been solicited by dozens of pressure groups attempting to influence government policy; and finally, they have been counted, courted, co-opted, and occasionally even corrupted by political parties seeking election victories for a wide variety of both noble and ignoble purposes. The result of all this lavish attention is what they do when they cast their ballots. At that moment, the voters are sovereign.

How do voters vote? That is perhaps the central issue in a democracy. Yet many of them don't vote at all. In the last half-century the percentage of the voting-age population that cast ballots in presidential elections has varied between 43.5 (in 1920) and 64.0 (in 1960).[35] Of those who do vote, what influences their choices when they stand alone with their consciences in the privacy of the polling booth? In varying degrees and combinations, at least three factors are involved: the candidates (especially for the major offices), party preference, and campaign issues.

Voting for the man   Many people say that they vote for the man and not the party. Perhaps they do, but only if they know

35 U.S. Bureau of the Census, *The Statistical Abstract of the United States: 1970*, p. 368.

something about the people who are running. Yet in 1970 only 53 percent of the voters knew the name of their representative in Congress and about a fifth of them knew how he or she voted on any major bill. Seven years earlier, 91 percent could identify Elizabeth Taylor, while only 72 percent knew who Senator Barry Goldwater was.[36] Although most people are aware of the candidates for major offices, chances are they "know" them in the sense that they have a "feel" for their personalities, projected by TV, better than they "know" their intelligence, executive ability, or even their stand on important issues.

Voters seem to sense the limitations of the information available to them. Since they know less about candidates for Congress than for President, the voter turnout in off-year congressional elections has been from 13 to 23 percent less than in presidential election years.[37] Moreover, in voting for congressional and state legislative candidates, who are generally unknown, voters seem to rely primarily on party affiliation in making up their minds. While the Democratic vote in presidential elections dropped 19 percent between 1964 and 1968, the Democrats lost only 1 percent of the seats in the House of Representatives and two tenths of 1 percent of all state legislative seats as a result of the 1968 balloting.[38] It seems clear that when voters know nothing about the candidates—in spite of what they may say—they vote their party preference; they do, in other words, the best they can.

The primacy of party Throughout the entire nation, there are more Democrats than Republicans. This is reflected by public opinion polls and by the long-standing Democratic majority in Congress. The importance of this numerical edge is somewhat offset, however, by a lower voter turnout among Democrats and independents than among Republicans. The key reason for this is probably the lower income of most Democrats; this is related to less education which is related in turn to a lack of knowledge concerning governmental affairs and little interest in political matters. Low income may also result in infrequent voting if it is tied to job changes which require people to move around a lot, making it difficult to meet voter residency requirements (although this is no longer very difficult). In most congressional or state legislative races, the importance of party affiliation is so predictable that if a district is about 52 percent Republican in voter registration (or close to 58 percent Democratic), it is assumed to be safe for the majority-party candidate.

Campaign issues Hardest to interpret is the effect of actual issues on voting behavior. To understand this factor, we must know what issues the voter thinks important, the candidates' positions on

36 Gallup Poll, *Los Angeles Times,* Sept. 20, 1970, Sec. H, p. 7, and Fred I. Greenstein, *The American Party System and the American People,* 2nd ed. (Englewood Cliffs, N.J.: Prentice-Hall, Inc., 1970), pp. 13–14.
37 Greenstein, op. cit., p. 10.
38 Philip E. Converse, *et al.,* "Continuity and Change in American Politics: Parties and Issues in the 1968 Election," *American Political Science Review* 63 (December 1969): 1084–1085.

Figure 23   Party Identifications

	Republican	Democratic	Independent	Other or Don't Know
National Totals	24%	49%	24%	3%
Sex				
Male	23	49	26	2
Female	25	50	22	3
Age				
21–29	19	47	31	3
30–49	20	52	25	3
50 and over	31	48	19	2
Education				
Grade school	20	58	18	4
High school	22	50	26	2
College	38	34	26	2
Income				
Under $5,000	21	55	21	3
$5,000–$9,999	22	50	26	2
$10,000 and over	39	34	25	2
Class Identification				
Propertied	54	22	23	1
Middle	33	38	26	3
Working	16	62	21	1
Occupation				
Professional, business	34	37	26	3
White-collar workers	25	45	29	1
Farmers	28	44	28	under .5
Blue-collar workers	17	57	24	2
Union Member				
Yes	15	60	23	2
No	27	46	24	3

these issues, and the degree to which the voter correctly understands their positions.

The issues stressed by the candidates may not be key determinants of voter decisions. In the 1960 campaign, for example, there was much debate over the so-called missile gap between the United States and Russia, while John F. Kennedy's Catholicism, which received less comment by the candidates, was a more important consideration to most voters. It is also necessary to recognize that the "real" issues may correspond neither to those that candidates talk about nor to those that voters think about. During the 1972 campaigns, for instance, the most important issue confronting the nation *may* have been environmental pollution, although candidates stressed school busing and tax loopholes, while voters fretted most about inflation and welfare.

The obligation to vote   Much has been written about the citizen's obligation to vote. Some argue that it makes no difference for whom you vote—just so you vote. This is patently absurd. It makes a great deal of difference if the majority votes for an embezzler for state treasurer, an extortionist for sheriff, or a fool for President. If one knows or cares only about a few candidates, one should vote only in the races in

	Republican	Democratic	Independent	Other or Don't Know
Religion				
Protestant	29%	45%	24%	2%
Catholic	12	63	22	3
Jewish	9	65	22	4
Ethnic Groups				
English	35	36	27	2
German	33	38	28	1
Scandinavian	31	37	30	2
Irish (Catholic)	14	59	26	1
Italian	14	63	22	1
Eastern or Central European	15	63	20	2
Race				
White	27	45	26	2
Negro	3	87	6	4
Ideological Spectrum[1]				
Liberal, completely or predominantly	8	66	25	1
Middle-of-road	16	60	21	3
Conservative, predominantly	30	42	25	3
Conservative, completely	40	30	28	2

[1]An explanation of President Nixon's 1972 victory lies in the results of a Gallup poll taken three months before the election: 41 percent of the voters view themselves as conservative, 30 percent middle-of-the-road, and 24 percent liberal, with 5 percent holding no opinion. At the same time, Nixon was viewed as substantially more conservative than Senator McGovern, his Democratic opponent. *Los Angeles Times*, August 27, 1972, p. 7.

Source: "Party Identification by Voter Characteristics" from *The Political Beliefs of Americans, A Study of Public Opinion*, by Lloyd A. Free and Hadley Cantril, Rutgers University Press, New Brunswick, New Jersey, 1968. Reprinted by permission.

which they are involved—and then go home. Otherwise, the vote becomes a menace to good government.

Another bit of nonsense is the allegation that to vote intelligently one must spend long hours of study, attend political meetings, and become—for all practical purposes—a political science major. It just isn't that hard. An intelligent voter is simply the man or woman who cares enough about the society to decide, with some thought, what issues are most vital and which candidates can best cope with them. If one knows too little about issues or candidates, it is not necessarily stupid to vote a straight ticket for the party of one's considered choice. This increases that party's chances of controlling both the executive and legislative branches, thereby facilitating cooperation between them and allowing the party to reap the advantages of legislative committee chairmanships.

A citizen doesn't have to do the job of intelligent voting without help. If one trusts one's union or the editorial policy of a newspaper, for example, there is nothing wrong with voting for the candidates they endorse. If one wishes to know how a congressman or state legislator voted on a particular issue, pressure groups such as the Chamber of Commerce probably know. If one wants to see brief biographies of the candidates and short statements of their major views, the League of Women Voters has compiled them. But before following others' recommendations, one should consider the interests and biases of those who make them. In the final analysis, intelligent voting springs as much from the spirit as the mind. It is the most solemn sacrament of democratic politics, a symbol of our common faith in our fellow citizens.

Voting Qualifications

The history of American voting laws is marked by two long-term trends. The first is the gradual elimination of restrictive requirements based on religion, property ownership, tax payments, race, sex, and literacy. The second is the transfer of considerable authority over voting regulations from the states to the national government.

When the Constitution went into effect, states were free to set up whatever voting restrictions they wished with one exception: Article I, Section 2 allowed anyone to vote for members of the U.S. House of Representatives who was permitted to vote for members of the lower house of his state legislature. In the next half-century, most of the states, having long since abandoned religious voting requirements, also repealed laws requiring the ownership of property. In 1870 the Fifteenth Amendment stipulated that no citizen could be prohibited from voting because of race. It took ninety-five years, until the passage of the Voting Rights Act of 1965, before this amendment was uniformly enforced and racial justice was brought, finally, to polling booths throughout the nation.[39]

Shortly before the 1920 presidential election, Amendment Nineteen banned voter qualifications based on sex. Women's suffrage, earlier granted in a few states as an act of chivalry, had become a demand the nation could no longer deny. Amendment Twenty-four, added in 1964, eliminated the payment of a poll tax, or any other tax, as a voting qualification. While once a barrier to the poor in many states, all but four had voluntarily abandoned the poll tax before the Constitution required it. Finally, in 1971, the Twenty-sixth Amendment lowered the nation-wide voting age to eighteen, following the trail blazed earlier only by Georgia in 1944 and Kentucky in 1955. The result was to enfranchise over eleven million people who otherwise would have been unable to vote in the 1972 elections. Politicians were perplexed regarding its implications. Young people were clearly more liberal than their elders, but the proportion who went to the polls was far lower.

Although the preceding developments have limited the states severely, four remaining requirements still deserve mention:

1) Citizenship. While aliens were once permitted to vote in some areas, usually because local machine bosses benefited thereby, citizenship is now a requirement in all states.

2) Residency. All states once had minimum residency re-

39 See Chapter 5, p. 114.

Figure 24   Age Differences

	Young	Old
Church Attendance[1]	33%	44%
Withdrawal from Vietnam by 1971[2]	63	55
Liberal[3]	61	34
Conservative[3]	26	52

[1] *Los Angeles Times,* Dec. 27, 1969, p. 19. Figures are for an average week. Young are 21–29, old are 50 and over.
[2] Ibid., Sept. 27, 1970, Sec. H, p. 3. Young 21–29, old 50 and over.
[3] Ibid., May 31, 1970, Sec. F, p. 8. Young are college students, old are general public.
Note: In 1968, only 51.1 percent of those between 21 and 24 said they voted, compared with 67.8 percent of the entire voting-age population. U.S. Bureau of the Census, *Statistical Abstract of the United States: 1970,* p. 369.
Source: Reprinted by permission of the American Institute of Public Opinion (The Gallup Poll).

quirements, ranging from two years in Mississippi to sixty days in West Virginia. The 1970 Voting Rights Act, however, set a thirty-day maximum as sufficient for voting for President and Vice President, and court decisions have ruled this to be adequate for the election of all officials.

3) Registration. A minimum period of residency is implicit in state laws that make voters register before the first election in which they wish to vote. Registration is relatively new as voting requirements go. It emerged toward the end of the last century to guarantee honest voting, especially in large northern cities, when fraud ran rampant: People ineligible to go to the polls were urged (and sometimes paid) to do so frequently, using fictitious names and addresses. "Vote early and vote often" seemed to be the motto of the corrupt politician. To obtain a list of persons eligible to vote, most states now use a system of permanent registration, requiring people to reregister only if they have moved, changed their name, or failed to vote in the last general election. Others require everyone to register at periodic intervals.

4) Literacy. About fifteen states have some sort of literacy requirement. Rather ironically, the practice began in Connecticut and Massachusetts to deal with immigrants in the 1850s, but it has been most frequently employed in the southern states to disenfranchise blacks. Literacy may mean anything from the simple ability to read and write to the ingenious capacity to "interpret" a provision of the state constitution. New York required a fifth-grade educational level. To prevent literacy tests from being used as a mask to conceal racial discrimination, the Voting Rights Act of 1965 suspended them in counties in which less than 50 percent of the adults were registered to vote, and the 1970 law mentioned earlier suspended them in all states until 1975. The literacy test created a special problem for substantial numbers of intelligent citizens who are unable to use the English language very well. This has been particularly true of the Puerto Rican population in New York and the Mexican-Americans in California.

At the root of all disputes about voting qualifications is a fundamental dilemma: Legally, voting is a privilege, but in democratic theory, it is a right. Should only the wise, the informed, or the successful

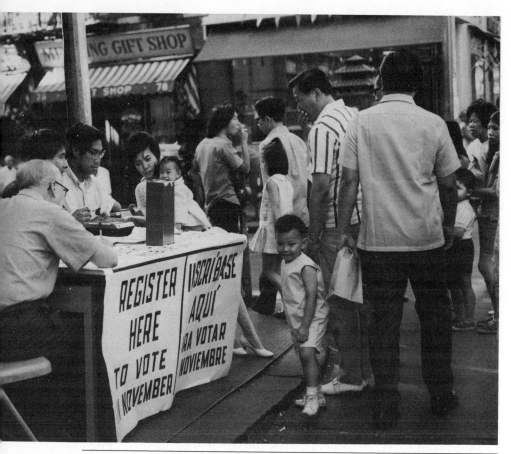

Rhyoda Galyn, Photo Researchers, Inc.

Voter registration in New York City's Chinatown.

vote? That group, depending on its definition, might be very small. Or on the other hand, should everyone affected by government policy be permitted to vote for government officials? Consider the implications.

Balloting

What happens on election day is influenced in some degree by the voting procedures and ballot forms prescribed by the election laws of the fifty states.

Voting procedures Prior to 1880, incredible as it seems to the modern citizen, it was relatively easy to find out how someone else voted. Ballots were printed by individual candidates or parties and varied in size or color. But the Australian or *secret ballot* is now used throughout the country and has almost eliminated the possibility that one person—a husband, employer, or creditor—can dictate the voting choices of another.

All ballots were printed on paper and marked by hand until Lockport, New York, introduced the use of voting machines in 1892. Over two thirds of the states now authorize their use, but the decision is often left to individual counties. There seems to be little doubt that voting machines, or a system of computerized punch-card ballots, help to prevent deliberate fraud or unintentional mistakes in the counting of votes. The chief objections to the use of voting machines center upon their expense and the relatively remote possibility of widespread mechanical failure.

Ballot forms   There are two basic distinctions involved in an analysis of ballot forms; one has to do with the way in which candidates' names are arranged and the other with the ballot's total length. About thirty states use the Indiana, or *party-column ballot,* with the candidates of each party listed in the same column. The voter may easily make a mark, or pull a voting machine lever, to vote a straight ticket for all candidates of one party. The remaining states use the Massachusetts, or *office-block ballot* on which candidates' names are grouped according to the offices for which they are running. Although party affiliations are listed, the voter must vote for each office individually, so it is just as time-consuming to vote a straight ticket as a split ticket.

Campaign strategy, as one might expect, is influenced by these facts. Especially in states with party-column type ballots, many lesser candidates might sweep into office on the coattail of a popular candidate for President, governor, or U.S. senator at the top of the party list. In the final analysis, the party-column ballot encourages party loyalty while the office-block ballot shifts attention to the qualifications of individual candidates. When Ohio changed to the latter form in 1950, the late Senator Taft estimated that he gained at least 100,000 votes.[40]

Partisan elections using the office-block ballot, like nonpartisan elections, present a special problem: How is the order in which names appear on the ballot to be determined? It is an important question, since many politicians believe that the top spot is worth as much as 5 percent of the vote, but state laws answer it in a variety of ways. In some places the incumbents' names are listed first, while in others the arrangement is alphabetical, or based on drawing straws, or rotated so that all candidates have their names in top position on an equal number of ballots.

The question of ballot length is important because, as indicated earlier, the average voter has neither the inclination nor the information needed for intelligent decisions among a long and bewildering array of choices. The long ballot may contain state constitutional amendments to be approved by the voters, certain proposed laws

---

40 V. O. Key Jr., *Politics, Parties, and Pressure Groups,* 5th ed. (N.Y.: Thomas Y. Crowell Company, 1964), pp. 641–44, has been very helpful for this section. A study of the 1952 and 1956 elections showed that 18 percent fewer voters who classified themselves as independents voted a straight ticket on office-block ballots than on party-column ballots. Angus E. Campbell and Warren E. Miller, "The Motivational Basis of Straight and Split Ticket Voting," *American Political Science Review* 51 (June 1957), p. 307.

required to be submitted to the electorate, and the names of candidates for numerous local, state, and national offices ranging from local coroner to President.

The antidote is simply a short ballot. The movement in that direction has concentrated on seeking two specific reforms: conversion of many state and local offices from elective to appointive ones, and the scheduling of local elections at different times of the year from state and national ones. The second, entailing what are called nonconsolidated ballots, has been the more successful.

Fewer people vote for local offices than for President or governor regardless of which system is used. On long, consolidated ballots there is ordinarily a drop-off of about 25 to 30 percent between the number of people who vote for the major candidates at the top of the ballot and those who bother to choose among local candidates at the bottom.[41] If local elections are separated from state and national ones, the turnout is often less than one quarter of those eligible to vote.

Direct Democracy: More Gods That Failed?

There was a time, around the turn of the century, when many big-city governments were in the clutches of graft-ridden, boss-controlled political machines and it was common knowledge that entire state legislatures were dominated by a few wealthy business corporations. California, it was said, had the best legislature money could buy, and the Southern Pacific Railroad had bought it. A succession of reformers under the Progressive label devised what they fervently hoped to be a solution to the problem. They proposed to take power away from the corrupt bosses and the bribed lawmakers and give it back to the people through a kind of political trinity: the initiative, referendum, and recall. Some would say these new gods have failed.

The initiative: for people or pressure groups? In 1898 South Dakota became the first state to adopt the initiative and referendum as methods of enacting state legislation. The initiative is a process whereby the registered voters can sign a petition proposing a new law or constitutional amendment. When sufficient signatures have been obtained, usually defined as a certain percentage of the vote cast at the last election, the proposal is submitted to the people as a ballot proposition at the next election. If a majority of the voters approve the measure it is adopted. The initiative therefore enables the people to enact laws whether the legislature likes them or not. It is now authorized in twenty states and in individual cities spread throughout many more.[42]

While the initiative was designed to thwart the influence of the powerful pressure groups and rich corporations that may have dominated elected legislators, there is some evidence suggesting that

41 Key, ibid., p. 646.
42 The states are Alaska, Arizona, Arkansas, California, Colorado, Idaho, Maine, Massachusetts, Michigan, Missouri, Montana, Nebraska, Nevada, North Dakota, Ohio, Oklahoma, Oregon, South Dakota, Utah, and Washington. Clyde F. Snider, *American State and Local Government*, 2nd ed. (N.Y.: Appleton-Century-Crofts, 1965), p. 169.

these same pressure groups and corporations are most skillful in utilizing the initiative process. For one thing, they have the money to pay professional petition circulators to obtain the required number of signatures, and the additional money necessary to wage highly effective campaigns to pass (or defeat) initiative measures that appear on the ballot. In the California general election of 1964, for example, four initiative propositions appeared on the ballot. Of the three that were passed, one was put there by railroads (to remove the legal requirement for a minimum number of crewmen on each train), another by theater owners (to ban pay television), and a third by the state Real Estate Association (to prevent state action eliminating racial discrimination in housing). The latter two were subsequently declared unconstitutional.

The case against the initiative, however, goes beyond the allegation that it doesn't control the influence of powerful lobbyists. It is said that it possesses certain inherent evils, including a reduction of the authority of legislative bodies, the possible enactment of poorly drafted or "crackpot" legislation, the lengthening of a ballot already too long, and the submission to the voters of highly technical and complex legislation that would baffle even the wisest of lawmakers.

On balance, however, these criticisms seem a bit too harsh. While it has not realized the idealistic hopes of its initial proponents, neither has it produced much horrible legislation. Most initiative measures, in fact, have been defeated by the voters and the process at least provides some psychic satisfaction as the purest form of direct democracy to be found in the American political system.

The referendum: limiting the legislatures In twenty-two states—all those with the initiative, plus Maryland and New Mexico—the referendum permits voters to repeal laws already passed by the legislature. There are several different varieties of the referendum. One involves the collection of signatures on a petition that will submit a state law or local ordinance to the voters for possible defeat. Another permits a state legislature or city council to place whatever proposals it wishes on the ballot, and thereby "pass the buck" to the electorate. A third requires that certain measures be put to the people, usually including amendments to state constitutions, bond issues to borrow money, and certain kinds of tax proposals. The first two types of referenda have been generally less significant than the initiative, and less frequently used. The last, however, has been important in shaping the structure of state and local governments and in granting (or denying) additional funds for schools and other publicly financed programs.

The recall: lest power corrupt Normally an elected public official can expect to serve out his prescribed term—two years, four years, or whatever—barring only death, voluntary resignation, or unlikely removal by impeachment proceedings. But officials in thirteen states, and in many cities in other states as well, face the possibility of defeat in special recall elections before their terms have expired.

The recall was first authorized at the local level in Los Angeles in 1903 and for state offices in Oregon just five years later. Like the initiative and one type of referendum, it requires the collection of signatures on a petition requesting a special election for the purpose of removing an official from office. It is rooted, perhaps, in the famous axiom of Lord Acton that power corrupts, and absolute power corrupts absolutely. If a majority of voters believe an official has indeed been corrupted, or has outrageously flouted the will of his constituents, the recall can be used to remove him promptly. While the initiative has been most important at the state level, recall elections have been confined largely to local politics and even here have been used rather sparingly. Nonetheless, mayors have been recalled in Detroit, Los Angeles, and Seattle, and the very possibility of such action, however remote, may help to keep officials on their toes.

Conclusion to Part Three

Democracy depends on a precarious balance between the power of the government and the power the people exert on the government. Unrestrained government power can produce tyranny; unrestrained popular power can produce anarchy; and both of these conditions jeopardize individual rights.

Since they have little force or authority compared to government, people must rely primarily on influence to persuade officials how to act. Here we confront a fact of overwhelming significance: Except for the vote, the political resources that can be converted into influence are distributed in a grossly unequal fashion. Money, prestige, access to the mass media, knowledge—all are concentrated in a minority of the population, although in the polling booths power is equalized.

The central thesis of Part Three is that people can remedy their relative powerlessness. First, they can organize pressure groups to advance their multiple and diverse interests. Second, they can seize, through democratic procedures and prodigious amounts of time and energy, the machinery of the major political parties. Imperfect as they are, they are the best instruments available for defining alternative solutions to the great problems confronting us. Third, the people can master the mechanics of campaign techniques and improve their skills in evaluating the candidates and issues on which they vote. Only then will election results reflect the real interests of the people rather than their manipulated preferences based on deceptive slogans, false fears, or the contrived glamor of candidate images. There are other ways average citizens can exercise influence. They can write letters to officials and editors, sign petitions, and nourish their children with the sense of participation, fair play, and respect for human dignity that are the staples of the democratic diet. But none is more important than support for pressure groups, participation in party activity, and intelligent voting.

Bibliography

Chapter 6

The People's Influence: Public Opinion and Pressure Groups

Binstock, Robert H., and Katherine Ely, eds., *The Politics of the Powerless* (Cambridge, Mass.: Winthrop Publishers, Inc., 1971).

Cirino, Robert, *Don't Blame the People* (Los Angeles: University Press, 1971).

Congressional Quarterly Service, *Legislators and the Lobbyists,* 2nd ed. (Washington, D.C.: Congressional Quarterly, Inc., 1968).

Dawson, Richard E., and Kenneth Prewitt, *Political Socialization* (Boston: Little, Brown and Company, 1969).

Graham, Hugh Davis, and Ted Robert Gurr, *Violence in America* (N.Y.: A Signet Book, New American Library, Inc., 1969).

Greenstein, Fred I., *Children and Politics* (New Haven: Yale University Press, 1965).

Report of the National Advisory Commission on Civil Disorders (N.Y.: Bantam Books, Inc., 1968).

Skolnick, Jerome H., *The Politics of Protest* (N.Y.: Ballantine Books, Inc., 1969).

Truman, David, *The Governmental Process,* 2nd ed. (N.Y.: Alfred A. Knopf, Inc., 1971).

Chapter 7

Government by the People: Political Parties

American Political Science Association, Committee on Political Parties, *Toward a More Responsible Two-Party System* (N.Y.: Holt, Rinehart & Winston, Inc., 1950).

Bone, Hugh A., and Austin Ranney, *Politics and Voters* (N.Y.: McGraw-Hill Book Company, 1963).

Campbell, Angus, et al., *The American Voter* (N.Y.: John Wiley & Sons, Inc., 1960).

Goldman, Ralph M., *The Democratic Party in American Politics* (N.Y.: The Macmillan Company, 1966).

Jones, Charles O., *The Republican Party in American Politics* (N.Y.: The Macmillan Company, 1965).

Key, V. O., Jr., 'Politics, Parties, & Pressure Groups,* 5th ed. (N.Y.: Thomas Y. Crowell Company, 1964).

Chapter 8

The Price of Democracy: Campaigns and Elections

Bullitt, Stimson, *To Be a Politician,* rev. ed. (Garden City, N.Y.: Anchor Books, Doubleday & Company, Inc. 1961).

Cotter, Cornelius P., ed., *Practical Politics in the United States* (Boston: Allyn and Bacon, Inc., 1969).

Lane, Robert, *Political Life* (Glencoe, Ill.: The Free Press, 1959).

McGinniss, Joe, *The Selling of the President, 1968* (N.Y.:Pocket Books, 1970).

Van Riper, Paul P., *Handbook of Practical Politics,* 3rd ed. (N.Y.: Harper & Row, Publishers, 1967).

PART FOUR

THE PEOPLE'S GOVERNMENTS

The political influence of the people is aimed at every level of government. In the next three chapters, we shall examine the national and state governments together, to emphasize their essential similarity of structure, as well as to simplify a comparison of their differences.

Like the national government, each of the fifty states displays a separation of powers among legislative, executive, and judicial branches, the primary purpose of which is to prevent too much power from falling into the hands of too few people. The three branches are constitutionally equal and, in most instances, the system of checks and balances makes the cooperation of all three essential. It does little good for the legislative branch to pass a law if the executive fails to enforce it, and executive enforcement is useless if the judiciary declares it unconstitutional. But in avoiding excessive concentrations of power, we run the risk that no branch can act with the speed and decisiveness necessary to cope with the crises of modern life.

The three branches are not always equally effective. In time of war, the national executive attains near dominance, after which legislators energetically reassert their authority; since the mid-1950s, a number of judicial decisions have had exceptional significance for American life. In the long run, the performance of the three branches would probably have pleased the Founding Fathers.

Chapter 9

Legislatures
Congress and State Legislatures

All government—indeed every human benefit and enjoyment,
every virtue and every prudent act—is founded on
compromise and barter.

Edmund Burke

Of the many roads to the White House, the winners of the last four presidential elections have traveled the same one. They all served in Congress, first in the House of Representatives and then in the Senate, before they became chief executive. The explanation is simple: Legislative bodies have a central place in American democracy and are more powerful than in any other nation in the world. To discover why the legislature is so central to democracy, we shall look first at the functions, the structure and membership, and the internal organization of these bodies, and then at dilemmas presented by the legislators' role in government.

LEGISLATIVE FUNCTIONS

The common tasks of the national and state legislatures are far more important than their differences. They all share four principal functions: (1) establishing public policy by passing laws, (2) controlling finance, (3) revising constitutions, and (4) checking the other two branches.

Policy Making

In passing laws, often known as statutes, legislatures are performing their best known and probably their most important function. By this means they formally establish official policy and the general methods by which it is to be implemented and enforced.

Congressional authority   The lawmaking authority of Congress is defined by the very first article of the Constitution and is broadly interpreted by the courts. The powers enumerated in Article I, Section 8 have spawned an astonishing array of implied powers deemed "necessary and proper" to carry them into effect.[1] On many occasions, Congress exercises its powers directly, as when it creates national parks or prohibits racial discrimination in hiring workers. Sometimes, however, Congress delegates substantial policy-making power to the executive branch, as when it authorized the President to impose wage and price freezes or the Food and Drug Administration to prohibit the sale of dangerous products.

State legislation   The legislatures of the various states can pass any laws not prohibited by the U.S. Constitution or the constitution of the state in question. The broad sweep of such authority is guaranteed by the reserved powers guaranteed to the states by the Tenth Amendment of the Constitution. State legislation, for example, may establish the scope of city and county power, determine what constitutes a crime, provide for colleges and universities, set licensing standards for people employed in numerous occupations, and regulate gambling, divorce, and abortion.

Controlling the Purse Strings

It does little good to pass a law without money to implement it. The legislature controls the purse strings through appropriation bills which allocate funds to all other agencies of government for their operating expenses. Naturally, it cannot appropriate money unless it raises it in some fashion, either by taxes or by borrowing funds through the sale of government bonds. Chief Justice John Marshall acknowledged long ago the scope of this sort of government power when he wrote that the power to tax is the power to destroy. Although the chief executive makes detailed budget recommendations, legislative bodies finally determine both where the money comes from and where it goes; in effect, they take from some what they give to others, a process that involves nothing less than the redistribution of wealth.

In bicameral legislatures, the lower house is often the most important in exercising financial controls. In Congress the House of Representatives has exclusive authority, under Article I, Section 7, to initiate bills to raise revenue. It has similar power, though only by

1 See Chapter 2, p. 35.

tradition, to introduce appropriation bills designed to spend money. Nevertheless, the Senate may exert considerable impact on money bills, and all are subject to amendment and final approval by both houses before they are sent to the chief executive.

There are two steps in the process by which Congress spends money. The first is the passage of legislation *authorizing* the expenditure of funds for a stated purpose and the second is the enactment of a bill actually *appropriating* money. Often the amount appropriated is smaller than that authorized; and in most cases the final figure is a compromise between the amounts approved by the Senate and by the normally more frugal House of Representatives. On appropriations for military aid to foreign nations, however, the Senate has threatened to cut off funds, in part as a protest against American involvement in Vietnam.

Constitutional Revision

It is normally the task of a legislature to propose whatever changes it thinks necessary in the state or national constitutions. In order to amend the United States Constitution, the proposed change is usually initiated by a two-thirds vote of Congress and takes effect only when approved, or ratified, by three quarters of the state legislatures. Alternative methods are also provided by the Constitution. In amending most state constitutions, some extraordinary vote in excess of a simple majority is also required in the state legislature, followed by the submission of the amendment to the voters in a referendum election. In Delaware, however, legislative action alone is sufficient.

Checking the Other Branches

In the system of checks and balances, legislative bodies have several ways to influence the other two branches.

Confirmation   One of the checks on the executive branch is the power of the senates to approve appointments made by the President or governor. In the national government, all top officials in the executive departments and agencies, plus all judges, are chosen by the President subject to the "advice and consent" of a Senate majority. In practice most presidential appointments are confirmed without much trouble, although there have been some notable exceptions. President Eisenhower, for example, appointed Lewis Strauss, former chairman of the Atomic Energy Commission, to be Secretary of Commerce, but the Senate failed to confirm him, and he withdrew the nomination of Mrs. Clare Booth Luce as Ambassador to Brazil after severe Senate criticism. Rather than risk Senate rejection, President Lyndon Johnson also withdrew his nomination of Abe Fortas as Chief Justice of the Supreme Court. More recently, the Senate rejected two of President Nixon's appointees to the U.S. Supreme Court.

Senatorial courtesy There are close to a thousand posts in the national government requiring Senate confirmation, including U.S. district attorneys, judges, ambassadors, tax collectors at various ports, and many postmasters. The President cannot possibly make so many selections on the basis of his own personal evaluations. Customarily, therefore, for the federal jobs located in the various states he appoints people who have been recommended by senators of his own party from the states where the job vacancies exist. If he does not, by tradition his choice will be rejected by the Senate. This practice, known as senatorial courtesy, was illustrated when President Truman appointed two men to U.S. district court judgeships in Illinois, neither of whom had been recommended by Senator Paul Douglas, a fellow Democrat from that state. The Senate refused to confirm the appointees. The practical effect of senatorial courtesy is to give U.S. senators who belong to the President's party a certain amount of patronage.

Gubernatorial appointments At the state level, many executive department heads are elected and thereby removed from both gubernatorial appointment and confirmation by state senates. Moreover, a big majority of states elect judges, similarly reducing executive and legislative control. Nonetheless, governors normally have some appointive power, subject to confirmation or rejection by state senates.

Impeachment Officials already in office may be removed by the legislature through a process known as impeachment. Technically, impeachment is a formal accusation against an executive official or judge, usually leveled by a majority vote of the lower house. The upper chamber then acts as a sort of trial jury, in which a two-thirds vote is most commonly necessary to convict and thereby remove the accused official from office.

This process has several variations. If the President is faced with impeachment charges, the chief justice of the United States Supreme Court presides over the Senate. In New York the judges of the state's highest court sit with the state senate in hearing impeachment cases; in Nebraska and Missouri impeachment charges are heard only by the state supreme court; and in Alaska the upper house impeaches and the lower house convicts or acquits. The Oregon legislature has no impeachment power at all.[2]

Since Andrew Johnson was impeached on politically inspired, trumped-up charges and acquitted by a margin of just one vote in the Senate, the impeachment process has been somewhat discredited. In our entire history, the House of Representatives has impeached only twelve national officials, and of these only four—all lower-court judges—were convicted.[3] At the state level, impeachment proceedings have been almost as scarce. New York, Texas, and Oklahoma removed

2 Clyde F. Snider, *American State and Local Government*, 2nd ed. (N.Y.: Appleton-Century-Crofts, 1965), pp. 215–16.
3 Henry J. Abraham, *The Judicial Process* (N.Y.: Oxford University Press, Inc., 1962), p. 42.

governors in this fashion, most recently in 1923, and Tennessee got rid of a judge by impeachment in 1958.

Treaty approval To some extent, the President's control over foreign policy is checked by the requirement that treaties with other nations be approved by a two-thirds vote of the United States Senate. This, along with its authority to confirm appointments, gives the Senate a larger role in limiting executive power than that possessed by the House of Representatives.

The expansion of government machinery Legislative power over the other branches also includes the authority to create government agencies. The increasing responsibilities of modern governments have resulted in the passage of new laws, requiring in turn a rather steady expansion of executive departments and commissions to implement them. Just as these are usually answerable to the President or to state governors, so the decisions of the lower federal courts created by Congress are subject to appeal to the Supreme Court.

Investigatory power Legislative bodies can, and often do, establish committees to look into the enforcement of the laws they pass. Usually this is done by permanent standing committees (or their subcommittees), but sometimes by special investigating committees. In any event, such inquiries enable Congress not only to supervise the executive branch but also to compete with it in getting public attention. During the 1950s, Senator Joseph McCarthy (R-Wis.) used the investigatory power as a springboard for flamboyant charges that Communists had infiltrated major executive agencies of the government, including the U.S. Army. When witnesses are required to testify before legislative committees, they may bring along a lawyer to advise them and may invoke the Fifth Amendment protection against compulsory self-incrimination. But they have no right to cross-examine earlier witnesses who may have made charges against them, nor to call other witnesses in their own behalf. Although legislative committees have no power to convict anyone of a crime, the allegations made in testimony before them can drag a good name through the dirt. It is important to note, in this connection, that *congressional immunity* protects members of Congress from being sued for what they say on the Senate or House floor or in committee hearings.

Most investigations, however, constitute a healthy examination of important problem areas in public policy. In June 1972, for example, various congressional committees held hearings on the trans-Alaska oil pipeline, health and accident insurance, the abuse of barbiturate drugs, and pesticide control. As usual, the leading witnesses were lobbyists, executive officials, and interested legislators. Such investigations are limited by two factors: First, tradition, along with the principle of separation of powers, has prohibited chief executives from appearing before legislative investigating committees; and second, questions directed to witnesses who are subpoenaed must have some relationship to facts about which there is power to pass laws. The investigating process, in other words, must not be used for the sole purpose of accusing or harassing witnesses. As former Chief Justice Earl Warren said in the case of *Watkins* v. *U.S.*, "there is no Congressional power to expose for the sake of exposure."[4]

Other checks on the courts   In addition to confirming court appointments or impeaching judges, there are two other legislative checks on the judicial branch. One is the power of Congress to change the number of judges serving on any federal court. The size of the Supreme Court has varied between five and ten, although it has remained at nine ever since 1869.

In 1937 President Franklin D. Roosevelt, unhappy over many court decisions handed down by a predominantly Republican tribunal, asked Congress to increase the number of judges from nine to a possible fifteen. The overwhelmingly Democratic Congress, usually eager to comply with Roosevelt's requests, construed this as a crude attempt to "pack" the Supreme Court and inflicted upon the President his most stinging legislative defeat in over twelve years in the White House. A nine-member Court seems destined to remain for a long time to come.

A second check on the Supreme Court is the authority of Congress to determine the kinds of cases that it can hear on appeal from lower courts. If the lawmakers don't like the decision of the Court in a certain kind of case, they can alter its appellate jurisdiction to prevent similar cases from reaching the high court in the future. Although this has not been done for more than a century, unpopular decisions involving school prayers, unequally populated legislative districts, and compulsory school busing have prompted such threats in recent years.

STRUCTURE AND MEMBERSHIP

Congress and forty-nine of the fifty state legislatures are two-house, or bicameral, bodies. Members of the lower house represent constituencies rather different from those represented by members of the upper house. Further, the way in which a state is apportioned into election districts makes a big difference in who gets elected to the legislatures.

Bicameralism

There were many reasons for the establishment of bicameral legislatures in the United States, including the example of the English Parliament and the necessity of two houses to gain the support of both the large and small states for the Constitution. But the survival of bicameralism indicates that it has some inherent advantages. The fact that a bill must pass two houses should theoretically produce better

4 354 U.S. 178 (1957).

legislation; the oversights, passions, or prejudices of one chamber can be corrected and counterbalanced by the other.

A one-house legislative body, however, is neither without precedent nor virtue in American government. Unicameralism characterized a few colonial legislatures, as well as the Continental and the Confederation Congresses. The overwhelming majority of city councils and county boards have only one house, although Nebraska, in 1937, became the only state legislature to have switched from bicameralism to unicameralism. Obviously, one house reduces costs and increases speed in the legislative process.

Some critics charge that bicameralism confers too much power on *conference committees.* When one house refuses to accept amendments that have been added to a bill by the other house, a conference committee is appointed, consisting of a few members of both chambers, whose task it is to come up with a compromise version. Sometimes entirely new provisions are added at this stage. Members of both houses usually conclude that the revised bill is better than none at all in this situation, and the conference committee compromise is enacted into law. Obviously, a one-house legislature eliminates the need for such a process.

The Allocation of Legislative Seats

Congressional apportionment   For a democracy, no characteristic of a legislative body is more important than the way in which seats are divided among the people to be represented. The Founding Fathers viewed the decision to grant the people of each state two seats in the Senate as immensely significant, for this is the only provision in the Constitution which they made immune from future amendment. They also provided that membership in the U.S. House of Representatives should be reapportioned among the states every ten years on the basis of an official population census, with the stipulation that each state would have at least one seat.

As the original thirteen states grew in population, and as new ones were gradually admitted to the Union, the total size of the House grew from sixty-five members to a total of 435 after the 1910 census. Congress then decided that if the House continued to grow it would be far too large to function efficiently. As a result, a law was passed freezing the size of the House at 435. Now when a state gains additional seats because its population has grown much faster than the national average, states with slower population growth lose seats. After the 1970 census, California gained five additional members of the House, and Florida three, while New York and Pennsylvania lost two each. Ten other states each gained or lost one seat.

After each state has been informed of the number of seats to which it will be entitled for the next ten years, it is the obligation of the state legislatures to determine the boundaries of the districts from which each representative will be elected. The inevitable result is a bitter redistricting fight.

State legislative apportionment Following each census, then, state legislatures emerge to a commanding position in our political system as they draw both congressional district boundaries and the boundaries from which their own members will be elected for the next ten years.

As indicated in Chapter 5,[5] this process produced rural-dominated legislatures until 1964, when the U.S. Supreme Court required members of both houses in state legislatures, as well as members of the House of Representatives in Congress, to be elected from districts of approximately equal population. Today all states elect almost all legislators except for U.S. senators, on a one-man, one-vote basis, and reapportionments are mandatory after each census.

In the apportionment of legislative seats, the chief difference between the national House of Representatives and the state legislatures is that voters in each congressional district elect only one representative whereas some members of fifty-six of the ninety-nine state legislative chambers are elected from multimember districts. Thirty members of the Arizona legislature are chosen from the same district and there are districts in Florida, Maryland, Texas, and Vermont where voters are expected to select fifteen or more state legislators.

The politics of gerrymandering When reapportionment is inevitable, nearly every conceivable interest group attempts to influence the reshaping of district boundaries to its own advantage. This process is known as *gerrymandering*.

The most influential groups concerned with redistricting are the political parties. The majority party in a state legislature usually can draw boundaries that will improve the chances of most of its candidates by a careful analysis of past election results in every part of the state. Assume that in Figure 25 each letter represents an equal number of voters, and that *R* stands for areas predominantly Republican, while *D*

Figure 25 Republican-controlled Gerrymander

stands for areas Democratic to the same extent. If the Republicans have a majority in the state legislature, they might draw boundaries to win in three of the four districts. But if there is a Democratic majority in the state capitol, the same region might be arranged to elect only one Republican and three Democrats, as shown in Figure 26.

Figure 26   Democratic-controlled Gerrymander

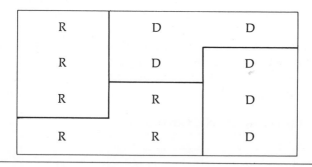

Compromise boundaries, favoring two Republicans and two Democrats, are shown in figure 27.

Figure 27   Compromise

Party considerations are not the only ones which are important in apportionment deliberations, however. Racial groups, for example, have an important stake in the matter. Given a certain area, black candidates may be elected in no districts, in one, or in two, as illustrated in Figure 28.

The interplay of personal ambitions is also a major factor. Members of the lower house of a state legislature may wish to have district boundaries drawn to help get them elected to the upper house, or to Congress. At a minimum, they would like to guarantee their reelec-

Figure 28   Racial Gerrymander

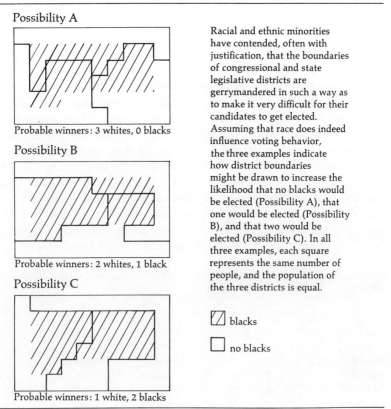

Possibility A

Probable winners: 3 whites, 0 blacks

Possibility B

Probable winners: 2 whites, 1 black

Possibility C

Probable winners: 1 white, 2 blacks

Racial and ethnic minorities have contended, often with justification, that the boundaries of congressional and state legislative districts are gerrymandered in such a way as to make it very difficult for their candidates to get elected. Assuming that race does indeed influence voting behavior, the three examples indicate how district boundaries might be drawn to increase the likelihood that no blacks would be elected (Possibility A), that one would be elected (Possibility B), and that two would be elected (Possibility C). In all three examples, each square represents the same number of people, and the population of the three districts is equal.

blacks

no blacks

tion.[6] One of the most predictable results of gerrymandering is the creation of many safe districts where incumbent legislators can hardly lose. Consequently, in congressional elections between 1950 and 1970 an average of 85 percent of the members of the House of Representatives won reelection.

City and county officials feel that they too have an interest in state legislative and congressional apportionment. In general, they believe that if units of local government are split by district boundaries a sense of community solidarity may be jeopardized and community interests inadequately represented.[7] The late Justice Frankfurter summed up the importance of the whole issue quite succinctly. The "practical significance of apportionment," he wrote, "is that the next election

6 Leroy C. Hardy and Charles P. Sohner, "Constitutional Challenge and Political Response: California Reapportionment, 1965," *Western Political Quarterly* 23 (December 1970): 733–51.
7 For a staunch defense of the community as an important and almost mystical basis of representation, see Alfred de Grazia, *Apportionment and Representative Government* (N.Y.: Praeger Publishers, Inc., 1963).

results may differ because of it."[8] So too may the kinds of legislation enacted.

Legislative Diversity

American legislatures vary enormously in membership, and from two to six years in length of legislative terms. When the term is four or six years, elections are usually staggered so that half or a third of the membership must seek reelection every two years. Another important difference among legislative bodies lies in the frequency and length of their sessions. About half the state legislatures meet every year and the other half every other year. Moreover, many states limit the length of sessions while others, especially the large industrial states, do not. The crucial distinction is that service in some state legislatures amounts to a part-time job, while membership in the rest, as well as in Congress, is a full-time occupation. Salaries and other financial reimbursements vary

Figure 29   The State Legislatures

State	Senate Size	Senate Term	Lower House Size	Lower House Term	Sessions Years Held	Sessions Duration Limit[1]	2 Year Compensation[2]
Alabama	35	4	106	4	Odd	36 L	$11,000
Alaska	20	4	40	2	Annual	None	17,495
Arizona	30	2	60	2	Annual	None	14,800
Arkansas	35	4	100	2	Odd	60 C	3,600
California	40	4	80	2	Annual	None	48,950
Colorado	35	4	65	2	Annual[3]	None	9,600
Connecticut	36	2	177	2	Annual[3]	147 C or 154 C & 84 C or 91 C	4,000
Delaware	19	4	39	2	Annual	June 30	12,050
Florida	48	4	119	2	Annual	60 C	33,600
Georgia	56	2	195	2	Annual	45 C & 40 C	10,775
Hawaii	25	4	51	2	Annual	60 L	28,860
Idaho	35	2	70	2	Annual	60 C	10,200
Illinois	58	4	177	2	Annual	None	24,000
Indiana	50	4	100	2	Annual	61 L & 30 L	11,725
Iowa	61	4	124	2	Annual	None	13,625
Kansas	40	4	125	2	Annual	None & 60 C	7,050
Kentucky	38	4	100	2	Even	60 L	9,850
Louisiana	39	4	105	4	Annual[3]	60 C & 30 C	16,500
Maine	32	2	151	2	Odd	None	4,100
Maryland	43	4	142	4	Annual	90 C	8,300
Massachusetts	40	2	240	2	Annual	None	23,000
Michigan	38	4	110	2	Annual	None	36,000
Minnesota	67	4	135	2	Odd	120 L	12,960
Mississippi	52	4	122	4	Annual	90 C & 125 C	14,500
Missouri	34	4	163	2	Annual	June 30/& May 15	18,750

8 *Baker* v. *Carr*, 369 U.S. 186.

State	Senate Size	Term	Lower House Size	Term	Sessions Years Held	Duration Limit[1]	2 Year Compensation[2]
Montana	55	4	104	2	Odd	60 C	$ 2,100
Nebraska	49	4	. . .	. . .	Annual	90 L & 60 L	9,600
Nevada	20	4	40	2	Odd	None	3,900
N. Hampshire	24	2	400	2	Odd	None	200
New Jersey	40	4	80	2	Annual	None	20,000
New Mexico	42	4	70	2	Annual[3]	60 C & 30 C	1,800
New York	57	2	150	2	Annual	None	36,000
North Carolina	50	2	120	2	Odd	None	10,000
North Dakota	49	4	98	2	Odd	60 L	3,590
Ohio	33	4	99	2	Odd[4]	None	25,500
Oklahoma	48	4	99	2	Annual	90 L	16,800
Oregon	30	4	60	2	Odd	None	10,500
Pennsylvania	50	4	203	2	Annual	None	24,000
Rhode Island	50	2	100	2	Annual	60 L	600
South Carolina	46	4	124	2	Annual	None	9,200
South Dakota	35	2	75	2	Annual	45 L & 30 L	5,000
Tennessee	33	4	99	2	Odd[4]	90 L	8,100
Texas	31	4	150	2	Odd	140 C	11,040
Utah	28	4	69	2	Annual[3]	60 C & 20 C	3,200
Vermont	30	2	150	2	Odd[4]	None	5,400
Virginia	40	4	100	2	Annual	30 C & 60 C	4,500
Washington	49	4	99	2	Odd	60 C	9,900
West Virginia	34	4	100	2	Annual	60 C	3,000
Wisconsin	33	4	100	2	Annual	None	21,000
Wyoming	30	4	61	2	Odd	40 C	1,640

[1] Duration limit means the number of days the legislature may meet in regular session. L means legislative working days. C is the number of calendar days between convening and final adjournment. In some states with no limit, legislators' expense allotments stop after a certain period of time. In other states with a limit, such a limit may be revoked by a special (e.g., 2/3) vote. Where two figures appear for the same state, one is for odd-numbered years and the other for even-numbered ones except for Mississippi, where the second figure applies every four years.
[2] For all states except Massachusetts, these figures include estimates of daily expenses for which the lawmakers were reimbursed, as well as salaries and other expense payments. The figures are based on January 1970 estimates.
[3] Every other year, the session is limited to budget and financial matters.
[4] Legislature may divide session by recess to meet in even year also; Ohio must.
Source: "The State Legislatures" from *The Book of the States.* Copyright © 1970 by the Council of State governments. Reprinted by permission. Information on sessions from 1972 edition, pp. 60–61.

accordingly. Figure 29 reports some of the most recent data on these and other variations.

Congress convenes each January, as required by the Constitution, and usually remains in session until the following autumn. Members of both houses receive annual salaries of $42,500, certain expense money, and the franking privilege which permits them to send postage-free mail.

What Manner of Men?

If legislatures are to represent accurately the interests and convictions of the people, as assumed in democratic theory, some have

Figure 30 Occupation of Legislators' Fathers, Legislators Themselves, U.S. Senators, and the U. S. Labor Force, 1950

Occupation	State Legislators' Fathers[1]	State Legislators[1]	U.S. Senators	Labor Force 1950
Professional, technical	18%	47%	64%	7%
Proprietors, managers, officials	29	35	29	7
Farmers, farm managers	25	10	7	16
Craftsmen, foremen, operatives	16	2	—	31
Clerical, sales	5	5	—	15
Unskilled labor, servants, farm labor	5	—	—	20
Other, not known	2	1	—	4
	100%	100%	100%	100%

[1] Data compiled from four states: California, New Jersey, Ohio, and Tennessee. Source: "Occupational Backgrounds" from *State Legislative Systems* by Wilder Crane, Jr., and Meredith W. Watts, Jr. Englewood Cliffs, N.J.: Prentice-Hall, Inc., 1968. Reprinted by permission. Note that "less than 10 percent of state legislators held occupations that were the same as those held by the majority of wage earners in the country." Ibid., p. 45.

argued that legislators must possess certain important characteristics in the same proportion as these characteristics are found in the total population. In fact, however, lawmakers are a rather special breed, unlike their fellow citizens in certain key respects.

Sex and race Women, to cite the most extreme example, constituted a little more than half the total population but only 2.4 percent of Congress in 1972 (13 out of 535). Blacks, comprising more than 11 percent of the population, also held only 13 seats. Furthermore, only in Ohio did the percentage of blacks in the legislature exceed the percentage of blacks in the state.[9]

Occupational background A comparison of the occupations of state legislators, legislators' fathers, U.S. senators, and the general public is shown in Figure 30. An analysis of the 1972 Congress discloses additional information about the types of people most likely to win election to this most exalted of legislative bodies. Of the 535 members, 462 had previous experience in public office, mostly state and local, while 387 were veterans.

Occupationally, lawyers constituted fewer than 1 percent of American workers, but well over half of all members of Congress. Other well-represented occupations on Capitol Hill were business and banking, 173; teaching, 72; farming, 47; and journalism, 36.[10] It is wise, if one wishes to run for legislative office, to have a secure occupation to which to return if one loses. As Bullitt observed:

9 *Congressional Quarterly Guide to Current American Government* (Fall 1970), p. 136. See also p. 138 for the number of blacks in each of the state legislatures.
10 *The New York Times Encyclopedic Almanac* 1972, p. 108.

A private calling is essential to the politician who is brave and wishes to be free. Like Cincinnatus, he should have a plow standing ready for him in a field at home. . . . Without a happy alternative, an acrobat's net, he cannot afford the independent judgment which he must have to do his duty. Through the window he sees the old men sitting on the courthouse lawn; unless he can afford to lose he may think, "There . . . go I," and keep a wetted finger in the air.[11]

Age Practical considerations prohibit young people from gaining their proportionate share of legislative seats. One can seldom hope to accumulate the acquaintances, money, or prestige necessary for a successful campaign before reaching middle age. The Constitution requires members of the House to be at least twenty-five and senators thirty years old. The average age of congressmen in 1971 was fifty-two in the House and fifty-six in the Senate.[12] Among committee chairmen, who attain their position by party seniority, the average age was sixty-six.[13]

The unrepresentative representatives Out of the welter of statistics, an overriding conclusion emerges: Legislative representatives are not very representative. Those who make our laws are generally male, white, professionally trained, business-oriented, and middle-aged. With inevitable exceptions, this means that legislators are rarely inclined to favor major alterations in the society in which they have attained such a high socioeconomic status.

INTERNAL ORGANIZATION

Within any legislature, some members have more power than others. Generally, maximum influence is exerted by presiding officers, committee chairmen, and party leaders.

Presiding Officers

The presiding officers have the authority to recognize speakers, interpret the rules of procedure, and decide on the committee to which each bill will be sent.

The Vice President, and a note on filibusters The Constitution authorizes the Vice President to preside over the U.S. Senate. But he is not considered a member of that body, may not participate in legislative debate, and may vote on bills only in case of a tie. If the Vice President is absent, the presiding officer is the president pro tem, a senator elected by his colleagues and usually the member of the majority party with longest Senate service.

Each legislative chamber adopts its own rules of procedure,

---

11 Stimson Bullitt, *To Be a Politician* (Garden City, N.Y.: Anchor Books, Doubleday & Company, Inc., 1961), p. 7.
12 *The New York Times Encyclopedic Almanac* 1971, p. 154.
13 *Congressional Quarterly Guide to Current American Government* (Fall 1970), p. 63.

and as those in the Senate are relatively few and informal, the Vice President rarely must render significant interpretations. Moreover, the Senate rules provide for unlimited debate. This means that each senator can normally talk as long and as often as he or she wishes on any bill before it can be brought to a vote. In such a situation, it makes little difference who is recognized at any particular time, since each will have a chance sooner or later anyway.

Unlimited debate permits a leisurely and thoughtful consideration of a bill but it also permits a small minority of the Senate to defeat a bill favored by a clear majority. This is accomplished by a *filibuster*—a colorful series of marathon speeches that can tie up the Senate for weeks and prohibit it from considering any other pending legislation. While talking a bill to death, a senator may speak about anything and may even read—as Senator Huey Long of Louisiana once did—the Bible, the Constitution, the Sears Roebuck catalogue, or recipes for "pot likker" sent him by his constituents.

Before 1917 there was no way to end a filibuster. In that year, however, Senate Rule 22 provided for the termination of debate through a procedure known as *cloture.* Sixteen senators must first sign a petition requesting that a filibuster be ended and then two thirds of those present must vote to stop debate.

Most senators are proud of their tradition of unlimited debate, justified as a means of arousing public opinion by dramatizing the depths of conviction displayed by those opposing the bill. The filibuster is frequently denounced, however, as an impediment to majority rule. There have been thirty-six cloture votes in fifty-three years, and only seven succeeded in shutting off debate.[14]

The Speaker of the House   The House of Representatives elects its own presiding officer on a straight party-line vote. Thus, the Speaker is accorded recognition as the most influential member of the majority party in the House. When the Speaker was at the pinnacle of his power, prior to certain reforms in House rules enacted in 1910, he ruled the chamber in a nearly dictatorial fashion. Even now, a strong one, like the late Rep. Sam Rayburn of Texas, is second only to the President of the United States in general political influence.

The sources of the Speaker's power are numerous. Because rules of procedure are far more intricate in the House than in the Senate, his authority to interpret them is more significant. Similarly, his power to recognize members to speak is important because severe time limitations on House debate prevent many representatives from speaking at all. He also appoints members to certain special committees (as distinct from standing committees, discussed below), names the Speaker pro tem to preside when he is absent, and performs personal but meaningful services for House members, such as the allocation of office space.

14 Lewis A. Froman, Jr., *The Congressional Process* (Boston: Little, Brown and Company, 1967), pp. 118–22.

Moreover, if the President belongs to his party, he plays a major role in engineering congressional approval of administration proposals.

Lieutenant governors and state speakers   At first glance, the presiding officers of state legislative bodies appear to have jobs patterned slavishly after their congressional counterparts. Indeed, this is often true, yet variation does exist. In more than thirty state senates the presiding officer is the popularly elected lieutenant governor, whose role is rather weak. In California and many other states, the president pro tem, a substitute presiding officer elected from among the senators, has greater influence than his national counterpart and more legislative power than the lieutenant governor. Tennessee provides an interesting deviation from the common pattern. There, whoever is elected presiding officer by the state senate becomes the lieutenant governor.

In state lower houses, as in the U.S. House of Representatives, the presiding officer is chosen from among the members and is called the Speaker. Usually, he has even more power than the House Speaker in Congress, especially in appointing the members and chairmen of legislative committees.[15] In Florida, Utah, and a few other states, however, legislative leadership is weakened and deprived of continuity by the regular rotation of the speakership among several legislators.

Standing Committees

Most of the work of modern legislative bodies is done in their standing committees. These provide for a division of labor which enables each lawmaker to acquire considerable knowledge in a particular area of public policy. Every legislator, national and state, is assigned to at least one standing committee which considers all bills dealing with its specialized field. Before he was elected President, Woodrow Wilson called the standing committees of Congress "little legislatures" with the power to bury a bill in "dim dungeons of silence whence it will never return."[16] In this respect, things haven't changed much.

Committee assignments and the seniority system in Congress   In both houses, there is nothing more important to the average legislator than his or her committee assignments. A preference will be dictated by three main considerations: the major concerns of the home district, his or her own background and interests, and the influence and publicity to be derived from committee membership. However, for freshmen congressmen there may be a wide discrepancy between the committee posts they would like and those they actually get. They can blame two factors for their disappointments: the party-ratio tradition and the seniority system.

15 Wilder Crane, Jr., and Meredith W. Watts, Jr., *State Legislative Systems* (Englewood Cliffs, N.J.: Prentice-Hall, Inc., 1968), pp. 57 and 61, and William J. Keefe and Morris S. Ogul, *The American Legislative Process* (Englewood Cliffs, N.J.: Prentice-Hall, Inc., 1964), p. 42.
16 Quoted by Bertram M. Gross, *The Legislative Struggle* (N.Y.: McGraw-Hill Book Company, 1953), p. 266.

On most of the standing committees, the ratio of Republicans to Democrats is roughly the same as in the whole chamber. Thus, if there are sixty Democrats and forty Republicans in the Senate, a ten-member standing committee probably will consist of about six Democrats and four Republicans. The seniority system is a bigger obstacle to a desired committee assignment. It usually means that legislators are given their choice of committees in order of their length of continuous service in the Senate or House. The chairman of each standing committee, moreover, is invariably the member of the majority party who has served longest on that committee.

The most obvious result of the seniority system is that it produces committee chairmen of long experience, advanced age, and—sometimes—questionable competence. More important, perhaps, is that legislators who accumulate enough seniority to become chairmen often are able to do so because they come from areas where the two parties do not compete on a very equal basis. Such noncompetitive, one-party regions tend to reflect social change and shifting opinion very slowly, and hence chairmen, with a few exceptions, are more conservative than most congressmen. When the Democrats are in a majority, as they have been since 1955, the seniority system naturally tends to elevate to chairmanships a disproportionately large number of congressmen from the South, where two-party competition is weakest. In 1972, Old Dixie could claim nine of the seventeen Senate standing committee chairmen, including both senators from Mississippi, Arkansas, and Louisiana, and eight of the twenty-one chairmen (including four Texans) in the House of Representatives.[17] This is an advantage no other section of the country enjoys and has been a major obstacle to Democratic Presidents such as Truman and Kennedy in their efforts for passage of liberal legislation.

The power of the chairmen   The seniority system would be less important if the committee chairmen were less powerful. They determine the agendas of committee meetings and frequently prevent bills from reaching the floor by pigeonholing them (refusing to schedule them for committee consideration). If a bill is not discussed in committee, or if the committee refuses to report it out to the floor, it is almost certainly dead. It can be revived only by a discharge petition in the House or a discharge motion in the Senate that will take it from the committee and place it before the whole House or Senate for further action. The discharge procedure requires the approval of a majority of the entire membership of either chamber, and is rarely used.

If a committee chairman decides not to pigeonhole a bill, he may refer it to a subcommittee which he alone can create and the membership of which he appoints, or he may schedule open public hearings at which lobbyists and officials from the executive branch have

17 *Congressional Quarterly Guide to Current American Government* (Fall 1971), pp. 61 and 63.

Paul Conklin.

Secretary of State Rogers defends the administration's foreign policy before the Senate Foreign Relations Committee.

opportunities to testify regarding the bill's alleged merits or defects. After public hearings have been concluded, the committee meets privately to consider the bill and to add whatever amendments it wishes.

Rounding out their authority, committee chairmen also play prominent roles in floor debate, participate in conference committees to iron out differences between the two houses, and hire most of the professional staff members who assist committees in their work. As the late Rep. Clem Miller once observed, "There are all sorts of ways to get things done in Congress. The best way is to live long enough to get to be a committee chairman."[18] Since the length of human life is not yet determined by majority vote, it is easy to see why reformers have worked for several decades to obtain a more democratic method than the seniority system for selecting committee chairmen.

Committees in the U.S. Senate   There are seventeen standing committees of the Senate, with members chosen by party committees, which are in turn selected by the Democratic floor leader and the chairman of the Republican Senate Conference.[19] As we have seen, seniority carries great weight, although if two senators from the same party have served an equal length of time, personal and political factors are also involved. When former President Johnson was the leader of the Senate Democrats in 1953, he broke with previous tradition by persuading his party's Committee on Committees to award each new Democrat one major committee assignment.[20]

Two committees have unique importance in the Senate because they deal with matters beyond the scope of any committees in the House of Representatives. One is the Foreign Relations Committee.

18 Clem Miller, *Member of the House* (N.Y.: Charles Scribner's Sons, 1962), p. 39.
19 These party leaders are discussed below, pp. 232–233.
20 Daniel M. Berman, *In Congress Assembled* (N.Y.: The Macmillan Company, 1964), pp. 144–50.

Figure 31   Senate Standing Committees Ranked According to Desirability

1. Foreign Relations	9. Banking, Housing and Urban Affairs
2. Finance	10. Labor and Public Welfare
3. Commerce	11. Public Works
4. Judiciary	12. Government Operations
5. Appropriations	13. Rules and Administration
6. Armed Services	14. Post Office and Civil Service
7. Agriculture and Forestry	15. District of Columbia
8. Interior and Insular Affairs	* Aeronautical and Space Sciences
	* Veterans' Affairs

Source: "Senate Standing Committees Ranked According to Desirability" from "The Seniority System in Congress" by George Goodwin from *American Political Science Review,* Vol. LIII (June 1959). Reprinted by permission of the American Political Science Association. *These committees were not ranked.

Because treaties with foreign nations must be approved only by the Senate, this is the only committee that has an opportunity to review them before they are put to a vote.

Somewhat similarly, the Senate Judiciary Committee has initial jurisdiction over presidential appointments to the federal courts—a matter over which the House of Representatives has no control. The Judiciary Committees in both houses have jurisdiction over most civil rights bills and proposed constitutional amendments.

Committees in the House of Representatives   There are twenty-one standing committees in the House, with Democratic members chosen by the Democrats serving on the Ways and Means Committee and Republican assignments made by a special Committee on Committees comprised of one Republican congressman from each state. The choices of both parties are influenced by their party leaders, and the Speaker has considerable impact upon the committee assignments of members of his party. Seniority, of course, is a major factor, but considerations of popularity, competence, and ideology also may be taken into account.

The most coveted committee posts in the House are on Rules, Ways and Means, and Appropriations. The Rules Committee is unique because its major function is to determine when and for how long bills approved by other standing committees will be debated on the House floor, and whether amendments may be offered there. While the power of the Rules Committee is supposed to facilitate action on pending legislation, it is sometimes employed to prevent any floor action at all if a bill is opposed by the committee chairman or a majority of its membership. The result of this whole process is that most bills must get through two committees before they reach the floor of the House, but only one to receive consideration in the Senate. Although the power of the Rules Committee is defended on the basis of the far larger number of bills introduced in the House than in the Senate, its abuse of authority has made it, along with the Senate filibuster and the seniority system, the most frequently criticized of congressional practices.

Figure 32 Standing Committees of the House of Representatives (in alphabetical order)

Agriculture	Internal Security
Appropriations	Interstate and Foreign Commerce
Armed Services	Judiciary
Banking and Currency	Merchant Marine and Fisheries
District of Columbia	Post Office and Civil Service
Education and Labor	Public Works
Foreign Affairs	Rules
Government Operations	Science and Astronautics
House Administration	Standards of Official Conduct
Interior and Insular Affairs	Veterans' Affairs
	Ways and Means

Source: *New York Times Encyclopedic Almanac* 1972, pp. 113–114. On a few matters, notably atomic energy and defense production, there are joint standing committees consisting of both senators and representatives, rather than separate ones in each chamber.

The Ways and Means Committee derives its special influence from that provision of the Constitution (Article I, Section 7) providing that "all bills for raising revenue shall originate in the House of Representatives. . . ." Most such measures are tax bills and all are referred to this committee to recommend ways and means of raising money. Since all expenditure bills are traditionally introduced first in the House, its Appropriations Committee has an advantage comparable to that of Ways and Means. No committees receive more attention from the President, interested in getting his proposed programs approved, or interest groups, interested in obtaining subsidies or avoiding taxes.

Finally, it should be noted that either house may appoint special *select committees,* usually for a one-year period, to investigate designated problems and provide information or recommendations to the entire body. In recent years, such committees have not been of great importance.

State legislative committees Although wide variations exist, all state legislatures employ a system of standing committees and most seem patterned after those in Congress. In a search for greater efficiency, their number has been generally reduced, although there are fifty in the Mississippi lower house.[21] In all but seventeen state senates and five lower houses, members and chairmen are appointed by the presiding officers.[22] Seniority plays a prominent role in determining committee memberships in less than half the states, although it is clearly dominant in New Mexico's senate and a few other chambers. In Iowa, it seems to be a downright liability, and in other states the presiding officer usually can make appointments on the basis of his personal political alliances, sectionalism, or other factors. The result may be the "stacking" of the most influential committees to benefit some particular group.

21 Crane and Watts, op. cit., p. 61.
22 John C. Wahlke, "Organization and Procedure," Alexander Heard, ed., *State Legislatures in American Politics* (Englewood Cliffs, N.J.: Prentice-Hall, Inc., 1966), p. 142.

In Florida, for example, rural interests known as "pork-choppers" have been notably successful in gaining prize committee assignments.[23]

By and large, committees seem to play a less important role in state legislatures than in Congress. One reason for this is a reluctance or inability to kill bad bills in the committees to which they are referred. As of 1968, both houses in fifteen states and one house in two others require committees to report out all bills.[24] A more important weakness among state legislative committees is the inadequacy of their professional staffs for such tasks as providing legal research and technical information. Joint standing committees are of considerably more significance in a few states, notably Connecticut, Maine, and Massachusetts, than in Congress. In Connecticut they are the only type of standing committees in existence.[25]

Party Leadership

It is hard to make general statements about the importance of the two major parties in determining legislative organization and procedure; too much seems to depend on the personalities of party leaders, differences between majority and minority party status, the variable degrees of competition between the two parties from state to state, the structural differences between the upper and lower houses, and the unique traditions of the Republicans and Democrats in each chamber.

Floor leaders in the U.S. Senate   About one thing, however, there can be little doubt: The *majority leader,* or floor leader of the majority party, in the United States Senate is the most powerful member of that body, and he thus ranks just below the President and the Speaker of the House in the total scheme of American politics. His preeminence stems from influence regarding committee assignments, control over the order in which the Senate will debate bills reported out of the various committees, the tradition that he will be recognized by the presiding officer whenever he wishes to speak, and his close relations with the White House—especially if the President belongs to the same party. In a sense, he has no comparable counterpart in the House of Representatives, since he combines some of the powers of the Speaker, the majority leader, and the Rules Committee in the lower chamber—all rolled into one.

The minority leader, who heads the numerically weaker party in the Senate, has only a little less power. He helps to determine committee appointments for members of his party, is consulted by the majority leader on the agenda for Senate debate, and, if the President belongs to *his* party may act as the semiofficial spokesman for the administration on pending legislation.

23 Keefe and Ogul, op. cit., pp. 164 and 171.
24 Crane and Watts, op. cit., p. 67.
25 Keefe and Ogul, op. cit., p. 151, and Wahlke, op. cit., pp. 141–42.

The majority and minority leaders are elected by a vote of all senators who belong to their respective parties, meeting in what are known as *caucuses* or (more recently) *conferences*. Although seniority may exert some influence, factors such as personality, intelligence, ideological commitment, legislative skill, and the accumulation of political debts play major roles in the final choices.

The Democratic conference allows its floor leader to accumulate more power than the Republican leader is permitted to muster. Both conferences elect an assistant leader, known as the majority or minority *whip*, to assist the leader in making sure party members are on the Senate floor when important matters come up for a vote. These positions are often a stepping-stone to bigger things. Sen. Mike Mansfield (D-Montana), the present majority leader, was previously the majority whip, and Sen. Hubert Humphrey (D-Minnesota), rose from whip to Vice President.

Party organization in the House   Here, as in the Senate, congressmen meet in party caucuses (conferences) to elect majority and minority leaders and majority and minority whips. In a sense, they play the same roles as their Senate counterparts, but with two important differences. One is that the most important member of the majority party is elected Speaker, with the majority leader ranking second, and the majority whip third. The majority leader is often considered the heir apparent to the Speaker, as when Rep. John W. McCormack (D-Massachusetts) and Rep. Carl Albert (D-Oklahoma) made this rather natural transition in 1962 and 1971 respectively. Similarly, the minority leader has a good chance of becoming Speaker if congressional elections shift control of the House from one party to the other.

The second major difference in the influence of House and Senate party organizations is that—as noted earlier—the order of business in the House is determined by the Rules Committee rather than by the party leadership.

Parties in state legislatures   Not much attention has been given to a systematic analysis of party organization in state legislatures, probably because it possesses so little uniformity. To cite rather extreme examples, Nebraska and Minnesota elect legislators on a nonpartisan basis, while party organization in the New York and New Jersey legislatures is normally more influential than in Congress. Available evidence indicates that the more two-party competition exists in state elections, the more important party leaders and alignments are in the legislatures.[26] Information regarding the legislative strength of the two parties is indicated in Figure 33.

Informal Power

Informal power is less easy to describe, but no less real than the various forms of formal authority. Almost every legislative body is

26 Crane and Watts, op. cit., Table 3–1, p. 42, and Keefe and Ogul, op. cit., p. 286.

**Figure 33   State Legislatures Classified According
to Degree of Party Competitiveness 1947–1966***

A 1   One-party States: Same party controlled the governorship and both houses throughout the period, and minority representation was negligible (all Democratic states).

Alabama   Arkansas   Louisiana   Mississippi   South Carolina

2   One-party States: Same party (Democratic) controlled the governorship and both houses throughout the period, and the minority representation was negligible (but Republicans were stronger here than in the group above, and this second group had developed a greater degree of two-party competitive politics).

Florida   Georgia   North Carolina   Tennessee   Texas   Virginia

B States with One Party Dominant: Same party controlled both houses throughout the period but did not always control governorship, and (except for Oklahoma) minority party occasionally had over one-fourth of the seats in at least one house.

Democratic: Arizona   Kentucky   Maryland   Oklahoma   West Virginia
Republican: Kansas   New Hampshire   Vermont

C 1   Limited Two-party States: Same party controlled both houses throughout most of the period and the governorship at least half the time.

South Dakota   Maine   Missouri   North Dakota   Iowa   Illinois
New Mexico   Wisconsin   Rhode Island   New York   Wyoming   Idaho

2   Limited Two-party States: Same party controlled both houses throughout most of the period but usually not the governorship.

Michigan   New Jersey   Ohio

3   Limited Two party States: Two houses controlled by different parties during most of the period.

Nevada   Connecticut

D Two-party States: Neither party had dominant legislative control, and in most cases party control of legislature approximated control of governorship.

Pennsylvania   Massachusetts   Oregon   Indiana   Delaware
California   Washington   Colorado   Utah   Montana

---

*Alaska and Hawaii are omitted because of their brief terms as states, and Nebraska and Minnesota are omitted because they have nonpartisan legislatures.
Source: Adapted from tables 6.1a. and 6.1b. in *The Legislative Process in the United States,* by Malcolm E. Jewell and Samuel C. Patterson. Copyright © 1966 by Random House, Inc. Reprinted by permission of the publisher.

characterized by informal alliances that may include the official leadership, sometimes challenge it, or simply exist as alternative centers of power.

In Congress, for example, over a hundred liberal Democrats in the House of Representatives belong to the Democratic Study Group. It raises campaign funds for its supporters, employs a small staff, and distributes pertinent information to gain support for bills important to its interests. The Wednesday Club is a somewhat similar group consisting of moderate and liberal Republicans. In addition, there is a Black Caucus in the House of Representatives which seeks to promote black interests, and the Members of Congress for Peace through Law (MCPL), a bipartisan, bicameral group that favors greater support for the United Nations, normalized relations with the People's Republic of China, and other comparable foreign policy objectives.

Sectional and economic groupings are even older among congressmen, but are less organized. There is, for example, a "farm bloc," a narrower "cotton bloc," an "oil bloc" and so on. The majority of congressmen tend to avoid frontal attacks on such groups. Representatives from the same state also meet occasionally in state caucuses. Of most importance is a loose coalition of Republicans and conservative southern Democrats which controls most major committees and has had a functional majority in Congress since World War II.

In the Senate, smaller and more intimate than the House, a kind of inner "club" has developed across party lines. It has no formal membership, consists of personal friends with considerable seniority, subtly enforces Senate traditions and behavior norms among younger members, and has considerable influence.

The sum total of formal and informal organization in the legislatures results in a considerable fragmentation of power. This decentralization creates numerous points of access for lobbyists, many obstacles to the passage of a bill into law, and hence a rather frustrating sluggishness in the legislative process described below.

THE LEGISLATIVE PROCESS

As President Kennedy observed in a 1962 television interview, "It is very easy to defeat a bill in the Congress. It is much more difficult to pass one."[27] He was neither the first nor the last President to be frustrated by that painful legislative truth. Of the "six great goals" announced in President Nixon's 1971 State of the Union address, four of them (revenue sharing, welfare reform, reorganization of the executive branch, and extended health insurance) had yet to clear Congress some twenty months later and only modest progress had been made on the other two (environmental protection and economic prosperity.) To as-

27 See Robert Sherrill, *Why They Call It Politics* (N.Y.: Harcourt Brace Jovanovich, Inc., 1972), p. 101.

certain why this can be, it is necessary to understand the obstacle course that confronts bills in Congress—and in most of the state legislatures as well. In the following sketch of a bill's passage in Congress, we see in sequence some of the procedures mentioned earlier.

Introduction of a Bill

Although congressional legislation must be introduced by either a senator or a representative, it may be suggested or even written by the President, some administration official, lobbyist, or influential constituent. (Tax, or other revenue bills, it will be remembered, can be introduced only in the House.) Occasionally, identical bills are introduced simultaneously by a senator and a representative to save time and so that both may receive whatever credit results. Important *public bills* may apply to the whole nation, but there are also *private bills* designed to admit a specific immigrant into the country or to provide some other assistance to an individual citizen. Each bill is given an identifying number and is referred by the presiding officer to the appropriate standing committee.

Committee Consideration

In ordinary circumstances, the committee has the power of life or death over bills assigned to it, and most receive the death sentence. It may never consider a bill (pigeonhole it); or refer it to a subcommittee; or consider it and then kill it; or amend it and send it on to the next pitfall awaiting it; or—in rare instances—send it on as originally introduced. In 1963–64, as an example, less than 12 percent of all bills were reported out by the committee to which they were sent.[28]

Once in awhile, as with the Civil Rights Act of 1964, a presiding officer will not send a bill to certain burial in the committee which would normally have jurisdiction over it, but will refer it instead to a committee known to be more favorably disposed toward it. If a bill is considered by the committee to which it is sent (a matter decided largely by the chairman) hearings are held at which interested persons may testify. Within a six-day period in June 1972, for example, witnesses testifying on a housing bill before the House Banking and Currency Committee included three congressmen, two lobbyists for retired persons' organizations, three housing industry lobbyists, two local government lobbyists, lobbyists for the American Bar Association and Americans for Democratic Action, and George Romney, Secretary of Housing and Urban Development.[29]

Compounding the frustrations for a President trying to get a bill passed is the fact that the enormously powerful committee chairmen

28 Froman, op. cit., p. 36.
29 *Congressional Quarterly Weekly Report,* June 24, 1972, pp. 1538–39.

support Presidents even of their own party less frequently than do most of their party colleagues in Congress.

Floor Action and Conference Committees

The relatively few bills that win a majority vote in committee (and sometimes in a subcommittee before that) usually have been subjected to grueling controversy and numerous amendments. In the House most important legislation must then go from a standing committee to the Rules Committee, which determines if and when the bill will arrive on the floor of the entire House. It is not uncommon for as many as thirty bills a year to die in the Rules Committee. In the Senate, the scheduling of debate for bills reported out of committee is primarily determined by the majority leader.

The Rules Committee normally limits debate by the entire House of Representatives to one or two hours per bill, and occasionally prohibits amendments from being proposed from the floor. In the Senate, any bill that gets out of committee may be brought to the floor by any senator, usually as scheduled by the majority leader. While it is easier to get a bill before the Senate than the House, the absence of time limits on debate make it harder to bring to a vote. If a bill's opponents resort to a filibuster—the ultimate weapon—it takes only one senator more than one third of those present to prevent cloture.

After a bill has passed one house of Congress, it is sent to the other where the procedure begins anew with a referral to a standing committee. If the second house passes the bill in the same form as the first, it is sent to the President for his signature. But if new amendments are added, the revised bill must be returned to the originating chamber for approval of the changes. Should it refuse to approve, which happens about one tenth of the time, both the Senate and House versions of the bill are sent to a conference committee. The members of this committee are usually chosen by the presiding officers from the two standing committees that had considered the bill earlier. Then, behind closed doors, about a dozen senators and representatives attempt to hammer out a compromise. When the compromise version goes back to the Senate and House of Representatives for a final vote, no further amendments are permitted and the bill is usually passed.

Presidential Action

By the time an important bill reaches the President's desk it has gone through a standing committee in each house, perhaps also subcommittees, the Rules Committee of the House, the Senate and House themselves, and often a conference committee. It may bear little resemblance to any bill the President initially requested and may indeed be a bill he never wanted at all. His options are discussed in the following

Steve Clevenger, BBM Associates.

To know the concerns of the people he or she represents, a legislator must listen. Senator Edward Kennedy hears the views of Vietnam war veterans.

chapter, but should he choose to veto it, a two-thirds vote is then required in both houses of Congress before it can become law.

LEGISLATIVE DILEMMAS
The Representative Function

There is considerable significance in the fact that one house of Congress is called the House of Representatives, for legislators are supposed to *represent* the people. As one scholar suggests, this means that lawmakers are to "stand for" or symbolize the people, just as a flag symbolizes a nation. Yet in another sense, a representative is one who "acts for" the people as well.[30] The representative's interests must be their interests, his desires their desires. The legislator, therefore, is required to play an ambivalent role: He or she is a part of the government, and at the same time a living link between the government and the people whom it is designed to serve.

The legislator as errand boy Frequently the legislator's role as a link between government and people makes him something of an errand boy. Many hours are spent helping constituents who have problems with some government agency. When the average citizen wants a visa for a relative in some foreign country, a draft deferment, a change in a proposed highway route, or reconsideration of an unemployment compensation claim, the first impulse often is to write his congress-

30 Joseph Tussman, *Obligation and the Body Politic* (N.Y.: Oxford University Press, Inc., 1960), p. 61.

man or state legislator. When a local businessman wants a government contract, he frequently does the same thing. A member of the House of Representatives in Washington, D.C., remarked that "[W]e spend too much time on errand boy activities. . . . But the real question is how we can avoid doing that. I think that . . . we cannot."[31]

Two recommendations have been made to lessen the errand boy burdens of lawmakers. One is to provide them with larger office staffs, which assume much of the responsibility for assisting constituents with their problems. The other, more drastic in nature, is for the legislature to appoint an ombudsman to investigate citizen complaints against executive agencies.

The office of ombudsman was created in Sweden over a century ago and has proved so effective in cutting bureaucratic red tape and righting administrative wrongs that it has spread to several other nations and to the state governments of Hawaii, Nebraska, and Iowa. Oregon also has an ombudsman, but appointed by the governor.[32] At least one congressman, Rep. Henry Reuss of Wisconsin, has proposed the establishment of such an office by Congress. Whether such an official would be as successful in a large and diverse country as in a small homogeneous one is problematical.

The legislator as representative	But there is much more to the representative function than being an errand boy. In a mystical way, for one to be elected a representative is to be transformed into those who elected him. A legislator is expected to respond so automatically to the constituents' wants and needs that the people—through him—rule themselves.

This concept of the representative function has encountered many objections and evoked more questions than can be answered here. Does it mean that only teen-agers or machinists or blacks can faithfully represent teen-agers or machinists or blacks? Does it mean the legislator should reflect only home district views, even at the expense of the rest of the nation? Does it mean ignoring his or her own judgment, even when the constituents are thought to be wrong on a certain matter?

Conscience or Conformity?

After several centuries of representative government, there is still little agreement on what it means to represent the people. Two schools of thought provide alternative explanations.

The agency theory	One view of the legislator's job, already noted, is that it is to do what the people who elected him or her would do themselves if they had the chance. Voters in Boston instructed their

31 Quoted in Charles L. Clapp, *The Congressman: His Work as He Sees It* (Garden City, N.Y.: Anchor Books, Doubleday & Company, Inc., 1963), p. 118.
32 Ed Meagher, "Ombudsman has Good 1st Year," *Los Angeles Times,* Aug. 30, 1970, Sec. B, pp. 4 and 5.

representatives how to vote as early as 1661,[33] and in his maiden speech to the House of Representatives, John Tyler, later to become President, defended such arrangements:

Is the servant to disobey the wishes of his master? How can he be regarded as representing the people when he speaks, not their language, but his own? He ceases to be their representative when he does so, and represents himself alone.[34]

Tyler expressed what is sometimes called the agency theory of representation, according to which the official is the agent of the voters and obligated to do their bidding. But whether such moral obligation exists or not, political expediency often dictates the same result. An unidentified congressman was recently quoted as saying

I take the position that "a politician's first duty is to get re-elected" and I think this sometimes requires casting votes you might prefer not to cast. The alternative to your re-election in most cases is the election of someone who would be diametrically opposed in conviction to what you stand for.[35]

The trustee theory Another concept of representation views the representative as a trustee to whom the voters have delegated the authority to act in their behalf in whatever way he or she sees fit. The classic statement of this doctrine was made by Edmund Burke, the great English scholar-politician. In a speech to the voters of Bristol in 1774, he said

Certainly, Gentlemen, . . . a representative [ought to be in] the most unreserved communication with his constituents. Their wishes ought to have great weight with him . . .; their business unremitted attention. It is his duty to . . . prefer their interests to his own. But his unbiased opinion, his mature judgement, his enlightened conscience, he ought not to sacrifice to . . . any set of men. . . . Your representative owes you not his industry only, but his judgement; and he betrays, instead of serving you, if he sacrifices it to your opinion.[36]

Legislators might well note that in the next election, Burke was defeated. Nonetheless, more than a century and a half later, a survey of congressmen found that 54 percent agreed with Burke while 37 percent believed they should vote in accordance with the consensus in their constituencies.[37] More recently, a study of four state legislatures revealed that the trustee conception was embraced by 81 percent of Tennessee lawmakers, 61 percent of those in New Jersey, 56 percent in Ohio, and 55 percent in California.[38]

Some writers impute a moral superiority to legislators who

33 Austin Ranney, *The Governing of Men* (N.Y.: Henry Holt and Co., 1958), p. 240.
34 Quoted in John F. Kennedy, *Profiles in Courage* (N.Y.: Pocket Books, 1957), p. 13.
35 Quoted in Clapp, op. cit., p. 427.
36 Reprinted in Hanna Fenichal Pitkin, ed., *Representation* (N.Y.: Atherton Press, Inc., 1969), pp. 174–75.
37 Alfred de Grazia, *Public and Republic* (N.Y.: Alfred A. Knopf, Inc., 1951), p. 158.
38 John C. Wahlke, Heinz Eulau, William Buchanan, and Leroy C. Ferguson, *The Legislative System* (N.Y.: John Wiley & Sons, Inc., 1962), p. 281.

"vote their conscience" to support an unpopular cause, rather than yielding to popular pressures. John F. Kennedy, for example, wrote a Pulitzer prize-winning book, *Profiles in Courage,* in which he lauded about a dozen such congressmen. Perhaps their rarity deserves recognition.

Legislators can most easily vote their judgment on controversial bills, disregarding possible constituency opinion, (1) if they have a few years (as in the case of U.S. senators) before reelection, (2) if last reelected by a big margin from a safe, noncompetitive district, or (3) if their judgment is strongly supported by the party or pressure groups most influential among constituents and most likely to make financial contributions to the next campaign.

Conflicting Demands

The actual behavior of a lawmaker is the product of many influences. How he or she votes on many bills, of course, reflects a general orientation (prolabor or probusiness, liberal or conservative) toward the issue at hand. Yet there are other bills (often of a somewhat technical nature) on which ideological preferences provide little guidance. In any event, the lawmaker is likely to be barraged by many cross-pressures. Constituents back home, the party leadership, powerful lobbyists, and trusted colleagues all may be clamoring for that vote—some for a bill and some against it.

The lawmaker knows exactly what vote each of these groups want with one exception: Seldom is it known for sure what a majority of the voters (the only group that controls his or her whole career) want on any given piece of legislation. Neither mail nor public opinion polls will reflect opinion accurately. Letter writers are not necessarily representative of the general population, and polls are fallible. One study showed an amazingly low relationship between what congressmen thought their constituents favored on certain issues and what their views really were.[39] Compounding this perplexity, lawmakers don't know what percentage of the voters are even aware of a particular issue, or whether the *intensity* of voters' convictions, if they are aware of it, is strong enough to cost a legislator the next election for voting the wrong way. Congressmen seem to believe that their voting records have a greater effect upon their chances of winning another term than is probably the case, even in the face of evidence that less than half of the people know anything about either candidate in most races for the House of Representatives.[40]

The importance of constituency pressure, then, lies partly in the fact that legislators are acutely conscious of it, no matter how inaccurately they may perceive it. It also lies partly in the population characteristics of the districts from which lawmakers are elected. It is

39 Warren E. Miller and Donald Stokes, "Constituency Influences in Congress," *American Political Science Review* 57 (March 1963): 45–57.
40 Loc. cit.

usually assumed, for example, that the United States Senate is more liberal than the House of Representatives because senators are elected from state-wide districts that almost invariably include some traditionally liberal voters (such as blacks or union members), while many representatives are chosen from small districts with virtually none.

It is difficult to generalize about the impact of either party leaders or lobbyists upon legislative votes, in part because legislators perceive their own roles in relation to these people in different ways. With respect to political parties, some lawmakers think of themselves as "loyalists" who place a high premium on party support while others, at the opposite extreme, are proud to be "mavericks." In spite of many exceptions, however, it is generally agreed that in Congress, party affiliation is the best single indicator of how lawmakers will vote. Similarly, with respect to pressure group lobbying, some legislators are "resistors" who believe such behavior unfortunate, while others are "facilitators" who believe it beneficial.[41]

The influence of a lawmaker's colleagues weighs heavily on the decision-making scales. Although the average legislator seems to have a local perspective, primarily concerned with the needs of his own district, the welfare of the entire state or nation is occasionally impressed upon him by legislators from other areas. Chances are that he has grown to like his colleagues and has come to realize, moreover, that unless he votes the way they wish upon occasion, he cannot expect to receive reciprocal treatment. This kind of vote trading is therefore not merely expedient, but an indication of mutual respect. In addition, a legislative body develops its own distinctive customs and behavior expectations. There is strong group pressure to remain loyal to these norms which, at least in the United States Senate, include courtesy and mutual assistance.[42]

The Legislature as Institutionalized Compromise

In conclusion, a legislative body, if truly representative, will consist of many lawmakers advancing as many conflicting interests as are found in the entire society. About the best a legislator can do for his constituents, therefore, is to fight as hard as he can for what they would like and then strike as good a bargain as possible for what they can actually get. This, of course, requires compromise among the competing interests—labor *vs.* business, city *vs.* suburb, and so forth. It is a process for which a legislative body is uniquely suited.

41 Wahlke, *et al.,* pp. 502–503 and passim.
42 Donald R. Matthews, *United States Senators and Their World* (Chapel Hill: University of North Carolina Press, 1960). For an interesting analysis of "deviant senatorial behavior" see Ralph K. Huitt, "The Outsider in the Senate: An Alternative Role," *American Political Science Review* 55 (September 1961): 566–75.

THE NEED FOR REFORM

The first congressional reform law in twenty-four years was passed in 1970. It required that all roll call votes taken in committee be made public, that more votes on the House floor be recorded, and that committee procedures be made slightly more democratic. But it did not deal with those procedures which have received the most bitter criticism: the seniority system for selecting committee chairmen, the power of the House Rules Committee to determine what can be considered by the entire membership, and the enormous difficulty of stopping a Senate filibuster. In short, it did not redistribute congressional power more evenly among the members nor seriously impede the capacity of a minority of congressmen to thwart majority action.

If reform is needed in Congress, revolution may be required in many state legislatures. They are, as one observer noted,

Figure 34 Rank Order of the 50 State Legislatures

Overall Rank	State	Overall Rank	State
1	California	26	Tennessee
2	New York	27	Oregon
3	Illinois	28	Colorado
4	Florida	29	Massachusetts
5	Wisconsin	30	Maine
6	Iowa	31	Kentucky
7	Hawaii	32	New Jersey
8	Michigan	33	Louisiana
9	Nebraska	34	Virginia
10	Minnesota	35	Missouri
11	New Mexico	36	Rhode Island
12	Alaska	37	Vermont
13	Nevada	38	Texas
14	Oklahoma	39	New Hampshire
15	Utah	40	Indiana
16	Ohio	41	Montana
17	South Dakota	42	Mississippi
18	Idaho	43	Arizona
19	Washington	44	South Carolina
20	Maryland	45	Georgia
21	Pennsylvania	46	Arkansas
22	North Dakota	47	North Carolina
23	Kansas	48	Delaware
24	Connecticut	49	Wyoming
25	West Virginia	50	Alabama

Source: Table 1, "Rank Order of the 50 State Legislatures" from *The Sometime Governments* by John Burns. Copyright © 1971 by the Citizens Conference on State Legislatures. Reprinted by permission of Bantam Books, Inc.

poorly organized and technically ill equipped. . . . They do not meet often enough or long enough; they lack space, clerical staffing, professional assistance; they are poorly paid and overworked; they are prey to special interests, . . . ; their procedures and committee systems are outmoded.[43]

Fortunately, improvements are under way in many states, and some legislatures are functioning quite efficiently. But the discrepancy among them is enormous. A massive study was recently made of the legislatures of all fifty states. On the basis of five criteria (functionality, accountability, informedness, independence and representativeness), they were ranked from best to worst, with the results shown in Figure 34.

43 Alexander Heard, ed., *State Legislatures in American Politics* (Englewood Cliffs, N.J.: Prentice-Hall, Inc., 1966), pp. 1–2.

Chapter **10**

Executives
Presidents, Governors, and Bureaucracies

*When I woke up this morning, the first thing I saw was a
headline . . . that our Navy was going to spend two billion
dollars on a shipbuilding program. Here I am, the
Commander in Chief of the Navy having to read about that
for the first time in the press. Do you know what I said to
that? . . . I said: "Jesus Chr-rist!"*
President Franklin D. Roosevelt

The President of the United States is the most powerful man
in the world. His counterpart in each of the fifty states is a sort of minor
league president, a governor who heads his own regional domain. It is
these officials—and the bureaucracies that serve them—with whom this
chapter is concerned.

THE PRESIDENT AND THE GOVERNORS
The Pomp and the Power

The President and the state governors have responsibilities
so awesome, challenges of such magnitude, and opportunities so unique,
that they are more than mere chief executives. They play many roles
or—as some say—"wear many hats." Moreover, their functions must be
performed simultaneously, for they overlap and each affects all of the
others.

Heads of State The first executive "hat" is almost crown-like, for Presidents and governors are heads of state who play a symbolically patriotic role, much like that of a royal monarch. It is they who embody the ties that bind us together, the links between a proud past and a perilous future. As a head of state, the chief executive may lay a cornerstone for a new government building, award medals of honor to heroic servicemen, greet foreign royalty, or throw out the first ball at the beginning of the baseball season.

In addition to gratifying our national appetite for pomp and ceremony, this function serves a number of other purposes, both for the people and for the chief executive. For the people, it permits a view of the President and state governors in a number of different circumstances and a better assessment of their qualities of leadership. For the chief executives, the head of state role keeps their thumbs on the pulse of the body politic and gives them politically priceless opportunities to improve their public images in what seem to be nonpolitical situations.

Many nations—England, West Germany, Japan, and others—have both a chief of state and a chief executive. One performs ceremonial functions; the other runs the government. In the United States, the President does both. A skillful leader exploits the prestige of the first role to enhance his power in performing the second. Thus, when a President issues a Labor Day proclamation, he is not only acting as chief of state but hopes also to be gaining additional political support from union members that will strengthen his position as head of the government.

But the ceremonial role can pose a hazard. People may confuse opposition to the chief executive's policies as a government leader with attacks upon him as a symbol of the nation itself. Although it is politically expedient for a President to encourage this confusion so as to minimize criticism, most people have learned to cherish the role of the President as head of state, while often deploring his performance as head of government. Few faulted President Nixon for conveying the congratulations of the nation to astronauts returning from the moon, but many criticized him for giving the space program priority over such domestic needs as improved health care.

Chief politicians   A chief executive must be, by definition, one of the most skillful politicians in the country. He has, after all, blended the ingredients of power—nomination by a major party, money, personal prestige and popularity, mastery of the mass media, and all the rest—into a consummately successful victory formula.

After his election, a President or governor does not cease to be a politician. In fact, if he does, he will seldom be an effective chief executive. To be a politician entails the skillful use of power—the ability to alter people's behavior in socially significant ways. If the leader is unable or unwilling to use the full range of his power—to threaten vetoes of extravagant appropriation bills, to promise Supreme Court appointments to Southerners, or to deploy troops to Thailand, for example—progress toward his goals will be slow indeed. On the other hand, to squander these power resources in behalf of trivial objectives is to demean the dignity of his office.

Among the power resources available to a President or governor is his position as leader of his own political party. As noted earlier, tradition permits the President to choose his vice-presidential running mate and the chairman of his party's national committee. Through his influence with the national committee he can affect the allocation of campaign funds to party candidates for Congress and through speeches at fund-raising dinners he can attract campaign contributions. He can personally endorse the congressional candidates he favors, as President Nixon did in 1970 by campaigning for Republican nominees in twenty-three states. He can attract instant publicity to whatever members of his party he chooses by news releases and in press conferences. He can allow congressmen to announce government contracts awarded to plants in their districts. By judicious use of his vast patronage powers he can reward the party faithful with prestige appointments and punish the party heretics by ignoring their existence. When two supporters of the President lost Senate races in 1970, one was appointed to the White House staff (Clark MacGregor) and another named as Ambassador to the United Nations (George Bush). But a third loser who had opposed the President slipped back into the shadows of private law practice (Charles Goodell). In politics, there is no isolation so bleak as that of a man without honor in his own party.

But why should a President bother himself with such petty partisan politics? The answer is that if he wishes his legislative program to be enacted into law, his vetoes upheld, his appointments confirmed, his military excursions financed, and his treaties approved, he needs congressional support. Since he can expect relatively little from members of the opposition party, he must secure as much as possible from his own. Besides, he may wish to seek reelection, and for that the full support of his party's machinery is essential.

A governor, too, is normally the leader of his own party within the state. For many of the same reasons mentioned above, his ability to elicit its loyalty is often essential to his success.

Managers of the economy   As each level of government has expanded, so too has its impact upon the economy. The force and direction of this impact is determined largely by the executive branch—by the state governors, and especially by the President. Governments now are major employers, landowners, purchasers, stockpilers, awarders of contracts, and producers of such commodities as electric power and nuclear weapons—all functions which are authorized by legislatures but directed and implemented by the executive bureaucracy. Although it is a cruel injustice, it is also symbolically significant of the President's potential influence on the state of the economy that the squalid shacks in which many Americans lived during the Great Depression of the 1930s were known as "Hoovervilles," after the President who was in office when the Depression began.

Executive influence on the economy was strengthened enormously in 1921 when Congress gave to the President the responsibility of submitting a unified budget proposing specific expenditures for all agencies in the national government. Beginning with Illinois in 1917, all states except Arkansas have also adopted this so-called executive budget, thereby giving the governor the major role in planning the allocation of state tax funds. Most governors possess a power which even the President lacks: They have an *item veto* on appropriation bills which enables them to veto expenditures for certain purposes while signing the rest of a budget bill into law.[1] Therefore, while legislative bodies still vote the money for government programs, they rely upon the executive for overall initial planning as well as for control through the veto power.

The President's obligations in the economic arena were further broadened by the Employment Act of 1946 which created the Council of Economic Advisers and required the President to send an annual economic message to Congress recommending measures needed to move the nation closer to full employment.

One of the more dramatic examples of presidential influence on the cost of living came in 1962 when John F. Kennedy was faced with an announced price increase by the nation's leading steel companies. Sure such an increase would be dangerously inflationary, he denounced the steel executives on television, threatened to transfer government contracts, and instigated antitrust investigations. Within a week, the steel corporations revoked the price boost.[2] When President Nixon exercised power which Congress had given him a year earlier to impose direct price and wage controls, it was a startling reversal of his administration's policy. He knew, certainly, that his success as a candidate in 1972 might well depend on his success as a manager of the economy in 1971.

The chief diplomat The President determines the official attitude of the United States toward every nation on earth. Constitutionally, he may sign treaties with other countries, recognize and exchange diplomatic representatives with other governments, and, with Senate approval, appoint American ambassadors abroad. In addition, through his control of other agencies in the executive branch, he directs American espionage and the content and scope of American propaganda abroad.

In most respects, the powers of state governors are somewhat comparable to the powers of the President; in the domain of foreign affairs, however, the authority of the President is unique. As he descends the steps of *The Spirit of '76* in Peking or Moscow, Bucharest or Bonn, he carries with him, as supreme diplomat, the prospects of survival in a nuclear world.

Commanders in chief The opening words of Article II,

1 Clyde F. Snider, *American State and Local Government,* 2nd ed. (N.Y.: Appleton-Century-Crofts, 1965), pp. 694, 261.
2 Louis W. Koenig, "Kennedy and Steel: The Great Price Dispute," Alan F. Westin, ed., *The Centers of Power* (N.Y.: Harcourt Brace Jovanovich, Inc., 1964), pp. 1–52.

Section 2 of the U.S. Constitution provide that "The President shall be commander in chief of the army and navy . . . and of the militia of the several states, when called into the actual service of the United States." In effect, this means that he can order troops anywhere, anytime, to fire on any foe. It is one of the most controversial provisions of the Constitution because its utilization nullifies the significance of the clause in Article I, Section 8 which gives Congress the "power to . . . declare war."

The growth of the President's role as commander in chief, ignoring the constitutional prerogatives of Congress, has been a gradual one, but full-scale "presidential wars" made their debut when Harry S Truman ordered U.S. forces to resist aggression against South Korea in 1950. The result, sanctioned by a United Nations resolution, was a period of hostilities lasting three years and killing more than thirty thousand Americans. These losses exceeded those of the Mexican and Spanish-American Wars combined, both of which were declared by Congress. Since President Johnson committed combat forces to Vietnam in 1965, nearly fifty thousand American lives have been sacrificed in a conflict lasting longer than any in our history.

It is probable that the Founding Fathers never intended to authorize the President to send troops into battle without either a congressional declaration of war or an enemy attack on American soil. Instead, it seems likely that they made the President commander in chief in order to authorize immediate retaliation in the event of aggression against the United States, and to insure civilian supremacy over the entrenched power of career military officials. The principle of civilian control over the military is a vital one, for if government policy yields to the wishes of the people with bombers and tanks, it cannot be directed by those armed only with votes.

In an era of hostile power blocs there is no doubt that the President must have the capacity to respond rapidly and reasonably to missile-laden provocations. But we must recognize that presidential authority as commander in chief has come dangerously close to dictatorship in military matters.

The military power of a governor seems trivial in comparison, yet significant by any other standards. He is commander in chief of his state militia, or national guard, except when the President has called it into national service. When race riots, hurricanes, or other disasters require action beyond the capacity of local police officials to control, a governor's judgment in sending in the additional forces he controls may be decisive in the restoration of an orderly peace.

Checking the Other Branches

Chief executives are influenced by legislative and judicial bodies and, in the total system of checks and balances, exert reciprocal influences upon them.

The legislative initiative   As we noted in the last chapter, many laws originate in the desire of some legislator to provide benefits to his district or to assist some local citizen. Paradoxically, however, chief executives are the source of most major legislative proposals. Article II, Section 3 directs that the President shall "from time to time give to the Congress Information of the State of the Union, and recommend to their Consideration such Measures as he shall judge necessary and expedient . . ." This process has now become rather ritualized, with an annual State of the Union message usually delivered in person each January. In this address, the President spends less time describing what the state of the union is than what he would like it to be. He uses it to outline very broadly the kind of new legislation he would like to see Congress enact. This is followed in close succession by a proposed budget of more than a thousand pages requesting specific amounts of money for each government agency, and an economic report recommending congressional action to insure general prosperity. In the months that follow, the President dispatches special messages to Congress, prepared by various executive agencies, in which he requests the passage of specific bills outlined in great detail. This recommended legislation is then introduced by sympathetic congressmen. Since 1953 no President has sent fewer than 170 legislative proposals to Congress in a single year, nor have fewer than 20 percent been enacted into law.[3] As a result, it is now commonplace to speak of much recent legislation in such terms as "Johnson's war on poverty," or "Nixon's revenue-sharing program."

State legislatures have come to rely upon governors for legislative leadership even more than Congress looks to the President. They are often poorly equipped with the staff assistance or research facilities necessary to formulate the detailed legislative solutions required by increasingly complex problems. The result is that

it has become customary to call the governor "the chief legislator," in spite of the . . . principle of separation of powers. . . . (G)overnors are now judged primarily by their legislative program rather than by their administrative ability, and most voters as well as most state legislators expect the governor to have a legislative program on the major issues of public policy.[4]

A variety of vetoes   Other checks that the chief executive can exert on the legislative branch are to call special sessions, to adjourn the legislature if the two houses cannot reach agreement on a date, and to exercise the veto power. Of these, the last is by far the most important.

When a chief executive receives a bill, he may sign it,

3 *The New York Times Encyclopedic Almanac* 1970, p. 172, and *Congressional Quarterly Weekly Report,* Feb. 19, 1972, p. 375. When President Johnson won approval of 69 percent of those he submitted in 1965, he had a larger congressional majority of members of his own party than any President in over twenty-five years. By contrast, in 1971 President Nixon, scoring only 20 percent, was faced with an opposition party majority of four in the Senate and thirty-seven in the House.
4 Wilder Crane, Jr., and Meredith W. Watts, Jr., *State Legislative Systems* (Englewood Cliffs, N.J.: Prentice-Hall, Inc., 1968), p. 99.

thereby completing its enactment into law, or veto it by returning it to the house where it was introduced. He is usually given a certain number of days in which to make up his mind (the President has ten), and if he chooses to veto it, the decision is usually fatal for the bill. It takes two thirds of those voting in both houses of Congress to enact a bill by overriding a President's veto. More stringent requirements prevail in most state legislatures; in Alaska, for example, a three-quarters vote is required, and in many states two thirds of the total membership. On the other hand, in six states a simple majority of the total membership can override a veto, and in North Carolina the governor is without any veto power.[5]

Should the chief executive neither sign a bill nor veto it within the time allotted him, the bill normally becomes law automatically. But if legislators have adjourned and gone home before the time limit for the regular veto has expired, the President and a few governors may kill a bill through what is called a *pocket veto* simply by refusing to sign it. The effects of the veto on legislation passed at the national level are summarized in Figure 35.

Figure 35   Congressional Bills and Presidential Vetoes, 1953–1970

Bills Passed	Regular Vetoes	Pocket Vetoes	Overridden Vetoes
12,671	108	135	4

Source: U.S. Bureau of the Census, *Statistical Abstract of the United States: 1971*, pp. 355–56.

All but eight state governors have a kind of check on the legislature which the President lacks. This is the *item veto*, mentioned earlier, which enables them to reduce or eliminate certain expenditures in an appropriations bill while signing the others into law.[6] The item veto gives governors more control over state budgets than the President has over the national budget and makes passage of *pork barrel* legislation more difficult in state legislatures than in Congress.

Since pork barrel measures benefit a particular region or district, rather than a larger area, they are particularly helpful in getting incumbent legislators reelected. A new court house or bridge or state college for the "home folks" will provide construction jobs and looks pretty impressive in the campaign literature of the candidate who can claim credit for getting the money to build it. Proposals for such appropriations are usually attached to more important bills as amendments, or *riders*, mainly because their sponsors fear that the chief executive

5 An unusually perceptive commentary on this topic may be found in Duane Lockard, *The Politics of State and Local Government*, 2nd ed. (N.Y.: The Macmillan Company, 1969), pp. 363–66. The six states are Alabama, Arkansas, Kentucky, Indiana, Tennessee, and West Virginia. *The Book of the States*, 1970–71 (Lexington, Ky.: The Council of State Governments, 1970), p. 78.
6 The eight states are Indiana, Iowa, Maine, Nevada, New Hampshire, North Carolina, Rhode Island, and Vermont. A few state governors have the authority to reduce the amounts of money appropriated for various "items" as well as to delete them entirely.

would veto them unless they were tied to the expenditure of more vital funds. Legislators tend to vote for each other's pork barrel measures in the vote-trading process called *logrolling.*

Special sessions The Constitution requires Congress to convene each January, and allows the President to call it into special session at his discretion. The mere suggestion that he may do so if action is not taken on certain bills is usually sufficient to prolong the regular session as long as is necessary. As a result, no President has called a special session since 1948. In over half the states, however, constitutions limit the length of regular sessions, and governors frequently resort to calling special sessions. Unlike the President, they can even limit the topics with which special sessions in about a third of the states may deal.[7]

The appointment of judges All federal court judges are appointed by the President, subject to confirmation by the U.S. Senate. Since these judges are chosen for life, the selections may influence the judicial branch long after the President who made them has slipped into the history books. One of the nine judges on the U.S. Supreme Court in 1972, for example, had been appointed by a President who died a quarter of a century earlier. Although the governor may appoint some judges in several of the states, this power is a less significant check upon the judicial branch than that of the President in the national government. The whole matter is examined in the next chapter.

Executive clemency Another check on the judicial process is the power of executive clemency which permits three kinds of orders: pardons, commutations, and reprieves. A pardon releases a person from further criminal punishment—usually a portion of a prison term. When whole groups of people are simultaneously pardoned, as frequently urged for draft resisters, the action is often called amnesty. A commutation is an executive order reducing a sentence imposed by the courts, and a reprieve simply postpones the time when a sentence is to begin.

The President has full powers of executive clemency over persons accused of violating national laws, but nearly half of the state governors have their authority over state law offenders curbed by constitutional restrictions, often involving approval by some pardon board. Yet the practical effects of the President's clemency powers are less significant, because most serious crimes are state, not national, offenses.

A Note on the Presidency

The similarities in the powers of the President and those of state governors have made it possible to discuss them together. In a deeper sense, however, the powers of the President are incomparable. Even if the mystique of his office can be penetrated and his authority categorized into its component elements, there is still the suspicion that

---

7 Donald R. Grant and H. C. Nixon, *State and Local Government in America* (Boston: Allyn and Bacon, Inc., 1963), p. 215.

the presidency, both as man and institution, somehow exceeds the sum of its parts.

The President's unique importance is best explained, perhaps, in terms of two curiously interrelated considerations: His authority is concentrated and his constituencies are numerous. On the first, it is well to note that Congress and the courts consist of many people, and their very multiplicity disperses the pressures brought by corporations, columnists, litigants, lobbyists, union leaders, and ordinary citizens throughout the nation. To influence national executive action, however, their ultimate target must be the man in the White House. He is the focus for the profusion of demands, desires, and fears that characterize this incredibly heterogeneous society.[8]

The President's constituencies, the groups which may affect his political future, are as varied as they are numerous. Most obviously, he is the only public official (discounting the Vice President) who is chosen by voters throughout the entire nation. This national constituency looks to him, as they have since the time of Washington, to transcend our infinite diversity by providing the moral leadership necessary to define our national purpose and attain our common goals. His international constituency, important only since World War II, sees in him the military assistance, trade concessions, or financial aid sometimes necessary for survival. Less broad but also significant are two domestic constituencies. One is the partisan coalition which supported his candidacy (campaign workers, party leaders, financial contributors, and so forth), and the other consists of congressmen and administrative officials—the bureaucracy—without whose help his efforts are doomed to failure.[9]

Taken together, these multiple constituencies impose on the President the obligation to meet an awesome array of sometimes contradictory expectations. His enormous power is scarcely commensurate with the demands made upon it, yet the very immensity of the challenge holds out a promise of greatness.

THE MAKING AND MAINTENANCE OF CHIEF EXECUTIVES
Room at the Top—for Whom?

The office of chief executive is the highest rung on the ladder of political success. What are the characteristics of those who have occupied it?

Qualifications for office The President and Vice President must meet constitutional standards set forth in Article II, Section 1. They must be citizens by birth, at least thirty-five years old, and must have resided in the United States for fourteen years or more. It seems doubtful

8 James MacGregor Burns, *Congress on Trial* (N.Y.: Harper & Bros., 1949), pp. 181–92.
9 Richard E. Neustadt, "The Presidency at Mid-Century," *Law and Contemporary Problems* 21 (Autumn 1956): 609–45.

Paul Sequeira.

His car well protected, President Nixon is acclaimed by supporters in suburbia.

that many political careers have been thwarted by these requirements. The state constitutional requirements for governors are somewhat similar, although less stringent, and are also of very little practical political consequence.

Characteristics of chief executives While millions of Americans meet the minimum legal qualifications for President, it is clear that few hurdle the informal barriers erected by an accumulation of traditions, myths, and considerations of political expediency. If the characteristics of the thirty-six persons who have become President are a guide to the kinds of people who have the best chance in the future, the field can be narrowed substantially. A composite description reveals that the "average" President is a male Caucasian, in his fifties, of English or Scotch-Irish descent. He is most often a lawyer who has previously served as a governor or U.S. senator.

The youngest ever to serve were Theodore Roosevelt at forty-two and John F. Kennedy at forty-three while the oldest were William Henry Harrison at sixty-eight and Dwight D. Eisenhower at seventy. There have been no non-Christians and only one Roman Catholic (Kennedy), although four had no formal religious affiliation. Methodists and Baptists, most numerous among Protestant denominations in the general population, have each sent only two to the White House, while among the churches of higher socioeconomic status, Episcopalians can claim nine Presidents, Presbyterians seven, and Unitarians four. All Presidents have descended from Irish, English, French,

Dutch, German, or Swiss stock.[10] Times, of course, are changing. Vice President Spiro Agnew is of Greek extraction and his opponent in 1968, Sen. Edmund Muskie, is of Polish parentage.

One can not be sure of the significance of these characteristics, or of the very similar ones shared by most congressmen and judges. It is plausible, however, that officials drawn so predominantly from the ranks of the relatively privileged may have difficulty understanding the problems, let alone the attitudes, of those less favored. Conversely, groups such as the poor, members of ethnic minorities, young people, and women may become increasingly alienated from a society that passes them by so frequently in recruiting its top leadership.

There was once considerable discussion about "availability" as a factor in choosing presidential nominees. The most available candidates were said to be those who possessed the characteristics of the previous Presidents, plus the advantage of coming from a large, politically doubtful state. The theory was that a party should nominate a man from a state with many electoral votes which the party might not win if it chose someone from somewhere else. But since television has demonstrated its ability to publicize almost anyone from anywhere in just a few weeks, this concept has been largely abandoned. Coverage by the mass media has also shifted attention from the presidential possibilities of governors, who cope mostly with state problems, to the potentialities of U.S. senators who speak out on national and international issues. Ideologically, a moderate image is an enormous asset. The "log cabin" tradition, moreover, occupies a nostalgic place in American political lore. It assumed that any boy could grow up to be President, and that a poor boy who made good had an even better chance. Recent history indicates that humble origins are neither a help nor a hindrance, as long as one can raise $25 million or so for a presidential campaign. There is another aspect of availability that still endures: the family man. No divorced man has ever been President (although this is no doubt a less serious liability than in the past), and we have elected only one bachelor.

It is reasonable to assume that many of the same characteristics that made for presidential availability also would improve one's chances for gaining a governorship. The backgrounds of governors, however, seem to reveal considerable diversity. A recent study shows that the largest number were lawyers in their late forties. Teaching ranked second as an occupational background.[11] Not surprisingly, all were males.

The Election Process

The procedures by which chief executives are chosen are sometimes complex and often controversial.

10 Most of this information came from *The New York Times Encyclopedic Almanac* 1972, pp. 62–63.
11 Grant and Nixon, op. cit., p. 213.

The electoral college   If every voter had to understand the whole process by which the President and Vice President are elected, chances are that we would never be able to choose them at all. The fact that we do is a triumph of common sense over legal technicalities, a conquest of function over form.

At the constitutional convention, a major controversy raged over who should elect the President. The compromise finally agreed upon provided that he should be chosen by an electoral college, but with the understanding that each state could select its members however it wished. It was further agreed that each state would have the same number of electors in the electoral college as it had members of Congress (two in the Senate plus as many in the House of Representatives as its population warranted).

Initially, each elector was to cast two votes. The person receiving the most votes would be President, and the person placing second would be Vice President. If no candidate received a majority, the election of the President was transferred to the House of Representatives, where all congressmen from each state were given a single vote. If the person finishing second lacked a majority in the electoral college, then the election of the Vice President became the responsibility of the U.S. Senate.

This procedure, outlined in Article II, Section 1, worked smoothly until 1800 when a tied vote in the electoral college between Thomas Jefferson and Aaron Burr (who belonged to the same party) threw the election into a long and bitter fight in the House of Representatives. After thirty-six ballots, and with the support of Alexander Hamilton, his long-time foe, Jefferson was elected President. This crisis prompted the ratification of the Twelfth Amendment which provided that each member of the electoral college should cast one vote for President and a second, separate vote for Vice President.

The actual implementation of these constitutional provisions was quite undemocratic originally. In the first place, until the ninth presidential election in 1824, members of the electoral college in most states were chosen by the state legislatures. The sequence is as follows:

Voters ⟹ State Legislatures ⟹ Electoral College ⟹ President

Gradually, however, state laws were changed to eliminate the state legislatures from this process and to permit the voters to elect members of the electoral college directly, as they do today in every state.

A second major change has democratized the process still more. Candidates for the electoral college are now nominated on political party tickets and pledged in advance to vote for the presidential nominee of their party. It was the rise of political parties, therefore, that transformed the role of the individual member of the electoral college from that of a free agent voting for whom he pleased to that of a political mirror, merely reflecting the voters' preference for his party's candidate. In each state, indeed, the electoral college selects the choice of the voters so automatically that in most states the ballots contain only the names of the presidential and vice presidential contenders, and not the names of the candidates for the electoral college who are committed to vote for them.

Political parties have had another effect on the process of electing the President: As a result of the two-party system, one of the major party candidates is almost certain to get a majority in the electoral college, thereby minimizing the possibility that a presidential election will be thrown into the House of Representatives. Only twice in our history, in 1800 and again in 1824, has there been a third candidate sufficiently popular to prevent an electoral college majority. It could, of course, happen again, and the third-party candidacy of George Wallace in 1968 came closer than any in more than fifty years to doing just that.

Electoral college reform   The electoral college, cumbersome and archaic as it is, might seem to be only a harmless relic of the dead past. Yet the number of reform proposals, pushed with great vigor, belies such a generous assessment. There are two major criticisms of the present system. One is that nothing can prevent a member of the electoral college, if he wishes, from voting for someone other than the candidate of his party. This has never altered the outcome of a presidential election, but to avoid this possibility, President Lyndon B. Johnson proposed that individual electors be eliminated and electoral votes be automatically awarded to the candidate with the most popular votes in each state.

The second, and more serious, accusation against the electoral college is that it permits the election of a President whose opponent received more popular votes. This objection cannot be dismissed lightly, for it actually occurred after the elections of 1824, 1876, and 1888. The voters' second choice became President. The cause of this perversion of the democratic process is that members of the electoral college are elected at large in each state. As a result, if a candidate carries a state by just one vote, he wins all of that state's electoral votes. This situation has had a profound effect on presidential campaign strategy and has enhanced the importance of populous urban areas in presidential elections, since it is the states with big cities that have many electoral votes.

Let us take a hypothetical example of how this situation might affect the next presidential election. Assume that the two candidates are running neck and neck throughout the nation as a whole, both in popular and electoral votes, and that the result will depend on the outcome of races in California and North Dakota. In California, each voter is voting for forty-five members of the electoral college and in North Dakota for three members. Finally, the vote count is completed, and results are announced:

Figure 36   How A Majority Can Lose

	Popular Vote		Electoral Vote	
	Republican	Democratic	Republican	Democratic
North Dakota	160,000	80,000	3	0
California	3,390,000	3,400,000	0	45
Total	3,550,000	3,480,000	3	45

Given such a distribution of votes, the Democratic candidate would win in the electoral college, even though his Republican opponent was favored by more people. Such an injustice can occur whenever one candidate carries the large urbanized states (*e.g.,* California) by even a few votes, while losing the small predominantly rural states (*e.g.,* North Dakota) by a substantial margin.

Several reforms have been suggested to eliminate this possibility. The Lodge-Gossett plan would split a state's electoral vote in the same proportion as the division of the popular vote. Former Senator Karl Mundt (R.-N. D.) would permit the people to elect one member of the electoral college from each congressional district and choose only two at large from every state. A final plan, already proposed as a constitutional amendment by a two-thirds vote of the House of Representatives, would abolish the electoral college completely in favor of a direct vote by the people. It includes the proviso that if no candidate receives at least 40 percent of the popular vote, a runoff election would be held between the two candidates with the most votes.

Those who favor the retention of the electoral college contend that its abolition would undermine the importance of the states and encourage the formation of minor parties. Some also suggest that since the U.S. Senate overrepresents small states in the Congress, the electoral college should be preserved because it enhances the importance of voters in the big states. People who want a direct popular vote for President rest their case chiefly on the grounds of simplicity and the assumption that it conforms most closely to the democratic theory of majority rule.

The choice of state executives   The President and the Vice President are the only officials in the entire national government who are chosen by and responsible to a nation-wide constituency. At the state level things are different. In addition to the governor and the lieutenant governor, the voters often elect four or five other state-wide executive officials, most commonly the attorney general, secretary of state, treasurer, and auditor (or controller). The number of officials appointed by the governor is correspondingly reduced.

The process by which state executives gain office is a simple one. They are nearly always nominated in party primaries and elected by a direct vote of the people. In Georgia and Vermont, however, the election is thrown into the state legislature if no candidate receives a majority of the popular vote.

Service and Succession

Many perils confront a chief executive, including death and defeat when seeking reelection. It is one measure of the hazards of the presidency that somewhat more than one in five have died in office. Four Presidents died naturally (W. H. Harrison, Taylor, Harding, and F. D. Roosevelt) and four were shot (Lincoln, Garfield, McKinley, and Kennedy). Governors seem to fare much better; they tend to be younger and make less dramatic targets.

Terms and salaries   Originally, no limit was placed on the number of four-year terms a President might serve. The examples of Washington, Jefferson, Madison, Monroe, and Jackson soon established a two-term tradition, however, and it was not until Franklin D. Roosevelt was elected to a third term in 1940 and a fourth in 1944 that this precedent was broken. Amendment Twenty-two was designed to prevent repetition of the Roosevelt example and limited the President to two terms or (if he had served a portion of his predecessor's term) no more than ten years in office.

A few state governors are elected for two-year terms, but a steadily growing majority are chosen for four. In some states, governors may be reelected without limitation, and in 1970 New York voters returned Nelson Rockefeller to an unprecedented fourth four-year term. Often governors are prohibited from seeking a second *successive* term out of fear that they may accumulate excessive power, and sometimes they face the same limitations as Presidents—no more than a two-term total. Only once, in North Dakota, was a governor removed in a recall election.

While in office, the President receives a salary of $200,000 per year, and the reimbursement for governors ranges from about $18,000 to $55,000. Housing accommodations and expense accounts are also provided.

Succession   The problem of an orderly succession process for filling vacant executive offices is still unsolved in many nations, where leadership often is seized by disgruntled military officers and consolidated by purges of all potential rivals. In the United States, the Constitution (Article II, Section 1) provides that the Vice President shall assume the powers and duties of the President in the event of his removal, death, resignation, or inability. It gives Congress the power to provide for succession if both the President and Vice President are disqualified and the Speaker of the House of Representatives is now next in line of succession, followed by the president pro tem of the Senate and cabinet officials beginning with the Secretary of State. Fortunately, only Vice Presidents have been summoned to fill a vacant presidency, and the torch has always been passed peacefully.

The presidential transition process might have proved more awkward if a President had died when the nation was without a Vice President. This situation has existed fifteen times—on the eight occasions when former Vice Presidents were forced to become Presidents, and during the periods immediately following the deaths of seven Vice Presidents. The possibility of a prolonged vice-presidential vacancy was eliminated by the Twenty-fifth Amendment, which requires the President to appoint a Vice President, should there be none, subject to the confirmation of a majority vote in the House and Senate.

When governorships become vacant before the term of office expires, the lieutenant governor fills the vacancy, except in ten states where there is no such official. In these states, the presiding officer of one of the state legislative chambers assumes the governorship.[12]

The problem of disability   Although the Constitution authorizes the Vice President to take over when the President is unable to discharge his powers and duties, it does not say what constitutes inability or who should determine whether it exists. As a result, no Vice President, no matter how sick or incapacitated the President has been, has dared to displace him. Thus, while President Garfield lay for more than two months in a coma, and again during the prolonged illnesses of Presidents Cleveland, Wilson, and Eisenhower, the ship of state drifted more or less aimlessly (although fortunately in placid waters).

The Twenty-fifth Amendment, in addition to providing a way to fill vice-presidential vacancies, establishes methods to cope with presidential disability. It permits the President to declare himself disabled, or—if he does not or cannot—it allows the Vice President and a majority of either the cabinet, or of some other body designated by Congress, to declare him disabled. Should the President object, the matter is submitted to Congress, with a two-thirds vote of both houses necessary to overrule him.

THE ADMINISTRATIVE BUREAUCRACY

Executives get their name from the fact that it has been their historic function, in the words of Article II, Section 3, to "take Care that the Laws be faithfully executed . . ." In other words, they administer, enforce, and thus carry out the laws. With thousands of statutes on the books, enormous administrative bureaucracies have been created to help them. They consist, in part, of the departments, commissions, and other agencies described below.

National Executive Organization

If the President spent just one hour a week supervising each of the agencies directly responsible to him in the executive branch, he would have about a sixty-hour work week, and would have to sign or veto bills, plan new legislative programs, grant pardons, appoint judges, discharge his ceremonial obligations, and perform all the rest of his

12 Ibid., pp. 218–19.

functions in what little time was left. Confronted with such overwhelming tasks, he does the best he can; he appoints people he trusts to head the various executive agencies, and usually intervenes personally only when troubles arise. Yet he knows that the ultimate responsibility is his.

The agencies reporting to the President may be grouped into four categories: (1) the departments headed by cabinet members; (2) agencies in the Executive Office of the President; (3) regulatory commissions; and (4) government corporations—with a substantial number left over. Only the most important can be mentioned here, but first, a few words on the vice presidency—an office too much maligned.

The vice presidency   John Adams, our first Vice President, complained that his was "the most insignificant office that ever the invention of man contrived or his imagination conceived." It has never quite recovered from that assessment. Theodore Roosevelt was put in the post to get rid of him as governor of New York, and John Garner, a salty old Texan who had the job for eight years, is said to have advised Lyndon Johnson not to take it because he believed the vice presidency wasn't "worth a bucket of warm spit."

Yet, since eight Vice Presidents (including Theodore Roosevelt and Lyndon Johnson) have assumed the presidency because of the deaths of their predecessors, the office obviously has great potential. But it is also important in itself.

In addition to presiding over the Senate and "checking the President's health," Vice Presidents have been delegated increased responsibility in the last quarter of a century. Perhaps the most powerful was Richard M. Nixon, whom President Eisenhower authorized to call cabinet meetings and exercise surveillance over the administration while he was recuperating from his several illnesses. Mr. Nixon also assumed many party campaign responsibilities for the President and represented him at a variety of ceremonial functions. The Vice President has increasingly become something of a world traveler, commissioned by the President to make various goodwill or fact-finding tours. He is also chairman of the National Space Council, director of the Office of Intergovernmental Relations, and a member of the National Security Council.

The point is not that the Vice President is an inherently powerful executive, but that he may become as important as the President wishes. His office is a largely untapped resource but one that has attained increasing public visibility in recent years. Vice President Agnew, for example, has succeeded in attracting more publicity and infuriating the political opposition to a greater degree than any Vice President in history—with the possible exception of Richard Nixon. The most important evidence of the growing stature of the vice-presidential office is its increasing effectiveness, demonstrated by both Nixon in 1960 and Hubert Humphrey in 1968, as a springboard to a presidential nomination.

The departments   The eleven departments now in the ex-

Figure 37   The Structure of the National Government

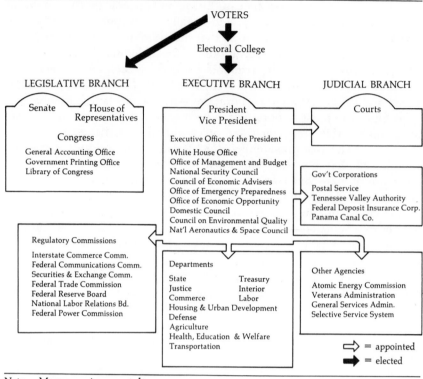

VOTERS

Electoral College

LEGISLATIVE BRANCH   EXECUTIVE BRANCH   JUDICIAL BRANCH

| Senate   House of Representatives | President Vice President | Courts |

Congress

General Accounting Office
Government Printing Office
Library of Congress

Executive Office of the President

White House Office
Office of Management and Budget
National Security Council
Council of Economic Advisers
Office of Emergency Preparedness
Office of Economic Opportunity
Domestic Council
Council on Environmental Quality
Nat'l Aeronautics & Space Council

Gov't Corporations

Postal Service
Tennessee Valley Authority
Federal Deposit Insurance Corp.
Panama Canal Co.

Regulatory Commissions

Interstate Commerce Comm.
Federal Communications Comm.
Securities & Exchange Comm.
Federal Trade Commission
Federal Reserve Board
National Labor Relations Bd.
Federal Power Commission

Departments

State   Treasury
Justice   Interior
Commerce   Labor
Housing & Urban Development
Defense
Agriculture
Health, Education & Welfare
Transportation

Other Agencies

Atomic Energy Commission
Veterans Administration
General Services Admin.
Selective Service System

⇨ = appointed
➡ = elected

Note: Many agencies are not shown.
Source: U.S. Bureau of the Census, *Statistical Abstract of the United States: 1971*, p. 371.

ecutive branch have been created by Congress over many years. These agencies are among the most prestigious in government, and their heads, usually called secretaries, constitute the nucleus of the President's cabinet. Traditionally, four departments (State, Defense, Treasury, and Justice) have been considered more important than the others, although expanded welfare programs and increased concern with environmental pollution have focused much attention on the Department of Health, Education and Welfare and the Department of the Interior. The relative influence of all the departments depends, in part, on the people who head them, and their distinctive relationships to the President. A list of the departments, with their major functions, appears in Figure 38.

The Executive Office of the President   The Executive Office is actually a collection of agencies which provide the President with advice, assistance, and coordinated effort in various fields. Among the more important are the Council on Environmental Quality, the Cost of Living Council, the Office of Emergency Preparedness, the Office of Economic Opportunity, and the four others whose descriptions follow.

The National Security Council integrates foreign policy formulation, in this respect eclipsing the functions of the State Department to some degree. It consists of the President, Vice President,

Figure 38   Executive Departments in the National Government

Department and date established	1971 Employees[1]	Major Functions
State, 1789	39,513	Supervises diplomatic personnel; advises on foreign policy; administers foreign aid.
Defense, 1947[2]	1,145,696[2]	Coordinates budgeting, logistics, and general administration of armed services; supervises Joint Chiefs of Staff; awards military contracts.
Treasury, 1789	98,173	Collects taxes; coins money; sells bonds; runs Secret Service to enforce laws in this area and protect government leaders.
Justice, 1870[3]	40,828	Administers F.B.I. to enforce acts of Congress; prosecutes court cases for U.S. government; maintains federal prisons; investigates violations of antitrust and civil rights laws; gives legal advice to government; supervises immigration.
Health, Education and Welfare, 1953[4]	110,100	Administers social security pension and Medicare programs, federal aid to education, pure food and drug laws, and public health research and assistance.
Interior, 1849	64,577	Administers Bureau of Indian Affairs, mine safety laws, conservation of mineral resources, national parks, overseas territories, some hydroelectric power facilities.
Agriculture, 1862	105,006	Guarantees minimum prices on certain crops; stores food surpluses; provides crop insurance; administers national forests; helps finance farm services.
Commerce, 1903	37,012	Awards patents; promotes exports of U.S. products; administers Bureau of the Census and Weather Bureau.
Labor, 1913[5]	11,246	Enforces minimum wage laws; administers unemployment compensation; mediates some labor-management disputes; compiles cost-of-living statistics.
Housing and Urban Development, 1965	15,544	Directs urban renewal financial grants, government-guaranteed home purchase loans, and public housing assistance.
Transportation, 1966	68,126	Administers interstate highway programs, air safety standards, automotive safety laws, the Alaska railroad, and Coast Guard.

[1] U.S. Bureau of the Census, *Statistical Abstract of the United States: 1971*, p. 389.
[2] The Defense Department replaced the War Department, in charge of army affairs, and the Navy Department, both established in 1789. The employment figure includes civilians only.
[3] The office of Attorney General was created in 1789 but he was given no departmental responsibility until 1870.
[4] The national government performed functions in these fields through separate agencies long before the department was created.
[5] The Labor Department was once a part of a Department of Commerce and Labor.

Secretaries of State and Defense, and Director of the Office of Emergency Preparedness; others may also participate. The Central Intelligence Agency, which gathers and interprets vital information concerning security matters, reports to the NSC.

The White House Office is an organizational extension of the President himself—it helps to manage his time, fill his brain, disseminate his thoughts, and execute his commands. More than any other agency, it is a monument to the institutionalization of the presidency. The nation's highest office, in a sense, has outgrown the man who holds it. It expands inexorably, as though reaching out to grapple with each new complexity in the nation it seeks to govern. To some degree, the White House Office is molded by the personal preferences of each President. Individual titles come and go; President Nixon has employed over fifty persons variously designated as counselors, assistants, special consultants, deputy assistants, deputy counselors, special assistants, and secretaries. The purposes for which the last few Presidents have used these officials have become rather standardized. Several are speech writers, one may act almost as a junior-grade president, and another serves as a press secretary in charge of press releases and news conferences. Usually included are a chief adviser for national security matters (the invaluable Henry Kissinger in the Nixon administration) and a congressional liaison man, who acts as the President's chief lobbyist. These men are closest to the President— they accompany him to Camp David on his weekend retreats and are privy to his deepest political desires. If one wanted to understand President Nixon's view of the world in 1972, one would need to inquire into the vistas opened to him by Kissinger, H. R. Haldeman, Ronald Ziegler, John Ehrlichman, Robert Finch, and other leading figures in the White House Office.

Perhaps the most important tool available to a President in establishing national priorities is his authority to recommend allocations of money to Congress. The proposed budget is prepared primarily by the Office of Management and Budget, to which all other government agencies must submit estimates of desired expenditures.

The Council of Economic Advisers is one of the smallest agencies in the national government, employing less than sixty people. Yet its three members are charged with the responsibility of providing the President with the most able economic advice about how to curb inflation and unemployment, while increasing both the living standard and the gross national product.

Regulatory commissions Among the many "independent" agencies of the national government—those not embraced by the eleven departments or the Executive Office of the President—are the commissions charged with protecting the public by regulating various phases of private business activity. In this area, a distinction should be made between those industries in which public policy has sanctioned monopolistic control by a single corporation, and those in which government has encouraged free and vigorous competition among many firms.

Monopoly is most common in the public utility industries whose services are vital to the entire population. If two electricity, natural gas, railroad, or telephone companies were competing in the same area, for example, there would be duplicate wires, pipes, and rails, thereby increasing costs, cutting the profits of each corporation, and resulting in higher rates for the consumer. In the radio and television industries, it is essential to grant each station a monopoly on a particular wave length so that the audience will not be plagued by two or more programs (to say nothing of commercials) simultaneously. Yet if consumer choice is limited by monopolistic control, as it often is, who is to grant the monopolies? Who is to protect the public from the abuses that may result—exorbitant rates, sloppy service, or poor programming?

The answers, presumably, are the regulatory commissions of the national and state governments which grant franchises, impose rate limitations, and establish minimum standards. Some of these agen-

Figure 39   Regulatory Commissions in the National Government

Commission and Date Established	No. of Members	Terms	Functions
Interstate Commerce Commission, 1887	11	7 yrs.	Licenses and fixes rates for railroads, trucks, buses, and domestic shipping.
Federal Reserve Board, 1913	7	14 yrs.	Controls supply of currency and certain banking policies.
Federal Trade Commission, 1914	5	7 yrs.	Assists in enforcing antitrust laws and prohibits false advertising.
Federal Power Commission, 1920	5	5 yrs.	Regulates prices and services in electric power and natural gas industries.
Federal Communications Commission, 1934	7	7 yrs.	Grants radio and television licenses and fixes rates for telegraph and telephone services.[1]
Securities and Exchange Commission, 1934	5	5 yrs.	Licenses stock and bond brokers and protects market investors.
National Labor Relations Board, 1935	5	5 yrs.	Holds elections to determine union collective bargaining rights and forbids unfair practices.
Civil Aeronautics Board, 1938	5	6 yrs.	Assigns airline routes and regulates rates and services.
Federal Maritime Commission, 1961	5	5 yrs.	Regulates dock charges and foreign routes for American merchant ships.

[1] Citing a shortage of funds and staff members, the FCC announced in December of 1971 that it was abandoning an attempt to investigate the fairness of rates charged for interstate phone calls. Its decision was widely criticized and later modified.

cies impose certain controls upon competitive industries as well. The functions of the major ones are indicated in Figure 39.

Regulatory commissions differ from most other executive agencies in four respects. First, they have what is sometimes called quasi-legislative and quasi-judicial powers, which simply means that they function somewhat like lawmaking bodies in formulating rules for the corporations they regulate, and somewhat like courts in holding hearings relative to those rules. Second, they are multiheaded agencies whose decisions, because of their complex nature, are made by groups rather than by single administrators. Third, they are bipartisan in membership to insure a representation of both parties and, it is hoped, diverse attitudes. Finally, they have considerable independence from the President, to make sure—among other things—that he cannot intimidate them into granting preferred treatment to corporations in which his friends own stock. Members of these commissions are appointed for specific terms of office and cannot be fired (except for demonstrated cause) until their terms have expired. In fact, these agencies are so independent that they are sometimes viewed as a fourth branch of the government.[13]

The major criticism levied against the regulatory commissions is that their relative independence from overall government control has allowed them to fall under the influence of the business interests from whose ranks their members are often chosen. Corporation-oriented wolves, it is argued, are sent to guard the defenseless chickens. As *Newsweek* magazine summed up the allegation, "the [regulatory] agencies seem more concerned with serving the industries they are supposed to regulate than with protecting the public."[14]

Government corporations   There are about twenty government-owned corporations in the national government created to sell some form of services that will defray all or a large part of their operating expenses. The newest of these—the U.S. Postal Service, created in 1970—is also by far the largest. Before the new corporation was established, the post office was operated as a government department whose 727,645 employees made it second only to the Defense Department among all government employers.[15]

Previously, the Tennessee Valley Authority, providing hydroelectric power, flood control, and recreation facilities in seven southeastern states,[16] was the largest government corporation, although the Federal Deposit Insurance Corporation, guaranteeing private bank de-

---

13 A mammoth collection of court decisions, official documents, and enlightened commentary on the regulatory commissions may be found in *Separation of Powers and the Independent Agencies: Cases and Selected Readings* (Washington, D. C.: U.S. Government Printing Office, 1970).
14 August 24, 1970, p. 45.
15 U.S. Bureau of the Census, *The Statistical Abstract of the United States: 1970,* pp. 396–97.
16 A favorable account of the TVA, often condemned as America's most socialistic enterprise, is found in David E. Lilienthal, *TVA: Democracy on the March* (Chicago: Quadrangle Books, Inc., 1944).

posits up to $20,000, and the Panama Canal Company are also important. Even more than the regulatory commissions, government corporations are largely independent of presidential control. They are also favorite targets of right-wing attacks upon socialistic programs.

Miscellaneous agencies   There are many other agencies in the executive branch that cannot be squeezed into neat administrative pigeonholes. One of these, the Veterans Administration, is next only to the Defense Department and Post Office in number of employees and dispenses G.I. college benefits, administers veterans' hospitals, and allocates funds for pensions. Lest it run low on clients, another government agency, the Selective Service System, has been busily providing new ones.

The General Services Administration is also too important to be ignored. It employs over 38,000 people, yet is engaged in activities that command no headlines and little attention. It is responsible for the purchasing of supplies and the management of property for many other government agencies in order to reduce the waste of tax money and duplication of government activities.

From spoils to merit: the civil service   During most of our early history, the victorious presidential candidate appointed his friends and supporters—almost always members of his own party—to public office. Although this *spoils* or *patronage* system is correctly associated with President Andrew Jackson, on a smaller scale its origins go back to 1801 when the control of the national government was first transferred from one party to another. Jackson justified the system by a principle of rotation in office, arguing that the potential corruption of government employees could be checked by replacing them with some frequency. He insisted, moreover, that almost any man had enough common sense to hold almost any job and that it was democratic, therefore, to give as many people as possible an opportunity to work for the government.

However worthy Jackson's intentions may have been, the spoils system deprived the government of experienced workers and often resulted in the appointment of men of dubious competence. An alternative system was available. The Prussian government had been hiring people on the basis of merit since late in the seventeenth century and England followed suit in 1853. In America, not until after the issue was dramatized by the assassination of President James A. Garfield by a disgruntled job seeker did any significant reform occur. In 1883 Congress passed the Pendleton Act creating a Civil Service Commission to supervise the selection of government employees on the basis of merit as demonstrated in competitive examinations. Although less than 15 percent of all jobs were initially covered, the merit system has gradually expanded to include more than 90 percent of the civilian employees of the United States government.

The Civil Service Commission consists of three persons appointed by the President, only two of whom may belong to the same party. From offices in ten cities scattered throughout the nation, it

**Figure 40   Some Characteristics of Civilian Employees
of the United States Government**

(by percent of total)

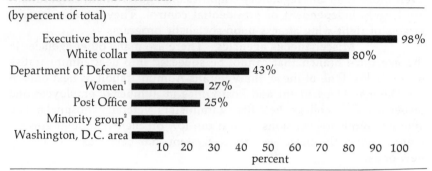

¹ Over half are employed in clerical, office, health, management, and library capacities.
² About 78 percent are blacks. Of government employees with the highest job classifications (GS 12–GS 18) 4.5 percent are members of minority groups.
Source: U.S. Bureau of the Census, *Statistical Abstract of the United States: 1971*, pp. 388–90.

coordinates employment, promotion, and dismissal procedures for most agencies in the executive branch, although some, such as the Foreign Service in the State Department, the F.B.I., and the Tennessee Valley Authority, maintain their own merit systems independently.

In 1971 there were 2,847,000 civilians employed by the national government, a number larger than the total populations of any of the twenty-six smallest states and nearly three times the number employed in 1940. These federal employees possessed a range of occupations almost as diverse as the entire economy, and included about 149,000 engineers and architects, 113,000 accountants and budget specialists, 94,000 medical personnel, 48,000 lawyers and legal assistants, 34,000 social scientists, 26,000 machine tool operators, 13,000 painters and paperhangers, and 65,000 manual laborers.[17] Related information about the federal civil service is found in Figure 40.

The overwhelming majority of government employees, after passing the appropriate examinations, are given job classifications in one of the General Schedule (GS) grades, numbered from 1 to 18 and paying, in 1971, from $4326 to $36,000 per year. Employment procedures include two important rules: The hiring officer in each bureau must fill each vacancy by employing one of the three persons scoring highest on the civil service examination, and on each examination disabled veterans, their wives, or their widows are given a ten-point bonus; any veteran receives a five-point bonus. After a probationary period, civil service employees cannot be fired without a public hearing, and under certain circumstances may appeal to the Civil Service Commission itself. All in all, government employment represents a potential career of considerable attractiveness.

17 U.S. Bureau of the Census, *The Statistical Abstract of the United States: 1971*, p. 390.

State Executive Organization

Not counting the cities, counties, and other agencies of local government, the fifty states employ over two-and-one-half million people—nearly as many as the civilians working for the national government. Even though the merit system has not gained so wide an acceptance at the state as at the national level, most employees in most states are recruited and protected by civil service procedures. State administrative organization, with few exceptions, differs most markedly from the national government in the dispersion and fragmentation of executive authority. In theory, the governor is a chief executive; in fact, there are many popularly elected "chiefs," each with his own staff of state employees.

The lieutenant governorships Although his office is generally modeled upon the vice presidency, the lieutenant governor's usually exceeds it in power. If the governor is out of the state, for example, many states give the lieutenant governor full powers as acting governor. In Indiana and Florida he may also serve as the head of some administrative department,[18] while in California, and many other states, he is an automatic *ex-officio* member of a number of commissions dealing with such matters as the management of state lands and the administration of the state university.[19] The lieutenant governorship differs from the vice presidency in another respect. In a majority of states, the lieutenant governor is elected separately, and therefore may even belong to a different party than the governor.

Other elected executives In forty-four of the states, the heads of five or more state agencies are chosen by the voters and in seven of them over ten agencies fall in this category.[20] At the other extreme, the governor has the widest discretion in appointing his executive subordinates in Alaska, Hawaii, Maryland, New Hampshire, New Jersey, and Pennsylvania.

The state executive posts most frequently filled by popular election, aside from governor and lieutenant governor, are secretary of state, attorney general, treasurer, and auditor. The secretary of state usually records official documents and laws, grants charters incorporating businesses, and supervises election machinery all the way from the printing of ballots to the counting of votes. The attorney general is the legal adviser to the governor, state legislature, and all executive agencies; he represents the state in court when it is suing or being sued, and usually oversees the prosecution of criminal cases. State treasurers have custody over tax receipts, allocate money to other agencies on the basis

18 Snider, op. cit., p. 269, and *The Book of the States*, 1970–71, op. cit., p. 138.
19 Winston W. Crouch, *et al.*, *California Government and Politics*, 4th ed. (Englewood Cliffs, N.J.: Prentice-Hall, Inc.; 1967), p. 161.
20 The seven states placing the most executive positions beyond gubernatorial control are Georgia, Louisiana, Mississippi, North Carolina, North Dakota, Oklahoma, and South Carolina. *The Book of the States*, 1970–71, op. cit., pp. 146–47.

of state legislative appropriations, and, in many cases, sell bonds when the state must borrow money. Auditors, often called state controllers, have the job of checking on state expenditures, much as the head of the General Accounting Office does in the national government. They also enforce financial restrictions on cities and counties.[21] The governor's authority is further diminished in several states by the popular election of public school superintendents, agricultural commissioners, and other executive officials.

Major departments and other agencies Most state executive departments are under the control of persons chosen by the governors, and employ a majority of the people on state payrolls. Combined employment figures for the fifty states reveal the relative significance of major state agencies:

1) Higher education   623,918
2) Hospitals   406,789
3) Highways   293,089
4) Natural resources   122,893
5) Financial administration   88,177
6) Public welfare   83,558[22]

In addition, each state has a public utility or public service commission, responsible for regulating rates and services within each state for the electric power, telephone, bus, natural gas, and similar industries. Other major state agencies license motor vehicles and drivers, enforce minimum standards for doctors, lawyers, pharmacists, barbers, morticians, and other occupations, and operate state parks and other outdoor recreational facilities.

The Problem of Bureaucratic Responsibility

At both the national and state levels of government, the central problem posed by administrative bureaucracies is how to make them accountable to the people—or to officials elected by the people. There is a widespread feeling that bureaucracies mean rule-bound, delay-filled indifference to the citizen and that they are unduly high in both operating costs and in project failures. The Federal Housing Administration has been criticized for granting mortgage insurance on "almost totally defective" homes,[23] compensatory education programs have been of little value in many instances,[24] and a subcommittee of the House of Representatives has reported that nearly $1.5 billion has been given to the states by the federal Law Enforcement Assistance Administration without any "visible impact on the incidence of crime." The

21 Snider, op. cit., pp. 277–80.
22 The Book of the States, 1970–71, op. cit., p. 180.
23 Congressional Quarterly Weekly Report, June 24, 1972, p. 1538.
24 Ibid., May 6, 1972, p. 1009.

Mary Rosenfeld, Nancy Palmer
Photo Agency.

At all levels of government, bucking bureaucracies has become a difficult problem. Here a young father complains of inaction on conditions in his rundown housing project in Somerville, Massachusetts.

report concluded that the program had been characterized by "inefficiency, waste, maladministration and, in some cases, corruption."[25] All too often, the bureaucracy seems to be a self-serving entity—too important to abolish and too complex to control.

Such charges are important because government directly touches most people's lives through the executive bureaucracies. Somewhere in an administrative office many decisions are made affecting the ordinary citizen's life—here will be granted or denied one's right to practice a profession, here will be set restrictions on where and how one can build his house, here will be determined how safe one's food will be, what textbooks one's children will read, where roads shall be constructed, and whether or not one is eligible for specific welfare grants and services. Thus, in applying general laws to concrete cases, administrators in effect have a policy-making role of great consequence.

There is no easy way for either voters or their elected officials to compel a vast bureaucracy to carry out its role in the public's interest. Random checks may be made, flagrant abuses may be investigated, but still the most constant vigilance is required. Here perhaps is one place where we rely on the pervasive influence of our political culture with its stress on the rule of law, the importance of fair treatment, and procedures for redress of grievances.

To some degree, the dozens of departments, bureaus, and commissions that make up the national and state bureaucracies can be made more efficient by reorganizing the executive branches. This was done in the early 1950s at the national level as a result of recommendations made by a commission headed by former President Herbert Hoover. Many agencies that previously had reported directly to the White House were consolidated, and the President's administrative task thereby lightened. But twenty years passed, new agencies were created, and President Nixon concluded that reorganization was again required. He created a Domestic Council within the Executive Office of the President to provide better coordination among various agencies and asked Congress, to no avail, for the legislation necessary to combine eight existing departments into four new ones. At the state level, there seems little progress toward consolidating executive agencies under gubernatorial control.

But true responsibility is more than efficiency. Executive agencies are filled with thousands of experts who are inherently irresponsible because their jobs are so specialized that neither the President and governors nor the voters can understand what they are doing. When physical and social scientists testify that they need X number of new employees or X number of dollars to develop a harmless pesticide, a new weapon, or a mass rapid transit system, few have the knowledge to verify or dispute their claim. Secrecy, too, is a barrier preventing an intelligent assessment of bureaucratic performance. If the voters, or even Congress, cannot be told what the Central Intelligence Agency is doing, how can they know if it is being done well, or even if it should be done at all?

The problem of holding bureaucrats responsible for their performance and accountable to elected executive officials is thus increasingly difficult. Sheer size, specialized expertise, and secrecy may be as big a threat to genuinely democratic government as any we now encounter.

Chapter **11**

Judiciaries
Courts and Judges

Scarcely any political question arises in the United States that
is not resolved, sooner or later, into a judicial question.
Alexis de Tocqueville

Every government must pass laws and enforce them. These
are the functions of legislative and executive bodies, sometimes called the
political branches of government because they are inevitably subject to
group pressures and properly swayed by public opinion. But among a
people who value justice, there must be a third branch, somewhat
independent of the other two, which applies the law to specific disputes
and alleged crimes in a humane and impartial fashion. This is the work of
the courts, the presumably nonpolitical judicial branch of the national
and state governments. Yet in the 1968 presidential campaign, Richard
Nixon charged (as have many before him) that courts were actually
making policy and that this tendency should be checked by the appointment of judges humble enough to defer more often to the decisions of
legislative and executive authorities. After his election, he made precisely
the kind of judicial choices he had urged, yet these appointments proved
just as controversial as the earlier ones he had deplored. When nonpolitical offices become political issues, they deserve close examination.

COURT JURISDICTION AND
PROCEDURE
The Reach of the Judicial Arm

Judges have authority over two types of cases; they settle
disputes between citizens, and they deal with violations of the law. The

first type of controversy is a civil case, and the second, far less common, is a criminal one.

Civil cases   In judicial controversies between two private parties, the government merely provides the court room, judge, and perhaps the jury to arbitrate the dispute impartially. It stands above the battle, while decisions are often rendered on the basis of judge-made common law decided in similar cases in the past.

Civil cases are either (1) contract cases in which the opposing sides have some legally binding relationship with one another, such as an employment contract, marriage, mortgage, lease, or will—although divorce is by far the most common type of contract case, or (2) tort cases in which there is personal injury or property damage but no legal relationship between the parties. Most numerous here are cases resulting from automobile accidents.

In civil cases, a plaintiff sues a defendant. Traditionally, the law requires that each side assume equal responsibility for justifying its position and that the decision favor the one with a preponderance of evidence. The Seventh Amendment to the U.S. Constitution, guaranteeing the right to trial by jury in civil cases involving over $20, is applicable only in federal courts although even there the defendant usually waives this right and prefers to let the judge render the verdict.[1] As Amendment Seven does not apply in state courts, there an even higher ratio of civil cases is decided by judges rather than juries. Still, much time is spent in both the national and state court systems in trying to select juries for civil cases.

Criminal cases   Although there are cases in which governments sue or are sued in civil cases, their direct courtroom involvement is most important in criminal cases. These pit the government, as the prosecution, against the accused defendant.

Criminal cases involve alleged violations of law and are of two broad varieties: felonies (major crimes), usually punishable by at least a year in prison, and misdemeanors (minor crimes), entailing less severe sentences. In all criminal cases the burden of proof falls exclusively on the prosecution. The government must prove the defendant's guilt beyond a reasonable doubt. A slight edge in evidence, therefore, is not sufficient for a conviction; the defendant is presumed innocent until *proven* guilty.

The Constitution guarantees the right of trial by jury in criminal cases in state as well as federal courts. Until the Supreme Court ruled otherwise in 1972, the common law required a unanimous verdict in criminal jury trials, and even now it appears that a vote of 8 to 4 would be too narrow a margin to reach a decision. If the jurors cannot agree, there occurs a mistrial, or hung jury. The prosecution has the option of either dropping the charges or beginning the trial again with a new jury.

---

1 In U.S. district courts in 1970, civil cases outnumbered criminal ones by an almost 3 to 2 margin. Of the civil cases, over 3000 were decided by a jury and about 6000 without one.

Figure 41   Cases in Federal Courts

Courts	1950	1960	1970
U. S. District Courts			
Civil trials	5663	6002	9449
Nonjury	3648	3161	6078
Jury	2015	2841	3371
Criminal trials	2314	3040	6583
Nonjury	825	943	2357
Jury	1489	2097	4226
Total	7977	9042	16032[1]
U. S. Supreme Court			
Total cases filed	1181	1940	3405[2]

[1] This represents an increase of over 100 percent since 1950.
[2] This figure is for 1969 and is an increase of nearly 200 percent since 1950. Chief Justice Warren E. Burger places the cases filed in 1970 at 4400. *U.S. News and World Report,* Dec. 14, 1970, p. 42.
Source: U.S. Bureau of the Census, *Statistical Abstract of the United States: 1971,* pp. 150–51.

Since the Constitution, in Amendment Six, requires a speedy trial in criminal cases, they take precedence over civil cases, with the result that it may take years before a civil suit is brought to court. Also, the constitutional guarantee of the right to legal counsel is limited to criminal cases.

Crisis in the courts   While Americans may be a notoriously lawless people, they have a paradoxical reverence for the law as a potential panacea for every problem. "There oughta be a law . . .," cries a massive chorus every time a wrathful public perceives a potential threat to its safety or even to its sensibilities. The result is many laws, many lawbreakers, and a staggering number of cases brought before the courts. Too many cases and too few judges have produced a judicial crisis of unprecedented magnitude.

One of the more dramatic manifestations of this crisis occurred in New York City in October 1970, when prisoners staged a five-day jail riot and seized thirty-two guards as hostages in protesting overcrowded conditions and delays of up to a year before trial. Manhattan Criminal Court was so overburdened that some judges heard nearly three hundred cases a day. "The result," as one reporter noted, "is turnstile justice in a subway rush-hour atmosphere."[2]

In the federal courts, too, the work load has increased dramatically. Among the reasons for overcrowded court dockets is our reliance on the courts to settle an excessive variety of problems. Chief Justice Burger has expressed doubts about

whether such things as divorce, child custody, adoptions . . . belong in the

2 John J. Goldman, "New York Facing a Breakdown in Criminal Justice," *Los Angeles Times,* Dec. 7, 1970, p. 1.

courts at all. . . . (T)he chronic alcoholic, the narcotic addict, the serious mental patient—there's a . . . question whether they should be dealt with in the judicial framework.[3]

Burger indicated that such problems, in addition to automobile accident cases, might be handled instead by administrative agencies. Others have suggested that private use of marijuana and homosexual activity by consenting adults should be legalized, if only to free the police, prison officials, and judges for the more pressing business of protecting life and property.

The more rigid enforcement of defendants' rights in recent years places additional demands on court time. This is especially true with respect to the guarantee of an impartial jury. Pretrial motions seeking a change of venue and prolonged questioning of potential jurors can take as long as the trial itself. Moreover, when an appeals court reverses a conviction, it often returns the case to the lower court for a new trial.

Finally, there has been not only the well-known increase in the rate of serious crime, but also a rapid rise in the number of cases involving welfare benefits and the protection of consumers from unsafe merchandise. These two categories are especially important because they affect the interests of the middle-class and poor Americans who are generally most defenseless against abuses by government or corporation bureaucracies. The neighborhood legal services program, administered by the Office of Economic Opportunity, has instituted *class-action* suits which represent not individuals, but entire categories of affected persons. So have nonprofit public-service law firms such as "Nader's Raiders," headed by Ralph Nader. Among recent class-action suits have been those that have attempted to restrict the arbitrary repossession of cars and other merchandise bought on credit, establish fair hearing procedures for those whose welfare payments have been cut off, and protect wilderness areas from environmentally destructive commercial development.

Besides removing certain matters from the jurisdiction of the courts, judicial burdens might be eased by an increase in the number of judges and "the appointment of para-judges to deal with the enormous mass of pretrial hearings, motions, and administration of court calendars, all of which take up a major portion of a judge's time."[4] Perhaps a small step in the right direction was the creation of an Institute of Court Management at the University of Denver Law School designed to train court executives in modern management methods. It graduated its first class in December 1970.[5]

3 *U.S. News and World Report,* Dec. 14, 1970, p. 35.
4 Judge Irving R. Kaufman, U.S. Court of Appeals, 2nd Circuit, "Court Crisis: A Matter of Volume and of Money," *Los Angeles Times,* Nov. 15, 1970, Sec. F, p. 3.
5 *U.S. News and World Report,* op. cit., pp. 32–33.

The Road to Justice

Original and appellate jurisdiction   Original jurisdiction is the authority to render decisions in either criminal or civil cases that have never been tried in court before. The lowest of the state courts and the federal district courts, at the bottom of the judicial branch in the national government, have original jurisdiction only. Appellate jurisdiction is the authority of higher courts to hear cases on appeal that have been tried before in a lower court.

The adversary system: legal warfare   The American people love a good fight. That may explain the popularity of plays, television series, and novels based upon courtroom drama. For the Anglo-American legal tradition conceives of a trial as essentially a battle between two adversaries, fair and honest, fought hard and tenaciously, out of which truth will somehow emerge and the best man will finally win. This is the essence of the adversary system. A leading authority has described it well:

(T)he judge will question a witness only to avert grave injustice, not to advance the case for either side. He is not in any sense an active elicitor of truth regarding the testimony presented. . . . (H)e is an independent arbiter. . . . This is a concept basic to the common law adversary proceeding . . . that "sets the parties fighting."[6]

While there is reason to believe that the adversary system is well suited to criminal cases where a defendant is simply innocent or guilty, it is possible that it is sadly inappropriate for settling more complex civil disputes, such as divorce or accident liability cases, where both parties may be at fault. If no one is committed to the active, disinterested search for truth, truth may not be found.

It is, therefore, encouraging to note that there is growing use of pretrial conferences in which judges encourage the opposing attorneys to agree on as many facts as possible and thereby limit the issues in dispute. A somewhat similar purpose is served by the procedure of discovery, which permits one lawyer to learn what evidence is possessed by the opposition in advance of the trial. In addition, many disputes are settled by informal negotiations between the opposing attorneys. In criminal cases, such negotiation often involves *plea bargaining* in which the defendant pleads guilty to a charge less serious than that for which he was initially arrested. In civil cases, a compromise financial settlement may be hammered out in the judge's private chambers. Such out-of-court solutions no doubt fall short of perfect justice, but they represent more or less voluntary agreements which reduce court time and provide pragmatic concessions that may well be as fair as those imposed by judicial decrees. On the other hand, plea bargaining may provide society with

6 Henry J. Abraham, *The Judicial Process* (N.Y.: Oxford University Press, Inc., 1962), p. 94.

too little protection from hardened criminals or induce innocent defendants to plead guilty to avoid a long prison sentence based on circumstantial evidence. Surely justice should not be sacrificed in the interest of convenience.

COURT STRUCTURE AND PERSONNEL
National Courts

Article III of the Constitution provides for a U.S. Supreme Court and whatever lower courts Congress may wish to establish. The resulting judicial system is relatively simple.

Federal district courts   The first year Congress met under the present Constitution, in 1789, it created United States district courts. There are now over three hundred judges serving on ninety-three district courts with at least one in each state and territory. In criminal cases, these courts have original jurisdiction over all acts—felonies and misdemeanors alike—prohibited by Congress. In addition, they have jurisdiction over most civil cases to which the United States government is a party, and those involving citizens of different states in which over $10,000 is at stake. In most instances, only one judge hears each case, and the defendant may claim the right to trial by jury.

Courts of Appeals   In 1891 Congress created the courts of appeals. Between the district courts and the U.S. Supreme Court, they have appellate jurisdiction in both criminal and civil cases. There are now about one hundred judges distributed among eleven courts. Three judges usually hear each case. The vast majority of cases reaching these courts come from the U.S. district courts, although a few arrive from other sources such as regulatory commissions in the executive branch.

The Supreme Court   The highest court in America is the United States Supreme Court. Here, at the judicial summit, nine judges (a number determined by Congress) exercise authority equaling that of the President or Congress. The Supreme Court has both original and appellate jurisdiction, although almost all of its cases fall in the latter category. Article III of the Constitution, as altered by the Eleventh Amendment, establishes original jurisdiction over suits involving foreign diplomats, those between states, or those between the national government and a state. All in all, the Court has heard an average of less than five cases a year under its original jurisdiction, mainly involving interstate disputes. The most notable in recent times have been those between Maryland and Virginia over oyster fishing and between California and Arizona concerning water from the Colorado River.[7] In 1947 a major dispute involving national versus state ownership of offshore (or tidelands) oil resources also reached the Supreme Court under its original jurisdiction.[8]

7 Ibid., pp. 157–58.
8 *United States* v. *California,* 332 U.S. 19.

Figure 42   The Judicial Branch

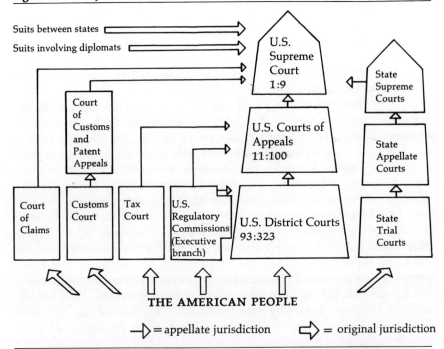

Note: In the federal pyramid, the first figure indicates number of courts, and the second indicates number of judges.**

The appellate jurisdiction of the Supreme Court consists of cases heard earlier by the various national courts of appeals, or by the state courts, although some cases involving important constitutional issues may arrive directly from the district courts. The only circumstance under which a case can be appealed from a state court is one in which someone has charged state or local officials with violating the U.S. Constitution or a law or treaty authorized by it. Such cases go directly from the highest state court to which it may be appealed to the U.S. Supreme Court.

Most cases reach the Supreme Court on *writs of certiorari,* which are court orders granting appeals from lower courts. These writs are usually issued when four Supreme Court justices feel a case to be of compelling importance. Of more than 3000 cases presented to it each year, the court renders decisions on three or four hundred, with less than half dignified by full written opinions.

Other federal courts   Various specialized courts complete the judicial branch of the national government. These are the Court of Claims, in which citizens may bring civil suits against the national government for damages of one kind or another; the U.S. Customs Court, which reviews administrative decisions on the tax to be imposed on merchandise brought into the country from foreign nations, and the Court of Customs and Patent Appeals, which hears appeals from the

Customs Court, the Patent Office in the Commerce Department, and the Tariff Commission.

State Courts

State court structures are similar to the federal one, but usually are organized in four or five levels.

Justices of the peace   Justice courts, at the bottom of the judicial structure and often charged with dishonesty, are being replaced in many states. The justices of the peace (J.P.s) are often part-time, without legal training, and reimbursed only from fines and costs they themselves impose. In order to encourage more civil suits and improve their business, J.P.s have a notorious reputation for ruling for the plaintiff—in 99 percent of the cases in Michigan, 98 percent in Tennessee, and 79 percent in Indiana at various times in the past. It is no wonder J.P. was said to stand for "judgment for the plaintiff." There is little indication that the few criminal cases J.P.s are permitted to hear elicit any more fairness than the civil actions. The jurisdiction of these petty officials is normally confined to civil cases involving no more than a few hundred dollars and the most minor of misdemeanors. They usually can pick up a few dollars by performing marriage ceremonies and often have the authority to hold preliminary hearings to determine whether persons accused of more important crimes shall be held for possible later action before a major trial court.

Other trial courts   In many states, the function of the J.P.s is exercised by full-time, salaried, professionally qualified judges serving on municipal courts, or similar tribunals with different names. They have original jurisdiction only.

In addition, every state has higher trial courts (generally known as county, superior, district, or circuit courts) with authority over all major cases. At this level a million-dollar damage suit or a murder case, for example, will be brought to trial. Supplementing this original jurisdiction is often appellate jurisdiction over cases heard first by J.P.s or municipal court judges.

At the trial court level, it is common to have a variety of specialized courts handling particular kinds of cases, or else general trial courts organized in specialized divisions. Either system permits judges to gain considerable experience and expertise in a certain field of law and presumably raises their level of competence. At the municipal court level, judges may specialize in traffic citations or in small claims cases, in which the plaintiff is suing for no more than a few hundred dollars and in which lawyers and juries may even be prohibited.

At the major trial court level, judges may specialize in juvenile cases, probate matters, or domestic relations. Juvenile cases are generally considered especially significant because the defendants may have a better chance of being rehabilitated. Probate matters involve wills, inheritances, and guardianship for dependent children and incompetent adults, while domestic relations cases embrace many of the traumatic disputes that pull families apart—divorce, child custody, alimony, separate maintenance, and parental visitation rights. Since the family is generally acknowledged to be the basic social unit, the highest of trial courts usually has jurisdiction over the legal battles affecting it.

Reform at the lower court levels has been sorely needed in many states, not only to root out corruption and gross incompetence, but also to reorganize courts with confusing and overlapping jurisdictions. It is heartening to note progress in that direction. Courts were reorganized in Colorado, Idaho, and Oklahoma (where J.P.s and county courts were abolished) in 1969, and significant court integration recently took place in Ohio, Pennsylvania, and Rhode Island as well.[9]

The appellate courts All states have a supreme court to hear cases appealed from the trial courts mentioned above, although it is called a supreme judicial court in Maine and Massachusetts, a supreme court of appeals in Virginia and West Virginia, and a court of appeals in Kentucky, Maryland, and New York. In addition, twenty-three states have intermediate appellate courts to help screen out and reduce the work load of the highest state court.[10] The number of state supreme court judges ranges from three (in Delaware) to nine (in seven states.)

The Selection of Judges

Judicial appointment While all federal judges are appointed by the President subject to confirmation by a majority vote of the U.S. Senate, the situation at the state level is both different and far more complex. State supreme court judges are appointed by the governor in sixteen states,[11] appointed by the legislature from nominations submitted by the governor in Connecticut, elected by the legislature in Rhode Island, South Carolina, Vermont, and Virginia, and elected by the voters in the remaining twenty-nine states. Most lower court judges are also elected, although some are chosen by higher courts, city councils or other local governing bodies.[12]

The case for appointing judges rests primarily on three arguments: (1) the voters know too little about prospective judges to be able to elect them intelligently; (2) to force a judge to seek office in an election campaign compromises the independence and integrity he needs to dispense justice impartially; and (3) good attorneys are more likely to be attracted to judgeships if they can gain them through appointment rather than through the rigors of a bitter, expensive, and acrimonious election campaign.

Even where judges are elected, the governor may appoint

9 William L. Frederick, "State Judicial Systems," *The Book of the States*, 1970–71 (Lexington, Ky.: The Council of State Governments, 1970), pp. 117–18.
10 *The Book of the States*, 1970–71, pp. 120–21.
11 Alaska, California, Colorado, Delaware, Hawaii, Iowa, Kansas, Maine, Maryland, Massachusetts, Missouri, Nebraska, New Hampshire, New Jersey, Oklahoma, and Utah.
12 *The Book of the States*, 1970–71, op. cit., pp. 124–25.

persons to fill judicial vacancies which occur between elections. This is of considerable significance, because in many states about one third of all judges die or resign before their elective terms have expired.

Judicial election   Among the states in which supreme court judges are chosen by the voters, in fifteen they are elected on a partisan basis, with candidates chosen by the opposing political parties,[13] and in fourteen they are elected on a nonpartisan ballot, with the party affiliation of the candidates unlisted.[14]

Election of judges is often justified on the grounds that judges apply the existing law to cases coming before them in a way which reflects their own values and preferences. The whole common law tradition, in fact, allows each judge to establish some legal principle whenever statutes and earlier legal precedents seem inapplicable. Hence, it is argued, democratic theory requires that judges, like all important policy-makers, be selected by the people. The discretion available to judges is indicated by a study of 298 national and state supreme court justices. It disclosed that in at least nine kinds of cases the decisions of Republican and Democratic judges differed to a statistically significant degree. This finding might seem to bolster the contention that people should be permitted to elect judges whose views are most similar to their own.

Yet the same study also revealed that judges who were appointed rendered decisions reflecting their party affiliation substantially less often than those who were elected.[15] Persons who value a politically independent judiciary more than one which is responsive to the wishes of the majority may cite this evidence, therefore, to support the case for appointed judges.

Another argument for elective judgeships is that chief executives use judicial appointments as a form of patronage to reward their supporters. As one honest, if somewhat cynical judge has admitted, "a judge is a lawyer who knew a governor."[16] And both governors and Presidents have a preference for their own party; among federal judges it is worth noting that President Franklin D. Roosevelt appointed 217 Democrats and 8 Republicans, Harry Truman 118 Democrats and 12 Republicans and Dwight Eisenhower, finally accorded the opportunity for sweet revenge, 175 Republicans and 11 Democrats.[17]

The California and Missouri plans   Out of the charges and countercharges in the debate over appointment *vs.* election have come two compromise plans promising the best of both worlds. The first plan,

13 Alabama, Arkansas, Florida, Georgia, Illinois, Indiana, Louisiana, Mississippi, New Mexico, New York, North Carolina, Pennsylvania, Tennessee, Texas, and West Virginia.
14 Arizona, Idaho, Kentucky, Michigan, Minnesota, Montana, Nevada, North Dakota, Ohio, Oregon, South Dakota, Washington, Wisconsin, and Wyoming.
15 Stuart S. Nagel, "Political Party Affiliation and Judges' Decisions," *American Political Science Review* 55 (December 1961): 843–50.
16 Quoted by Fred Rodell in A. N. Christensen and E. M. Kirkpatrick, eds., *The People, Politics, and the Politician* (N.Y.: Henry Holt and Company, 1941), p. 542.
17 John J. Kennelly, "Elect Judges?—Yes," *The Rotarian,* June 1961, pp. 40, 54, 56. President Kennedy chose 111 Democrats, 11 Republicans, and 1 Liberal.

adopted by California in 1934, requires that judges on the higher courts be appointed by the governor subject to the approval of a special judicial commission. At the next election the voters are permitted to vote, yes or no, on whether such judges shall have a full term in office. No opposition candidates are permitted. The voters have never rejected a judge selected in this way.

The Missouri plan works in much the same way, but requires the governor to make his initial appointment from among three persons whose names are submitted by a judicial nominating committee. A few states, including Alaska, Iowa, Kansas, and Nebraska have adopted variations of this method.[18]

The Care and Characteristics of Judges

Few jobs in our society carry the prestige and honor of a judgeship, especially on a higher court. It is well to examine some of the factors affecting the judicial life style, as well as the characteristics of the men and women who enjoy its rewards.

Judicial tenure and salaries Judges in the national court system have life-time jobs, subject only to their unlikely removal on impeachment charges. At the state level, however, few are so lucky. The vast majority of the state higher court judges have terms ranging from six to twelve years, and those on the trial courts from two to six years. However, most elected judges have relatively little difficulty getting reelected. The voters in many states, distracted by better publicized races for other offices, tend to vote for incumbent judges almost automatically unless they have been involved in some recent scandal or a highly unpopular decision.[19]

The Chief Justice of the U.S. Supreme Court receives an annual salary of $62,500; the eight associate justices get $60,000, court of appeals judges $42,500, and district court judges $40,000. At the state level, supreme court judges receive from a low of $19,000 in Mississippi and Wyoming to a high of $42,500 in New York, and major trial judges earn from $10,500 in Oklahoma, to $39,100 in New York. While judges hardly go hungry on such salaries, they earn far less than thousands of lawyers. Why, then, would one want to become a judge? There are perhaps as many reasons as there are judges, but among them are the prestige and relative security of judicial office, its usefulness as a springboard to even higher office, and a desire for public service. In addition, there are fringe benefits. Most judges do not have to pay for their office space, secretarial assistance or other professional necessities.

Characteristics of judges Except for justices of the peace,

---

18 Abraham, op. cit., pp. 34–39, and *The Book of the States,* 1970–71, loc. cit.
19 In Kansas, for example, of the 309 district court judges seeking reelection between 1930 and 1956, less than 40 percent were opposed and fewer than 8 percent defeated. Duane Lockard, *The Politics of State and Local Government,* 2nd ed. (N.Y.: The Macmillan Company, 1969), p. 451.

nearly all jurists are lawyers. Oddly enough, this is true in the federal courts only as a result of tradition, common sense, and the political influence of bar associations. Although the Constitution prescribes rather detailed requirements for legislative and executive officials regarding age, citizenship, and residency, it imposes none of any sort on judges. At the state level, judges untrained in the law were once rather common, but a long drive to professionalize the judiciary has diminished their number substantially and many states now make admission to the bar a constitutional requirement for judges. One effect of the attorneys' monopoly over the judicial branches is that judges have a higher socioeconomic background than the average American.

The courts are not only dominated by lawyers, but by a specific kind: male lawyers. No woman has ever served on the U.S. Supreme Court, and a survey of the names of state supreme court justices reveals only four women among the fifty states combined.[20] It is probable that this situation is less the result of deliberate discrimination than of a sort of institutionalized sexism within the legal profession. In 1970 only 9000 of 315,000 lawyers in America were females.[21]

THE SUPREME COURT AND JUDICIAL REVIEW

Courts in all countries have the job of settling disputes, acquitting the innocent, and punishing the guilty. But American courts have the unique additional power of judicial review, which means that they can declare legislative and executive acts unconstitutional and therefore invalid.

In the hands of state courts judicial review becomes a sort of two-edged sword, cutting down government actions which violate either the state or federal constitutions. But whenever any action is declared contrary to the federal constitution, it will result, almost inevitably, in an appeal to the Supreme Court of the United States.

The Court of Last Resort

The Supreme Court is well named; it is the final interpreter of the law, the ultimate watchdog of the whole governmental process, the court of last resort. It is the final arbiter of what the Constitution permits and what it prohibits. If one dislikes the Court's decision, one has but three choices: defy it, wait patiently in the hope the Court will reverse itself later, or seek a constitutional amendment nullifying its ruling.

The politics of judicial selection   Many factors influence a President's nomination of Supreme Court judges. One is partisan

20 *The Book of the States,* 1970–71, op. cit., pp. 562–611. Much of the other data regarding state court systems in this chapter has come from Section III of this source.
21 U.S. Bureau of the Census, *The Statistical Abstract of the United States: 1971,* p. 153.

loyalty; another is general political philosophy. In either case, a President may be disappointed to find his appointee voting against his expectations once cloaked with black-robed independence, prestige, and life tenure on the Supreme Court. President Theodore Roosevelt was quickly angered by Justice Oliver Wendell Holmes, shortly after he had appointed him, and President Eisenhower was thought to regret his selection of Chief Justice Earl Warren. President Nixon apparently made his appointments more carefully. During the 1968 campaign, he emphasized his intention to choose justices with a preference for a "strict construction" of the Constitution. Seldom has a campaign promise been kept with such frequency or fidelity. Before he had completed three years in office, he had the rare opportunity to make four such selections. His choices have consistently justified his confidence. As a result, constitutional interpretation in the areas of police power, press freedom, trial by jury, and race relations may be altered for several decades. Ten Supreme Court justices have held their posts for more than thirty years.

Emphasis is sometimes placed on the maintenance of a balance on the Supreme Court, both in terms of geographical sections of the country and religion, but balance is a relative concept. Less than a quarter of all Supreme Court justices have come from west of the Mississippi River, and New York, Ohio, and Massachusetts have produced nearly a third of the total number.[22] President Nixon appointed three persons from the South, on the grounds that this section was underrepresented on the Court, before one of them won Senate confirmation. The concept of a religious balance has traditionally meant seven Protestants, a Catholic, and a Jew, but this tradition is a relatively recent one and has resulted in only six Catholics and five Jews out of the one hundred justices who have served on the Court. President Nixon explicitly repudiated religion as a legitimate factor in judicial recruitment, and as a result our highest court is now without a Jew (with Justice William Brennan the lone Catholic) for the first time since 1916. President Lyndon B. Johnson may have broadened the ideal of a balanced Court by selecting the first black, Justice Thurgood Marshall, to sit on that body.

In making his choice, the chief executive relies in large measure upon the recommendation of his attorney general who, in turn, has usually sounded out the Committee on the Federal Judiciary of the American Bar Association.[23] Of necessity, the likelihood of Senate opposition must be considered also, as well as pressures brought to bear by influential interest groups. The rejection of two Nixon appointees reflects the close scrutiny the Senate, especially its Judiciary Committee, gives to Supreme Court nominations. It also indicates the influence of the labor and civil rights lobbies, both strongly opposed to the Pres-

22 Much of the material in this section, somewhat updated, has come from Abraham, op. cit., pp. 47–81.
23 John R. Schmidhauser, *The Supreme Court* (N.Y.: Holt, Rinehart & Winston, Inc., 1961), pp. 77–91.

ident's choices. Another factor involved in Supreme Court appointments is prior judicial experience. Over a third of the justices throughout our history have had none at all—including such notable ones as Chief Justices John Marshall, Roger Taney, and Earl Warren.

The most likely result of all these considerations is a Supreme Court justice who is

probably Protestant; of Anglo-Saxon stock . . .; a background of upper-level social status; reared in an urban environment; a member of an economically comfortable, civic-minded, politically active family; with B.A. and LL.B. degrees; experienced in some public or civic office.[24]

In 1972, six of the nine justices were over sixty years of age.

The mystique of court procedure   If majestic rituals and symbolic procedures enhance the legitimacy of government bodies, the prestige of the Supreme Court is not difficult to explain. It is big on ceremony, both public and private.

Opposing attorneys in each case present written briefs to the Court. In addition, at least eight days a month are devoted to oral arguments, in which each side of every case is usually permitted an hour to emphasize its most persuasive contentions. At the beginning of each of these sessions, a court crier intones an impressive chant: "Oyez, oyez, oyez! All persons having business before the Honorable Supreme Court of the United States are admonished to draw near and give their attention, for the Court is now sitting. God save the United States and this Honorable Court." The chief justice takes the middle chair, and the eight associate justices arrange themselves, in order of seniority, on either side of him. During these sessions, each of the nine justices may direct questions, sometimes sharp, to the opposing lawyers. Occasionally, to the delight of the press and public present, the justices exchange verbal barbs with one another.

Then, on Friday, the Court meets in secret conference, each justice first shaking hands with each of his judicial brethren. The chief justice presides and summarizes the cases on the agenda. Each of the associates, in order of seniority, makes additional comments, and then voting begins, in reverse order, with the most recently appointed associate voting first and the chief justice last.

The assignment of opinions   When the votes are tallied, the chief justice assigns the responsibility of writing the majority opinion of the Court. This explains the case briefly, describes the issues it presents, and justifies the Court's decision so that it may provide guidance to lower courts in deciding similar cases and persuade the nation of its correctness. Just as the Constitution is the heart of American law, Supreme Court opinions are its lifeblood, applying constitutional principles to the gravest disputes in the nation.

If the chief justice has voted with the minority, the task of

24 Henry J. Abraham, *The Judiciary* (Boston: Allyn and Bacon, Inc., 1965), p. 96.

assigning the majority opinion falls to the senior associate justice who voted with the majority. Once written, the opinion is circulated among other members of the majority. If any justice should disagree with its reasoning, he may write a concurring opinion giving his own reasons for reaching the same conclusion as the majority. Similarly, any justice who voted with the minority may write a dissenting opinion in which he states why he believes the majority was wrong. These dissenting opinions are sometimes very influential, fanning a spark of doubt regarding the majority's wisdom that may lead the Court on some future occasion to reverse its earlier decision. This has happened about a hundred times since the adoption of the Constitution.

The Nature of Judicial Review

Although judicial review has been controversial since the doctrine was first used in the case of *Marbury* v. *Madison,* it has now become deeply entrenched in our constitutional system. Judicial review is used to declare government acts unconstitutional primarily under three circumstances: if one level of government (national or state) exercises power properly belonging only to the other; if one branch of the government exercises power properly belonging only to either of the other two; or if any government agency or official exercises power that violates the constitutional rights of an individual. But two broadly different interpretations of judicial review have staunch supporters on the Supreme Court.

Judicial self-restraint One group of judges, now led by Chief Justice Burger, contends that the power of judicial review should be used with great restraint and only against laws or actions that are blatantly unconstitutional. They complain that too often judges interpret the Constitution to reflect their own views, thereby invalidating government acts simply because they don't like them. President Nixon clearly advocated judicial self-restraint when he asserted his intention to appoint judges who

would be strict constructionists who saw their duty as interpreting law not making law. They would see themselves as caretakers of the Constitution and servants of the people, not superlegislators with a free hand to impose their social and political viewpoints upon the American people.[25]

Perhaps the essential spirit of judicial self-restraint was best captured in a remark Justice Oliver Wendell Holmes addressed to Justice Harlan Fiske Stone:

Young man, about 75 years ago I learned that I was not God. And so, when the people . . . want to do something I can't find anything in the Constitution

25 Alan Barth, "Strict Constructionism—the Illusory Quality of Labels," *Los Angeles Times,* April 19, 1970, Sec. E, p. 3.

expressly forbidding them to do, I say, whether I like it or not, "Goddamit, let 'em do it."[26]

This spirit has taken flesh in the form of specific rules the Court imposed upon itself to minimize the use of judicial review. Mr. Justice Brandeis summarized them in a concurring opinion in the case of *Ashwander* v. *Tennessee Valley Authority* in 1935:

1) The Court will not pass upon the constitutionality of legislation in a friendly, non-adversary, proceeding. . . .
2) The Court will not anticipate a question of constitutional law in advance of the necessity of deciding it. . . .
3) The Court will not formulate a rule of constitutional law broader than is required by the precise facts to which it is to be applied. . . .
4) The Court will not pass upon a constitutional question . . . if there is also present some other ground upon which the case may be disposed of. . . .
5) The Court will not pass upon the validity of a statute upon complaint of one who fails to show that he is injured by its operation. . . .
6) The Court will not pass upon the constitutionality of a statute at the instance of one who has availed himself of its benefits.
7) When the validity of an act of the Congress is drawn in question, and even if a serious doubt of constitutionality is raised, it is a cardinal principle that this Court will first ascertain whether a construction of the statute is fairly possible by which the question may be avoided.[27]

To these so-called Ashwander rules, two others must be added that serve also to reduce the frequency with which government acts are declared unconstitutional: The Court will not decide "political questions" that are within the proper domain of the other two branches (although what these are is sometimes disputed), and the burden of proof rests on those claiming that a particular act is unconstitutional. Yet in spite of all these indications of reluctance, the Supreme Court has in fact declared 87 acts of Congress and 733 state laws unconstitutional between 1789 and 1969.

Judicial activism   A somewhat different interpretation of the power of judicial review is held by those sometimes called judicial activists, or (to use President Nixon's preferred term) loose constructionists. This group, now including Justices William J. Brennan and William O. Douglas, contends that it is difficult to construe "strictly" such essentially "loose" terms of the Constitution as *"unreasonable searches and seizures," "cruel and unusual punishments,"* and *"due process of law."* The broad language of the Constitution, they argue, requires broad latitude for the Court in interpreting it and in enforcing its provisions. Activists stress the importance of judicial review in protecting individual

26 Charles P. Curtis, *Lions Under the Throne* (Boston: Houghton Mifflin Company, 1947), p. 281.
27 297 U.S. 288.

rights. They see it as a refuge for minorities from oppressive government action provoked by age-old prejudices, current political pressures, or the fleeting passions of the moment.

Here it is important to note two quite different kinds of provisions in the Constitution. First, there are those that *grant* power to government officials, such as the "necessary and proper" clause concerning congressional authority, or the "commander in chief" clause conferring presidential prerogatives. To interpret these provisions broadly or loosely would *increase* governmental power and result in fewer acts declared unconstitutional.

But, secondly, there are constitutional provisions, such as the Bill of Rights, that *limit* the power of government in the interests of protecting the liberty of the individual. To interpret these broadly would *diminish* governmental power and result in more acts declared unconstitutional. Thus, judicial activism, implying a readiness to exercise judicial review, is furthered by *a strict construction of power grants and a loose construction of power limitations.* Few judges are entirely consistent on the matter, although it is generally agreed that judicial activism reached its zenith during the era of Chief Justice Earl Warren (1953–1969). It is equally clear that the Burger Court, under the impetus of the Nixon appointees, shows a dominant preference for judicial self-restraint.

Judicial politics Whether the courts pursue policies of activism or self-restraint, it seems inevitable that their decisions will have a greater political impact than has been assumed in classical legal theory or desired, perhaps, by President Nixon. The Warren Court rendered important policy decisions by interpreting the Constitution to ban prayer in the public schools, to require that criminal suspects be informed of certain rights, and to prohibit the election of lawmakers from unequally populated districts. Although such decisions have represented triumphs of judicial activism, they have also revealed disputes over legal theory and policy preferences which have pitted some judges against others.

In controversies such as these, even the long robes of judicial authority cannot obscure essentially political splits of a profound and persistent nature. Within the Supreme Court itself, attitudes coalesce, coalitions form, and ideological animosities emerge which can be measured by a quantitative analysis of judicial voting behavior. In 1957, for example, activist Justices William O. Douglas and Hugo Black voted together in 89 percent of the cases on which the Court was divided, but sided with Justice John M. Harlan, noted for his self-restraint, only 29 and 33 percent respectively.[28] In 1972 the four Nixon appointees, Chief Justice Warren Burger and Justices Harry Blackmun, Lewis Powell, Jr., and William Rehnquist, voted together in thirteen out of eighteen (or 72 percent) of the cases decided by a 5 to 4 vote.[29]

The truth is that judges could not stay out of politics, even if

28 Glendon A. Schubert, *Constitutional Politics* (N.Y.: Holt, Rinehart & Winston, Inc., 1960), p. 159.
29 *New York Times,* July 2, 1972, p. 18.

they wanted to, because politics involves making decisions about government policy. The higher the court, the more frequent and important are the policy decisions it is required to make. For example, when judges exercise their power of judicial review, they pass judgment on the constitutionality of a law or executive procedure which is already established. If they uphold the challenged action, they are *perpetuating existing policy.* If they declare the action unconstitutional, they are *changing existing policy.* A fundamental issue between activism and self-restraint may not be, therefore, whether the courts should intervene in the action of other government agencies, but on whose side. But, although judicial interpretation can either affirm or invalidate existing policy, it has its limits: It can seldom make new policy.

Even when a case involves no question of constitutionality, it may reflect some of the enduring conflicts in our society: employers *vs.* employees, manufacturers *vs.* consumers, whites *vs.* blacks, prudes *vs.* pornographers. When the courts render a decision, they incorporate into public policy a legal preference favoring the interests of one group and opposing those of its adversary. That is a policy decision which is profoundly political in nature.

Finally, judges are trapped in a political web woven around them by external political pressures. Interest groups exert influence for and against the appointment of particular judges, and their lawyers intervene in specific cases through the submission of *amicus curiae* legal briefs on behalf of one side or the other. Presidents and governors use judicial appointments to reward the party faithful or to perpetuate their own political attitudes. Courts must also be sensitive to public opinion, puzzling as it often is. They have no armies, few jobs, and little money to help them gain compliance with their decisions. Devoid of force and influence, the power of judges stems from authority rooted in the faith and confidence of the people. If these judges "follow the election returns," as was once alleged, it is because they realize that when the public no longer acknowledges the legitimacy of their decisions, then the rule of law ends and barbarism begins.

Judicial review, democracy, and freedom   The chief attack on judicial review is that it is undemocratic. And so it seems to be, if democracy means majority rule. It is difficult to imagine anything less democratic, in fact, than a law passed by an overwhelming majority of elected congressmen, enthusiastically signed by the elected President, and then declared unconstitutional by a 5 to 4 vote of the appointed Supreme Court.

Yet the American political system is dedicated to individual freedom as well as to democracy, and in defense of this freedom judicial review can make its greatest contribution. Since legislative and executive officials are elected by majorities, they are compelled both by moral obligation and by political expediency to do what the majority wishes. The protection of minority rights against a prejudiced and hostile majority, therefore, is the responsibility of an independent court system, armed with judicial review, and staffed by judges neither selected by majorities nor in danger of removal by them. The American Constitution is preeminently an experiment in the limitation and control of power—whether exercised by a majority or a minority—through the rule of law. Without the protection of judicial review, it is doubtful whether that great experiment can succeed. If it does not, both majority rule and minority rights will perish with it.

Conclusion to Part Four

Each of the three branches of government possesses a characteristic kind of power. The legislative branch wields influence, especially through the power of the purse. By appropriating or refusing to appropriate money for the vast variety of government programs it exerts not only a potent check on the other two branches but also an enormous impact on the distribution of wealth among the people and on the priorities of the government among competing demands for better health care, greater national security, more effective control of pollution, and innumerable other goals. Power is more diffuse in the legislature than in the other branches and this branch is the most accessible target for influence from the public.

The executive branch controls force: the armed forces, national guard units, state police forces, the F.B.I., the secret service, highway patrols, federal prisons, and state penetentiaries. Because coercion is the ultimate form of power, the executive is the most dangerous branch. It is also the biggest, and its bureaucracies affect the citizens most frequently. In addition, as activities have multiplied, executive agencies have developed a new influence—specialized knowledge—on which the other branches must depend. The old system of checks and balances strains to render the executive safe for a free people.

The judicial branch must rely almost exclusively on authority, especially on the Constitution, that supreme source of authority which pledges equality of legal protection. If the courts are unable to gain voluntary compliance with their orders, only the executive has the power to enforce them. If that branch refuses, races will remain segregated, contracts will be violated, alimony will be unpaid, suspects will be forced to confess, and law will be washed away in a sea of anarchy, with only the strongest or richest remaining afloat.

Bibliography

Chapter 9

Legislatures: Congress and State Legislatures

Burns, John, *The Sometime Governments: A Critical Study of the 50 American State Legislatures* (N.Y.: Bantam Books, Inc., 1971).
Clapp, Charles L., *The Congressman: His Work as He Sees It* (Garden City, N.Y.: Anchor Books, Doubleday & Company, Inc., 1963).
Crane, Wilder, Jr., and Meredith W. Watts, Jr., *State Legislative Systems* (Englewood Cliffs, N.J.: Prentice-Hall, Inc., 1968).
Davidson, Roger H., *The Role of the Congressman* (N.Y.: Pegasus, The Bobbs-Merrill Co., Inc., 1969).
Froman, Lewis A., Jr., *The Congressional Process: Strategies, Rules, and Procedures* (Boston: Little, Brown and Company, 1967).
Keefe, William J., and Morris S. Ogul, *The American Legislative Process: Congress and the States* (Englewood Cliffs, N.J.; Prentice-Hall, Inc., 1964; 2nd ed., 1968).
Wahlke, John C. et al., *The Legislative System* (N.Y.: John Wiley & Sons, Inc., 1962).

Chapter 10

Executives: Presidents, Governors, and Bureaucracies

Book of the States (Lexington, Ky.: Council of State Governments, biennial).
Corwin, Edward S., *The President: Office and Powers,* 4th ed. (N.Y.: New York University Press, 1957).
Koenig, Louis W., *The Chief Executive,* rev. ed. (N.Y.: Harcourt Brace Jovanovich, Inc., 1968).
Neustadt, Richard E., *Presidential Power* (N.Y.: John Wiley & Sons, Inc., 1960).
Rossiter, Clinton, *The American Presidency,* rev. ed. (N.Y.: Harcourt Brace Jovanovich, Inc., 1960).
Sorensen, Theodore C., *Decision-Making in the White House* (N.Y.: Columbia University Press, 1963).
U.S. Government Organization Manual (Washington, D.C.: U.S. Government Printing Office, biennial).
Woll, Peter, *American Bureaucracy* (N.Y.: W. W. Norton & Company, Inc., 1963)..

Chapter 11

Judiciaries: Courts and Judges

Abraham, Henry J., *The Judicial Process* (N.Y.: Oxford University Press, Inc., 1962; 2nd ed., 1968).
Friedman, Leon, and Fred L. Israel, eds., *The Justices of the United States Supreme Court 1789–1969* (N.Y.: R. R. Bowker Co., 1969).
Jackson, Robert H., *The Supreme Court in the American System of Government* (N.Y.: Harper & Row, Publishers, 1955).
Jacob, Herbert, ed., *Law, Politics, and the Federal Courts* (Boston: Little, Brown and Company, 1967).
Roche, John P., and Leonard W. Levy, eds., *The Judiciary* (N.Y.: Harcourt Brace Jovanovich, Inc., 1964).
Schmidhauser, John R., *The Supreme Court* (N.Y.: Holt, Rinehart & Winston, Inc., 1961).

Epilogue
Where Do We Go from Here?

"If I were dying my last words would be: Have faith and pursue the unknown end."
                              Justice Oliver Wendell Holmes

Is the people's power sufficient to control the government's power? In an age of rapid change, the answer to that question (like so many others) is always tentative, for every year, nearly every day, issues emerge which demand that it be answered anew. It has been common and even fashionable in academic circles to view the future of representative government with some skepticism. Moreover, the people themselves seem to have lost faith in their own power to influence official policy. A recent survey reveals that within only six years the number of Americans who distrusted their government had nearly doubled, reaching 39 percent of the population.[1]

It is far too early, however, for the people to throw in the towel. There is little reason for them either to accept the loss of their power with resigned despair or to burn the system down. On the contrary, the survival of American political institutions for nearly two centuries displays a resilience and flexibility, a capacity for change and regeneration, too great to be abandoned now. If government is remote and secretive, callous to considerations of moral decency, or insensitive to the concerns of a troubled people, it is not because something is wrong with our basic political

1 *Los Angeles Times*, Sept. 21, 1972, p. 3. The survey results were reported by Professor Arthur Miller of Ohio State University in a paper presented to the 1972 convention of the American Political Science Association.

principles but because we have permitted their perversion or distortion. Chapter 2 identified four of those central ideas which now require rededication and revitalization.

1) *Federalism.* The states and the communities within each state must resume their historic function of pursuing the varied policies demanded by their diverse populations and unique needs. Perhaps a vastly expanded program of revenue sharing by the federal government will make that financially possible, but administratively it may require that local governments be consolidated or at least reorganized to permit more simplified control by the voters. At the same time, we must recognize that at every level of government—city, county, state, and national—there is a different coalition of groups, a majority comprised of different interests, that will attempt to shape official policy to its own advantage. It is a risk as necessary as government itself.

2) *Separation of Powers.* The three branches of government must be required to respect the roles and prerogatives of the other two. Legislators, especially, have been weakened by subservience to wealthy interests, a lack of expert assistance and specialized knowledge, undemocratic procedures, fragmentation of authority among powerful and independent committees, and at the level of Congress, a surrender of their influence over foreign affairs to the encroachments of an ambitious and ever stronger presidency.

3) *Freedom.* Slowly, awkwardly, sometimes reluctantly, American government has usually done what a majority of the people want it to do. Minorities have fared less well, generally because they lack sufficient votes, money, or other basic political resources. Occasionally, however, a minority is powerless because an intolerant majority has restricted its freedom. Minority rights must be protected, then, if only because new ideas, by definition, are at first propounded only by a minority—initially, perhaps, by a minority of one. Ironically, the freedom to advocate those new ideas on which progress depends, those that are unpopular, is the very freedom that is most often in jeopardy. No regime in human history has threatened the freedom to praise its wisdom. Yet when freedom for the critics of society is abridged, the validity of their criticism can never be fairly judged. In that event, freedom for the rest of us is neither very significant nor, in the long run, very safe.

4) *Democracy.* The people's power must rest its hopes on majority rule—though a majority consisting of, and enlightened by, the many minorities that uneasily coexist in this wondrously diverse society. That is the essence of democracy. But if a majority is to exert political power, it must

muster the resources and master the skills (which are perhaps the most important resource of all) that are essential to democratic politics. This requires some intelligence and considerable work. It means going to meetings, distributing literature, and contributing money. It demands that the people organize in pressure groups to advance their interests, that they learn to control the political parties that vie for governmental office, that they demand election laws that give the poor candidate a fighting chance against the rich one. At minimum, it demands that before they vote they identify the policies they most want, their own basic interests, and the candidates most likely to advance both.

Will it do any good? If all these prescriptions are filled, or others that may be offered by wiser heads, can the people's power prevail over that concentrated in the elites whose political resources so far exceed their own?

These are variations of the same question with which this epilogue began. No one knows the answers, but if they are affirmative, if American democracy can realize its promise, it will require that the people have confidence that it can. When black leaders of the 1960s admonished their followers to "keep the faith, baby" they were expressing a fundamental psychological truth: There is no progress without faith that progress is possible.

While faith in the perfectability of ancient political principles has no sure reward, three things seem certain. One is that experience justifies more faith in democracy than in aristocracy or dictatorship. A second is that American government is already more democratic than many of the social and economic institutions it sometimes seeks to regulate. A third is that the only alternative to faith is the cynicism and despair that become self-fulfilling prophesies of doom, destroying hope and paralyzing action. But if the people define a vision of the society they want, if they learn all they can about controlling the government that may help bring it about, if they work diligently to improve the mechanisms of that government, if they demand decency and honor in their officials, and if they treat one another with the compassion and dignity necessary for concerted action, then there is cause for optimism. Spiritual salvation, according to some Christian theologians, comes from faith and good works. The former inspires the latter. So it must be if the people's power is to prevail.

The Constitution of the United States

We the People of the United States, in Order to form a more perfect Union, establish Justice, insure domestic Tranquility, provide for the common defence, promote the general Welfare, and secure the Blessings of Liberty to ourselves and our Posterity, do ordain and establish this Constitution for the United States of America.

ARTICLE I

Section 1. All legislative Powers herein granted shall be vested in a Congress of the United States, which shall consist of a Senate and House of Representatives.

Section 2. The House of Representatives shall be composed of Members chosen every second Year by the People of the several States, and the Electors in each State shall have the Qualifications requisite for Electors of the most numerous Branch of the State Legislature.

No Person shall be a Representative who shall not have attained to the Age of twenty five Years, and been seven Years a Citizen of the United States, and who shall not, when elected, be an Inhabitant of that State in which he shall be chosen.

Representatives and direct Taxes shall be apportioned among the several States which may be included within this Union, according to their respective Numbers, which shall be determined by adding to the whole Number of free Persons, including those bound to Service for a Term of Years, and excluding Indians not taxed, three fifths of all other Persons. The actual Enumeration shall be made within three Years after the first Meeting of the Congress of the United States, and within every subsequent Term of ten Years, in such Manner as they shall by Law direct. The Number of Representatives shall not exceed one for every thirty Thousand, but each State shall have at Least one Representative; and until such enumeration shall be made, the State of New Hampshire shall be entitled to chuse three, Massachusetts eight,

Rhode-Island and Providence Plantations one, Connecticut five, New-York six, New Jersey four, Pennsylvania eight, Delaware one, Maryland six, Virginia ten, North Carolina five, South Carolina five, and Georgia three.

When vacancies happen in the Representation from any State, the Executive Authority thereof shall issue Writs of Election to fill such Vacancies.

The House of Representatives shall chuse their speaker and other Officers; and shall have the sole Power of Impeachment.

Section 3. The Senate of the United States shall be composed of two Senators from each State, chosen by the Legislature thereof, for six Years; and each Senator shall have one Vote.

Immediately after they shall be aseembled in Consequence of the first Election, they shall be divided as equally as may be into three Classes. The Seats of the Senators of the first Class shall be vacated at the Expiration of the second Year, of the second Class at the Expiration of the fourth Year, and of the third Class at the Expiration of the sixth Year, so that one third may be chosen every second Year; and if Vacancies happen by Resignation, or otherwise, during the Recess of the Legislature of any State, the Executive thereof may make temporary Appointments until the next Meeting of the Legislature, which shall then fill such Vacancies.

No Person shall be a Senator who shall not have attained to the Age of thirty Years, and been nine Years a Citizen of the United States, and who shall not, when elected, be an Inhabitant of that State for which he shall be chosen.

The Vice President of the United States shall be President of the Senate, but shall have no Vote, unless they be equally divided.

The Senate shall chuse their other Officers, and also a President pro tempore, in the Absence of the Vice President, or when he shall exercise the Office of President of the United States.

The Senate shall have the sole Power to try all Impeachments. When sitting for that Purpose, they shall be on Oath or Affirmation. When the President of the United States is tried, the Chief Justice shall preside: And no Person shall be convicted without the Concurrence of two thirds of the Members present.

Judgment in Cases of Impeachment shall not extend further than to removal from Office, and disqualification to hold and enjoy any Office of honor, Trust or Profit under the United States: but the Party convicted shall nevertheless be liable and subject to Indictment, Trial, Judgment and Punishment, according to law.

Section 4. The Times, Places and Manner of holding Elections for Senators and Representatives, shall be prescribed in each State by the Legislature thereof; but the Congress may at any time by Law make or alter such Regulations, except as to the Places of chusing Senators.

The Congress shall assemble at least once in every Year, and such Meeting shall be on the first Monday in December, unless they shall by Law appoint a different Day.

Section 5. Each House shall be the Judge of the Elections, Returns and Qualifications of its own Members, and a Majority of each shall constitute a Quorum to do Business; but a smaller Number may adjourn from day to day, and may be authorized to compel the Attendance of absent Members, in such Manner, and under such Penalties as each House may provide.

Each House may determine the Rules of its Proceedings, punish its Members for disorderly Behaviour, and, with the Concurrence of two thirds, expel a Member.

Each House shall keep a Journal of its Proceedings, and from time to time publish the same, excepting such Parts as may in their Judgment require Secrecy; and the Yeas and Nays of the Members of either House on any question shall, at the Desire of one fifth of those Present, be entered on the Journal.

Neither House, during the Session of Congress, shall, without the Consent of the other, adjourn for more than three days, nor to any other Place than that in which the two Houses shall be sitting.

Section 6. The Senators and Representatives shall receive a Compensation for their Services, to be ascertained by Law, and paid out of the Treasury of the United States. They shall in all Cases, except Treason, Felony and Breach of the Peace, be privileged from Arrest during their Attendance at the Session of their respective Houses, and in going to and returning from the same; and for any Speech or Debate in either House, they shall not be questioned in any other Place.

No Senator or Representative shall, during the Time for which he was elected, be appointed to any civil Office under the Authority of the United States, which shall have been created, or the Emoluments whereof shall have been encreased during such time; and no Person holding any Office under the United States, shall be a Member of either House during his Continuance in Office.

Section 7. All Bills for raising Revenue shall originate in the House of Representatives; but the Senate may propose or concur with Amendments as on other Bills.

Every Bill which shall have passed the House of Representatives and the Senate, shall, before it become a Law, be presented to the President of the United States; If he approve he shall sign it, but if not he shall return it, with his Objections to that House in which it shall have originated, who shall enter the Objections at large on their Journal, and proceed to reconsider it. If after such Reconsideration two thirds of that House shall agree to pass the Bill, it shall be sent, together with the Objections, to the other House, by which it shall likewise be reconsidered, and if approved by two thirds of that House, it shall become a Law. But in all such Cases the Votes of both Houses shall be determined by Yeas and Nays, and the Names of the Persons voting for and against the Bill shall be entered on the Journal of each House respectively. If any Bill shall not be returned by the President within ten Days (Sundays excepted) after it shall have been presented to him, the Same shall be a Law, in like Manner as if he had signed it, unless the Congress by their Adjournment prevent its Return, in which Case it shall not be a Law.

Every Order, Resolution, or Vote to which the Concurrence of the Senate and House of Representatives may be necessary (except on a question of Adjournment) shall be presented to the President of the United States; and before the Same shall take Effect, shall be approved by him, or being disapproved by him, shall be repassed by two thirds of the Senate and House of Representatives, according to the Rules and Limitations prescribed in the Case of a Bill.

Section 8. The Congress shall have Power To lay and collect Taxes, Duties, Imposts and Excises, to pay the Debts and provide for the common Defence and general Welfare of the United States; but all Duties, Imposts and Excises shall be uniform throughout the United States;

To borrow Money on the Credit of the United States;

To regulate Commerce with foreign Nations, and among the several States, and with the Indian Tribes;

To establish an uniform Rule of Naturalization, and uniform Laws on the subject of Bankruptcies throughout the United States;

To coin Money, regulate the Value thereof, and of foreign Coin, and fix the Standard of Weights and Measures;

To provide for the Punishment of counterfeiting the Securities and current Coin of the United States;

To establish Post Offices and post Roads;

To promote the Progress of Science and useful Arts, by securing for limited Times to Authors and Inventors the exclusive Right to their respective Writings and Discoveries;

To constitute Tribunals inferior to the supreme Court;

To define and punish Piracies and Felonies committed on the high Seas, and Offences against the Law of Nations;

To declare War, grant Letters of Marque and Reprisal, and make Rules concerning Captures on Land and Water;

To raise and support Armies, but no Appropriation of Money to that Use shall be for a longer Term than two Years;

To provide and maintain a Navy;

To make Rules for the Government and Regulation of the land and naval Forces;

To provide for calling forth the Militia to execute the Laws of the Union, suppress Insurrections and repel Invasions;

To provide for organizing, arming, and disciplining, the Militia, and for governing such Part of them as may be employed in the Service of the United States, reserving to the States respectively, the Appointment of the Officers, and the Authority of training the Militia according to the discipline prescribed by Congress;

To exercise exclusive Legislation in all Cases whatsoever, over such District (not exceeding ten Miles square) as may, by Cession of particular States, and the Acceptance of Congress, become the Seat of the Government of the United States, and to exercise like Authority over all Places purchased by the Consent of the Legislature of the State in which the Same shall be for the Erection of Forts, Magazines, Arsenals, dock-Yards, and other needful Buildings;—And

To make all Laws which shall be necessary and proper for carrying into Execution the foregoing Powers, and all other Powers vested by this Constitution in the Government of the United States, or in any Department or Officer thereof.

Section 9. The Migration or Importation of such Persons as any of the States now existing shall think proper to admit, shall not be prohibited by the Congress prior to the Year one thousand eight hundred and eight, but a Tax or duty may be imposed on such Importation, not exceeding ten dollars for each Person.

The Privilege of the Writ of Habeas Corpus shall not be suspended, unless when in Cases of Rebellion or Invasion the public Safety may require it.

No Bill of Attainder or ex post facto Law shall be passed.

No Capitation, or other direct, Tax shall be laid, unless in Proportion to the Census or Enumeration herein before directed to be taken.

No Tax or Duty shall be laid on Articles exported from any State.

No Preference shall be given by any Regulation of Commerce or Revenue to the Ports of one State over those of another: nor shall Vessels bound to, or from, one State, be obliged to enter, clear, or pay Duties in another.

No Money shall be drawn from the Treasury, but in Consequence of Appropriations made by Law; and a regular Statement and Account of the Receipts and Expenditures of all public Money shall be published from time to time.

No Title of Nobility shall be granted by the United States: And no Person holding any Office of Profit or Trust under them, shall, without the Consent of the Congress, accept of any present, Emolument, Office, or Title, of any kind whatever, from any King, Prince, or foreign State.

Section 10. No State shall enter into any Treaty, Alliance, or Confederation; grant Letters of Marque and Reprisal; coin Money; emit Bills of Credit; make any Thing but gold and silver Coin a Tender in Payment of Debts; pass any Bill of Attainder, ex post facto Law, or Law impairing the Obligation of Contracts, or grant any Title of Nobility.

No State shall, without the Consent of the Congress, lay any Imposts or Duties on Imports or Exports, except what may be absolutely necessary for executing its inspection Laws: and the net Produce of all Duties and Imposts, laid by any State on Imports or Exports, shall be for the Use of the Treasury of the United States; and all such Laws shall be subject to the Revision and Controul of the Congress.

No State shall, without the Consent of Congress, lay any Duty of Tonnage, keep Troops, or Ships of War in time of Peace, enter into any Agreement or Compact with another State, or with a foreign Power, or engage in War, unless actually invaded, or in such imminent Danger as will not admit of delay.

ARTICLE II

Section 1. The executive Power shall be vested in a President of the United States of America. He shall hold his Office during the Term of four Years, and, together with the Vice President, chosen for the same term, be elected, as follows

Each State shall appoint, in such Manner as the Legislature thereof may direct, a Number of Electors, equal to the whole Number of Senators and Representatives to which the State may be entitled in the Congress: but no Senator or

Representative, or Person holding an Office of Trust or Profit under the United States, shall be appointed an Elector.

The Electors shall meet in their respective States, and vote by Ballot for two Persons, of whom one at least shall not be an Inhabitant of the same State with themselves. And they shall make a List of all the Persons voted for, and of the Number of Votes for each; which List they shall sign and certify, and transmit sealed to the Seat of the Government of the United States, directed to the President of the Senate. The President of the Senate shall, in the Presence of the Senate and House of Representatives, open all the Certificates, and the Votes shall then be counted. The Person having the greatest Number of Votes shall be the President, if such Number be a Majority of the whole Number of Electors appointed; and if there be more than one who have such Majority, and have an equal Number of Votes, then the House of Representatives shall immediately chuse by Ballot one of them for President: and if no Person have a Majority, then from the five highest on the List the said House shall in like Manner chuse the President. But in chusing the President, the Votes shall be taken by States, the Representation from each State having one Vote; A quorum for this Purpose shall consist of a Member or Members from two thirds of the States, and a Majority of all the States shall be necessary to a Choice. In every Case, after the Choice of the President, the Person having the greatest Number of Votes of the Electors shall be the Vice President. But if there should remain two or more who have equal Votes, the Senate shall chuse from them by Ballot the Vice President.

The Congress may determine the Time of chusing the Electors, and the Day on which they shall give their Votes; which Day shall be the same throughout the United States.

No Person except a natural born Citizen, or a Citizen of the United States, at the time of the Adoption of this Constitution, shall be eligible to the Office of President; neither shall any Person be eligible to that Office who shall not have attained to the Age of thirty Five Years, and been fourteen Years a Resident within the United States.

In Case of the Removal of the President from Office, or of his Death, Resignation, or Inability to discharge the Powers and Duties of the said Office, the Same shall devolve on the Vice President, and the Congress may by Law provide for the Case of Removal, Death, Resignation or Inability, both of the President and Vice President, declaring what Officer shall then act as President, and such Officer shall act accordingly, until the Disability be removed, or a President shall be elected.

The President shall, at stated Times, receive for his Services a Compensation, which shall neither be encreased nor diminished during the Period for which he shall have been elected, and he shall not receive within that Period any other Emolument from the United States, or any of them.

Before he enter on the Execution of his Office, he shall take the following Oath or Affirmation:—"I do solemnly swear (or affirm) that I will faithfully execute the Office of President of the United States, and will to the best of my Ability, preserve, protect and defend the Constitution of the United States."

Section 2. The President shall be Commander in Chief of the Army and Navy of the United States, and of the Militia of the several States, when called into the actual Service of the United States; he may require the Opinion, in writing, of the principal Officer in each of the executive Departments, upon any Subject relating to the Duties of their respective Offices, and he shall have Power to grant Reprieves and Pardons for Offences against the United States, except in Cases of Impeachment.

He shall have Power, by and with the Advice and Consent of the Senate, to make Treaties, provided two thirds of the Senators present concur; and he shall nominate, and by and with the Advice and Consent of the Senate, shall appoint Ambassadors, other public Ministers and Consuls, Judges of the supreme Court, and all other Officers of the United States, whose Appointments are not herein otherwise provided for, and which shall be established by Law; but the Congress may by Law vest the Appointment of such inferior Officers, as they think proper, in the President alone, in the Courts of Law, or in the Heads of Departments.

The President shall have Power to fill up all Vacancies that may happen during the Recess of the Senate, by granting Commissions which shall expire at the End of their next Session.

Section 3. He shall from time to time give to the Congress Information of the State of the Union, and recommend to their Consideration such Measures as he shall judge necessary and expedient; he may, on extraordinary Occasions, convene both Houses, or either of them, and in Case of Disagreement between them, with Respect to the Time of Adjournment, he may adjourn them to such Time as he shall think proper; he shall receive Ambassadors and other public Ministers; he shall take Care that the Laws be faithfully executed, and shall Commission all the Officers of the United States.

Section 4. The President, Vice President and all civil Officers of the United States, shall be removed from Office on Impeachment for, and Conviction of, Treason, Bribery, or other High Crimes and Misdemeanors.

ARTICLE III

Section 1. The judicial Power of the United States, shall be vested in one supreme Court, and in such inferior Courts as the Congress may from time to time ordain and establish. The

Judges, both of the supreme and inferior Courts, shall hold their Offices during good Behaviour, and shall, at stated Times, receive for their Services, a Compensation, which shall not be diminished during their Continuance in Office.

Section 2. The judicial Power shall extend to all Cases, in Law and Equity, arising under this Constitution, the Laws of the United States, and Treaties made, or which shall be made, under their Authority;—to all Cases affecting Ambassadors, other public Ministers and Consuls;—to all Cases of admiralty and maritime Jurisdiction;—to Controversies to which the United States shall be a Party;—to Controversies between two or more States; between a State and Citizens of another State;—between Citizens of different States;—between Citizens of the same State claiming Lands under Grants of different States, and between a State, or the Citizens thereof, and foreign States, Citizens or Subjects.

In all Cases affecting Ambassadors, other public Ministers and Consuls, and those in which a State shall be Party, the supreme Court shall have original Jurisdiction. In all the other Cases before mentioned, the supreme Court shall have appellate Jurisdiction, both as to Law and Fact, with such Exceptions, and under such Regulations as the Congress shall make.

The Trial of all Crimes, except in Cases of Impeachment, shall be by Jury; and such Trial shall be held in the State where the said Crimes shall have been committed; but when not committed within any State, the Trial shall be at such Place or Places as the Congress may by Law have directed.

Section 3. Treason against the United States, shall consist only in levying War against them, or in adhering to their Enemies, giving them Aid and Comfort. No Person shall be convicted of Treason unless on the Testimony of two Witnesses to the same overt Act, or on Confession in open Court.

The Congress shall have Power to declare the Punishment of Treason, but no Attainder of Treason shall work Corruption of Blood, or Forfeiture except during the Life of the Person attainted.

Section 1. Full Faith and Credit shall be given in each State to the public Acts, Records, and judicial Proceedings of every other State. And the Congress may by general Laws prescribe the Manner in which such Acts, Records and Proceedings shall be proved, and the Effect thereof.

Section 2. The Citizens of each State shall be entitled to all Privileges and Immunities of Citizens in the several States.

A Person charged in any State with Treason, Felony, or other Crime, who shall flee from Justice, and be found in another State, shall on Demand of the executive Authority of the State from which he fled, be delivered up, to be removed to the State having Jurisdiction of the Crime.

No Person held to Service or Labour in one State, under the Laws thereof, escaping into another, shall, in Consequence of any Law or Regulation therein, be discharged from such service or Labour, but shall be delivered up on Claim of the Party to whom such Service or Labour may be due.

Section 3. New States may be admitted by the Congress into this Union; but no new State shall be formed or erected within the Jurisdiction of any other State; nor any State be formed by the Junction of two or more States, or Parts of States, without the Consent of the Legislatures of the States concerned as well as of the Congress.

The Congress shall have Power to dispose of and make all needful Rules and Regulations respecting the Territory or other Property belonging to the United States; and nothing in this Constitution shall be so construed as to Prejudice any Claims of the United States, or of any particular State.

Section 4. The United States shall guarantee to every State in this Union a Republican Form of Government, and shall protect each of them against Invasion; and on Application of the Legislature, or of the Executive (when the Legislature cannot be convened) against domestic Violence.

The Congress, whenever two thirds of both Houses shall deem it necessary, shall propose Amendments to this Constitution, or, on the Application of the Legislatures of two thirds of the several States, shall call a Convention for Proposing Amendments, which, in either Case, shall be valid to all Intents and Purposes, as Part of this Constitution, when ratified by the Legislatures of three fourths of the several States, or by Conventions in three fourths thereof, as the one or the other Mode of Ratification may be proposed by the Congress; Provided that no Amendment which may be made prior to the Year One thousand eight hundred and eight shall in any Manner affect the first and fourth Clauses in the Ninth Section of the first Article; and that no State, without its Consent, shall be deprived of its equal Suffrage in the Senate.

All Debts contracted and Engagements entered into, before the Adoption of this Constitution, shall be as valid against the United States under this Constitution, as under the Confederation.

This Constitution, and the Laws of the United States which shall be made in Pursuance thereof; and all Treaties made, or which shall be made, under the Authority of the United States, shall be the supreme Law of the Land; and the Judges in every State shall be bound thereby, any Thing in the Constitution or Laws of any State to the Contrary notwithstanding.

The Senators and Representatives before mentioned, and the Members of the several State Legislatures, and all executive and judicial Officers, both of the United States and of the several States, shall be bound by Oath or Affirmation, to support this Constitution; but no religious Test shall ever be required as a Qualification to any Office or public Trust under the United States.

ARTICLE VII

The Ratification of the Conventions of nine States, shall be sufficient for the Establishment of this Constitution between the States so ratifying the Same.

Done in Convention by the Unanimous Consent of the States present the Seventeenth Day of September in the Year of our Lord one thousand seven hundred and eighty seven and of the Independence of the United States of America the twelfth. In witness whereof We have hereunto subscribed our Names.

(The first 10 Amendments were ratified December 15, 1791, and form what is known as the "Bill of Rights.")

AMENDMENT 1

Congress shall make no law respecting an establishment of religion, or prohibiting the free exercise thereof; or abridging the freedom of speech, or of the press; or the right of the people peaceably to assemble, and to petition the Government for a redress of grievances.

AMENDMENT 2

A well regulated Militia, being necessary to the security of a free State, the right of the people to keep and bear Arms, shall not be infringed.

AMENDMENT 3

No Soldier shall, in time of peace be quartered in any house, without the consent of the Owner, nor in time of war, but in a manner to be prescribed by law.

AMENDMENT 4

The right of the people to be secure in their persons, houses, papers, and effects, against unreasonable searches and seizures, shall not be violated, and no Warrants shall issue, but upon probable cause, supported by Oath or affirmation, and particularly describing the place to be searched, and the persons or things to be seized.

AMENDMENT 5

No person shall be held to answer for a capital, or otherwise infamous crime, unless on a presentment or indictment of a Grand Jury, except in cases arising in the land or naval forces, or in the Militia, when in actual service in time of War or public danger; nor shall any person be subject for the same offence to be twice put in jeopardy of life or limb; nor shall be compelled in any criminal case to be a witness against himself, nor be deprived of life, liberty, or property, without due process of law; nor shall private property be taken for public use, without just compensation.

AMENDMENT 6

In all criminal prosecutions, the accused shall enjoy the right to a speedy and public trial, by an impartial jury of the State and district wherein the crime shall have been committed, which district shall have been previously ascertained by law, and to be informed of the nature and cause of the accusation; to be confronted with the witnesses against him; to have compulsory process for obtaining witnesses in his favor, and to have the Assistance of Counsel for his defence.

AMENDMENT 7

In Suits at common law, where the value in controversy shall exceed twenty dollars, the right of trial by jury shall be preserved, and no fact tried by a jury, shall be otherwise reexamined in any Court of the United States, than according to the rules of the common law.

AMENDMENT 8

Excessive bail shall not be required, nor excessive fines imposed, nor cruel and unusual punishments inflicted.

AMENDMENT 9

The enumeration in the Constitution, of certain rights, shall not be construed to deny or disparage others retained by the people.

AMENDMENT 10

The powers not delegated to the United States by the Constitution, nor prohibited by it to the States, are reserved to the States respectively, or to the people.

AMENDMENT 11
[RATIFIED FEBRUARY 7, 1795]

The Judicial power of the United States shall not be construed to extend to any suit in law or equity, commenced or prosecuted against one of the United States by Citizens of another State, or by Citizens or Subjects of any Foreign State.

AMENDMENT 12
[RATIFIED JULY 27, 1804]

The Electors shall meet in their respective states and vote by ballot for President and Vice-President, one of whom, at least, shall not be an inhabitant of the same state with themselves; they shall name in their ballots the person voted for as President, and in distinct ballots the person voted for as Vice-President, and they shall make distinct lists of all persons voted for as President, and of all persons voted for as Vice-President, and of the number of votes for each, which lists they shall sign and certify, and transmit sealed to the seat of the government of the United States, directed to the President of the Senate;—The President of the Senate shall, in the presence of the Senate and House of Representatives, open all the certificates and the votes shall then be counted;—The person having the greatest number of votes for President, shall be the President, if such number be a majority of the whole number of Electors appointed; and if no person have such majority, then from the persons having the highest numbers not exceeding three on the list of those voted for as President, the House of Representatives shall choose immediately, by ballot, the President. But in choosing the President, the votes shall be taken by states, the representation from each state having one vote; a quorum for this purpose shall consist of a member or members from two-thirds of the states, and a majority of all the states shall be necessary to a choice. And if the House of Representatives shall not choose a President whenever the right of choice shall devolve upon them, before the fourth day of March next following, then the Vice-President shall act as President, as in the case of the death or other constitutional disability of the President.—The person having the greatest number of votes as Vice-President, shall be the Vice-President, if such number be a majority of the whole number of Electors appointed, and if no person have a majority, then from the two highest numbers on the list, the Senate shall choose the Vice-President; a quorum for the purpose shall consist of two-thirds of the whole number of Senators, and a majority of the whole number shall be necessary to a choice. But no person constitutionally ineligible to the office of President shall be eligible to that of Vice-President of the United States.

AMENDMENT 13
[RATIFIED DECEMBER 6, 1865]

Section 1. Neither slavery nor involuntary servitude, except as a punishment for crime whereof the party shall have been duly convicted, shall exist within the United States, or any place subject to their jurisdiction.

Section 2. Congress shall have power to enforce this article by appropriate legislation.

AMENDMENT 14
[RATIFIED JULY 9, 1868]

Section 1. All persons born or naturalized in the United States, and subject to the jurisdiction thereof, are citizens of the United States and of the State wherein they reside. No State shall make or enforce any law which shall abridge the privileges or immunities of citizens of the United States; nor shall any State deprive any person of life, liberty, or property, without due process of law; nor deny to any person within its jurisdiction the equal protection of the laws.

Section 2. Representatives shall be apportioned among the several States according to their respective numbers, counting the whole number of persons in each State, excluding Indians not taxed. But when the right to vote at any election for the choice of electors for President and Vice President of the United States, Representatives in Congress, the Executive and Judicial officers of a State, or the members of the Legislature thereof, is denied to any of the male inhabitants of such State, being twenty-one years of age, and citizens of the United States, or in any way abridged, except for participation in rebellion, or other crime, the basis of representation therein shall be reduced in the proportion which the number of such male citizens shall bear to the whole number of male citizens twenty-one years of age in such State.

Section 3. No person shall be a Senator or Representaive in Congress, or elector of President and Vice President, or hold any office, civil or military, under the United States, or under any State, who, having previously taken an oath, as a member of Congress, or as an officer of the United States, or as a member of any State legislature, or as an executive or judicial officer of any State, to support the Constitution of the United States, shall have engaged in insurrection or rebellion against the same, or given aid or comfort to the enemies thereof. But Congress may by a vote of two-thirds of each House, remove such disability.

Section 4. The validity of the public debt of the United States, authorized by law, including debts incurred for payment of pensions and bounties for services in suppressing insurrection or rebellion, shall not be questioned. But neither the United States nor any State shall assume or pay any debt or obligation incurred in aid of insurrection or rebellion against the United States, or any claim for the loss or emancipation of any slave; but all such debts, obligations and claims shall be held illegal and void.

Section 5. The Congress shall have power to enforce, by appropriate legislation, the provisions of this article.

AMENDMENT 15
[RATIFIED FEBRUARY 3, 1870]

Section 1. The right of citizens of the United States to vote shall not be denied or abridged by the United States or by any State on account of race, color, or previous condition of servitude.

Section 2. The Congress shall have power to enforce this article by appropriate legislation.

AMENDMENT 16
[RATIFIED FEBRUARY 3, 1913]

The Congress shall have power to lay and collect taxes on incomes, from whatever source derived, without apportionment among the several States, and without regard to any census or enumeration.

AMENDMENT 17
[RATIFIED APRIL 8, 1913]

The Senate of the United States shall be composed of two Senators from each State, elected by the people thereof for six years; and each Senator shall have one vote. The electors in each State shall have the qualifications requisite for electors of the most numerous branch of the State legislatures.

When vacancies happen in the representation of any State in the Senate, the executive authority of such State shall issue writs of election to fill such vacancies: *Provided,* That the legislature of any State may empower the executive thereof to make temporary appointments until the people fill the vacancies by election as the legislature may direct.

This amendment shall not be so construed as to affect the election or term of any Senator chosen before it becomes valid as part of the Constitution.

AMENDMENT 18
[RATIFIED JANUARY 16, 1919]

Section 1. After one year from the ratification of this article the manufacture, sale, or transportation of intoxicating liquors within, the importation thereof into, or the exportation thereof from the United States and all territory subject to the jurisdiction thereof for beverage purposes is hereby prohibited.

Section 2. The Congress and the several States shall have concurrent power to enforce this article by appropriate legislation.

Section 3. This article shall be inoperative unless it shall have been ratified as an amendment to the Constitution by the legislatures of the several States, as provided in the Constitution, within seven years from the date of the submission hereof to the States by the Congress.

AMENDMENT 19
[RATIFIED AUGUST 18, 1920]

The right of citizens of the United States to vote shall not be denied or abridged by the United States or by any State on account of sex.

Congress shall have power to enforce this article by appropriate legislation.

AMENDMENT 20
[RATIFIED JANUARY 23, 1933]

Section 1. The terms of the President and Vice President shall end at noon on the 20th day of January, and the terms of Senators and Representatives at noon on the 3d day of January, of the years in which such terms would have ended if this article had not been ratified; and the terms of their successors shall then begin.

Section 2. The Congress shall assemble at least once in every year, and such meeting shall begin at noon on the 3d day of January, unless they shall by law appoint a different day.

Section 3. If, at the time fixed for the beginning of the term of the President, the President elect shall have died, the Vice President elect shall become President. If a President shall not have been chosen before the time fixed for the beginning of his term, or if the President elect shall have failed to qualify, then the Vice President elect shall act as President until a President shall have qualified; and the Congress may by law provide for the case wherein neither a President elect nor a Vice President elect shall have qualified, declaring who shall then act as President, or the manner in which one who is to act shall be selected, and such person shall act accordingly until a President or Vice President shall have qualified.

Section 4. The Congress may by law provide for the case of the death of any of the persons from whom the House of Representatives may choose a President whenever the right of choice shall have devolved upon them, and for the case of the death of any of the persons from whom the Senate may choose a Vice President whenever the right of choice shall have devolved upon them.

Section 5. Sections 1 and 2 shall take effect on the 15th day of October following the ratification of this article.

Section 6. This article shall be inoperative

unless it shall have been ratified as an amendment to the Constitution by the legislatures of
three-fourths of the several States within seven
years from the date of its submission.

AMENDMENT 21
[RATIFIED DECEMBER 5, 1933]

Section 1. The eighteenth article of amendment to the Constitution of the United States is
hereby repealed.

Section 2. The transportation or importation
into any State, Territory, or possession of the
United States for delivery or use therein of
intoxicating liquors, in violation of the laws
thereof, is hereby prohibited.

Section 3. This article shall be inoperative
unless it shall have been ratified as an amendment to the Constitution by conventions in the
several States, as provided in the Constitution,
within seven years from the date of the submission hereof to the States by the Congress.

AMENDMENT 22
[RATIFIED FEBRUARY 27, 1951]

Section 1. No person shall be elected to the
office of the President more than twice, and no
person who has held the office of President, or
acted as President, for more than two years of a
term to which some other person was elected
President shall be elected to the office of the
President more than once. But this Article shall
not apply to any person holding the office of
President when this Article was proposed by the
Congress, and shall not prevent any person
who may be holding the office of President, or
acting as President, during the term within
which this Article becomes operative from holding the office of President or acting as President
during the remainder of such term.

Section 2. This article shall be inoperative
unless it shall have been ratified as an amendment to the Constitution by the legislatures of
three-fourths of the several States within seven
years from the date of its submission to the
States by the Congress.

AMENDMENT 23
[RATIFIED MARCH 29, 1961]

Section 1. The District constituting the seat
of Government of the United States shall appoint in such manner as the Congress may
direct:

A number of electors of President and Vice
President equal to the whole number of Senators and Representatives in Congress to which
the District would be entitled if it were a State,
but in no event more than the least populous
State; they shall be in addition to those appointed by the States, but they shall be considered, for the purposes of the election of
President and Vice President, to be electors

appointed by a State; and they shall meet in the
District and perform such duties as provided by
the twelfth article of amendment.

Section 2. The Congress shall have power to
enforce this article by appropriate legislation.

AMENDMENT 24
[RATIFIED JANUARY 23, 1964]

Section 1. The right of citizens of the United
States to vote in any primary or other election
for President or Vice President, for electors for
President or Vice President, or for Senator or
Representative in Congress, shall not be denied
or abridged by the United States or any State by
reason of failure to pay any poll tax or other tax.

Section 2. The Congress shall have power to
enforce this article by appropriate legislation.

AMENDMENT 25
[RATIFIED FEBRUARY 10, 1967]

Section 1. In case of the removal of the
President from office or of his death or resignation, the Vice President shall become President.

Section 2. Whenever there is a vacancy in
the office of the Vice President, the President
shall nominate a Vice President who shall take
office upon confirmation by a majority vote of
both Houses of Congress.

Section 3. Whenever the President transmits
to the President pro tempore of the Senate and
the Speaker of the House of Representatives his
written declaration that he is unable to discharge the powers and duties of his office, and
until he transmits to them a written declaration
to the contrary, such powers and duties shall be
discharged by the Vice President as Acting
President.

Section 4. Whenever the Vice President and
a majority of either the principal officers of the
executive departments or of such other body as
Congress may by law provide, transmit to the
President pro tempore of the Senate and the
Speaker of the House of Representatives their
written declaration that the President is unable
to discharge the powers and duties of his office,
the Vice President shall immediately assume the
powers and duties of the office as Acting President.

Thereafter, when the President transmits to
the President pro tempore of the Senate and the
Speaker of the House of Representatives his
written declaration that no inability exists, he
shall resume the powers and duties of his office
unless the Vice President and a majority of
either the principal officers of the executive
department or of such other body as Congress
may by law provide, transmit within four days
to the President pro tempore of the Senate and
the Speaker of the House of Representatives
their written declaration that the President is
unable to discharge the powers and duties of his
office. Thereupon Congress shall decide the

issue, assembling within forty-eight hours for that purpose if not in session. If the Congress, within twenty-one days after receipt of the latter written declaration, or, if Congress is not in session, within twenty-one days after Congress is required to assemble, determines by two-thirds vote of both Houses that the President is unable to discharge the powers and duties of his office, the Vice President shall continue to discharge the same as Acting President; otherwise, the President shall resume the powers and duties of his office.

AMENDMENT 26
[RATIFIED JUNE 30, 1971]

Section 1. The right of citizens of the United States, who are eighteen years of age or older, to vote shall not be denied or abridged by the United States or by any State on account of age.

Section 2. The Congress shall have power to enforce this article by appropriate legislation.

Index of States, Counties, and Cities

General Index

5 6 7 8 9 10 11 12 –KP– 80 79 78 77 76 75